My Sicilian Legacy

*The Struggles and Joys
of Three Generations*

❧

Richard F. Cavallaro

authorHOUSE®

AuthorHouse™
1663 Liberty Drive, Suite 200
Bloomington, IN 47403
www.authorhouse.com
Phone: 1-800-839-8640

©2008 Richard F. Cavallaro. All rights reserved.

No part of this book may be reproduced, stored in a retrieval system, or transmitted by any means without the written permission of the author.

First published by AuthorHouse 11/25/2008

ISBN: 978-1-4343-0244-1 (sc)

Library of Congress Control Number: 2007908443

Printed in the United States of America
Bloomington, Indiana

This book is printed on acid-free paper.

Dedication

I dedicate this book to my father, Alfred Cavallaro. Many of the stories included came from him, and I recall him sharing them with me over the years. He loved Sicily and he expressed that sentiment often as he spoke with his family and friends. After he left Sicily at the age of fifteen, he never returned to visit the land where he grew up and loved so much. It is because of him, and the dedication he had to his family and to his Sicilian roots, that this book exists. I only wish he could have lived long enough to read the book and enjoy reliving his past that he so freely yielded to me.

As a little boy, growing up in my Sicilian family, I remember my father singing a favorite song of his many times. It was one he learned in Sicily and brought with him to America. When I began to play the piano, he took me to the Sciabarazzi Music Store to buy the sheet music so I could play many of his favorites at home. Located on either North Clinton or Joseph Avenue, they specialized in selling various musical instruments and Italian sheet music. They also gave private music lessons in their studios, so as you shopped, you could always hear students playing some of the popular Italian songs that we all knew so well.

When I asked him why he sang that particular song all the time, his answer to me was, "My grandmother in Sicily sang this song to me all the time and, when I left to come to America, she told me to never forget her. She must have known that she would never see me again. I sing it now to remind me of her and hope that my family will never forget me either." This song brings tears to my eyes each time I hear it, and listen to the beautiful words. There are times when I play it on the piano that, if I listen hard enough, I can still hear him singing as he stitched on his sewing machine in the kitchen.

Non Ti Scordar Di Me
(In the original Sicilian Dialect)

Versi Italini di Domenico Furnò
Mùsica di Ernesto De Curtis

Non ti scordar di me, la vita mia legata è a te.
Lo t'amo sempre più, nel sogno mio rimani tu.

Non ti scordar di me, la vita mia legata è a te.
C'è sempre un nido nel mio cor per te,
Non ti scordar di me!

Don't Forget About Me
(Translated into English by Anna Bahr)

Words in Italian by Domenico Furnò
Music by Ernesto De Curtis

Don't forget about me, my life is tied to you.
I love you always forevermore, in my dreams you always remain.
Don't forget about me, my life is tied to you.
There is always a place in my heart for you,
Don't forget about me!

I still have the sheet music for this song that he bought me over fifty years ago, and I play this song often. It reminds me of my father and the things that he said to me. He had a tremendous impact on my life. Whether it's this song, a photograph of a special time in our lives, or just a card that he signed in his own unique way, "From Me," I have memories of him that have lasted a lifetime; I shall always remember him with love and pride in my heart.

This book is just for you, and as the song says,
I have a place in my heart for you and I will never forget you, Dad!

With much love from your son,
Richard F. Cavallaro

*"Men like my father cannot die.
They are with me still,
real in memory as they were in flesh,
loving and beloved forever."*

---

*Ford, John (Director). (1941). *How Green Was My Valley* [Film}. Hollywood: 20th Century Fox Studio

Contents

Acknowledgments
5

Prologue
11

Sicilian Proverbs
13

Introduction
17

The Sicily of My Ancestors
23

Italian Migration
41

Peasant Life in Sicily
55

The Trip to America
59

The Voyage on the Principe di Piemonte
63

Principe di Piemonte
71

America – At Last!
73

Arrival on Ellis Island
77

An Advocate of the Immigrants
95

The Journey Continues…….
99

Angelo Cavallaro
107

Angela (Gravagna) Cavallaro
125

Angela (Angelina Cavallaro) Lamanna
141

Alfio (Alfred Michael) Cavallaro Sr.
157

Maria Catena (Mary Cavallaro) Lizzio
235

Giuseppe (Joseph P.) Cavallaro
257

Orazio (Roger Joseph) Cavallaro
281

Giovanna (Jennie / Joan Cavallaro) D'Amanda
311

Life on the Farm
329

The Annual Cavallaro Family Picnics
341

The Legacy They Left Us
349

Appendix
353

The Cavallaro Surname
355

Italian Influence on American Life
363

A Lifetime of Memories
395

Bibliography
411

Acknowledgments

As I recorded this account of our family history, I tried to adhere to the actual names and dates so it would be as accurate as possible. The people, incidents, and events recounted in this book are a collection of my childhood memories, stories my parents shared with me, and personal accounts from other family members. Therefore, this collaborative effort of interweaving memories adds to the richness of the Cavallaro legacy.

First, I need to express my debt to my parents, my grandparents, and my aunts and uncles whose lives made this book possible. Their struggles to succeed and search for a better life are traits, which I hope, have been passed on to each of us. Their love for each other and the importance they placed upon family closeness are qualities, which I have tried to weave throughout this book as I wrote the history of my family. I shall forever be grateful to them for showing me how they embraced the family and for giving me the rich heritage, which I have been able to pass on to my children.

I express deep gratitude to my cousins, Jennie Romeo, Angelo Lizzio, Joe Cavallaro, and Roger Cavallaro who played major roles in adding to the story sequence and providing some of the pictures, which I have used in this book. They shared the details to the anecdotal stories, exact place names, and the sequence of incidents, which were necessary to chronicle this historical account.

My special thanks are extended to my nephew, Bob Barone, who spent hours with me at the Holy Sepulchre Cemetery in Rochester, New York, searching out gravesites and obtaining information on my deceased relatives. Thank you to my great-niece, Anna Bahr, who helped me with some of the translations of songs from Italian to English. I express deep gratitude to my cousin, Frank Siracusa, who searched Ellis Island records in order to find the correct dates of departure and arrival, passenger lists, and genealogy charts. His interest, direction, and encouragement fed my passion and inspired me to complete this book.

I also want to thank to the North San Diego County Genealogical Society, for their support, guidance, classes, and access to their research materials, as they assisted me in my quest for more information. For the many others, whom I have not mentioned here, I give my sincere thanks.

It is important for me to express sincere thanks to my cousin, Angelo Lizzio. He was instrumental in providing early historical information about our ancestors. During each of my many trips to Rochester, from the time I began archiving the information for this book in 1980, to my last trip in 1995, he spent hours driving me to various sites that are mentioned in this book, including the farm location, and various homes where the Cavallaro's had lived. He shared some old photographs, and many of the stories that he remembered while growing up. I offer my heartfelt thanks to him and I am forever grateful for his tireless efforts and his important role in this journey.

Additional thanks to my daughter, Lisa Cavallaro, for all the time, patience, and effort she spent in helping me edit the entire book; also, for her positive suggestions on how to make the book better and more readable. Her computer savvy helped me complete this manuscript into the correct format for the publishers. I could not have done this without her assistance.

Last, but not least, I extend my sincere thanks to my wife, Aggie Cavallaro, for the continued encouragement she gave me, and for her patience in having me spend hours, days, and months at the computer while I was writing this book. Thanks to her, also, for diligently joining me as we traveled all over San Diego and Orange Counties, to the many Genealogy classes and seminars as I searched for more information and contacts to include in this book.

Molti grazie a tutti voi!

(Thanks so much to all of you!)

The New Colossus

❦

"Give me your tired, your poor, your huddled masses yearning to breathe free,
the wretched refuse of your teeming shore.
Send these, the homeless, tempest-tost to me,
I lift my lamp beside the golden door!"
Emma Lazarus, New York City 1883 (1849-1887)

Statue of Liberty and Ellis Island Coloring Book, A. G. Smith, Dover Publications, N.Y., 1985.

My Sicilian Legacy

The Struggles and Joys of Three Generations

Prologue

Picture yourself on a perfect moonlit night on the patio of a Sicilian café in Taormina that overlooks the beautiful blue Mediterranean Sea. The moon and stars are brilliant as their lights reflect off the waves that are rushing to the shore. You are sitting at a table, all alone. You're quietly enjoying the beauty that can only be experienced from these magnificent Sicilian shores. A soft, warm breeze is blowing across the patio. You can smell someone roasting peppers; the aroma of tomato sauce cooking accompanied by the smell of sweet basil escapes from a nearby ristorante to let you know that anytime is mealtime in this Sicilian town. In the distance, you can hear someone playing <u>Come Back to Sorrento</u> on the mandolin. What a perfect evening for you to be relaxing in the area where your own ancestors once walked.

On your table, sits a large, steaming cup of cappuccino that the waiter just delivered to you. A single candle glows on your table and its flame flickers as the gentle breezes come and go. You take a sip of your cappuccino, and close your eyes as you enjoy the rich tastes of this magnificent coffee. You pick up a book you brought with you to read........a history of the Cavallaro family. You open to the first chapter and you are captured by the story that is being revealed about your family, and other paisani that you know. You can close your eyes and picture your ancestors sitting with you at your table with a smile on their faces. As you begin to read, you are immediately brought back to the end of the nineteenth century in old Sicily, to the rural areas where your family lived, near the rich vineyards on the northern slopes of Mt. Etna. You know this is the beginning of a great adventure. It will bring you a new understanding of what encompassed the lives of your ancestors. As you read the incidents in the story, you'll experience many emotions; joy, anxiety, fear, and sadness, just to mention a few. Above all, you'll experience a new level of pride for being a Sicilian and for being part of the Cavallaro family. As you turn from page to page of each chapter, may you be reintroduced to our rich Sicilian culture and may the legacy that is yours be unfolded into reality.

Lettore, spero che godiate il vostro viaggio con la nostra Famaglia!
(Readers, I hope you enjoy your journey with our family as you read this book!)

Sicilian Proverbs

Sicilians brought with them to America, many proverbs which reflected their culture. They used these proverbs to illustrate a point, to encourage, or to give advice to others. These listed, best illustrate the theme of this book

Chi lascia la via vecchia per la nuova,
sa quel che lascia ma non sa quel che trova.

He who takes the new path rather than the old,
knows what he leaves behind but not what will unfold.

Dio chiude una porta e apre un portone.

God may close one door, but He will always open a larger one.
Keep your chin up and good fortune will come your way.

Lungo è il cammino, ma l'amore è forte.

Long and difficult is the road, but love conquers all.
Love knows no barriers it cannot overcome.

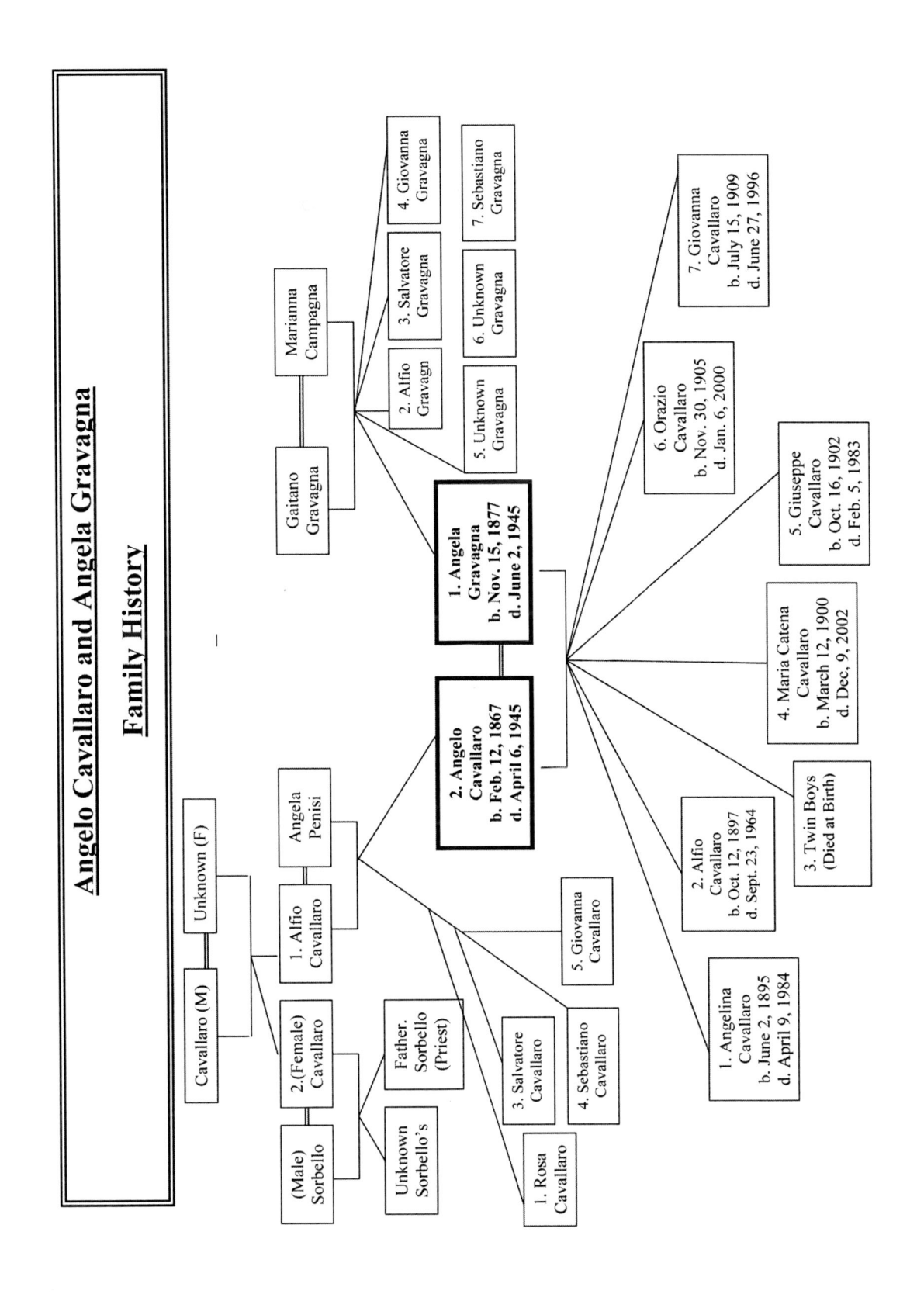

Angelo Cavallaro and Angela Gravagna

Family History

- Cavallaro (M) — Unknown (F)
  - 1. Alfio Cavallaro — Angela Penisi
    - 2. Angelo Cavallaro, b. Feb. 12, 1867, d. April 6, 1945
    - 1. Rosa Cavallaro
    - 3. Salvatore Cavallaro
    - 4. Sebastiano Cavallaro
    - 5. Giovanna Cavallaro
  - 2. (Female) Cavallaro — (Male) Sorbello
    - Unknown Sorbello's
    - Father. Sorbello (Priest)

- Gaitano Gravagna — Marianna Campagna
  - 1. Angela Gravagna, b. Nov. 15, 1877, d. June 2, 1945
  - 2. Alfio Gravagn
  - 3. Salvatore Gravagna
  - 4. Giovanna Gravagna
  - 5. Unknown Gravagna
  - 6. Unknown Gravagna
  - 7. Sebastiano Gravagna

Children of Angelo Cavallaro (b. Feb. 12, 1867, d. April 6, 1945) and Angela Gravagna (b. Nov. 15, 1877, d. June 2, 1945):

1. Angelina Cavallaro, b. June 2, 1895, d. April 9, 1984
2. Alfio Cavallaro, b. Oct. 12, 1897, d. Sept. 23, 1964
3. Twin Boys (Died at Birth)
4. Maria Catena Cavallaro, b. March 12, 1900, d. Dec, 9, 2002
5. Giuseppe Cavallaro, b. Oct. 16, 1902, d. Feb. 5, 1983
6. Orazio Cavallaro, b. Nov. 30, 1905, d. Jan. 6, 2000
7. Giovanna Cavallaro, b. July 15, 1909, d. June 27, 1996

Now the Lord said to Abram,
"Go forth from your country,
And from your relatives,
And from your father's house,
To the land which I will show you;
And I will make you a great nation,
And I will bless you,
And make your name great;
And so you shall be a blessing;
And I will bless those who bless you,
And the one who curses you I will curse.
And in you all the families of the earth shall be blessed."
So Abram went forth as the Lord had spoken to him; …..
Genesis 12:1-4a (NAS)

…..and so it was with the Cavallaro's, as our story begins.

Introduction

I can remember the day well. It was a warm afternoon in July 1980. I had traveled from my home in California to visit my mother who still lived in our hometown of Rochester, New York. Prior to my two-week visit, my mother was busy arranging for me to visit all my aunts and uncles, other relatives, and some friends while I was there. We were invited to their homes for dinner and enjoyed some quality time together. Although I had a full schedule, I looked forward to this with much anticipation. I knew it would be a fun trip.

One of these many invitations came from my Aunt Mary Lizzio. I always enjoyed seeing her at each of my visits. She had so much to share with me each time we saw her. This time, she was anxious to show me her new apartment located on Fernwood Park. My mother and I drove to her house and found that she had invited other family members for dinner also. Her son and daughter-in-law, Angelo and Audrey Lizzio, Aunt Jennie Cavallaro, and Uncle Roger and Aunt Lucy Cavallaro all joined us for dinner on that Sunday afternoon. After showing us her new apartment, she took great pride in sharing her crocheting, knitting, and embroidering projects, she had recently completed. Her apartment was lovely and I recognized many of the pictures, knick-knacks, and furniture from her former residence in Webster. Then we sat down at her large dining room table for dinner. It was quite an arduous task for a woman who was eighty years old to cook a complete dinner for eight people. I must admit, it was a delicious Italian meal complete with all the traditional favorites.

After dinner, we sat around the large dining room table and talked. They wanted to know about what was happening in California with me and my family. I shared pictures of my family and brought them up-to-date on our many activities. Since we were the first of the Cavallaro family to leave Rochester and move to the west coast, it was quite an adjustment for everyone. Although it had been ten years since I had moved to California, the conversation centered on how difficult it was to keep family ties strong when family members move away from their hometown. Aunt Mary quickly compared it to the time when her parents left Sicily. She told how they traveled with a family of six children to a foreign land, never more to return to see their family and friends they had left behind in their hometown. With that, the conversation escalated to much reminiscing about the old country. Stories were shared about the *paisani* that remained in Sicily and those who immigrated to the United States in later years. It was fascinating to hear about incidents they remembered as children growing up in the rural areas of northeastern Sicily.

I immediately became enthralled with all the information that was crossing back and forth across the table. I wanted to capture this information down on paper; to only talk about it was not enough, and I knew there were more details than I could remember to write down later. I asked Aunt Mary if she had a large sheet of paper that I could use to record the information. It was my intent to make a genealogical chart at that moment with the information they remembered. I wanted to know who my ancestors were and how they fit into my family tree. She searched for a few moments and finally returned with a piece of gray cardboard from the backing of a man's new dress shirt. I told her that would be fine and I began drawing boxes and connecting them with lines to see who belonged to whom.

Of course, we started with the relatives who were still living and their children; that was the easy part. Then, we began to work backwards to previous generations. My aunts and uncle could recall the names of most of their parent's siblings, the names of their grandparents, and other related people. Some of the names were unknown; however, they remembered how many siblings were in each family we discussed. The excitement was building around the table; they were so interested in capturing every detail. They watched me very closely to be sure that I spelled the names correctly and that I was connecting the right person with the correct family. There were times when Aunt Mary and Uncle Roger would disagree about a particular person's name or their placement in the genealogical sequence of the chart. At that point, and at numerous times during that conversation, Angelo was on the phone to his Aunt Grace Trovato. She had just returned from a trip to Sicily and visited the town they came from, and had even spoken to many of the people they knew while they were there. She, too, was very clear on her information and backed it up with conversations she had with them on her recent trip.

During this discussion, they shared many stories and their memories of things that happened in Sicily prior to their voyage to America, the actual trip on the boat, and their Ellis Island experiences. I wrote furiously to keep up with the excitement and laughter that dominated that conversation. As they told some of the stories, tears were shed because of the hard times they had on the boat and at Ellis Island. They made it very clear to me that it was a tremendous sacrifice that was accompanied by many difficult experiences. Taking a trip of that magnitude to a foreign country, for peasants traveling with six young children was a courageous endeavor; especially since they had never ventured out of Sicily.

As the day progressed and it became dark outside, I had completed the chart with as much information as I could glean from them. I also had a memo pad filled with hurriedly written notes of the stories they shared. As I left Aunt Mary's house, with my materials in my hands, she came up close to me and asked, "Now, what are you going to do with all this?" I told her and the others who were standing at the door with me, that I would transcribe all my notes, and try to put it in some order while I continued to collect more information on the family. I promised them that, eventually, I would write it into a book and make them all famous. They all laughed and wished me well. As I made this statement to them, they became more excited about what was to be birthed. On each subsequent visit I made to Rochester, they would ask me about my progress with the book and shared more information that they thought should be included.

On my six-hour flight back to California, I secured the notes in my carry-on bag. I didn't want to take any chance that they'd get lost with my luggage. These notes were a treasure and I could never duplicate them. While in flight, I took them out and began to read and rewrite them. As I read, a surge of excitement welled within me. I could close my eyes and visualize life, as it was when our family lived in the rural areas of Sicily, when they were young boys and girls playing on the scenic hillsides. I could see it and owned the vision as they did. It became a real place in my mind, a land of beauty.

I was so impressed that my aunts and uncle had not forgotten all the scenes and moments that had passed over all these years. In reality, the Sicily they left was no longer as they knew it. It was different now; but in their minds, they remembered it as it was then. The land they knew as children was so beautiful; they could never compare it to anywhere else they lived. As they recalled, in all of Sicily, there was no land as beautiful as the area around Mt. Etna, which was abundant with orange trees, grape vineyards, olive, and fig trees. They remembered the air always smelled of orange blossoms, rosemary, and basil growing in the gardens. They recalled the countryside being covered with various colors of bougainvillea growing along fences that lined the roads, up the trunks of huge trees, and up the sides of houses and onto their roofs. They described it so beautifully to me that I could see it as vividly as they did. Could I believe all the stories of these men and women, long since dead that they shared with me? I can only attribute them to the voices of those who told the stories with deep passion and clarity as though each incident happened just yesterday. The stories were real and each incident actually happened; they remembered every detail.

Shortly after I arrived home, I completed the rewriting process. I was so excited to be able to fill many of the gaps and put it into formal writing for others to appreciate. Was there enough to complete my quest? No. I soon discovered that this was just the tip of the iceberg; however, I needed to collect more information. Would I have enough information to tell their story? Yes. I would be able to write it in a story format; but there was much more research to uncover. I wanted to write a book about the Cavallaro family and the little corner of Sicily that they called home. I was determined to make this a goal for myself.

Over the years, each trip I made to Rochester, I researched more information about the family history. I made trips to the cemetery to take photographs of my relatives' monuments so I would have a record of the actual dates of their birth and death. Over five or six visits, I toured the old neighborhoods, collected maps of the area, and took photographs of landmarks where they worked and lived. On one trip, my cousin Angelo Lizzio and I spent many hours traveling through neighborhoods where our family lived; also, to see the farm that the Cavallaro family once owned. I have included the directions to the farm and pictures as it looks today in another chapter. I was able to see the original, barn where my father worked and where they kept the horses and chickens. Although it didn't look very sturdy, it was still on the grounds of the farm. That was a thrill for me to see.

On each of my trips, I would visit with Aunt Jennie Cavallaro (who came from the same town in Sicily) and she gave me more information that I needed. I'd also visit with Uncle Roger and Aunt Lucy Cavallaro to get additional information. From California, I would call my cousins in Rochester, Joe and Roger Cavallaro, Jennie Romeo, and Angelo Lizzio, and they gave me more family details. I began going through my parent's old photo albums to collect pictures of the family. My cousins also sent me pictures that enhanced the stories. Along with the documents my parents had given me, it was finally coming together.

In the ten years that followed, I enrolled in writing classes, attended many genealogical conferences, and visited the National Archives to obtain more information on the family. My cousin, Frank Siracusa, assisted me from the east coast by searching out other information that I was unable to locate. Little by little, each tidbit that I found filled in the missing gaps about my family history. I was slowly putting the pieces of the puzzle together. Throughout this process, an excitement was building up within me to the point that it was, and still is, an all-consuming project. It became the focus of my life; every book I bought and read, every documentary I taped, and every bit of research I collected, was for the purpose of getting more information about the rich history of Sicily These activities broadened my view of the unique characteristics that shaped my family.

I am about to publish this book, twenty-seven years after I started all the research on this project. I have been writing this book for about three years and I'm finally at the point where I see this story ending. I know that I could continue writing; however, it's important for me to share this information with all my living relatives in the Cavallaro family. The family is growing and many of the younger generations are not aware of their beginnings. It is my desire that everyone who reads this book is filled with the awe, gratitude, and respect that I experienced as I wrote the information about my family into a story. I hope that this will remind us all of our genealogical roots; that we may go back in time, examine our beginnings, and honor our family ancestors, as they well deserve. When you finish reading this book, you should feel proud to know more about where we came from. Our ancestors worked hard for what they had and we can thank each of them for where we are today in our careers, for our families, and for possessing the unique morals and characteristics of being a "Cavallaro." As you begin this historical journey, my hope is that these sequential chapters will truly enhance your understanding of family roots. When you finish reading the book, share it with a friend or read it to your children so they may know more about the struggles that immigrants experienced when they risked everything for the sake of their families. May it serve as road map for future generations.

As I sit here with my manuscript ready to go to the publisher's office, I hold it close to my heart and wrap my arms around it as a symbol of the love I have for my family. I love the Cavallaro family; my grandparents, my aunts and uncles, my dad and mom, my brother, my cousins, my nieces and nephews, and all that make up our Cavallaro lineage. I submit this to you as it has been my passion for many years, and I hope it becomes yours also; it has been my privilege to be able to write this history of my family and to share it with you. It has been my intent to honor each family member. Being a part of this family has filled me with great pride and my heart overflows with love for each of them. I hold my head a little bit higher today knowing that I am a Sicilian, and that I am a "Cavallaro." I hope those in my family feel likewise; and will pass that pride onto their children and grandchildren!

The Sicily of My Ancestors

I have some very dear friends who have one parent from Sicily and the other from mainland Italy. You might think they would consider themselves 100% Italian; however, they jokingly describe themselves as "half-Italian, half-Sicilian." That was always humorous to me because I always believed that Italy and Sicily were one nation, both flying the same Italian flag. After I visited Italy, I knew that there was some truth behind that statement, and I now know why they separated the two nations. Though they are both under the Italian flag, they are similar in many ways; however, they are also very proud of their differences. Some of the differences go back many centuries and they have become inbred within the people.

Of course, Italy and Sicily have much in common. They both possess breathtaking views of the crystal, clear and azure Mediterranean Sea; cuisine unequaled to any other European nation; and a generosity among the people that goes beyond the common hospitality that often is not seen elsewhere. Their expression of love for their family, friends, and other Italians is unequaled. Yet, the differences make these places and their inhabitants endearing in their own right. Visitors flock to Florence to view its Renaissance architecture; those visiting Palermo are charmed by its quaint Norman-Arabic dwellings. In Agrigento, people greet each other with *Buon Giorno* in the morning and *Buona Sera* in the evening; however, in Sorrento, it's *Ciao*, both day and night. Pompeii, conquered by the mighty Mount Vesuvius many years ago, still draws many tourists; Taormina, unaffected by the rumblings of the beautiful Mount Etna, continues to be a prime resort community. One trait Italians and Sicilians have in common is their leisurely attitude. They don't rush anything. They savor life as they savor their delicious pasta. You can apply *La Dolce Vita* (The Sweet Life) mentality to your experience when you visit the country.

During my stay in Italy, I found that Italians could identify Sicilians very easily. As we drove into Italy from the north, having been in Monaco previously, we approached the border crossing on our way to Genoa. At the Border crossing, I used what I thought was my perfect Italian in communicating with the inspectors, thinking I'd pass for a local citizen. However, the officers checking my passport gave me a very discriminating look and said, "You're Sicilian, aren't you?" I was astounded, because, at that time I had always considered myself as 'Italian' as anyone one else from Italy. I answered, "Yes, my parents were born in Sicily. But, how did you know I wasn't from Italy?" He said he could tell from my name, Cavallaro, and by my appearance; my olive complexion and dark hair gave me away. I was amazed.

After this incident, I was resolved that, yes, there were differences in the two cultures, and yet, there were many similarities. Therefore, I began to do some research to find out what made Sicily so different and what was in my background to identify me as Sicilian. What follows, is a brief research of where my family came from, and the historical significance of Sicily's culture. I am a part of what transpired in Sicily so many years ago. This is not something I can deny, nor can I fail to acknowledge any of its truth. It is all a part of Sicilian history and its richness lives within me. Now, let us examine a closer, more intimate view of my motherland; the land of my parents, grandparents, and ancestors; My Beautiful Sicily – *La Mia Sicilia Bella!*

Sicilia

Sicilia, or better known as Sicily in English, is an Italian island in the Mediterranean Sea off the tip of the Italian peninsula. On the east coast and at the Strait of Messina, it is only about two miles from the mainland of Italy. At the southwest coast, it is about ninety miles from Tunisia on the North African coast. It has a roughly triangular shape and is the largest region of Italy. There are nine provinces in Sicily, namely: Agrigento, Caltanissetta, Catania, Enna, Messina, Palermo, Ragusa, Siracusa, and Trapani.

Perhaps the Strait of Messina and the waters of the Mediterranean have protected Sicily from modernizing in the same ways its mainland neighbor, Italy, has progressed. Though cars may crowd the streets in Palermo, the remote roads that wind over the island cross wide expanses where your only companion may be a lone shepherd and his grazing flock of sheep and goats. Mountains and hills cover most of Sicily. Lush trees, laden with oranges, lemons and olives, sway gently in the breeze in all the coastal communities. Pink and yellow pastel-colored walls line medieval streets as they wind aimlessly over and around the hills. Bougainvillea in shades of peach, red, violet, and purple covers many of the houses. Mount Etna looms in the distance and is the island's highest point. It is an active volcano, and occasionally it will bellow and bring forth charcoal smoke that will frame Taormina into a Sicilian heaven. My ancestors grew up, and lived in this area until they immigrated to the United States. Mount Etna erupts periodically and in the 1908 earthquake, my father, only eleven years old at the time, said that he saw the lava as it oozed down the side of the mountain. He described it as being red hot and burning everything in its immediate vicinity. This heavily populated area was valuable because the volcanic ash made the soil extra fertile and it was perfect for farming and raising grapes in the vineyards. The 1908 eruption and earthquake destroyed the city of Messina; rebuilding efforts turned it into a thriving metropolis. Mount Etna is ever-present, though local Sicilians have adjusted to life in the shadow of an active volcano; a place the Greeks believed was the dwelling place of Vulcan, the god of fire and Homer's one-eyed monster, The Cyclops.

The climate of Sicily is very mild and temperatures average 50° in the winter and 85° in the summer. Most of the rain occurs during the winter, with little rain falling between the months of March to October. During the summer, they experience drier air with hot winds called, *sirocco*. This wind blows across the Mediterranean Sea from the deserts of North Africa, which cause many of the Sicilian rivers to dry up during the hot summer months. The land, parched in areas, is not totally irrigated. At one time, Sicily was a heavily wooded area, but most of the trees were cut down leaving the mountainsides bare, causing them to erode easily. Farmers used much of the island for growing wheat and for grazing goats and sheep. Along the coast, irrigation provides water for crops, such as, almonds, grapes, lemons, olives, oranges, and potatoes. The coastal areas are heavily dependant upon their fishing industry.

I remember when my Aunt Angie and Uncle Fritz moved to southern California. They lived in Westminster and they wrote back saying that the weather was just like Sicily. Now that I live here myself, I can easily see that we have almost the identical climate and we raise the same kinds of crops. For this reason, my Aunt Angie and Uncle Fritz loved living in California for the short time they were there.

An Island of Many Cultures

Though Sicily may appear to be isolated now, its location in the near-geographic center of the Mediterranean Sea made it a crossroads of invasion for as many as fifteen different empires over a period of 2,000 years. Greek Tyrants, Arab Emirs, Norman Knights, Byzantine Bishops and Holy Roman Emperors had all turned their eyes to Sicily, leaving traces of their reign speckled all over the island. Sicilians have a cultural makeup unequaled to any other population of the European continent. A perfect example of this is to view the people of Palermo, the capital city of Sicily. There is no other city in Europe that has such diverse roots as Palermo. They just do not fit the image of what Sicilians usually look like. It is common to see blond-haired, blue-eyed *bambini* playing in the streets of Palermo. As viewed by Sicilians from the east coast, they believe that blond-haired, blue-eyed people do not fit the image of most Sicilians. This is especially true when contrasted with the Provincia di Catania, where people with their dark hair, dark eyes, and olive skin occupy the area. However, looking at the history of Sicily, having a variety of physical characteristics can be attributed to William the Conqueror and the Normans.

Prior to 1060, the Normans (the French and Scandinavians) launched a campaign to gain control of Sicily from its Arab residents. The Norman influence remains in both the buildings and bloodlines of Palermo; thus, blond haired, blue-eyed, and fair-skinned people are present there today. Later, in 1066, William the Conqueror set his sights on another island to conquer – England. Many of the cathedrals and churches that survived the 1943 Allied bombings highlight their Arab and Norman roots.

Searching Sicily's very early beginnings and as early as 700 B.C., the Greeks colonized the eastern part of the island; the western part of the island was colonized by the Carthaginians. The Romans conquered Sicily in the 200's B.C. and made it their first province. Sicily was important to the Romans because they supplied all the grain for the Roman Empire. Under their rule, the island became an important food supplier and slaves worked the many great estates. In general, Sicily was subject to exploitation during these years and was under the control of a variety of different rulers.

After the decline of Rome during 400 A.D., the Vandals (wandering Germans) and the Goths conquered Sicily. In 535 A.D., it was under the control of the Byzantine Empire (eastern part of the Roman Empire – Russia, parts of Asia, and Greece). The official language of Sicily became Greek. Sicily has more ancient Greek temples than Greece itself. Nearly all of them are Doric in design – the same style as the Parthenon in Athens, Greece. During the 8th Century, the Greeks and Carthaginians arrived from Rhodes and Corinth to colonize Naples, Calabria, and the entire eastern area of Sicily. The colonies of Catania and Siracusa thrived and encouraged Greek trade routes to the west. Throughout the occupation of the Greeks and the Carthaginians, there was constant fighting among them; however, the Greeks always prevailed. During the latter years of the 8th Century, the Arabs began making raids on Sicily to capture the island from Greece.

About three hundred years later, North African Muslims replaced the Byzantine rulers and Sicily flourished again for about 200 years under Muslim rule. They were responsible for the introduction of irrigation and a variety of crops, such as, cotton, lemons, and oranges to the island. The Muslim's art, literature, and science influenced the Sicilian culture as well.

In time, Arab rule weakened by internal decay and conflict, and in 1060, the Norman's began to occupy Sicily. Under Roger II (1130-1154 A.D.), Palermo was the capital of the kingdom that included not only southern Italy, but also parts of Greece. During this time, the capitol had the reputation as a great intellectual and cultural center where the Christian and Islamic cultures were blended. Under the Norman rule, the island's culture gradually became one with western European influences. Later, during the 1200's A.D., the German, and French who ruled the island added to the mixture of traditions in Sicily. In 1282, an uprising called the Sicilian Vespers, resulted in the massacre of nearly all the French on the island, which ended French rule forever.

During the next 400 years, Spain and Austria ruled Sicily. When Sicily came under Spanish rule in the 1300's, Peter IV of Aragon, acquired the island. Spanish rule was inefficient, cruel, and corrupt. Sicily was finally freed from Spanish rule in the nineteenth century. In the 1700's, a Spanish branch of the royal Bourbon family began to rule Sicily. Sicily and Naples joined as the Bourbon ruled Kingdom of the Two Sicilies in 1816 A.D. The Kingdom of the Two Sicilies played an important part in the movement for a united Italy. In 1820, there was an uprising in Naples and King Ferdinand was forced to grant the Neapolitans a constitution. After 1860, when the Italian patriot Giuseppe Garibaldi invaded Sicily, the island revolted against Bourbon rule and it became a part of the Kingdom of Italy in 1861. Garibaldi conquered the Kingdom of the Two Sicilies for the Kingdom of Italy, which was just coming into being. Later that year, it all became part of the total domain of Victor Emmanuel II, who became King of Italy in 1861. There is a huge white marble building erected near the center of Rome and dedicated to the memory of Victor Emmanuel II. It is one city block long and one city block wide in size; it is the location of the site of the Italian Unknown Soldier. It is important to remember that when Victor Emmanuel II became King of Italy in 1861, it was only six years prior to the birth of my grandfather, Angelo Cavallaro, in Sicily. Therefore, he grew up in the new Sicily with all the difficulties that any new nation would experience at their birth.

When Garibaldi invaded Sicily in 1860, the Sicilians were more than ready to welcome him and his Redshirts. They consisted of a thousand volunteers to help fight for Sicily's freedom from its Bourbon rulers. Garibaldi landed at Marsala, Sicily (known for its Marsala wines) on May 11, 1860, and he occupied Palermo on the west coast by June 6, 1860. By July 27, 1860, he overtook Messina on the east coast. He conquered the island of Sicily for the Kingdom of Sardinia at that time; eventually, the island was transferred to the Kingdom of Italy in 1861, and under the rule of Victor Emmanuel II.

Recent History of Sicily

During World War II, all of the Axis powers used Sicilian ports and airfields. This was beneficial for them, as they needed to be close by in order to support their armies in northern Africa. On July 23, 1943, American forces invaded Sicily by air and naval bombardments. They took control of Palermo on July 23; the Germans abandoned Catania on August 5; and the Americans captured Messina on August 17, 1943. At this point of the European Campaign, only Allied forces occupied Sicily. This successful invasion of Sicily brought about the immediate fall of Benito Mussolini and Sicily became the springboard for the Allied invasion of Italy. Italy made peace with the Allies on September 8, 1943. During that invasion of Sicily, Sicilian and Italian immigrants living in the United States were very concerned for the people. They still had friends and relatives who lived there and they feared for their lives. During the 1950's, Sicily began a major road construction program on the eastern portion of the island. Their first super highway, linking Catania and Messina, opened in 1971. They have continued to build better roads and highways to this day, making travel much more enjoyable to the many tourists who visit the country.

In conclusion, the historical development of Sicily has affected the ethnicity of the people. Sicilians represent a mixture of many elements, including Sicilian, Greek, Carthaginian, Roman, Arab, Berber; Norman, French, German, and Spanish to name a few. During the period of Muslim rule, one third of the population was of North African origin. In general, they tended to be short, stocky, and olive-complected, with dark hair and eyes. This was a contrast to the people who inhabited Sicily earlier and to those living on the mainland of Italy. Much of these same characteristics are present in the southern Italians; however, as one travels through Italy toward the northern borders of Switzerland and France, the people are seen to be much taller, thinner, lighter skinned and with very light hair (blonds and redheads).

The People of Sicily

Because the Sicilians are a mixture of many ancient civilizations, the people speak many local dialects (forms of speech) that have traces of Arabic, Greek, Spanish, and other languages. Regardless of their individual dialects, they all share strong bonds of family and personal relationships. The hundreds of years of invasion, foreign rule, and poverty discouraged the people's trust in the government and they were encouraged to follow a code of ethics called the *Omertà*. The *Omertà* is a code that identifies a person who cooperates with the government as being dishonorable. This code, which supports the Mafia code of ethics, is a tradition of personal and private justice for the people. Sicilians and Italians who ever needed help, whether in their home country or in their new home of America, called upon the services of the Mafia to protect them, help them through difficult times, or with people who were dealing with them unfairly. They always could depend on the Mafia to support them; however, in turn, the Mafia used their assistance as a means to gain support from these people when needed. At that time, Sicilians felt the Mafia to be a very helpful and useful group; but also, one where you could not question any of their policies, beliefs, or tactics; most of which were unwritten codes, such as the *Omertà*. They viewed the Mafia as engaging in various illegal activities. Many Sicilians became increasingly opposed to Mafia involvement. During the 1980's, the Italian government waged a campaign to fight organized crime and convicted hundreds of people associated with the Mafia.

Of course, we all remember the name made famous by the Martin Scorsese classic, <u>The Godfather</u>; the name of Don Vito Corleone. Corleone derives its name from a town located at the top of a hill in central Sicily. It is in this small community of Corleone where the true Sicily can be revealed. Brown-eyed, black-haired children play in the streets among the houses chiseled into the hillside. Cheese makers in the local street markets offer their *pecorino* and *provolone*, favorites of Sicilian chefs for use in pastas. Corleone's Mafia heritage is evident throughout the city; however, it has softened during the past fifty years.

During the years that Angelo Cavallaro was growing up, many Sicilians were farmers and worked the land. Others worked as fishermen, stonecutters, wine makers, and tailors of fine clothing. A lack of jobs was one of the chief reasons for the high rate of emigration from 1890 to 1915. More than one million Sicilians moved to the United States from 1876 to 1925. Since the end of World War II in 1945, many Sicilian workers settled in the industrial cities of northern Italy, France, Germany, and Switzerland.

Most Sicilians are Roman Catholics and their religious celebrations often include colorful parades where men throughout the town carry statues of the Blessed Mother or of their favorite patron saints on flowered platforms. As the procession weaves in and out of the tiny streets, members of the church follow it and/or the *società* (society) affiliated with the celebration to the central piazza. It is there that they have a full day's festival with food, music, and dancing climaxed by a fireworks display in the evening.

Italian, like French and Spanish, is a romance language; one of several languages that came from Latin roots. The standard Italian language evolved from the true Italian Tongue, which is spoken in the province of Tuscany. Its use in public schools, television, and radio has helped make it the principal language of most Italians. However, some people still speak the regional dialects, which differ greatly from one another. Italians in northern Italy speak an Italian dialect closely related to the French and Germanic languages and contains different accents in many words. Italians in the southern provinces of Italy speak a dialect that is very different and closely related to the dialects spoken in Sicily. It is in these Sicilian dialects that many of the words are shortened, their sounds slurred together, and many of the words end with the 'u' sound, rather than the regular vowel sounds that end most Italian words. Some of these are words such as *figliu* - child (fĕg'-you), or *sangu* - blood (san'-goo). In correct Italian, they would be pronounced *figlio* (fil-lee-o) and *sangue* (son-gway). Consequently, when one listens to Sicilian people speaking to each other, they will hear many words ending in the 'u' sound, making it sound quite different from the true Tuscan Italian language.

In my younger years, I was privileged to hear both English and Sicilian spoken in my home and many of the words my family used continue to be very special to me. When Sicilians spoke about anything, they could always back it up by a common Sicilian phrase that would firm up the particular point they were making. These phrases were referred to as Sicilian Proverbs. One Sicilian proverb my father used comes to mind, which demonstrates the predominance of the 'u' sound in the language. Whenever he'd open a new barrel of wine that he had made, he would say, "*u vinu ti fa sangu*" (oo vee-noo tee fa son-goo) meaning "wine will improve your blood." Sicilians truly believed that adage, so much so, that it was a common practice for adults to offer little sips of the new wine from the recently opened barrels to toddlers and pre-schoolers each spring.

The Way of Life

Life in northern Italy differs significantly from that in southern Italy and Sicily. Since many of the Italian industrial centers are located in the northern part of Italy, it is financially richer, and more urbanized, than the south. Manufacturing, major industries, and construction companies employ most people in the north; but the percentage of people who work in agriculture is much higher in the southern farming communities. Although the younger generations of Italians dream of moving to the larger metropolitan areas, most Italians are strongly attached to the towns of their birth, neighborhoods, and families. Many people, who leave their homes in southern Italy in search of greater opportunities in the north, hope to return eventually to the communities of their birth, sometime later in their lives.

My Cavallaro ancestors left Sicily with this same plan in mind. They believed they would travel to America, make the promised money, and then return to Passopisciaro to live like kings. For over 90% of the emigrants that left Sicily, that dream never happened. When they arrived in America and settled in the same area as their other *paisani*, this new community was the closest thing that resembled their former home in Sicily and they fell in love with it. They quickly became acclimated to their new surroundings and they saw this was an acceptable place for them to live; therefore, their decision was to settle in and take up residence. This emerged as a new *Sicilia* for them – a home away from home.

Sicilian Foods Become Part of the American Culture

Coming to America brought many changes in the lives of the immigrants. The new way of life and the different American customs they had to encounter became a challenge for them. Although they began to learn how to use the new American money system and started to learn some new words in their new language, some of the customs they brought with them gave them comfort. One of these was their style of cooking. They had memorized all their favorite recipes and could put together an Italian meal in a short amount of time. Because they did not rely on written recipes, they would use 'a handful of this' and 'a pinch of that,' or 'a little bit of this,' and 'a little bit of that.' Although they understood these unusual measurements, it was difficult to teach this way of thinking to someone else.

In no time at all, the neighborhood became alive with the aromas of Italian foods that were being prepared in each household. One could walk down the street and take in the distinctive smells of the various foods prepared by the newly arrived immigrants. From the Italian homes, the fragrances of fresh tomato sauce, eggplant parmigiana, or sausage and peppers being prepared for the evening meal filled the air. There were also many Jewish families living in the area and they too were cooking favorites, including kugels or pastrami for their evening meal. These unique aromas were intermingled throughout the neighborhood. As people walked down the street, their appetites were stimulated by all the savory smells coming from each of the homes.

Sicilians take great pride in the quality of their specialty recipes and general cooking skills. They traditionally eat their main meal at midday. Large meals usually consist of a pasta course, followed by a main course of meat or fish. Sometimes a course of antipasto is served before the pasta. The antipasto would consist of a variety of vegetables, cold meats such as prosciutto and salami, olives, artichoke hearts, anchovies, and various cheeses.

One of the main differences in Italian and Sicilian cuisine is in the cooking of their pastas and pizzas. In the north of Italy, flat, ribbon-shaped pastas are served with cream sauces and are embellished with fish and expensive cheeses. In the south, macaroni is served with tomato-based sauces, with meat or without meat as a marinara sauce, or primavera style with many vegetables. Pasta made with any type of tomato sauce is fondly referred to as *pasta cu sucu* (pas'-ta coo soo'-coo). Sometimes, soups of many varieties are substituted for pasta as a first course. In southern Italy and Sicily, where most of the farms are located, they would contain many varieties of yellow and green vegetables.

Sicilians make special soups called *verdure* (ver-doo'-rah), *minestra* (min-es-tra) or *minestrone* (min-es-trō-nā). One of the favorite side dishes they eat is called *cicoria* (chee-cor'-ree-a) which is a bitter type of dandelion plant. Most of their soups and side dishes are made with any variety of vegetable that is available to them.

Living in an agricultural area and in the midst of many varieties of vegetables being grown, one of their specialties and a staple with Sicilian families was, and still is, *pasta è fagioli* (*ditalini* - 'short macaroni' with beans and vegetables). This humble dish used to be particularly popular during the religious observance of Lent and on days of fasting. Many types of beans can be added, but most times, *ceci* beans (chick-peas/garbanzo beans) are used with red lima beans.

When making their *pasta è fagioli*, Sicilians include all the basic ingredients; then, embellish it with a variety of vegetables already at their home. Color is an important component to consider when preparing meals; many different types of vegetables are used to make each dish pleasing to the eye, as well as to the tongue. The following rendition of this popular staple dish offers a healthy dose of food value as well as color: tomatoes (red), spinach and zucchini (green), carrots (orange), onions and garlic (white), pasta (yellow), and don't forget the *fagioli*, (beans - deep red), and/or *ceci* (garbanzo beans - light beige). Here is a basic recipe for Pasta è Fagioli Soup; so, you too, can enjoy the popular dish that was made famous among the immigrant Sicilians.

Pasta è Fagioli Soup
(Makes 8 Servings)

- 1 tablespoon olive oil
- 2 cloves garlic, minced
- 1 onion, chopped
- 2 carrots, chopped
- 1 small zucchini, quartered lengthwise, then sliced ¼" thick
- 1 (14.5 ounce) can diced tomatoes
- 2 (14.5 ounce cans fat-free, beef broth
- 2 cups water
- 1 teaspoon dry basil leaves
- ½ teaspoon dry oregano leaves
- ¼ teaspoon ground pepper
- 1 (15 ounce) can red kidney beans, and/or garbanzo beans, drained and rinsed
- 1 cup loosely packed, fresh spinach leaves, minced or whole
- 2 tablespoons minced fresh parsley
- ¾ cups pasta, either small shell or small elbow macaroni (so it can be eaten with a spoon)
- ½ cup grated parmesan cheese

Heat the olive oil in a large saucepan over medium-high heat. Add the garlic, onion, and carrots. Cook the ingredients, stirring frequently, until the onions are tender. Stir in the zucchini, tomatoes, broth, water, basil, oregano, and pepper (salt to taste). Cover and heat to boiling. Reduce heat and cook fifteen minutes. Stir in the kidney beans and/or garbanzo beans, spinach, and parsley. Cover and cook fifteen minutes. Increase heat to high. Add pasta and cook about ten minutes more, or until the pasta is tender. Ladle into large soup bowls and top each with grated parmesan cheese. Now, sit and enjoy this wonderful meal.

A legend that surrounds this famous soup and is often told to young Sicilian children:

On March 31, 1282, the citizens of Palermo, Sicily began a revolt against the French occupation forces. The Sicilians, who had long desired independence, turned on the French with a bloody vengeance. Anyone who was French was slaughtered. The popular legend claims that to determine who was and who wasn't French, the Sicilians asked possible suspects to say the word ceci, which means chickpea or garbanzo bean. Ceci is loosely pronounced "cĕ'-chēē." If your pronunciation was off, you were exposed. The use of the ceci bean was very popular so all the Sicilians would have known how to pronounce it correctly. Because of the popularity of this legend, Sicilians chose to use it in much of their cooking; it was mainly featured in their hearty soup, which is known today as pasta e fagioli.

Being more agricultural and always on the brink of poverty, the southern Italians and Sicilians ate more vegetables than meat. Vegetables were cheaper because they could be grown on their own land. Meat was customarily served on feast days, holidays, Sundays or at special events. At these special times, lamb was used for the main meal, while beef or pork were usually used in the making of meatballs – *polpetti* (pol-pet'-tē); veal - *scalapini* (scă-lă-pē'-nē); or *brisciola* (brē-shall'-lă) (rolled meat stuffed with salami, hard-boiled eggs, celery and herbs). These were some of the favorite dishes my ancestors made in Sicily. Once they arrived in America, they continued to make them for their families. Because of their popularity, they now appear on most menus in Italian restaurants. Pizza, which has become very popular in America, is very different in Italy. In northern Italy, it usually consists of a very thin crust, tomato sauce, vegetables, various meats, and a little cheese. Many times in northern Italy, tomato sauce is replaced with a creamy, white sauce and then it is called *pizza bianco* (white pizza). It is enjoyed as a snack or as a substitute for bread. This is contrasted in southern Italy and Sicily where pizza takes on a much different appearance. It is usually prepared with a type of bread dough. In the process of preparation, the dough is allowed to rise twice. Then, it is liberally covered with fresh tomato sauce, vegetables, and cheese. It is baked in oven a little longer than a thin crust pizza. Here it is eaten as a basic staple or main dish, which is more economical and affordable for the poorer people of the south.

A meal would not be complete without a variety of Sicilian desserts. Many of the desserts which have been made famous in America are items such as, *cannoli* stuffed with ricotta or cream; rum cakes; *pizzelle* (anise flavored lace cookie), and plain flour and egg cookies often shaped in an 'S' or the letter of a person's name. Other desserts may include *biscotti, tiramisu*, sesame cookies, and fruitcake made with the Italian liqueur, sweet Vermouth.

Italians have had a great affect on the foods eaten in America. Italian restaurants are in abundance throughout the United States and are favorites for Italians and non-Italians alike.

It is very common for many children to choose pizza as their favorite food. The cooking channels on television have programs showing chefs who demonstrate how to make Italian dishes every day. Whichever way you look at it, Italian food has had a tremendous impact on this country.

The Arts of Sicily

We have much to be proud of when we consider what the Italians have given the world in the field of The Arts. Three great Italian writers shaped the Italian language with their writings. In the 1300's, Dante, Petrarch, and Giovanni Boccaccio shared their writings with the world. Dante's The Divine Comedy is a masterpiece of poetry; Boccaccio's Decameron is one of the most popular collections of short stories ever written, and Petrarch's love poetry served as a model for poets around the world for centuries.

Italian composers have played a major role in music since the Middle Ages. Much of the classical Italian music is attributed to the music of Scarlatti, Antonio Vivaldi, and operas composed by Giuseppe Verdi, Giacomo Puccini, Gioacchino Rossini, Ruggiero Leoncavallo, and Pietro Mascagni. When we hear the strings playing The Four Seasons, The William Tell Overture, and The Intermezzo from Cavalleria Rusticana, we can thank our Italian composers. We can also thank them for the beautiful and melodic operas, such as, La Traviata, La Bohemè, Pagliacci, and Rigoletto among others of equal fame.

Some of our great Italian Artists and sculptors include Fra Angelico, Leonardo da Vinci, Raphael, and Michaelangelo. The beautiful paintings of the Sistine Chapel in St. Peter's Cathedral, the Mona Lisa, and The Last Supper; sculptures of La Pietà and The David are beautiful examples of art that have truly blessed the world.

These are but a few of the most famous artisans from Italy. Their contributions have made a significant impact to the world.

The Sicily of the Cavallaro Family

Although Sicily is an island with many cities and towns, our Cavallaro family lived only in the northeastern section of Sicily, in towns near the coast and very close to Mount Etna.

The towns that I mention here are the larger towns that my parents spoke of many times; however, it was common for all Sicilians to have used the name of the larger town in their conversations, even though they really lived in the countryside, somewhere near that town. Using the name of the larger town made it more recognizable to others so they could tell the general location of their residence. I remember my father mentioning the town he came from, Passopisciaro and it was always followed by, La Provincia de Catania; meaning that it was somewhere in the Province of Catania, located on the east coast of Sicily. Some thought that he actually came from Catania; however, I doubt he ever visited there.

Giarre: I will begin with the community of Giarre. When I tried to investigate the birthplace of my grandfather, Angelo Cavallaro, his children all said that he was born in Giarre. However, after further discussion, they all agreed that it was probably in a small township just outside the city of Giarre. My father spoke of Riposto and Mascali located just outside of Giarre. It could have been any one of these. Giarre is approximately fifteen miles north of Catania and on the east coast of Sicily. It's important to note that Giarre is quite a large city now. It has a population of approximately 30,000 people. The lava from Mount Etna paves the streets. It has many eclectic buildings and a huge 18th century church. Giarre was once part of the feudal estate belonging to the Mascali, bestowed upon the Bishop of Catania by Roger II in 1124 A.D. Giarre's name comes from the Sicilian word that means 'jars,' in which the tithes on the harvest due to the bishop were collected. The jars were called *giarre*. Il Duomo is an imposing neo-classical building with twin square-set bell towers. The town's main *piazza* is Via Callipoli, which is lined with elegant shops and townhouses, including the Palazzo Bonaventura, and the Palozzi Quacttrocchi, which is very ornamental with traces of Moorish designs.

Giarre is the wine producing center of Sicily. It is the first coastal stop on the Circumetnea Railway. One of the most popular streets is Via L.S. Turzo, which is lined with handicraft shops. It is here where many of the town's ceramics and Sicilian folk art are sold. It is also the site of the famous shop of Giuseppi Cicala, at number 59, who is one of the last artisans to make authentic Sicilian puppets. Sicilian puppets are seen all over the island and puppet shows are very common on street corners in both Sicily and southern Italy. It is usually on these street corners where you would find the infamous 'Hurdy-Gurdy Man' with his trained monkey begging for coins. As he plays his organ grinder, the monkey dances around and passes a tin cup among the people to gather coins. Life in the piazzas of Giarre is full of music, shops with folk art, and puppet shows for the children to enjoy.

Piedimonte Etneo: This is the community where my grandmother, Angela Gravagna Cavallaro was born. Although she did not live there very long, she always listed that city as the place of her birth. All information I found, including the Manifest (passenger list) from the boat, lists Piedimonte Etneo as her birthplace. It is located approximately twenty-five miles northwest of Giarre and on the slopes of Mount Etna. It continues to be a small community to this day, with barely over 6,000 inhabitants. It is known for its rich production of citrus fruits, floral plants and all varieties of grapes. Each autumn, they have a vintage feast, called *La Vendemmia*. Held at the end of September, the people display wood and iron handicrafts, preserved fruits and fine, hand embroideries of all sorts. People from all over the eastern coast of Sicily frequent this event.

The original name of the town is Piedimonte. In 1687, its founder, Ferdinando Gravina, changed it to Piedimonte Etneo because the town was situated at the foot of the volcano. The town was under the dominion of this noble family until the abolition of the feudal rights. It is interesting to note that the founder's name of this town was Gravina. My grandmother Angela's last name was Gravagna. In the two hundred years that passed until she was born, it could very possibly be that the spelling of the name was changed, altered or misspelled to the present spelling of Angela's name. If that is the case, her family may be direct descendents of Ferdinando Gravina and inherit that nobility.

Castiglione di Sicilia: This community has become a part of my family history because it appears on the legal documents of many of my relatives. It appears on the birth records of Joseph, Roger, and Jennie Cavallaro, indicating that they were born in Castiglione di Sicilia. When I was gathering the information from my Aunt Mary, Uncle Roger and Aunt Jennie, they insisted that all the children, with the exception of Aunt Angie, were born in Passopisciaro. Upon further research, I found out that Castiglione di Sicilia was the largest and closest city that was near Passopisciaro and the only one that had a town hall where legal documents could be filed. This is where the people from all the small surrounding communities went to file documents for births, marriages, and deaths; however, it doesn't necessarily mean that they were born in that particular community. In my research, I found that the village of Passopisciaro belongs to the larger city of Castiglione di Sicilia.

Castiglione di Sicilia is situated about five miles east of Passopisciaro and on the hilly slopes of Mount Etna. The name, derived from the Latin *Castrum Leonia*, means 'Castle of the Lion' because of the presence of a cliff called Leone (lion) in the town's higher area. Because of this, it was called Castel Leone for many years. The Castel Leone of the Norman era is a clear and graphic example of the bridge to Arab roots along with some traces to the Middle Ages. The castle is now in ruins, yet it still dominates the town's view. Set as it is, on an amazing rocky hillside, it appears it be fused to the earth. The site of the castle has been a lookout point since ancient times. From there, one can view the entire town including Mount Etna. To the east, lie the ruins of a fortress dating from 750 B.C. The main monuments are clustered around the highest part of the town.

This section of Sicily is outstanding for its rich production of grapes used for wine, vegetables, citrus fruits, and excellent olive oil, as well as for large varieties of cheeses. Goat and pig ranches flourish along with large plantations of walnut and almond trees.

Passopisciaro: This is the place that I had heard my father refer to repeatedly, "Passopisciaro! Passopisciaro! Passopisciaro!" I heard it so often, that I thought it was the capitol of Sicily. In fact, I thought that everyone who came from Sicily came from Passopisciaro. It was the town where five of the six Cavallaro children were born, where they grew up, and lived until they immigrated to the United States. One can view some of the most beautiful scenery in all of Sicily here. In the hills, there are numerous russet-colored houses, many of which are now abandoned. There are excellent views of the volcano, and to the north are the wooded mountains of Alcantara. Only three miles apart, Passopisciaro is a suburb of Randazzo in the Alcantara valley. It is located ten miles west of Taormina, and one of approximately ten towns that sit closest to the crater of Mount Etna. It is located about five miles from Linguaglossa, another town I heard mentioned repeatedly. These communities are built on lava beds, making the soil in that area very rich.

The population of Passopisciaro is not very large and according to my recent research, it shows a population of only 500 inhabitants. In the past, when the small village had known a certain economic prosperity, it had reached 1,500 inhabitants. Legends say that its name dates back to the beginning of the 1700s. A fishmonger (*pescatore* – in Italian, and *pisciaro* in Sicilian) was assassinated at the hands of an adventurous brigade of that period. This community had been the path of many fishermen upon their return from fishing trips; therefore, it was called, 'The Way of the Fishermen' or Passopisciaro.

The majority of the residents, which make up the population, are not natives of Passopisciaro. The landowners, in order to defend their interests, brought workers from their own region to work the land. Most of them came from the nearby city of Acireale. This explains why the people from this community all speak different dialects or a combination of three or four different local dialects. The landowners came to these places because they bought up all the land to plant vineyards. The ground was very rich and the climate was perfect for growing all varieties of grapes. They invested in the region, bringing in large groups of workers from other communities and it became the largest wine producing area in all of Sicily. The low growing vineyards in this region produce excellent red and white wines – Etna Rosso and Etna Bianco. These wines are exported into Italy and all over the European continent. This large production of wine brought work to the entire village for many years.

With the inception of World War II, the fighting in Sicily and its eventual occupation by the allied forces, affected them greatly. There was great destruction in this area and the economy of the tiny village was greatly affected. At the conclusion of the war, there was nothing but misery present and it pushed many people to the sad choice of emigration again; mainly to the Americas and Australia. This small community, which has had a tumultuous history, continues to survive on an essentially agricultural economy, wine, and oil production above all. The people continue to seek a re-emergence with its old splendors and respond to the economic crisis that affects the entire valley. They are currently attempting to create an interest in tourism, which will help them conquer their continuing despair.

The community has many churches, four of which I would like to address at this time. Santa Mona is a 13th century church and is the town's major Cathedral currently. Santa Nicola is a church built during the 16th and 17th centuries. The church was badly damaged by the bombings in 1943 during World War II. It was in this church that the Germans made the strong point of their last resistance on the island. Santo Martino, built in the 14th century, was damaged during World War II; however, the *Campanella* (bell tower) is still used to this day. During the medieval times, there was great rivalry around these three churches. The parishioners were Greek, Latin, or Lombards. Each church spoke in a different dialect. The last church I want to mention is the *Chiesa Madre di Colonna* (Church of Mother Colonna). This church was completed in 1897, the year that my father was born. It was in this church where the Cavallaro family attended Sunday mass. It was also at this church where my father received special training to become an altar boy at the age of nine years old. He attended school up to third grade at the church school.

Although Passopisciaro does not claim great works of art, their churches contain most of the art that is located in the town. The architecture of these churches offers much artistic and creative interest. Most of their churches contain rose windows, and in the niches around the interior, are frescoes painted by artists from Rome, Florence, and Sicily. Many of the statues in the niches have been carved out of lava stone and limestone indigenous to the area.

Closing Comments

With this short history of the island of Sicily, I have tried to share with you a little bit of the background from which my ancestors emigrated. Many have toured Sicily and returned with glowing reports of the scenic views that are some of the most beautiful that they have ever viewed. Many writers have repeatedly vacationed in Sicily and have returned saying that it was their favorite place to visit. Others have lived in Sicily for long periods because there was nowhere on earth that could equal its beauty, way of life, and cuisine. Some of those whom you may recognize and had their residence in Sicily were Ernest Hemmingway, Henry Faulkner, Bertrand Russell, Tennessee Williams, and Roald Dahl. Johann von Goethe (1749-1832) after one of his visits to Sicily 1787 writes,

"I am happy to think that I now carry in my soul a picture of Sicily; that unique and beautiful island."

After that same trip, he wrote,

"To have seen Italy without having seen Sicily is not to have seen Italy at all, for Sicily is the clue to everything."

My ancestors raved about the beauty of Sicily and that it could not be equaled anywhere. I have heard many vacationers, upon their return from trips to Sicily, enthusiastically share their comments about its beauty. Because of the warmth of its people, the beauty of its countryside, and the cuisine that is associated only to this island, Sicily bids us all an affectionate welcome to visit her. It was a magical country to my ancestors, and it continues to tempt people to her shores to this day.

Italian Migration

As we begin our discussion on Italian Migration, it is important to note that when I refer to 'Italian,' I also am including the Sicilian population. I, as most people, consider them one in the same. However, when I was in Italy, I became aware of a definite difference between their meanings among the native Italians. Some Italians still have not accepted Sicily as part of the mainland. They still carry some of the old prejudices of their ancestors, in that, Sicilians are not as cultured, educated, or prosperous as mainland Italians. Therefore, for our purposes, when I refer to 'Italians,' I am considering them all as one nationality of people.

In order to offer clarification for two words I frequently use throughout this book, I have included definitions for 'emigrate' and 'immigrate.'

Definitions

Emigrate: to leave one's country or the departure from their native land. Therefore, *emigrants* are the Italians who left their native Italy to travel to another land.

Immigrate: to enter and settle in a country where they are not a native. When my relatives reached the American shores, they were considered *immigrants* to this new world.

So many times, we tend to use these words synonymously, when they really have very different meanings.

Early Italian Migration

The great wave of Italian migration to the United States began during the 1880s, only a few years after the creation of the Republic of Italy. Unification dissolved ancient borders and enabled many residents of Italy's poor, agricultural south to find work in the cities and factories in the Northern provinces. These sections of Italy had always been more industrial, more highly sophisticated in terms of fashion, foods, and culture, and where many of the major universities were located. The south of Italy, including Sicily, was known as the poorer part of the country. Winemaking was perfected in the agricultural south where most of the vineyards were located. The southern cities consisted of small hamlets and villages that contained wholesome people who were poor and lived on the day-to-day existence of their labors. This view of southern Italy's economic conditions continues to be very prevalent in the minds of many Italians on the mainland to this day.

Internal migration provided for only a portion of the rural southerners who sought better opportunities. Large numbers of young southern Italians, and even from the industrial north, began immigrating to other countries, especially to the United States and Argentina. They settled primarily in the major ports of New York City and Buenos Aires. Since many Italian immigrants arrived with little or no education, and with the tradition that each family should take care of its own members without intervention by the legal and judicial systems, they often appeared to native-born Americans and other ethnic migrants, as uncouth, unruly, and even dangerous. By 1914, Italian immigrants living in New York City numbered 370,000 and Italian immigrants living in Buenos Aires consisted of 312,000. It was in 1913, at the height of the migration movement of all Italians that the Cavallaro family migrated to America and was part of the 370,000 embarking on New York City.

The newcomers fared differently in New York than in Buenos Aires partly because the cities differed in their cultures and in their economic development. In the United States, which possessed a full array of highly developed industries and businesses, the main demand was for unskilled and casual labor, especially factory workers, stonecutters, grocers, peddlers, construction workers, or as laborers on the docks. Some took jobs in railroad construction, which brought them into the small towns of the Hudson River valley and the central portion of New York State.

Sharp differences in their dialects, cultures, educational levels, and economic backgrounds hampered the people of Italy, because most North American views were biased on their contact with poor, southern Italians and Sicilians. Although southern Italians were a numerical majority of the immigrants to both the United States and Argentina, (80% of those in the U.S. and 55% of those in Argentina), the greater proportion of southern Italians in the United States migration meant a slightly lower level of overall education, since the Italian south was the poorer, less developed region.

Like the masses of Irish immigrants, the Italians were subjected to stereotyping. For example, it was common to accuse an Italian of being a member of a criminal gang like the Mafia. Many of the Italians in New York were single men, who would return to Italy to marry and settle down, compared with Argentina, where a larger proportion of immigrants consisted of families who saw their new home as being more permanent. For their part, immigrants found comfort and a sense of security by settling in Italian ghettos, which served the same social, economic, and psychological functions as the ghettos of other ethnic groups. A shared culture and language reinforced the belief that only through mutual support could immigrants protect themselves against a hostile society. The Italians in Buenos Aires were far more successful in obtaining good jobs and housing, and in achieving social mobility, owing it mainly to the more receptive local economy and culture of Argentina.

Italian Migration from 1871 – 1914

Based upon the publications of Professor Sam Baily of Rutgers University, the conditions in the receiving countries were as important as the characteristics the immigrants brought with them in determining their future socioeconomic success in their new homes. The following are some statistics to ponder:

- During this time, Italy's population decreased from 35 to 28 million.

- Of the numbers that left Italy, 44% went to other European countries, 30% went to North America, and 24% went to South America (13% to Argentina and 9% to Brazil) which accounts for the large Italian populations in South America to this day.

- During this time, Argentina's population increased from 1.7 million to 7.9 million, which was considered tremendous for a period of only 43 years.

- By 1910, the foreign-born population in the United States climbed to 16%; Argentina escalated to 30%. Eighty years later, in 1990, the foreign-born population in the United States decreased to 7.9%.

Other Statistics to Ponder

- 1846   The Great Potato Famine of 1845-50 prompts a surge in emigration from Ireland.
- 1855   New York State opens Castle Garden Immigration station in lower Manhattan.
- 1858   Monetary crisis and famine in Sweden cause large-scale migration to U.S.
- 1869   Central Pacific and Union Pacific Railroads span North America, built by Irish and Chinese laborers.
- 1880-1900   Nine million immigrants start arriving in great numbers to U.S. from Italy, Austria-Hungary, and Russia. Many are Jews fleeing persecution in Russia.
- 1892   Ellis Island opens; federal immigration stations are established in other major ports, including San Francisco, Boston, and Philadelphia.
- 1907   Federal law raises the head tax on immigrants and adds to the excluded list the following: persons having physical or mental defects that may affect their ability to earn a living; those with tuberculosis; and children, unaccompanied by adults.
- 1907   Expatriation Act states that any woman who marries an alien looses her citizenship.
- 1910   More than 25% of foreign-born Italians over the age of ten can speak no English.
- 1913   California law prohibits ownership of land by illegal aliens ineligible for citizenship. The majority of Asians will be excluded from ownership.
- 1914   Outbreak of WWI ends mass migration to the Americas. Labor needs of U.S. industry, a major supplier to warring nations in Europe, draws southern blacks to northern cities.
- 1917   Congress requires that each immigrant older than sixteen be literate in a language; the requirement does not apply to persons fleeing religious persecution. Virtually, all Asian immigration is banned.
- 1900-1920   The peak years of immigration - more than 14 million people enter the U.S. A growing proportion of immigrants come from southern and Eastern Europe. First large wave of Mexican immigrants arrives in CA to work on farms and railroads. In 1907, more than 1,285,000 people are admitted into the United States, a record for any one year.
- 1921   Federal law establishes quotas limiting the number of immigrants of each nationality to 3% of each nationality living in the U.S. in 1910. The law also limits European immigration to about 350,000 persons annually.

- 1924   The Johnson-Reed Act set temporary annual quotas at 2% of each nationality's U.S. population in the 1890 Census; also set an upward limit of 150,000 in any one year from any Western Hemisphere countries. The law reduces immigration and controls its ethnic character by excluding Asians and setting low quotas for countries in eastern and southern Europe. Immigrants are processed abroad, under the direction of U.S. consulates.
- 1930s   Economic depression, combined with a rigorous enforcement of current immigration laws, further reduces immigration. For the first time, people leaving the U.S. outnumber those arriving.
- 1940   Immigration is perceived more as a national security issue; oversight is transferred to the Attorney General in the Justice Dept. where it now remains.
- 1940   Alien Registration Act requires finger printing and annual registration of all resident aliens as a national security measure.
- 1943   Chinese Exclusion laws are repealed.
- 1940-1960   Approximately 3.5 million people immigrate to U.S.
- 1942   Alien Italians in the U.S. were no longer designated with enemy-alien status; only 228 alien Italians are interred; 500,000 Italian Americans served in the armed forces during World War II.
- 1946   War Brides Act allows GI's to bring foreign-born wives home to America.
- 1950   The Internal Security Act requires all aliens to register annually with the INS.
- 1950s   After the Korean Conflict, about 8,000 Korean refugees, war brides and orphans come to the U.S. Refugee Acts admit more than 250,000 eastern Europeans, including 30,000 Hungarians.
- 1960-1980   U.S. immigration tops 8 million; uncounted illegal immigrants add significantly to total number of aliens. Immigration from Latin America and Asia steadily rises. By 1980, more than 41% of immigrants come from Latin America and 34% come from Asia. More than 440,000 Cuban refugees immigrate to the U.S.
- 1965-72   President L.B. Johnson and Fidel Castro sign a 'Memorandum of Understanding' and 275,000 Cubans are airlifted to the U.S.
- 1975   The Fall of Saigon to the Viet Cong. About 130,000 refugees from Vietnam, Laos, and Cambodia are admitted to the U.S.
- 1986   Immigration Reform and Control Act establishes sanctions against employers who hire illegal immigrants and offers amnesty for illegal immigrants who request legal status. An agricultural guest worker program is established for alien laborers.

- 1990   The Ellis Island Museum of Immigration opens.

Sources: Ellis Island Museum, <u>The Peopling of America</u> exhibit
Thomas Kessner, <u>Today's Immigrants, Their Story</u>, New York: Oxford University Press, 1981

Who Were These New Immigrants?

What dangers and desires were powerful enough to move immigrants from their family homes, their roots, and their ties? Why would they leave the area where their personal history was rooted and their families had lived, generation after generation? For each individual, the decision to come to America was unique; each based upon the special circumstances of their lives. Yet, each person's reasons and feelings reflect millions of others who decided to leave their homes to try for a new and better life in America…..when the old country promised only more of the same poverty, oppression, and starvation.

Many people came to this country seeking the traditional American freedoms of life, liberty and the pursuit of happiness. Such freedoms were rare in the Europe of the early years of the 20th century. A Europe that was different from the one we know today. The old country - the land the immigrants left and the life-style they lived there - no longer existed, except in their memories. Even the names on the landscape were different. Empires they knew no longer existed; new countries had been created, some only to disappear within a generation. Their familiar hometowns were called by different names now, and some were gone forever.

There is no argument that our lives today are dramatically different from our grandparents' generation. Nevertheless, for peasants like the Cavallaro family, who lived in Sicily during the 17th through the 20th century, one generation's lifestyle was remarkably like the next and probably no different from the generations who came before them.

Some Immigrants' Comments

(Taken from: <u>*The Making of an Insurgent: An Autobiography 1882-1919*</u>, LaGuardia, Fiorello H., J. B. Lippincott Company 1948; New York.)

- *"Meet you in America."*

- *"There was absolutely no chance for the common man over there to get ahead. You just lived, and you finally died, and probably the county had to bury you."*

- *"We have meat about once a year. We had goats and we had a cow, but most of the time we were brought up on goat's milk, me, and my three younger sisters. And once in a while, Mother would buy one of those short bolognas, cut it up, put it in the soup, and everybody would get a little piece. I used to think, 'If I could get enough of that to fill my stomach!"*

- *"Well, when we came to America, for a few cents, we ate like kings compared with what we had over there. Oh, it was really heaven!"*

- *"I remember that we left in a cart, a two-wheeled cart with a big homemade trunk, I would say perhaps five feet wide, three feet deep, and three feet high. It was well made, because it lasted for the whole trip to America, and we had that trunk for many, many years in America. I think I can remember it being in my family even when I got married, and for twenty-five years after we got to America. So in the trunk was our baggage. It was in the cart, plus my mother, brothers and sisters that came with us. We started off for Palermo with one horse and a driver. We stayed overnight in a small town, where we slept in a stable, where the horse slept, on top of the hay. Even my dear mother slept there with us. And we started the same way the next morning and we got to Palermo. I do remember that we took a small launch. We hopped onto it. There was no such thing as a dock. And the Mediterranean Sea was very rough. We had to travel some distance to get to the boat. It was an overnight trip and I remember so well that there was really a lot of crying going on because of the frightfulness of the Mediterranean Sea. Now, this boat was not a boat to come across the ocean. You had to go to Naples first...... there you take the big ship. We were leaving Naples about five or six in the evening and as we left I could see on my left the Mt. Vesuvius....... and that stood out so vividly with big smoke coming out of the mountain."*

- *"Seeing the Statue of Liberty was the greatest thing I've ever seen. It was really something. What a wonderful sight! This was the end of our voyage to the Golden Door of America. To know you're in this country. God, just think of it! I remember as a child people used to say to me, 'In America you'd find gold in the streets.' The streets of gold! And as a child, I said to myself, Gee, we're in America. Now I can go out in the streets and pick up gold."*

Traveling out of the rural areas through the hills of Sicily was not so easy in those days. There were no fancy suitcases, and hotels were an unthinkable luxury. So many, like the Cavallaro family, carried homemade trunks or huge bundles made of sheets or blankets to hold their belongings. They rode in carts when they could, walked when they had to, and slept wherever they found themselves, until they reached a railroad center or a port city.

That was a tremendous shock for these immigrants. They were wrenched from an isolated country life and set on a trek to the seaport, followed by a lengthy ocean voyage, a passage through the "Tower of Babel" at Ellis Island and their final arrival at a country of bustling cities, with skyscrapers and elevated trains. *(The Tower of Babel refers to a city in the Book of Genesis where the construction of a heaven-reaching tower was interrupted by the confusion of many languages..... referred to as 'Babel.')*

Many people who came to America were indeed poor people, with little or no resources but an enormous capacity for hard work. Poverty was not unique to any nationality. For many Italians, being an ethnic minority under an alien government, was perhaps less important than being poor. Poor people from all over Europe came to America looking for food, work, maybe even gold in the streets, and most of all, and a chance for a better life.

Making the Move

The usual pattern of immigrating to another country was for just one person in the family to make the first journey. This was usually the father or mother, or an older brother or sister; anyone who could be a breadwinner. If it happened to be a younger person to migrate, they would get the traveling expenses from another member of the family; usually an older uncle or brother would provide most of the money it took to finance the trip.

Sometimes, the move to America was a planned family move. The family would sacrifice and save enough money to send one person across to America; that person would then begin to work and save enough money to bring a second person in the family across; then a third, and then a fourth; until finally, the whole family was together again.

To this end, the fathers would save every penny they earned. They worked very hard, in the sweatshops of the tailoring and needle industry, or in button or tobacco factories. In the tailoring sweatshops, the migrants never had decent, up-dated machines to sew on; younger and shorter workers had to stand on wooden fruit boxes in order to reach the machines. They would make great sacrifices to bring their families to America. At that time, families were large. A family of six children or more was very common and they had to earn enough money to pay for the passage for every child in their household.

Such a pattern posed tremendous hardships for everyone. The first person, often the father, suffered loneliness, and deprivation along with the shock of adjustment to the new country, as he tried to save up enough money for the rest of the family to make the voyage. The mother, left behind with the children, had to run the family farm or business, and deal with the normal problems of growing children without the aid of her husband. Just prior to World War I, she had to rely on uncertain mail service to keep in touch with her husband; a service that eventually broke down completely once the war began.

Immigration was a big business, involving millions of immigrants and hundreds of thousands of others who made their livings while assisting them. These workers included immigration agents working as freelancers. Some took jobs as proprietors and employees of the immigrant hostels that were privately run and/or by governments all over Europe; these were largely seen in many of the port cities. The railroad, ferry, and steamship companies who transported the immigrants from place to place employed others. Hundreds were employed as border guards, health officials, and customs workers who regulated and inspected each passenger coming into the country. Then, there were the people who sold them food and other necessities en route. There were those who befriended the immigrants on-board; however, were really thieves who preyed upon them while they slept.

The difficulties surrounding land transport often made it impossible for immigrants to schedule travel to meet the specific dates of their ship sailings. Those arriving at a port city sometimes made very quick connections with ships to America; however, there were times when some had to wait as long as a week or two for the proper connections. Those arriving who were already ticketed, were sent on ahead as quickly as possible by the steamship companies from whom they had purchased tickets; by sending them on ahead, it saved the steamship company money since they wouldn't require the care and feeding while waiting for tickets or connections on other ships. In some ports, the governments ran hostelries for the immigrants and charged the ship companies for their keep; some steamship companies built their own facilities for the immigrants and made more money from the inexperienced travelers.

Since 1891, shipping companies were required to abide by the laws set forth by the American Immigration Service, which required the shipping companies to vaccinate, disinfect, and examine their immigrant passengers before sailing. The law also stated that they pay for the housing of detained passengers at Ellis Island and other American Ports of Entry. It continued to require them to return the rejected immigrants back to their Ports of Embarkation free of charge. The shipping companies complied with cursory, quick, and often remarkably ineffectual inspections, vaccinations, and disinfection procedures, usually preferring to pass prospective immigrants and take their chances on the acceptance of most of their passengers in America. Had they known, tens of thousands of immigrants who may have cured their physical problems prior to their emigration to America would not have made the trip. The shipping companies hastily passed them on to make the voyage. Once on American shores, they found that they were only to be rejected and sent back to Europe from Ellis Island and other American inspection stations. Thousands of others, who had sold everything they owned, and were accepted for passage, arrived in America to find that they had incurable physical conditions that barred them from entrance into the United States. All of these people were forced to return to Europe, landless, jobless, and infinitely worse off than they had been before they left their homes.

Italy was the only country that was a major exception to this policy prior to start of World War I. Fiorello H. La Guardia, as American counsel in Fiume, Italy from 1903-1906, insisted on careful medical examination of all immigrants bound for the United States. He battled the shipping companies, and made his rulings stick to the considerable benefit of those emigrating. The Italian government, seeing the success of La Guardia's experiment in Fiume, adopted his approach, and conducted careful medical examinations of emigrants after 1908, sharply curbing the number of those rejected in the United States, and preventing them from being sent back to Italy penniless.

Birds of Passage

The emigration trail was not all one way. Considering the distance that needed to be traveled, the difficulty, the cost of the journey, often the sale of property back home, we might think that the move to America was final and virtually irrevocable. Not so! People traveled back to their homeland more often than we might suppose. Many who did this often were fondly known among the immigration officials as Birds of Passage.

Some Italian men were labeled as Birds of Passage immigrants who went back and forth between America and Italy several times before deciding to bring their families to America. Southern Italians had a high rate of return migration from America. Thirty percent went back to Italy after five years and remained there. Their major goal was to earn enough money in America so they could return to Italy to buy some land and have a better life. Many Birds of Passage never became American citizens because it was not their intent to stay in America, since they felt their time in America was only temporary. Many stayed because they couldn't afford to return..... not even to get their families; thus, many loved ones were separated permanently. My grandfather, Angelo Cavallaro, was considered a Bird of Passage because of the more than seven trips he made back and forth to Sicily. However, he finally decided in 1913 to return with his family. Even then, after they arrived and the family settled in Rochester, New York, he still made two more trips to Sicily before he chose to remain in America.

Finding work became more difficult in southern Italy. Many of those who left for America had planned to stay only long enough to earn money and return to Italy to buy land rather than pay rent to absentee landlords. These Birds of Passage, or seasonal migrants, made the transatlantic voyage several times, working a few months in America and returning to Italy in time for the harvest. Italians were among the top three ethnic groups with the highest return migration rate. In 1903, for example, more than 214,000 Italians came to this country; about 78,000 went back to Italy the same year.

Emigrants who returned to the United States did not always sail into the same port when they migrated back at a later date. Sometimes they came to New York, and the next time they may have arrived in Boston, Philadelphia, or New Orleans. Should they decide not to return to Italy, they would remain in their newly arrived city and settle there. To this day, these cities are largely populated by Italians due to the Birds of Passage immigrants who never returned to their native homeland of Italy. Significant gaps of more than two years in the births of a family's children are a good indication that papa may have been away from home and might be a Bird of Passage.

For most Italians, however, the higher wages in America were an enticement to remain in their new home. Therefore, after earning enough money, which was usually three to five years later, they sent for their families. Along with better wages, what interested more and more southern Italians to leave their homeland was the availability of jobs and the opportunity to own land. In what historians have termed as 'Chain Migration,' villagers, who already immigrated to America, encouraged others to join them by sending them money and providing temporary lodging for the newcomers. Some of these chains were so strong that nearly an entire village might follow over a period of years. For example, people who had left Roseto Valforte, Apulia in Italy, settled the town of Roseto, Pennsylvania almost entirely.

In the early decades of the 20th century, those who later wanted to return to the United States, had to go through the complete immigration check again – with the risk of being turned back – unless they had become American citizens on an earlier visit. Clearly, these people had not burned their bridges, but had been able to raise the fare without selling everything they owned. Often they had family back home to keep watch over their interests there; although some found to their sorrow, that families are not always as completely reliable as they thought.

A Decision to Emigrate from Sicily

You will see many similarities in what I have just outlined, to what happened to my family. Angelo Cavallaro was a Bird of Passage and traveled numerous times to America to make money; however, it was never his intent to remain there. He would always return to Sicily to find that the poverty, lack of jobs, and poorer lifestyle had not changed since he had been gone. Then he would return to America to earn more money. This would have worked for him, except that he managed his money poorly and never went back to Sicily with enough money to bring his family back to America. When he finally made the decision to bring his family to America, he had to borrow the money from his brother, Sebastiano, who was already living in Rochester. This made it possible for them to make the trip.

When Angelo and Angela were married and they began their own family in the late 1800s, Italy was undergoing political changes that ultimately had an effect on their decision to emigrate. Before 1860, Italy was divided into eight separate states, with all but one ruled by foreign governments or the papacy. The movement, known as Il Risorgimento, was to unite Italy and remove foreign rule. While the movement reached success and the north and central parts of Italy prospered, the south, including Sicily, remained unaffected, and the peasant class continued to sink further and further into poverty. Starting a decade after the unification, peasants began to leave the country in substantial numbers. Statistics show that over 100,000 people left per year and in a short amount of time, six million Italians were living abroad while thirty-five million remained in Italy.

Keep in mind that the Cavallaro family made their emigration journey to America in 1913. They, like so many other Italians, were tempted by the opportunity of a better life in America. For many southern Italian peasants like the Cavallaro's, the decision to leave Italy and head for a new country across the Atlantic was the result of several factors; most of them economic. In the old country, *contadii* (farmers) and *taglierine delle pietre* (stonecutters) earned about twenty cents a day; in America, they could earn one dollar a day as laborers. This was a significant increase in their salary and an incentive for them to travel to a new country.

The peak years of immigration to America were between 1901 and 1914. This was the time span when Angelo was a Bird of Passage, and was making all his trips back and forth to Italy. This is when he chose to bring his family to America. However, prior to their decision to leave Sicily, other *paisani,* and relatives had already immigrated to America. It was a common pattern for people involved in 'Chain Migration,' if they were the first arrivals to America, to pay for their relatives' passage, and provide temporary lodging when newcomers arrived. They usually left from different ports and they didn't always travel on the same ships as their relatives. Hence, regardless of their city of arrival, they followed the same pattern of travel to arrive eventually in Rochester, New York. One factor they all had in common was that they traveled in third class or steerage. Their travel experiences are identical to other immigrants during this mass exodus. With Angelo having made the trip many times prior to their 1913 voyage, he was well aware of the conditions they would have to endure on the ship and knew how to make all the necessary arrangements for passage. He also had arranged with *paisani* and *parenti* (relatives) in Rochester concerning sponsorship, and lodging when they arrived. This made it easier for Angela and the children, knowing that Angelo had prepared them well for the trip.

Peasant Life in Sicily

We can all agree that our lives in the twenty-first century are considerably different from the lives of our grandparents and the generations of Sicilians that lived before them. Nevertheless, for peasants like the Cavallaro family, who lived in Sicily for many centuries, one generation's life style was remarkably like the next and probably no different from the generations who came after them.

The Cavallaro family had a long history of peasant life. Accessible information from relatives and records that are still available from the Provincia di Catania (Province of Catania), where most of them lived, indicate that they were peasants and either worked the land as *contadini (con-tă-dē´-nē)* (peasant farmers) or *taglierine delle pietre* (tă-gā-rē´-nā děl´lā pē-ě´-trā) (stonecutters) and remained so throughout their lifetimes. The peasant farmers worked for small landholders and generally lived in rural villages. They rented land from absentee landlords. Most *contadini* and *taglierine delle pietre* had a one to three hour walk to and from their work. Each day, the men of the family left their homes before the break of day and didn't return until after dark because of the long distances.

Surviving everyday life was a challenge in itself. Along with natural disasters, they had to encounter such as, earthquakes, droughts, and floods, nineteenth-century peasant families also had to deal with frequent outbreaks of smallpox, meningitis, typhoid, cholera, and malaria. Malnutrition was another problem for peasant families. They rarely ate meat; their diet consisted mainly of rice, fava beans, bread, pasta, and polenta (a type of corn meal mash). Many of the villagers ate a diet that was low in protein and caused common deficiencies known as pellagra.

In the Province of Catania, where the Cavallaro's lived, earthquakes were prevalent and severe because they were so close to Mt. Etna, 'The Mother of All Volcanoes.' Being so close to the epicenter, made the disasters even more devastating. To withstand these earthquakes and tremors, the homes were built of stone and the walls were very dense; usually eight to ten inches in thickness. The rooms were tiny so that the walls could better support smaller spans of roofing that covered them; however, when the lava flowed, nothing would remain in its path. Mount Etna, which dominates the northeastern coast of Sicily, was considered a thing of beauty and something to be feared. The Sicilians say the volcano is taken for granted and they are immune to its terrifying splendor. It became a very important part of their lives because it provided fertile soil and building materials, creating picturesque beauty to the surrounding cities, while enticing tourists to come and visit *La Bella Sicilia* (Lă Bĕl´ lă Sē-chē´-lē-ă) (Beautiful Sicily). During the early 20th century, it became a Mecca for various famous authors, movie stars, and political celebrities.

Records show that Mount Etna had many eruptions over the years. During the years that the Cavallaro family lived at the northern edge of the volcano, there were repeated earthquakes from 1899-1907 that produced strong tremors and created some lava flow. Other earthquakes that were accompanied with significant lava flow occurred in 1908 and 1909. In 1910, there were two earthquakes and eruptions; one was on the southwest side of the volcano and the lava flow lasted for twenty-six days. In 1911, there were two more eruptions. In 1912 and again in 1913 (the year our family immigrated to America), the volcano erupted again. It was during the eruption of 1912, that my father remembered the lava flowing down the mountainside and coming very close to their home. He told me that the molten rock threatened their village of Passopisciaro and was flowing at a rate of five to six yards an hour. At that rate, it would hardly allow the villagers to gather their meager belonging and evacuate to a safer location. Their home was never lost to any of the earthquakes.

Passopisciaro, located at the very edge of the volcano, was always in constant danger of being affected by earthquakes, eruptions, and lava flow. The people were within earshot of the continuous exploding and crashing sounds created by the mini eruptions. Whenever there was an eruption, they were able to view it from their homes. They could see the fountains of red lava that shot up into the sky and landing on the summit's slopes causing clouds of hot dust upon impact. Whenever this began to happen, the sky would darken because of the volcanic ash that was created by the chunks of rock and molten lava being thrown onto the dusty hillsides and upper slopes. Eventually, they would experience a light precipitation of ash and would have to take cover because it could come down as heavy as a rain or snow shower. They could hear it making a ticking sound on the metal roofs of their homes. When the eruptions were over, they would go outside and sweep all the ash that had fallen onto the streets. It was part of their lives, and as my father would always say, in a comical manner, to me, *"Non è sempre così"* (Nōn è sē-ĕm´-prā cō-sē´) "It's not always like this." There were weeks, and sometimes months, when there would be no volcanic activity; however; at other times, they could expect earthquakes and eruptions every couple of days or so.

With such diseases, malnutrition, and natural disasters working against them, many families lost several young children during their lifetime. Parents were considered fortunate if they lived long enough to see any of their children marry and have families of their own. Angelo and Angela were one of the fortunate couples who only lost a few of their children during the early years of their marriage. They lived to see all six of their surviving children marry and have children.

While death may have been a frequent aspect of the peasant family's life, it was never taken lightly. The death of a child caused parents extreme grief. The custom of naming children after grandparents and the use of necronyms (naming the next-born child with the same name as the deceased child who carried a grandparent's name) further demonstrated the importance of procreation and perpetuation of *la famiglia (lă-fă-mē´-glē-ă)* (the family). It is for this reason why so many Sicilian families have children with the same name scattered throughout the family and the extended family. It is also for this same reason that when researching genealogical records, finding a person's name in your family tree needs to be accompanied by other confirming data. There should be verification of such data as their birth date, place of birth, parent's names, and any other identifying information. Only by thoroughly examining genealogical records can one be sure that the person listed is the exact person for whom you are searching. Sometimes, it can turn out to be a sibling with the same name that was born years later.

The Trip to America

As soon as Angelo and Angela Cavallaro decided to prepare for their passage to America, they immediately began the process of acquiring their passports for travel. They were required to provide identity papers and passports for each family member. Having done this for his previous trips, Angelo made the necessary arrangements while Angela prepared the children for the trip to America. After they had packed their simple belongings, which consisted mainly of clothes, they traveled to the port city of Palermo, the capitol city of Sicily. They had to arrange for transportation from Passopisciaro in la Provincia de Catania to Palermo; this meant they had to travel from the eastern coast of Sicily to the northwestern coast to the city of Palermo. They traveled by a horse-drawn cart on the main roads and then boarded a railroad train destined to Palermo. Once in Palermo, they walked as a family to the area designated for travelers going to America and they rested in a tiny, mock village set up by the steamship company. Here, they were quarantined for five days in a pest house and given antiseptic baths. The men were given short haircuts and both men and women had their scalps washed with a soft soap, carbolic acid (a disinfectant), and petroleum. Since the steamship companies had to absorb the cost of return passage for anyone who did not pass the health inspections in America, the emigrants were given medical examinations and vaccinations before departure.

After a stay at the pest house for at least five days, the Italian family was herded by foot, to the shipping docks. Each member of the family carried their small bundles of clothes, and my father, Alfred, being the oldest son, carried the one trunk they brought; it contained most of their belongings and he carried it on his shoulder. Imagine the scene of this family walking down the streets of Palermo in single file; Angelo and Angela at the head of the line, then older children carrying the younger children, and bringing up the end of the line were the middle-aged children dragging their bundles behind them. The eight of them walked very close to each other for fear of getting lost in the crowds of other immigrants, headed in the same direction - toward the shipping docks at the harbor.

Steamship representatives compiled the ship's Manifest, or list of passengers, for each departure. At the gangplank, they waited in long lines into the night, as each person was required to answer the same questions; the information was recorded on the ship's Manifest sheets. They recorded such information as I have listed below for each person who was to board the ship:

- Name
- Age
- Sex
- Occupation
- Marital status
- Last residence
- Final destination in U.S.
- If ever in America before:
    - *when
    - *where
    - *for how long
- If going to join a relative:
    - *relative's name
    - *address
    - *their relationship
- Were they able to read and write in Italian?
- What was the amount of money the passenger was carrying?
- Were they in possession of a train ticket to their final destination?
- Who paid their passage?
- Had the passenger ever been in prison?
- Had they ever been in an almshouse or poorhouse?
- Had they ever been in an institution for the insane?
- Was the emigrant a polygamist?
- What was the passenger's state of health?
- A personal description that includes the following:
    - *height   *complexion
    - *color of hair   *color of eyes
    - *identifying marks   *place of birth
- What was the name and address of the closest living relative in Sicily?
- What was the name and address of the person who was their sponsor in America?

There were to be 1,960 people boarding this ship. With a minimal number of clerks available to record the information, it took a very long time to complete this phase of the trip. My family, as all others, had to wait in long lines for many hours awaiting their turn. Waiting in the lines went beyond the regular meal times and the hungry children ate snacks they carried with them from home. Even the lengthy distance to the bathroom facilities was an inconvenience; usually, a friendly immigrant would kindly hold their place in line. Through this, they became very weary and tired, and they had not even begun their twenty-three day voyage yet.

Most steamship companies were capable of carrying about 1,500 third-class passengers, but many vessels were overcrowded in steerage, transporting several hundred more than capacity. The Cavallaro family quickly found this out as they were herded down the narrow hallways and steps; they were eventually shoved into the steerage compartment. They tried to stay together, but that was very difficult because the conditions were so crowded. There was a lot of noise made by unhappy people as they entered this abyss in the depths of the ship that had neither windows nor fresh air. They immediately knew that this was not going to be a pleasant trip. Angelo, having traveled this way before, was accustomed to the uncomfortable living conditions; however, this was very difficult for the children who had never known confinement in all their lives. This was just a foreshadowing of what was ahead of them. The name of the ship on which they traveled was Principe de Piemonte and sailed from Palermo, Sicily on June 30, 1913.

The Start of the Trip

For people who lived in or near the port cities, the ship's departure was an event in its own right. Many people and whole families turned out to bid goodbye, and often to say, "Soon, I'll meet you in America!" This was not the case with my family. Angelo and Angela, along with their six children, were already tired and worn out even before boarding the ship. The dock where they waited was a very windy, wooden pier that led to their large ship. As they stood on the dock for what seemed like hours, the lines slowly began moving forward. At noon, a call for all passengers to board the ship blared from the loud speakers and the people shouted in anticipation of the beginning of their voyage. As they walked up the gangplank and boarded the ship, they looked behind them to their glorious Sicily, the land where they were all born, and the land that had been their home for as long as they could remember. Knowing that they had made the right decision to leave this poor country and to migrate to the land of opportunity – America, they walked with renewed anticipation of a new life. However, as Angelo looked back at his beloved *Sicilia*, he always felt he would return and that this would not be goodbye, but rather *Arrivederci*, (until we meet again). He was right, because he did make numerous trips back to Sicily after his family was settled in America; however, neither Angela nor the children ever returned to live in Sicilia. Only one of their children, Joseph, returned as an adult with his wife, Vincenzina, to vacation in and around their glorious home in Passopisciaro in La Bella Sicilia.

The Voyage on the Principe di Piemonte

Sir James Laing & Sons Limited from Sunderland, England built the Principe di Piemonte in 1889. It was 430 feet long and 52 feet wide. It had a steam triple expansion engine with a twin screw. The service speed was fourteen knots. At capacity, it serviced 1,960 total passengers; 60 in first and second class, and 1,900 in third class or steerage. The ship was built primarily for service from Italy to New York and return trips. In 1913, it carried the Cavallaro family to the harbor in New York. In 1914, it was sold to the Uranium Steamship Company, renamed Principello, and provided service from Rotterdam to New York and return trips. In 1916, it was sold a second time to the Cunard Line under the British flag and was renamed Folia. On March 11, 1917, during World War I, it was torpedoed and sunk by a German submarine off the Irish coast.

According to the ship's Manifest, the ship was to leave Palermo, Sicily on June 30, 1913 and arrive in New York Harbor, Ellis Island on July 23, 1913. On the passenger list, the following names were recorded for that particular voyage and they are listed below with the exact spelling as they appeared:

Name	Gender	Age	Status	Ethnicity	Residence
0009 Gravagno, Angela	F	34	M	Italy, South	Castiglione di Sicilia
0017 Cavallaro, Angelo	M	46	M	Italy, South	Castiglione di Sicilia
0018 Cavallaro, Angelina	F	18	S	Italy, South	Castiglione di Sicilia
0019 Cavallaro, Alfio	M	16	S	Italy, South	Castiglione di Sicilia
0020 Cavallaro, Maria Catena	F	13	S	Italy, South	Castiglione di Sicilia
0021 Cavallaro, Orazio	M	8	S	Italy, South	Castiglione di Sicilia
0022 Cavallaro, Giovanna	F	4	S	Italy, South	Castiglione di Sicilia
0023 Cavallaro, Giuseppe	M	11	S	Italy, South	Castiglione di Sicilia

The Manifest indicated that Angela was the first to register and Giuseppe was the last in line. Note the registration numbers next to the names are in numeric sequence as they passed the registrar, except for Angela.

In a careful examination of the ship's Manifest, it showed very clearly that Angelo Cavallaro, along with his six children, boarded the ship together and were going to travel in steerage. Their assigned numbers on the Manifest are in sequential numeric order. I searched long and hard and could not find Angela's name on the Manifest anywhere. Finally, I was able to locate her. I knew that she traveled on that same ship and on that same voyage; however, I found out that she chose to use her maiden name, Gravagna, instead of her married name, Cavallaro. This was a common practice for women who were traveling from Europe at that time. The boarding crew personnel were made up of people who were non-Italian and could not speak the Italian language. As a result, they made many mistakes spelling names and recording accurate answers to the questions on the Boarding Questionnaire. Although Angela said "Gravagna," ending her name with an 'a,' they wrote Gravagno, ending it with an 'o;' making it very difficult to find a passenger if their name was misspelled. In addition, I found that she did not travel in the steerage compartment with the rest of the family. Her name was on another Manifest list for first class passengers only, which accounts for her having a different registration number, and not in sequence with the rest of the family. She was listed with different passengers because she traveled in what was referred to as the 'Saloon,' or another word for first class passage. Why she traveled separately from the rest of the family is a continuing mystery. Although I asked many relatives for the answer to that question, they could never give a reason why it happened. At times, I felt they really knew the reason, but were unwilling to share that information. Therefore, during the entire trip, neither Angelo nor the children ever saw her. When they occasionally went up on deck, they would walk around looking for her, but she couldn't be located. Angelo stayed with the children and traveled the entire trip with them. He ate his meals with them, slept in the same area as they did, and cared for their daily needs. Angelina, being the oldest at eighteen years of age, was also a great help to him. She, and Mary at fourteen years of age, cared for the younger children. My father said that Mary could be seen at any time of the day either holding Giovanna in her arms or by her hand as they walked the deck. The whole family, including Angela, finally met up on the last day of the trip as they were sailing into New York Harbor toward Ellis Island. At that point, everyone was required to be on deck with their luggage and belongings because it was never certain at what time they would dock and disembark the ship. My father remembered that his mother said she had met some *paisani* in first class and had spent most of her time there with them. She had brought some sewing with her to pass the time during the voyage.

Once they had passed the tables where information was taken to be placed on the ship's Manifest, they were ready to begin their journey. As they walked up the gangplank to the steamship, The Principe di Piemonte, they approached the area where passengers were separated into first, second, and third class travel (third class was also known as steerage and was located in the bowels of the ship). This was where most of the immigrants were assigned. As the Cavallaro's went past the officials, struggling with their bundles, boxes, and one trunk, their heads were checked for lice. If they wore hats, they were pushed back by the officials to see if any lice were present. The steamship lines had little or no respect for immigrants who were traveling, especially those who were traveling in steerage. One way or another, most people eventually got past that final pre-boarding check and settled in for the voyage; going from the old life to the new life. It would be a voyage that would leave a permanent imprint on nearly all who experienced it. As they walked up the gangplanks and scraped the European mud from their shoes, the immigrants knew that it was finally happening. America would be the next solid ground they would step on and finally, they would arrive at their new home.

After they embarked on the ship, they quickly became settled into their steerage facility. The children were bedded down for the night and everything was quiet. Very abruptly, they were awakened in what seemed like the middle of the night, as the ship's motors were activated and they were ready to leave the harbor of Palermo. In addition to all the uncomfortable conditions I mentioned earlier, they immediately found that being in steerage was a very noisy place. It was right next to the large motors and machinery that moved the ship and the noise continued day and night; it did not end until they got off the ship in New York.

As they sailed westward across the Mediterranean Sea toward Gibraltar, everyone was feeling fine. The sea was calm and they made friends with others who were in steerage. After they passed Gibraltar, the sea became rough and, one by one, they all started to get seasick, spending most of the days on their cots. Shortly after, those who were sick and needed medical attention, decided to go to the ship's infirmary. They climbed the steps to the deck. It was windy and cold; the steel steps were wet and slippery from where others had become sick. They held onto the railings just to keep from slipping and sliding. By the time it took to arrive to where the ship's hospital was located, the lines were so long that they couldn't even see the door that entered the facility. Therefore, they trudged back to the depths of the ship to lie in discomfort on their cots.

At this point of the voyage, steerage was not a comfortable place to be. It contained no ventilation of any sort, so the air was always hot and muggy; it reeked with the stench of seasickness. The cots were close and very uncomfortable, usually covered with a very thin mattress and with no pillows or sheets. No one from the crew was assigned to the steerage area to clean up after the people who had become sick, so the stench and odor for the others became a major discomfort. When they felt the least bit better, they would force themselves to go up the three flights of stairs and sit on the deck floor just to get some fresh air. It was cold and windy there, so they usually huddled together for protection from the weather. These conditions continued throughout the twenty-three days as they traveled on that turbulent and stormy sea.

The harsh North Atlantic Ocean took a heavy toll on the well-being of most of the travelers. They were land creatures, temporarily uprooted from their familiar soil, and were passing through an alien environment. In those days, the ships were built like huge traps. The passengers would need to go down many flights of steps to get to steerage, not really knowing how many floors they were descending into the bottom of the ship. When they went there to sleep at night, they felt trapped. Then, when a heavy storm would begin, the ship's crew would close everything up; all the doors and gates were chained shut and no one could get out of steerage. They were truly trapped. In the event of an emergency, they would be corralled in the deepest core of the ship behind chained, steel gates that blocked the stairways to the upper decks. In later years, many of these memories were indistinct to the voyagers. Only flashes of fear, uncertainty, and severe illness could be recalled. My father shared part of the experience to us. It went something like this:

> *"It was so rough! I didn't see or eat anything but water for days. A lot of times, I'd just lie on my bed when I didn't feel so good. I didn't get up and go anywhere because, if I did, I'd get dizzy and then I'd get sicker than before, because the water was so rough. It was rough weather and the waves were so high, and the wind so strong, that the water would spray on the deck so it was always wet. There were days when the ship rocked so much, we thought that it would turn over, but it didn't."*

As a young boy listening to this description, I could never relate to this description, and thought that my father was exaggerating a bit. However, after my research and the extensive reading I've done concerning the experiences immigrants had while they traveled, this became very real to me and I could appreciate so much more the sacrifices my father, my grandparents, and my aunts and uncles made to come to a new world for a better life.

Midway through the voyage, on July 15th, it was Giovanna's birthday. She was turning four years old. As sick as they were, they were able to celebrate her birthday on the ship at their regular mealtime. In later years, she told me that she remembered receiving a small piece of cake at the mealtime. Another Italian passenger on the ship had given it to her to help celebrate her birthday.

The overwhelming majority of the immigrants from southern Europe traveled in steerage because it cost a great deal less than first or second-class passage. Before World War I, steerage fare from Atlantic and Mediterranean ports cost as little as ten to fifteen dollars during some years, but never more than thirty-five dollars per person. During and after the war, it increased, but still was, by far, the lowest priced way to travel to America; and for poor immigrants who had limited funds, this was the only way many of them could afford to travel at all. Passengers in steerage rarely socialized with passengers from other countries, nor did they see any wealthy people in their travels. They only knew their fellow-countrymen who were passengers in steerage, who suffered seasickness together with them. They would meet on board and speak of their trips to the port cities, or talked with great anticipation of the relatives that were waiting for them in America. They would exchange impressions, reminisce and compare notes on their backgrounds and where they came from, where they were going, their expectations, and hopes in the golden land of Cristoforo Colombo – the great Italian that had discovered the new world. The wealthy, those in first and second-class passage compartments, never mixed with steerage passengers. The steerage passengers were not permitted to enter any cabins of people who were not their social equals; they had to confine themselves completely to the steerage area at the bottom of the ship.

Therefore, as they sat on the deck sharing their own dreams, some would talk about getting wealthy. There were legends that in America, gold was available to gather on the streets. This legend must have survived from the days of the so-called 'Gold Rush' of 1849, just sixty years earlier, which brought thousands of people from all over the world to dig for gold. That must have been the origin of the expression, "In America, gold could be picked up from the ground."

Transporting immigrants from the European countries to America was extraordinarily profitable for the steamship companies. In the early years of mass immigration, the only real difference between traveling on an old, slow boat in steerage, and in traveling in steerage on one of the super-liners of the day, was that the super-liner went faster and was somewhat more stable. Not major differences, but to the travelers, the lower cargo hold of a superliner was much like a cargo hold of a smaller ship. Some of the larger ships crossing the Atlantic jammed as many as 2,000 men, women, and children into quarters unsuited for any habitation by anyone and they were poorly fed; this practice resulted in enormous profits for the steamship companies.

A typical steerage area consisted of a space indistinguishable from any upper cargo hold, without portholes or any other effective ventilating mechanism. There were no partitions; just one huge space to accommodate all of the people. The compartment was six to eight feet high, crammed with two or more tiers of narrow metal bunk beds, sometimes covered with mattresses of a minimal thickness. Men and women were separated, sometimes on different decks, sometimes by nothing but a few blankets tossed over a line in the middle of a compartment. Children usually stayed with their mothers throughout the voyage. However, as I related earlier, this was not the case with my family. All the Cavallaro children remained with Angelo as they traveled in the steerage compartment for the entire voyage.

Toilet facilities were always inadequate; cleanup was almost nonexistent; and the combined smells from the ship's galleys and human excrement gave a nauseating odor to the entire steerage compartment. The food was monotonous, poorly prepared, and bland. Fresh water was usually available only on the upper deck. The main kind of food provided, was barrel after barrel of salted herring, the cheapest food available that might be relied upon to keep the immigrants alive for voyages that lasted up to three or four weeks. Strangely, this common, little fish grew into a truly memorable creature in the memories of the immigrants. So many people remember their voyages in terms of the herring; a remarkable link that is retained by nearly all of the steerage passengers who came to America. Their ships could be as different as night and day, their passage decades apart, but herring was the great unifier. The shipping companies provided herring because it was cheap; also because it was nourishing and seemed to help combat seasickness. With herring, bread, and little else, millions made it to America in steerage. Occasionally, they were served garlic to put on their bread. They were told that garlic would help prevent seasickness also. For my Sicilian ancestors, this was great because eating a lot of garlic with their meals was a way of life for them. However, for people from other European and Asian countries, it was scoffed at and left on the plates to be thrown away.

Under these conditions, people still got seasick and remained ill for the entire voyage. During the trip, it was common for people to get so sick, that they died. The passengers watched the ship's crew as they threw the dead overboard into the water. It was a pathetic thing to watch because the passengers wanted to keep their dead relatives and give them a proper burial on land – but this was not permitted. You can imagine how many of the women carried on, especially when they would forcibly take a dead child away from them. The crew would just toss them into the sea. It was a sad time for everyone. Mothers, many times would hide babies in their aprons to prevent them from getting sick and to prevent this from happening to them. It was a part of the trip they had not expected to experience. Hearts were broken on those trips and many immigrants arrived to the new world in sadness rather than with the happiness and anticipation they had when leaving their port cities in Sicily and Italy.

As they got closer to America, the waves subsided, the winds were not as violent, and the people began to feel better. The seasickness was still prevalent among the old and the weak, but most of the others were able to walk around and they begin to eat the herring again to regain their strength as they continued on to the next stage of their long voyage.

The ship arrived in New York Harbor on July 23, 1913. The entire trip lasted twenty-three long and horribly, difficult days.

Principe di Piemonte

This ship was built by Sir James Laing & Sons Limited, in Sunderland, England.
Its specifications include that it was 6,560 gross tons; 430 feet long; 52 feet wide;
it ran on steam triple expansion engines which contained a twin screw.
Its service speed was 14 knots.
It could accommodate 1,960 passengers
(60 second class passengers, 1,960 third class (steerage) passengers;
however, it carried many more people on most of its trips.

It was built for The Uranium Steamship Company, in 1889 and was originally
named Principe Di Piemonte. It provided service from various ports in Italy to New York City
It was sold to The Uranium Steamship Company, in 1914
and was renamed Principello, which provided service from Rotterdam to New York City.
It was later sold to The Cunard Line, and flew under the British flag in 1916
and was renamed Folia. It was torpedoed and sunk by a German submarine
off the Irish coast on March 11, 1917*

*(no author). ("n.d."). Ship Image. (Online), October 18, 2002
http://www.ellisislandrecords.org/search/shipImage.asp

America – At Last!

Finally, after braving the stormy seas, the misery of steerage, and after eating far too much of the salted herring, the tired and weary immigrants entered New York Harbor. After all the years of talking, preparations, and dreaming about it, they were finally beginning to see some land and tall buildings on the horizon. It was July 23, 1913, and the sun was just coming up over the horizon, when loud and thunderous voices shouted over the loud speakers that everyone in steerage was to get up, get dressed, and pack all their belongings because they would be leaving the boat that day. Cheers and shouts of joy echoed all over the ship. Everyone was so happy. They had finally reached their destination. My father remembered that he was already awake when the announcement was made. He was sitting up on his cot. He knew that the ship's motors were not running as strong as they were before, and that the ship was going much slower. He knew they were getting closer to America and the time would be short when they would arrive. That night, he went to bed with his clothes on and even wore his shoes to bed because he didn't want to take the time to dress in the morning. As soon as he heard the announcement, he shook his brothers to awaken them and began packing all their baggage. He did not want to be late. Angelina and Mary began dressing the younger children who were still half-asleep and not aware of what was happening.

Everyone in steerage was rushing and there was a lot of activity. People were so excited this day had finally arrived. Some people had brought special clothes to wear on this day and they pulled them out of their bags to dress up for this big event. Others found that as they put on their special outfits, they did not fit since they had lost a considerable amount of weight. They had to use pieces of string or rope to hold their clothes up so they would not fall off. As the anxious travelers prepared themselves and packed their bags, they began their trek up the numerous flights of steps to the upper deck. My father remembers dragging by himself, their one big trunk up the steps to the upper deck. Once they were on deck, that trunk served as a seat for them and as a meeting place for the family.

As recounted to me, my father observed the following scene. When they had arrived to the top of the last flight of steps, the deck was filled with many people from the steerage compartment. They all wanted to get their first glimpse of New York City. My father said that he and his brothers and sisters ran to the railing so they could get a better look at the harbor and see sights that were new to them. Giovanna, his youngest sister who had just turned four years old, sat on the trunk with her father. As they approached New York Harbor, Angelo put Giovanna on his shoulders so she could see over the heads of the other people that were on deck. My father said as they stood there, that they were filled with such excitement as they saw other ships at the dock and long wharfs filled with people waving and shouting at them. They were still far away and the people looked very small. They gazed, as if in a trance, at the tall buildings of the New York City skyline. Coming from their small communities in Sicily, they had never seen such a magnificent sight. Not even in Palermo had they seen such a magnificent skyline. He and his siblings pointed out various interesting objects and kept saying, "Vedi! Vedi! Vedi!" which meant, "See! See! See!" The wind was very cool on their faces as the boat was still traveling at a quick rate of speed on that sunny July morning.

Then it happened. As the boat made a slight turn in the harbor, they could see they were approaching the Statue of Liberty. They had heard so much in Sicily about the 'Lady with the Torch' who would be greeting them. As the people on the ship saw the statue, the shouts and cheers rose to a deafening level. People began to cry and kiss each other; they even began to hug strangers. Fathers lifted young children on their shoulders so they could see. There was so much joy. Many were on their knees praying and thanking God that they had finally arrived to the land with the golden streets. My father remembered the children were so happy, they didn't know what to do except to jump up and down in place and hit each other on the top of their heads with their caps. Then, he could hear some of the people on the upper decks as they began to sing. On his deck, the people wanted to rejoice also, so they began singing one of their favorite Italian songs. As soon as they started, people from the other decks all over the ship joined in and sang <u>O Sole Mio</u>, meaning <u>O Sun of Mine</u>. There were people from other countries on board this ship, but this particular voyage had mostly Italians as passengers, so they sang the Italian song over and over again. There was so much joy on the ship at that time, that people could not contain themselves. My father said that the boat passed right in front of the Lady with the Torch while they were all singing; tears were streaming down their faces. They continued to sing as their voices were mixed with sobs; yet, the familiar melody continued. As a gesture of love and as though she could see, they began to wave to her as they passed. Hundreds of hands in the air, waving without stopping, many holding white handkerchiefs or scarves in their hands, they were waving *Buon Giorno* to the Lady with the Torch. Hands in the air waving, hands that were rough – rough from tilling the soil of their farms in Sicily; hands that were weak – weak from being seasick during the voyage; hands that were thin – thin from malnutrition of not eating the proper foods for twenty-three days; hands that were uncertain – uncertain of what was lying ahead of them in this new land; hands that were strong – strong enough to come across the Atlantic Ocean, to face all the hardships of establishing themselves in a new country that they knew nothing about; hands that were determined – determined they were going to succeed, to achieve a better life for themselves and their children; and hands of commitment – a commitment to become good Americans – never to forget their Italian heritage, but to learn a new way of life and to raise their children to become citizens in this new nation and to be part of giving America some of their rich Italian culture. As they continued singing, their voices became stronger and, by the time they were passing the Lady with the Torch, their voices could be compared with a professional choir that had been cultured and rehearsed at La Scala in Milan…..now they sang with a purpose and determination. This was their commencement – their graduation day – things would never be the same for any of them again. America would never be the same again either. They were here! The Italians had arrived!

****

To understand why they chose to sing the song, *O Sole Mio*, it is important to read the English translation of the words. They had genuine meaning for these brave travelers.

Che bella cosa, na giornata e sole,	What a beautiful thing, one day of sun,
N'aaria serena, doppo na tempesta!	A cool breeze, after a tempest storm!
Pe'll'aria fresca, pare gia' na festa….	The fresh breezes, are like a feast this day….
Che bella cosa, na giornata e sole.	What a beautiful thing, one day of sun.
Ma n'atu sole – chiu'bello, oi ne,	But no other sun, none is more beautiful,
O sole mio – sta 'nfronte a te!	Oh sun of mine, I'm in front of you!
O sole, O sole mio,	Oh sun, Oh sun of mine,
Sta 'nfronte a te! Sta 'nfronte a te!	I'm in front of you! I'm in front of you!

Having spent twenty-three days in steerage, in the filth, bug-infested compartments, and with only stale air to breathe, their dark surroundings were finally gone; they were out with their warm sun that they were accustomed to seeing every day in their *Bella Sicilia*. They continued waving their white handkerchiefs and sang vigorously with contentment as the tears of joy dripped from their faces onto the wooden deck of the ship. Yes, they had arrived in America; their prayers had been answered.

Arrival on Ellis Island

As they approached the shore, the boat slowed to a complete stop. Everyone waited to see what was going to happen next. By that time, it was mid-afternoon and they had not eaten since early morning. Finally, they began passing plates to all the people on board that included only herring or sardines and a crust of stale bread. As unappetizing as it was, there was enough for everyone to eat. Angelo Cavallaro and his six children sat on their trunk on the ship's deck as they ate what they thought was to be their final meal of the salted herring. When they finished, they waited a long time. There was no word as to what was going to happen next. As dusk was approaching, the passengers wanted to go back down to steerage to retire for the evening on their cots; however, they were not allowed to do so. The gates were chained shut with large locks to prevent the people from entering. The restrooms were the only places that remained open and accessible. Finally, an announcement came over the loud speakers. A voice they were used to hearing announced they would not be leaving the ship that night because the boat that was scheduled to bring them to Ellis Island had broken down and other provisions would have to be made.

Therefore, they had to spend the night on the ship once again. Of course, they were very disappointed and moans and groans could be heard throughout the crowds; however, the people took it in their stride and began to find places on deck where they and their families could sleep. Fortunately, it was a warm, balmy July night in New York – one of those nights when it doesn't cool off when the sun goes down, so the people made themselves as comfortable as they could. Many of them could not sleep; they were fascinated by all the flickering lights on Manhattan Island that reflected on the waters of the Upper Hudson Bay. They could see the Statue of Liberty behind them and Ellis Island lay just a few yards in front of the ship. They were so close, yet still so far away from being processed into their new country.

Early the next morning, the people were instructed to line up because the inspectors were coming to give physical inspections to all passengers before they left the ship. This needed to be accomplished before they were cleared to board the smaller ship that would take them to Ellis Island. They were given bread pudding for breakfast and then got in lines for the inspection. That morning, they were told that the people who were in steerage were the only passengers who had to remain on the ship overnight. The people who had traveled in first or second-class were able to leave the ship the night before to either meet family members or sponsors who were waiting for them, or to begin their processing at Ellis Island. Isn't it strange, that here they were coming to a country where there was complete equality, but not quite so, for the newly arrived immigrants who traveled in steerage? This was only the beginning of the discrimination they were to experience in the years to follow.

The people were instructed to line up as families, couples, or in small groups depending upon the port city where they had originated. The Cavallaro's gathered their trunk, bags of belongings, and moved as a family to the end of the long line. At this point, Angelo was still alone with the children. When they moved closer to the front of the line, the inspectors checked the tags that were tied to their clothing. Each person had been given a tag when boarding the ship and was required to wear it for the entire trip. The tag was made of strong cardstock and attached to their clothing with a safety pin and a six-inch piece of heavy, white twine. On the card, the immigrant's identifying information was given. It included their name, age, port city, city of birth, date of departure, destination, and the amount of money they had with them. The officials checked the tags and gave them a quick visual inspection to see if they had lice or any outward appearances of having any illness, which would prevent them from entry into America. The health checks were not as important because the inspectors knew the passengers would have another, more rigorous health inspection at the Ellis Island Receiving Station. Once they passed inspection, they were loaded onto a smaller boat that took them to Ellis Island. The smaller boats made many trips that day, taking a few passengers at a time from the larger ship to Ellis Island.

Ellis Island was little more than a sandbar, a small, flat, low island in Upper New York Harbor, one of a group known as Oyster Islands, named after the oyster beds found there in the early days of the American colonies. The Immigration station was still unfinished when it first opened on January 1, 1892. The main station was a large, two-story wooden building, 400 feet by 150 feet, with a large baggage handling area occupying the first floor. On the second floor were the main processing and handling facilities, including the inspection areas, holding enclosures for those who had passed inspection, railroad ticket offices, money exchange counters, food stands, and several administrative office areas. The Island facility, by then substantially enlarged, included a dormitory for those detained, a hospital, bathhouses, a restaurant, and other service and staff residence buildings.

The entire installation was capable of processing 10,000 immigrants a day. The original buildings were lost in a great fire on June 14, 1897. New buildings were constructed and the rebuilt facility was much larger than the old, original buildings. It grew from three acres to twenty-seven acres. The entire facility was able to process several thousand more immigrants a day; to hold, feed, and house hundreds of detainees; and to treat hundreds more in the hospital section. During the peak immigration years of 1900 to 1914 and 1919 to 1921, it needed this extra space to accommodate the tremendous increase in immigration to America and for future years.

For many immigrants, the processing procedure through Ellis Island was an outrageous shock. They anticipated that their arrival in New York Harbor meant it would be a safe haven for them. Despite the millions of people who had come before them and some who were eventually sent back to the old country, few were really prepared for the process that awaited them. They had heard the negative words about Golden America, and the hazards of the Castle Garden and Ellis Island experiences, but they never thought they would have to endure the ensuing hardships also. Many of the steerage passengers were infuriated at learning they would have to go to Ellis Island for a special immigration inspection, from which most first and second-class passengers were exempt. The immigrants became very fearful, and terribly afraid of what awaited them. Even if they had relatives waiting for them, the relatives could not accompany them to Ellis Island. The immigrants had to do this alone.

The transfer barges that brought the immigrants to Ellis Island were crowded, often with little protection from the elements, and without seats for most people. Once moored at the Island, immigrants waited on the barges, sometimes for hours, while others ahead of them were being processed. If the barges were needed elsewhere, the immigrants were unloaded on the landing docks and stood outside in a long line waiting to enter the main building. If they were still waiting in line at noon, all the personnel inside the building went for their lunch; this included just about everyone, the clerks, the doctors, and inspectors. The immigrants would have to wait until three or four o'clock in the afternoon to be processed; they would not have the opportunity to get into the building because it was either full, or everyone in authority was out to lunch. They were fed while they were waiting outside. People from the Island would bring cans of milk, coffee, some brown bread cut up into fancy slices, and the usual boxes of sardines or herring to the immigrants waiting in line. They thought they had seen the last meals of herring on the ship, but here they were in the land of plenty, and they were still eating this dreadful fish. These meager amounts of food were passed around to the waiting immigrants. There were usually two to three hundred people in line by this time.

Once they arrived to the door of the main building, they were formed into groups by ship name and Manifest number. A canopy just outside the main entrance offered them some protection against the elements as they stood in line. This was the first of many such lines – while they all waited and talked with other immigrants, curious as to what was going to happen next.

Eventually, the immigrants were allowed into the building and were led up the main stairway by an interpreter into the Great Hall and onto the central examining area on the second floor. At the base of the steps, Angelo and the children saw Angela waiting for them. She had been there for hours, waiting for her family. There was great joy among the children when they saw their mother and they wanted to talk to her all at once in order to tell her about their experiences on the boat. However, they were not allowed to do so, because they were quickly rushed upstairs to the Great Hall of Ellis Island.

At the top of the stairs, the first stop of a two-step medical examination took place. Immigrants were spaced apart so the doctors could study them as they approached the examining section. They moved in single file past a team of two doctors, placed some distance apart. The men and boys were in one line, and the women and girls were sent to another. These lines were separated by black drapes so they could not see each other.

The doctors examined as many as 5,000 immigrants a day, checking for a wide range of abnormalities and diseases (some treatable, and some not), which might cause an immigrant to be excluded from America. They checked for symptoms of mental problems, both specific and general. They checked for such disabilities as very poor eyesight or partial blindness, senility, lameness, deafness, general weakness and for physical deformities. They also checked for many specific illnesses; which included, trachoma (a kind of conjunctivitis that causes eventual blindness), favus (a scalp disease) and tuberculosis which were all causes for rejection, and meant that they'd be returned to Italy and not allowed to stay in America with their families.

In 1913, one of the peak years of immigration, the two doctors spent no more than two minutes to inspect each immigrant and often much less. The resulting examination was therefore, rather minimal. They looked generally at the people as they approached the front of the line, and then more closely at their hands, faces, and throats. If they saw any basis at all for further examination, they'd put chalk marks on the front or back of the immigrant's clothing, in a code indicating the nature of the suspected physical condition. The code for the chalk-marks indicated the follow problem areas:

X = suspected mental illness	F = face	CT = Trachoma
O = definite sign of mental illness	H = heart	Sc = scalp (favus)
K = hernia	N = neck	Pg = pregnancy
G = goiter	S = Senility	FT = feet
L = lameness	C = Conjunctivitis	
E = eyes	P = physical & lungs	

The doctors also looked for signs of nail biting, unusual smiling, and facetious behavior as signs of mental illness. During 1913, at least 20% of the immigrants were detained and returned to their port cities in Europe. Many of the immigrants, knowing what it meant to be chalk-marked, could be seen turning their coats inside out to hide the marks; many immigrants got away with this method of hiding their chalk marks and proceeded to the next station.

Because of the wide range of possible medical exclusions and the brevity of this primary medical examination, it is not surprising that hundreds of thousands of people were chalk-marked and held aside for further examination.

It was at this point of the examinations that the Cavallaro family experienced quite a difficult time. All the boys were in line with Angelo; one by one, the doctors examined them. When it came time for Angelo to be examined, the boys could see that the doctors put chalk marks on the front of his coat – a large 'E' and a 'C;' meaning that he had a problem with his eyes – specifically Conjunctivitis. The children did not understand what the letters stood for except that he was receiving a chalk mark and that was not a good thing. It meant detention and/or return to Sicily – and if he was to return, so were his children. Uncle Roger recalled the incident to me very vividly. Remember that the boys were the following ages at this time: Alfred was sixteen, Joseph was eleven, and Roger was eight years old. Uncle Roger said that as soon as they saw the chalk marks made on their father's coat, they started to yell and scream loudly. The boys moved closer to hug their father. The two doctors immediately proceeded to separate them. Then, Uncle Roger jumped up, wrapped his arms around his father's waist and his legs around his father's legs, and would not let go. This caused quite a commotion in the men's line. As a result, many of the women were tempted to peek over the black drape to see what was happening. Angela recognizing her son's voices, and with Giovanna in her arms, scooted under the drapes to their aid. Angelina and Maria followed her. The doctors tried to calm the family down, while others wanted Angelo to go to a separate area where he would be examined for a second time. An interpreter went with them to explain what was happening. The family pleaded with the doctors that his eyes were red and bloodshot due to lack of sleep and that that the salt water splashed into his face every day of the trip. The doctors made a concession for them and allowed the entire family to accompany Angelo to the second inspection station and to wait with him, which was not the normal procedure. Angela and the girls went back to the other side of the black curtain to continue their inspection. The boys eventually calmed down as they proceeded with their father to the next station of inspection.

Once past the first team of doctors, the immigrants encountered another team at the end of the examining aisle. These doctors used buttonhooks to conduct the next eye examination. A buttonhook can be described as a long handled tool with a curved metal hook on the end that was designed to pull a button through the hole in fabric or a shoe. Imagine the horror the immigrants experienced when they first saw these strange instruments, not knowing how they were going to be used. They experienced more fear when they realized that the buttonhooks were to be used to turn their eyelids inside out in order for the doctors to see the underside of their eyelids. My father remembers when they performed this procedure on Angelo. He said that Angelo screamed with utter anguish; the doctors physically had to hold him down so they could continue the procedure.

This second step of the medical inspection, mainly directed at discovering Trachoma, was another frightening experience. The examination was quite painful, and left his eyes hurting and sensitive for many days after. The immigrants had no preparation for this type of examination except for the stories that were told to them by earlier immigrants, and the very real pain that was experienced by others ahead of them in line, which was heard by their screams throughout the Great Hall.

After the second inspection station, it was determined that the Cavallaro family had passed and did not need to be detained any longer. They found that Angelo did not have Conjunctivitis or Trachoma. They were finally approved to continue through the rest of the inspection stations. They left that area, feeling relieved; however, the whole family had experienced some things they talked about for many days later. It left them with memories etched into their minds that remained with them for the rest of their lives.

Those detained were held in screened detention areas, clearly visible to other immigrants as they passed from station to station. They felt like they were caged animals, on display. Later, they were moved into special inspection areas for further examination, to dormitories for detention, to bathhouses for disinfecting and delousing, and sometimes directly into hospitals, as thought necessary by the examining doctors.

If not detained for medical reasons, the immigrants were moved, still in groups by ship Manifest number, to benches between the medical examination area and the main inspection area. When their group was called, they moved to another series of benches arranged in long, narrow aisles. There they waited until, one by one, they were called for examination by one of the immigration inspectors who sat at the end of each aisle at a raised desk, as does a judge in a courtroom; an interpreter was usually present also.

The immigration inspector had before him the ship's Manifest, listing the basic information about each passenger that had been filled out by the ship's officer at the Port of Origin. The basic questions contained in the Manifest were set by the Immigration Law of 1903, and focused on identification, marital status, individual skills, personal history, financial responsibility, and plans for prospective employment.

If no problems arose during this review of the Manifest information, immigrants who passed were free to board the boat that brought them to the Battery. The Battery was a collection area on the mainland where relatives were waiting for them. Once at The Battery and they had no relatives waiting for them, they were taken by numbered groups to make railroad connections for the remainder of their journey inland. Those not examined before nightfall, were held overnight at the Island, and inspected the following morning. Immigration policy precluded nighttime inspections or clearance.

Those remaining for additional inspections were dismissed to dormitories. The physical aspects were worse than being in prison. The four main dormitories held about four hundred wire cages each. They contained three-tiered steel bunks, set in long rows with narrow aisles between them. Each steel bunk had a blanket, but when they went to find their bed, they found that not all of them had mattresses, pillows, or sheets. The space between the bunks was about two feet high, and ventilation was minimal. New York's humid and sweltering summer nights made it very uncomfortable for the people who were required to stay in that place.

Despite Ellis Island's rough-and-ready delousing procedures, the main building and the dormitories were lice-infested. My father remembers lying down on the cot with the blanket and he immediately threw it off the cot and to the floor. There were louses all over it and on the thin mattress. He said that he spent most nights sitting on the trunk that he carried with his back to the wall, sleeping up right. He said that shortly after he got up to sit on the trunk, his brothers Joe and Roger joined him as they leaned on each other for support and tried to get some sleep. They feared contact with lice and that they would get into their clothing or in their hair. They had seen others during the initial inspections that had been found to have lice and were not allowed to get on the ship. Regardless of the beautiful hair, many passengers had to shave their head if they were suspected to have lice. This included children, men, and women. The immigrants were required to remain on Ellis Island until they were cleared of lice; yet, they had to continue to live in the filth and under the unhygienic conditions.

Some people were detained for many days and, sometimes for weeks. They were not allowed to join their families and some were eventually returned to their city of origin in Europe. If a person or a family was not detained and allowed to process through the inspection stations at a normal rate, it would take anywhere from two to five days. What I have written in these previous paragraphs may appear to be a quick and easy method of going through these stations, but remember that there were thousands of people at Ellis Island every day thus creating long lines and additional waiting for the immigrants. A majority of the time used during the processing of immigrants was dedicated just to translating everything that they needed to know. They had translators there from all nations to interpret for the immigrants and this extended the time needed for processing. Every day forms needed to be filled out for people, such as: those transported to hospitals for serious illnesses; those being deloused; those sent to the infirmary for short term illnesses; those arriving without money or sponsorship; those sent to holding stations for various reasons; and many other special problems. Just filling out forms for each of these situations created long waiting lines for the immigrants. It was very common for people to be detained because of other special problems, such as a female immigrant who was not met by the American sponsor listed on her forms. Sometimes, the sponsor would send a friend to pick her up in their place. The Immigration Service did not let immigrants leave the Island with people who were not relatives or bona fide sponsors – they were especially careful not to let young women go with unknown men; so these people were met with further delay.

Many times, just prior to or during the inspections, one could hear loud crying. They were crying because of a loved one being chalk marked or detained; someone having to go to the hospital; a young girl traveling alone may have been found to be pregnant; these were automatically returned to their port city. Crying, as is laughing, is very contagious. Many immigrants, fearing the worst, often cried because others were crying and did not want to experience any of the hardships of their friends. For this reason, Ellis Island was often referred to as 'The Island of Tears.' The immigrants saw it as an island of bars, cages, and callousness. They saw iron railings covering most of the Great Hall. The bars were there to create aisles for orderly movement within the Hall; however, the immigrants saw them as the iron bars of a prison. They saw wired detention areas, which they identified as cages. They believed people should not be put in cages – cages were for animals. Seeing all of this would also make them cry. The crying epidemic was fed by exhaustion, fear, confusion, and tragedy; the Island personnel observed this behavior. When the Island personnel were interviewed, they were no worse than bureaucrats everywhere. They, themselves, were exhausted by an enormous and never-ending workload, and had to work under conditions of extreme crowding and tension - and the crying that never stopped.

Meals on Ellis Island

One of the things that most people remember about Ellis Island is the kind of food that was offered to them. Some thought it to be wonderful and others described it as terrible. Some felt the food facilities were very clean and others described them as being filthy. Concessionaires, working under government contracts, supplied the food at Ellis Island. Two sets of kitchens were maintained; one for all immigrants and another kosher kitchen for those of the Jewish faith. The steamship companies paid for the food consumed during the examination and detention periods. Food for their further journey was bought by the immigrants themselves or provided by various social service organizations.

When it was dinnertime, the immigrants sat down at long tables in the large dining halls. The steerage immigrants went to a dining room that was very plain and the food was already on plates that were brought out from the kitchen to the people. In great contrast, the people who had traveled in first or second class, had tablecloths on their tables with cloth napkins, nice silver service, and specially prepared meals that were served family style. Many of the inspectors, doctors, and employees also ate there. The dining room where the steerage passengers ate had a very strong odor of disinfectant. In the steerage passenger dining hall, there were long, narrow tables set up. The tables were set up end to end, from one side of the room to the other. There were at least eight to ten rows of tables set up in one dining hall;

therefore, making it possible to have as many as six hundred or more people in the room at one time. People sat on both sides of the tables making the aisles between the tables only large enough for the diner's chairs and for one server to squeeze through to bring in the plates of food. People sat shoulder to shoulder in very cramped quarters to eat. Sitting on both sides of the table, there could be as many as sixty or more people at one table. On the walls in the dining halls, they had signs that read, "No charge for food here." These signs were written in several languages to cater to all the different languages spoken by the immigrants on Ellis Island; however, they didn't realize that many immigrants from southern Italy and Sicily could not read them because they were illiterate and couldn't read Italian. Many times, the interpreters would go into the dining halls and read the signs aloud in the various languages so everyone would know what was written on them.

Everyone agreed that there was plenty of food. Another item of agreement was that there were new varieties of food and new ways of serving familiar foods each day. My father recalls seeing and eating his first banana. Bananas were not grown in Sicily; neither were they imported. As a result, Sicilians had never seen nor tasted bananas before. Although my father had never seen bananas before, they looked very attractive to him as they were placed in the bowls on the tables. One of those bowls of bananas was on the table right in front of where he was eating, so he took one. He bit into it, skin and all; it felt it a bit chewy. Others at the table laughed at him because it looked so strange to be eating a banana in that manner. He knew that something was wrong, so he stopped eating it, began to squeeze it out like toothpaste from a tube, and finished eating it that way. He said it was too chewy to eat with the skin. Before long, he watched others eating the bananas and he took another one, peeled it, and ate it the correct way. He found he really did not like the flavor or consistency of the banana, so he threw it down and did not finish it. As I remember, he never liked bananas after that incident and never ate them as an adult.

On several occasions, the immigrants were served sandwiches to eat. In Sicily, or even in other parts of Europe, sandwiches were unheard of at that time. It was something like ham or bologna between two slices of dark bread. They were not accustomed to eating this kind of food but they ate it because they were hungry. At every meal, they had large cookies to eat and everyone liked those. Another difference for them was large quantities of milk. They liked this. They could have as much milk as they wanted and this was the first good nourishment many of the immigrants had since the beginning of their journey.

After dinner, the immigrants would linger in the dining hall or go to their sleeping quarters. Again, men and women were separated in the sleeping areas. People slept with their clothes and shoes on because there was no place to put them. They slept on cots, one stacked on top of another to resemble bunk beds, but they were stacked three high. This also was new to immigrants. They had never seen this kind of bed and didn't know how to get up to the top cot. Those that remained in the dining hall would talk, reminisce about the old country, or share their dreams about what was waiting for them in the new America. Some of the immigrants brought musical instruments with them. They brought guitars, mandolins, concertinas, harmonicas, zithers, or a *friscaletto* (frē-skă-lĕt´-ō) (similar to a high-pitched piccolo). They would take out their instruments and begin playing many of their favorite songs from their own native country. People would dance and sing, and make new friends. It would be common to see an Italian gentleman dance with a German woman to a waltz, or other Italians dancing a *tarantella (tă-răn-tel-tă)* together. The time would pass in a very pleasant way and would remind them of how they relaxed after dinner when they were at home. It would give them the opportunity to forget about their fears or concerns about what the next day would hold for them. They had to stop playing and singing at ten o'clock in the evening. By that time, everyone had to be in his or her cot. The lights were turned off in all compartments at that hour.

They Changed our Names at Ellis Island

We have often heard someone say that inspectors at Ellis Island changed their name. It is believed that immigrants had one correct way to spell their name in the old country that was accepted by all; however, when they encountered the clerk at Ellis Island, many were changed and spelled differently upon their arrival. In reality, the immigrants spoke little or no English, so either the immigrant inadvertently gave an incorrect reply to the question of "What is your name?" or, the clerk misunderstood the name, or decided it was too complicated and wrote it in a shortened, Americanized way. The records from The Immigration and Naturalization Service show that the clerks at Ellis Island didn't write down names. They worked from lists that were created by the shipping companies. What usually happened was that the immigrant brought a ticket from an office that was not near his home. Therefore, the seller, being from another area of Sicily, probably spoke another dialect and transcribed the name incorrectly. In cases where the name was recorded incorrectly, it likely occurred in the old country, not at Ellis Island. The spellings of the same name could be different, depending upon the level of education of the clerk writing the names on the forms.

At least 75% of those passing through Ellis Island came through with their names unchallenged. After passing through the medical examination, immigrants waited in the main line inspection area conducted by Immigration Service inspectors. In that line, only one question was asked. This was usually done in haste and under conditions of mutual exhaustion and overcrowding. That question was simply: "What is your name?" If the name were changed in any way, it would later cause a great deal of trouble to the immigrants seeking citizenship in America. As a result, it makes it difficult for thousands of genealogists today to get beyond the barrier of their Ellis Island research as they try to trace the histories of their families. They must be creative in spelling the names in a variety of ways until the correct person for whom they are searching is found.

Some immigrants wanted their names changed, and accomplished that at Ellis Island, simply by responding with shortened and altered versions of their original names. Tens of thousands of others had their names changed for them by the immigration inspectors or by the ship's officer who had filled out the Manifest, often in ways that were objectionable to them. However, most did not object, feeling they could not object to anything the inspector did. The inspector seemed to have unlimited power over their futures, and in fact, did have enormous discretion as to acceptance or rejection of an immigrant. Other immigrants didn't know what was happening, especially the approximate 20% who were illiterate in the years before the mandatory literacy law of 1917.

Many inspectors were careful and conscientious in the matter of getting names spelled correctly. Some leaned heavily on the interpreters who were normally present during the main line inspections. They made a concerted effort to get the names pronounced and spelled correctly. Nevertheless, some immigration inspectors were casual and uncaring on the matter of names. These inspectors misunderstood replies to the "What is your name?" question. They misspelled, and often assisted the immigrants with suggestions for Americanized names they could use. Some even capriciously changed names, with little or no concern for the feelings of those they were mishandling.

Listed below are the names of the Cavallaro family, as they appear on the Manifest for the Principe de Piemonte, along with the English names that that they used in America. The ship's Manifest was created in Palermo, Sicily, the port city of departure, and written by Sicilian nationals. These appear on Page # 0309, List # 28, Section 228, in the list for steerage passengers.

Line #	Name on Ship's Manifest	Name Used in America	Age
0017	Angelo Cavallaro	Angelo Cavallaro	46
0018	Angelo Cavallaro	Angelina	18
0019	Alfio Cavallaro	Alfred	16
0020	Maria Catena Cavallaro	Mary	13
0021	Orazio Cavallaro	Roger	8
0022	Giovanna Cavallaro	Jennie (Joan)	4
0023	Giuseppe Cavallaro	Joseph	11

On the ship's Manifest for the Principe di Piemonte (same ship), for first class passengers, the following is listed:

Line#	Name on Ship's Manifest	Name Used in America	Age
0009	Angela Gravagno	Angela (Gravagna) Cavallaro	34

By examining the name of Angela (Gravagna) Cavallaro, note that on the ship's manifest, her last name (her maiden name) ends in an 'o'. That was an error because she always said her name ended with an 'a'. This may appear to be a slight error; however, it became very difficult to locate her on the Manifest because of this one letter and since she was traveling alone and as a first class passenger. In addition, her daughter, Angelina had her first name listed as 'Angelo' rather than 'Angela.' This error did not create as much confusion since she was listed in numerical order with the rest of the family.

As you can see, many of the names of the Cavallaro children were Americanized. However, I know that they all used their given Italian names for any legal purposes, which included applications for naturalization/citizenship certification. In the case of Roger, I'm not sure how that change was made. The Americanization of the name, Orazio would actually be, Horatio. Uncle Roger may have done this on his own or they may have even done it when he began attending school in Rochester; they could have changed it upon entering and it stuck with him. I do know that Aunt Joan selected her name as she grew older. She did not like to be called Jennie and, because she worked in the fashion world, Joan just seemed to fit much better for her needs; to all of us she became known as Aunt Joan. I remember when I was a little boy, sometimes slipping, and calling her Aunt Jennie, and she'd always correct me to use her name, Joan. Her brothers and sisters, being true-blooded Italians, didn't like the change, so they continued to call her, Jennie. It was always a point of contention with her.

Money on Ellis Island

From the early 1900s, immigrants all over Europe understood that one of the main hurdles of admission into the United States was the matter of money – twenty-five dollars to be precise. The information as to the twenty-five dollar rule came from various sources; it came from agents working in the cities and countryside, searching out prospective immigrants from the steamship companies; from returning emigrants; from newspaper and magazine articles; and in letters from family and friends who were in America. They were told that they could gain admission to America only if they could show twenty-five dollars for each person entering at Ellis Island. They eventually found this to be true through their own experiences. During the journey to America, the twenty-five dollar rule was verified when the ship's officer was filling out the Manifest required by American law and asked about money. So immigrants immediately assumed that America required a show of money before opening its doors to them.

Oddly enough, it was only partially true. What was entirely true was that an administrative regulation was unevenly applied, resulting in intentional gross discrimination against poor immigrants from southern and eastern Europe. Not all immigrants entering Ellis Island were asked about the amount of money they were carrying.

Commissioner of Immigration William Williams, an outspoken foe of what he called 'low grade immigrants' from southern and eastern Europe, required as early as 1904 that all immigrants show ten dollars and tickets to their destinations if they were going beyond New York City. When he left office in 1905, his successor, Robert Watchorn, formally repealed his ten-dollar regulation. Four years later, Williams returned as Commissioner of Immigration, and immediately instituted a new regulation that was in no way supported by any of the immigration laws; it required that all immigrants show twenty-five dollars plus tickets to their next destination.

The resulting storm of protest from outraged immigrant organizations, coupled with court challenges, forced him to pull down the notices he had posted at Ellis Island, announcing the new regulation. Two years later, he was ordered to eliminate reference in the regulation to the specific twenty-five dollar amount. Nevertheless, his retreat was a simple sham – the regulation was not repealed. In fact, the regulation stayed fully in force until he left office in 1914 – the year after the Cavallaro's immigrated to America.

As a result, immigrant fathers, older sisters, and brothers continued to work in New York sweatshops, or on railroad gangs to produce that extra twenty-five dollars per person to bring the rest of their family to America. Twenty-five dollars may not sound like much today, but during the immigrant years, it was a good deal of money, often representing months of painful penny-by-penny saving, denial and continued separation from their family who still remained in Europe. At that time, people were making about two dollars a week in tailor factories. Some, in the bigger cities were making as much as four to five dollars a week as full-time unskilled sweatshop workers. Rentals in New York's terrible tenements were relatively high - eight to ten dollars a month for a three-room apartment or a few dollars a month for a room with only a bed in a stranger's crowded apartment. Although you could buy a herring for two cents and you might walk to work, it was still very difficult to save anything at all on seasonal sweatshop wages.

For immigrants with families still in the old country, that twenty-five dollars for each of perhaps six members of a family meant a dollar a week saved for 150 weeks – if they were working steadily. Often that twenty-five dollars was the difference between bringing a family over this year or next year; bringing two older children or just one child; reuniting only a portion of a family; or waiting almost a decade until after the storms of war and revolution had swept Europe. Yet, while the whole world knew you needed twenty-five dollars to get into America, administration of the rule was inconsistent and sometimes even intentionally directed to the southern and eastern Europeans that Williams and others were trying to keep out of the United States.

Some immigrants related a different sidelight on how they got through the lines. Sometimes the procedure was not followed exactly as the officials had planned, because some immigrants did not have twenty-five dollars available upon arrival. You can be assured that envelopes containing twenty-five dollars were passed along from one passenger to another to help those that did not have it and this had to be done with a quick motion of the hand so no one would be caught. Actually, it was a very real part of the whole procedure. Immigrants would help each other in those trying moments, as they all wanted to leave Ellis Island and enter the mainland of America.

In my research, it appears this may be the way in which Angelo Cavallaro and his six children entered into the United States. According to the ship's Manifest, he was carrying sixty dollars. Because there were seven people in his family, he was required to have a minimum of $175.00. Whether he had money secretly passed to him that was not seen by the authorities, or if he was not asked to show the money, is not known. Of course, the steamship company would not bar passage to him because they didn't require the twenty-five dollars per passenger amount – this was only a requirement on Ellis Island in order to enter the United States. One immigrant arriving on that same ship in 1913 recounts his Ellis Island activity as follows:

> *"I thought we were sent to a concentration camp because they didn't land us in New York, but landed us on Ellis Island. There you had to sit, and they called you and pushed you. There was a barricade so that you could walk in a row. You walked up, they asked you your name, and they asked you this and they asked you that, and they asked you if you had any money so that you could take care of yourself. We said "Yes" and my father wanted to show it, but they said, "Oh, no, no, you don't have to show." They believed him; and they made a white cross on a yellow card and we went on a small boat there and the small boat took us to New York…"*

Now, remember that Angela was traveling in first class and went through this part of the line on her own. The ship's Manifest recorded that she was carrying forty dollars. Because this was more than the required amount, she had no problem at that station.

The twenty-five dollar rule continued for many years after the Cavallaro family arrived in the United States. Records show that this was still being required until at least 1925. Word of this spread throughout the immigrant communities and they all came to the United States with great fear about having to show twenty-five dollars, hoping that they would find an inspector who was kind and understanding, and would not ask them to show their money. Immigrants from southern Europe (specifically Italy and Sicily) were especially targeted to comply with this requirement. This would be their first exposure to the bias and discrimination they would experience after they arrived in America. Immigrants not having the money were detained on Ellis Island for as long as a month, waiting for their relatives or sponsors in America to send them the required amount of money.

Some Final Thoughts

While doing my research, another issue surfaced which brought about much discontent to my relatives. They remembered being herded from place to place, and in the process, they were pushed and shoved so they would move faster. They didn't dare speak out because they were all in constant fear of being returned to Sicily. They could not afford that risk. They had left their jobs, they had spent most of their money, and they didn't have a home there anymore. This was to become their new home; therefore, they had to learn to conform and accept things that they had not been accustomed to in their beautiful Sicily.

It was known that most of the people who did the shoving and pushing were foreigners and former-immigrants themselves, who delighted in the fact that they could lord over the new entries, the new immigrants. They had very unusual accents and acted how people do when they have recently acquired some power. Uncle Roger said that one time he was pushed and picked up to move and his feet actually left the ground. As angry as they would get, they never said a word. Aunt Mary said that close to the time when they were ready to leave Ellis Island, they found out from other immigrants, that there were signs on the walls that read, *"Employees are required to be civil to immigrants. Employees are required to be helpful to immigrants."* After some other immigrants who could read English told them this, you could be sure the Cavallaro's were not pushed around much anymore, and they did voice their concerns about the abuse all the immigrants were receiving. Other immigrants did the same, and soon, the pushing, shoving and mistreatment lessened.

When the Cavallaro family landed on Ellis Island, they knew it would be for more than one day. They had just endured a twenty-three day trip across the Atlantic Ocean under deplorable conditions, including poor sleeping quarters, unsanitary restroom facilities, unhealthy and insufficient meals, and general discomfort for all the voyagers. Little did they realize when they arrived on Ellis Island they would have a new set of conditions and challenges that needed to be dealt with during their extended stay. None of the Cavallaro children could remember how long they were detained on Ellis Island when we discussed this part of their trip. They only knew that it was approximately five or six days before they were allowed to leave. Neither could they clearly understand why they had to wait that long in detention. All they could remember was that they could not wait to get off the Island and get to Rochester.....wherever that was.

An Advocate of the Immigrants

The following is an excerpt from Brownstone, David M., Franck, Irene M. Brownstone, Douglass; *Island of Hope, Island of Tears*; MetroBooks, 1979, 2000.

Between the years of 1910 and 1913, someone arrived at Ellis Island that would make a significant difference as to the treatment of the people and procedures that had been considered as law on the Island. His name was *Fiorello La Guardia*. After working as the American consul in Italy, he came to the Island and worked as an interpreter for the Immigration Service. Always a man of extraordinary depth and compassion, he describes some of the terrible scenes that resulted in the long years before his advice was adopted. One of the special problems they had to face was when an adult had to accompany a child that needed to be returned to Italy, because they had all passed the inspections except for the one child. A situation like this created a terrible decision that many families had to face.

"The immigration laws were rigidly enforced, and there were many heartbreaking scenes on Ellis Island. I never managed during the three years I worked there to become callous to the mental anguish, the disappointment, and the despair I witnessed almost daily. Some of the employees did become callous to the suffering after a while, but on the whole they were a hardworking lot, conscientious and loyal…"

"Several hundred immigrants daily were found to be suffering from trachoma, and their exclusion was mandatory. It was harrowing to see families separated because the precaution had not been taken of giving them prior examinations on the other side. Sometimes, if it was a young child who suffered from trachoma, one of the parents had to return to the native country with the rejected member of the family. When they learned their fate, they were stunned. They had never felt ill. They had never heard the word trachoma. They could see all right, and they had no homes to return to. I suffered because I felt so powerless to help these poor people, and I did what I could by writing letters to Senators and Representatives telling them of my experiences at Fiume, and urging legislation to remedy the situation. Everyone seemed to agree that the law should require a physical examination at the port of embarkation. But nothing was done about it officially until 1919, when such a law was passed."

"The physical requirements for immigrants were very high, and a large percentage of them were excluded for medical reason. In addition to trachoma, cases of favus and other scalp diseases were common. I always suffered greatly when I was assigned to interpret for mental cases in the Ellis Island hospital. I felt then, and I feel the same today, that over fifty percent of the deportations for alleged mental disease were unjustified. Many of those classified as mental cases were so classified because of ignorance on the part of the immigrants or the doctors, and the inability of the doctors to understand the particular immigrant's norm, or standard."

Immigrants, because of lack of knowledge, not understanding the English language, and fear, had to deal with many other difficulties on Ellis Island also. One of the classic problems they faced was the question about contract labor. Prior to their arrival in America, American businesses had actively advertised for labor from Europe; by 1885, because of American workers protecting their own jobs and the rates of pay increasing, a bill was pushed through and passed which outlawed the importation of "contract labor" – immigrants who had been promised jobs by American companies prior to their leaving the old country. The problem faced by immigrants was, if they said they had a job, they might be sent back home as "contract laborers"; if they said they had no prospects for a job, they might be sent back as likely to become public charges. Weary and forewarned, immigrants had to answer the questions – as well as they could through interpreters, since most knew no English – by conveying that they had "good prospects of a job." In fact, that was usually the truth, but that didn't make it any easier for the immigrant. Fiorello La Guardia describes that and some of the other problems that came before the Boards of Special Inquiry:

"It is a puzzling fact that one provision of the Immigration Law excludes any immigrant who has no job and classifies him as likely to become a public charge, while another provision excludes an immigrant if he already has a job! Common sense suggested that any immigrant who came into the United States in those days to settle here permanently surely came here to work. However, under the law, he could not have any more than a vague hope of a job. In answering the inspectors' questions, immigrants had to be very careful, because if their expectations were too enthusiastic, they might be held as coming in violation of the contract labor provision. Yet, if they were too indefinite, if they knew nobody, had no idea where they were going to get jobs, they might be excluded as likely to become public charges. Most of the inspectors were conscientious and fair. Sometimes, I felt, large batches of those held and deported as violating the contract labor provision were, perhaps, only borderline cases and had no more than the assurance from relatives or former townsmen of jobs on their arrival..."

"Persons convicted of offenses involving moral turpitude were excluded from the country also. Immigrants were required to present certificates to show them free from penal offenses. Some did not have them, and others would not present them. That created a presumption of guilt, and then, the immigrants were questioned very closely. I discovered that many were being deported for minor offenses, or because of incorrect interpretation of their answers, or inaccurate translations of their penal certificates. I got the translators together, and we brought about some uniformity in the translation of these crimes, and that prevented a lot of injustice."

"There were rare cases of husbands who had sent for their wives after two or three years of hard working and saving from their small wages, only to earn for the first time that a child had been born in the meantime. We also witnessed scenes of great generosity, understanding and forgiveness…"

"On the whole, the personnel of the Immigration Service were kindly and considerate. At best, the work was an ordeal. Our compensation, besides our salaries, for the heartbreaking scenes we witnessed, was the realization that a large percentage of these people pouring into Ellis Island would probably make good and enjoy a better life than they had been accustomed to where they came from…"

Fiorello La Guardia brought many changes to the Immigration Service that significantly changed the procedures at Ellis Island. All immigrants benefited from these changes; however, Italian immigrants found the procedures worked extremely well for them because of all the extra interpreters that were hired who could speak the Italian language. Fiorello La Guardia's entire career, was highlighted by his affective innovations and personal involvement, transformed the procedures for Ellis Island for many, many years. Out of a poorly organized system that was full of bureaucracy and discrimination, he created a system that gave immigrants a fair opportunity to gain admittance into America, which was organized, and gave needed assistance to all newcomers. Immigrants from all nations appreciated him for this. He was, and still is, long remembered for his faithful work and sincerity in the Immigration Service.

The Journey Continues.......
.....On To Rochester, New York

Once the family had been completely cleared and processed, which meant that they had been physically examined; questioned as to the identification and location of their sponsors; declared the amount of money they had on hand; identified their job prospects; and had all the paper work completed, they were ready to leave Ellis Island. This was a great day for the Cavallaro family as it was for many of the immigrants. They were all anxious to get on with their journey and to make contact with their waiting relatives and sponsors. Considering all the Immigration Laws and red tape they had to surmount, only about one-third of the immigrants were admitted to the United States. Once entrance was granted, they went out the back doors of the Great Hall, down the stairs, and into the first-floor baggage room, where they made the necessary arrangements for the delivery of their baggage. Then, they walked down a wire-enclosed path to a door bearing the simple, yet emotion-filled sign that read, "PUSH......To New York." Indeed, they would find that to make it in New York they *would* have to PUSH. For now, they felt a moment of relief as they passed through the door to the cheering reception of waiting friends and relatives. That landing was, for most of four decades, the scene of extraordinary and joyous reunions; families, long torn apart, were made whole again; lovers, who had almost given up hope, were reunited; fathers and children, who had never seen each other before, started a new life together.

However, for the Cavallaro family and for about two-thirds of the other immigrants on that landing, there were no welcoming relatives to greet them. Everyone the Cavallaro family knew lived in the Rochester area, many miles away. Therefore, as they exited the door, they followed the raised wooden planks to the ferry, which would bring them from Ellis Island to the Battery. Then, they would board the ferry for another short ride to the mainland. When they exited the ferry, their feet finally touched the solid ground of New York, and they were in Manhattan – *L'America*. It was truly a time of joy for all immigrants to be on the land that would eventually become their new home and the home for all their future generations. From the Manhattan area, immigration officials would guide those who were traveling further inland, to a train that would take them to their next destinations. Of course, they still could not believe it, but the tears of joy that cascaded down their pale cheeks spoke for them. Their heart-felt joy expressed, "At last, thanks to '*La Madonna*,' we have made it to our new home!"

The first thing they did was to exchange all their money into United States currency at the moneychanger counters at the train station. Then, if they had their tickets for the train, they proceeded to the Waiting Room in another building to wait for their trains. Those who had not purchased their tickets yet, went to the first floor ticket offices and the immigration officials helped them to purchase the correct passes for their destination. In the Waiting Room, they had the opportunity to purchase box lunches for the trip. While they sat and waited, they saw a section called, The Railroad Clearing House. It was a pool of twelve railroads, which shared all traffic originating at Ellis Island. At that point, they had tags attached to their clothing which read, 'P.R.R.,' or 'L.V.R.R.,' indicating that they would be taking either the Pennsylvania Railroad or the Lehigh Valley Railroad.

From there, the immigrants were grouped according to destination and according to the railroad station, they were to depart from to get to their destinations. Therefore, from the Waiting Room and wearing their new tags, they were taken in groups to travel by barge to their designated railroad stations for their trip further into New York State. Once they arrived at the railroad station, it only meant more waiting. The Cavallaro family had to wait overnight for their train so they had to sleep on the hard benches in the New York Railroad station. Not knowing the language, it was difficult for them to understand the announcements coming over the loud speakers. They had no conception as to what was being announced or as to when their train to Rochester would arrive. However, they found other immigrants at the railroad station who would help them. They were not traveling alone. It appeared that all the immigrants traveled together because they were traveling on, what was known as, Immigrant Trains. Immigrants were transported on these trains, with no other passengers on board; they were old, poorly lit, badly ventilated cars. The Immigrant Trains would travel to larger cities, and usually on non-direct routes. Many times, these trains were put on holding tracks to let other commercial trains pass through. They were generally handled like the slowest of freight trains. For all this, the immigrants were charged first-class fares, for supposedly 'direct service' to their eventual destinations. This was another example of how they were taken advantage of during the trip.

Angelo, having gone through this procedure a number of times previously, seemed to know the location of the specific gate where they needed to wait for their train. He went to the

Dispatch Window and asked for the time when the train to Rochester would arrive. He could not speak English, but he knew Rochester as, *Rochesterre*, pronounced (Rō-kĕ-stĕ-rrĕ), the Italian pronunciation of Rochester. He could read numbers, so they wrote the time on a piece of paper for him. He and the family listened intently for the voice that echoed over the loud speakers throughout the huge train station for the word, *Rochesterra*. Finally, the train arrived; they hurriedly climbed on board, got the children settled in seats near each other, and prepared for their long voyage northward to the city that would become their new home.

Arriving in Rochester was another uneventful experience for them.....similar to when they arrived in New York City. There were many people at the station greeting other immigrants as they stepped off the train. There were shouts of joy, the waving of arms, and all you could hear in Italian was, *"Siamo Qui! Siamo Ca!"* ("We are here! We are here!") *"Turido, Maria, Luigi, Antonio...Siamo Qui!"* In addition, from others, you could hear *"Aspettate La! Siamo venendo!"* ("Wait there! We are coming"). People were running all over to meet loved ones, some dropping their baggage and bundles so they could hug two or three relatives at a time. There was great joy and excitement among the people as they hugged and kissed their newly arrived relatives and loved ones. Little children were swept up off their feet and into the arms of relatives, and smothered with kisses as shouts of praises were heard all over the station: *"Figlia Bedda!" "Tu sei Bedduzza!"* ("Beautiful Child!" "You are a Cutie!"). The Cavallaro family watched all of this and they were happy also; even though they had no one to greet them at the station, they were still so happy to have arrived at their destination.

Angelo and Angela made certain that all the children were accounted for and that they all had their bundles, sacks, and the big trunk they had been carrying. The children all showed their parents that they had their bundles; however, with my dad being the oldest son at sixteen years old, and being quite strong, he continued to carry their one trunk. He stood at the end of the line as they prepared to leave the station. As he had done throughout the trip, he hoisted the trunk upon his shoulder and off they went.

They left the station looking like they were on a safari with Angelo in the lead. Having been there before, Angelo knew exactly where to go. They exited the main train station that was located on Court Street at that time. They left the train station and walked down Court Street to South Clinton Avenue. They turned north onto South Clinton Avenue and continued their journey. They knew it was going to be a long walk. They knew they had to get to North Clinton Avenue and that was quite a distance past Main Street before they would reach their destination of Albow Place.

As my father explained to me, they suddenly had a renewal in strength and they were filled with great anticipation at seeing some familiar faces. Angelo and Angela led the group with the children following behind, each of them carrying their sacks and bundles, wearing old coats and hats, and looking a bit different from the first people they saw in Rochester. My dad said that they walked down the middle of the street the entire way. There were no cars or vehicles to watch for; yet each of their eyes were searching every person that they saw, "Was there someone out there that they knew?" As they passed Ward Street and walked northward, they suddenly began to see familiar faces. People sitting on their front porches began to shout to them, *"Benevenuto! Siete Arrivati! Che cosa li ha prese così lungamente?"* ("Welcome! You finally arrived! What took you so long?"). Some came to the street to hug them and talk to them as they continued to walk. Soon they passed a meat market that was owned by Peter Quagliata, a close *paisano* they knew. Once he saw them from inside the market, he ran outside, shouting their names as he greeted them. He was their first contact of any of the *paisani* and they were very happy to see each other. They hugged and danced in the middle of the street. As they approached Albow Place, they saw more families that were *paisani* from Sicily also. They passed another shop of their good friends Alfio Maccarone and his family; they, too, came out joyously to greet them. The La Rocca, La Rosa, and Musameci families also greeted them. *"Ai Angelo, Ai Angela! Siete Arrivati!"* ("Hey, Angelo, Hey Angela! You finally arrived!") They finally received the welcome that they had expected many days earlier. They were filled with many emotions, but they mainly felt very secure and confident that they were finally in Rochester, which was where they belonged. They were with *paisani* and it was as if they were back home in Passopisciaro again. The Cavallaro family turned the corner into Albow Place, toward the home of Angelo's younger brother, Sebastiano, with great smiles on their faces, tears on their cheeks, and with renewed joy in their hearts.

The Cavallaro Family Establishes Residency

According to the ship Manifest, Angelo Cavallaro was to go to the home of Sebastiano Cavallaro, his brother, who lived at 20 Albow Place. It also showed that Angela was to go to the home of Sebastiano Cavallaro, her brother-in-law, who lived at 21 Albow Place. The addresses may be incorrectly written on the ship Manifest, but I know that Sebastiano owned property on Albow Place and there were two houses on one lot; one house behind the other. As I understand it, Sebastiano lived in the front house and, Sam Raymond, another *paisano*, lived in the back house. Sam Raymond operated a shoe repair shop located at the house. His shoe repair business was later relocated to a store on Lowell Street where he became a community landmark in that Italian section of Rochester. They stayed with Sebastiano for a short while, but having eight more people in a small three to four room house was difficult. Prior to their arrival, Sebastiano had arranged for them to rent a house on Lowell Street, which was within walking distance from his house. Sam Raymond owned that house and kept it empty for them until they arrived. They lived on Lowell Street for a short time and began moving from house to house until they found the one they liked. All the houses they lived in were in the general area of North Clinton Avenue, and within a street or two of each other. Listed below are the locations of the homes, in chronological order, with a brief description of each. This information was received from Roger Cavallaro and Mary Lizzio.

1. 20/21 Albow Place: Home of Sebastiano Cavallaro. They lived here for only a few weeks until they relocated to their next home. This was during the last week of July and first few weeks of August 1913.

2. Lowell Street: Sam Raymond, a paisano, and shoe repairman, owned this home. Sebastiano Cavallaro had arranged for them to live here upon arrival in America. It had no central heating furnace, so they kept warm that first winter by putting wood or coal in the kitchen stove that was converted to a heater.

3. Emmett Street: This was a large house and two to three families used the same bathroom. The toilet seat hung on the wall and had to be placed on the toilet each time someone wanted to use it. The room was lined with carpet fabric. It was always wet because of urine and had a foul odor.

4. Baden Street: No information on this house. They lived here for a very short time.

5. Rauber Street: This was a dilapidated, run-down house. It had an indoor and outdoor bathroom and the family used both.

6. Hoeltzer Street: They bought this house and it was the first home they owned. It was newer and cleaner than the other houses. It had a furnace, but it was unusable. They used the kitchen stove to heat all the rooms in the house. As a result, the bedrooms were always cold during the winter months. They would order a half-ton of coal, but the furnace had many cracks and leaks in it. Gas fumes filled the basement and came up through the heat registers located in the floor of each room, and into the whole

house. They would have to flee the house often and open all the doors and windows get some fresh air into the house before they returned. Because it was so cold outside, all the heat escaped from the house while it was being aired out. When they returned, there was no heat in the house at all. In the spring, Angelo and the boys had to seal the cracks with cement so they could eventually use the furnace the following winter.

Note: None of the houses they lived in had bathtubs; however, the next-door neighbor at the Hoeltzer Street house had a round, portable tub in the back yard. It was 1915, Uncle Roger was ten or eleven years old, and he said he had never taken a bath in a bathtub. The next-door neighbor invited him to go over to take a bath. He sat in the tub full of water. He just sat there and didn't know what to do. So, after a while, he just got out of the tub, wiped himself off, and went back home, telling his mother that he had finally taken a bath. When he told us this story in 1984, there were many questions asked which resulted in a lot of laughter around the table.

7. The Farm in West Bloomfield: After a few years, they sold the house on Hoeltzer Street and they bought the farm in West Bloomfield. This happened in 1917. At the conclusion of World War I, they decided to sell the farm. Angela received some cash for the farm, but the rest of the value she received for the sale of the property was for a home that was given in trade. The home was located on Electric Avenue in Rochester. It was a very nice, two story home with a large front porch, but they stayed there only a short time. They found out that they couldn't afford to pay the taxes on the house, so they traded it back for the farm they originally had in West Bloomfield. Within a few weeks, they began to look for another farm to purchase. They found one in Springwater that they considered buying. It was located on the west side of Hemlock Lake. According to Uncle Roger, he said that it was a very nice farm and the buildings were in very good condition. It totaled about 200 acres. He said it contained a lot of timber on the land; however, they waited too long to make a decision to purchase it and they lost it to another buyer. They eventually sold the original farm in West Bloomfield again and moved back to the city where they bought their next house.

8. 49 Moulson Street: This house was located just off Norton Street, between Hudson Avenue and North Clinton Avenue. They lived there from 1921 to about 1926. I remember my father telling me that he really liked living there. It was at this house where he was practicing and improving his tailoring skills and began working in the various tailor factories in Rochester. In 1926, he married Theresa Siracusa and they

moved to an apartment on Martin Street, which was in the same neighborhood and close to Bond Clothing factory. It was just after his marriage when Angela moved the family to their next house.

9. <u>680 North Clinton Avenue:</u> This house was located next door to a large firehouse. I remember visiting this house a couple of times when I was young. The firehouse was very large and was constructed entirely of red brick. The house my grandmother purchased was located on the left side of the firehouse. There was a large dress shop located in front of her house; it was here where her teenage daughter Giovanna, obtained her first job.

On the other side of the firehouse and facing North Clinton Avenue, was Gitlin's Jewelry Shop. It had been at this location for many years. When my father visited his family at the North Clinton Avenue address, he developed a close relationship with Mr. Gitlin. It was at this jewelry store where my father bought his wedding rings when he married my mom. When my brother and I were ready to be married and needed diamond rings for our brides-to-be, my father brought us both in to meet Mr. Gitlin. Naturally, we bought our wedding rings there also. My dad knew Mr. Gitlin for so many years, that he trusted him in every transaction he made. He would always ask, "Mr. Gitlin, this is a real blue- white diamond with no flaws, isn't it?" Mr. Gitlin would give him a reassuring smile and say, "You're like a son to me, Alfred. Would I ever give you anything but the best?" He always reassured him that it was the best and over the years, we all felt a close relationship with Mr. Gitlin and his family.

Angela lived in this house for quite a few years. Most of her younger children were married while they were living in this house. When Angela saw more of her children being married and leaving her home, it became obvious that the house was too expensive for her to keep on her own. It was also too large for those that remained. Eventually, Angela became ill with the first stages of Parkinson's disease. As the disease progressed, the older children decided that she needed to live with one of them. So the decision was made that Angela would go to live with her daughter Mary, and Angelo, who had just recently returned from another trip to Sicily, would go to live with his daughter Angelina. From this point on, Angelo and Angela would never live under the same roof as a family again.

The Cavallaro family always resided in the same general area of Rochester. They found comfort and joy in being near their *paisani*. They had created a new home in that section of

Rochester that could be likened to the little area they were from in Sicily – Passopisciaro, only larger and with more conveniences. Even after they left the area to live on the farm in West Bloomfield, they returned to the North Clinton Avenue area often. When the children married, they too, located in that same area to be near their parents, brothers, and sisters. The streets that have been mentioned earlier bring fond memories to the Cavallaro's. In addition, the neighborhoods where they lived….. Almira Street, Oakman Street, Martin Street, Galusha Street, and Albow Place…… are also imbedded into their memories. They lived happily there; they shopped in all the local stores, visited with neighbors and *paisani* and those streets were and are an important part of the lives of the next generation. For Angelo and Angela, their journey began and ended in the same neighborhood.

Now that we have traced their journey from Sicily to Rochester, It is time to take you on another journey through each of their lives. The chapters that follow will give you an in-depth view of each member of the family. As you read, they will help explain much of what happened prior to and after their immigration to America. These next sections will also help fill the gaps of how the lives of the next generation of children were interwoven with each other as they grew, married, and had children of their own. As you read, the true characteristics of the family will be revealed, the individual traits they possessed will unfold, and the close ties they maintained with one another through the years will be described. They were such unique individuals; yet, they were also very much alike. The value of their family ties was a priority to each of them, and they passed this down to their children, the next generation of Cavallaro's. As you read on, I know that you will understand them better; I hope the incidents I have recounted will help you to fall in love with each one of them, as they were loved by their families.

Angelo Cavallaro

February 12, 1867 – April 6, 1945

Prologue

Angelo Cavallaro, my grandfather, was someone that I did not know well since he was not in America very much while I was a child. My most vivid memories of him were during the years of my adolescence through my early teens. During the late 1920s and 1930s, he took many trips back and forth to Sicily to see family or to take jobs that interested him. Although he immigrated to America, he always had the desire to return and live in Sicily. Much of the information I have to share with you are from stories that were told to me by my father, Alfred Cavallaro, and by my aunts and uncles in later years after my grandfather had passed away. I wrote these anecdotes down as they were told to me and I have kept them for the past 20+ years. My cousin Jennie (Lamanna) Romeo shared some other specific information with me. My grandfather lived with Aunt Angie on Oakman Street and on Norton Street; his granddaughter Jennie helped care for him. Angelo and Jennie developed a very close relationship during those years.

Angelo lived a different lifestyle because he came from a foreign land where social standards were not the same as we know them today. Although I didn't know him well, I was told he was a happy-go-lucky person who was jovial all the time. This accounting will help give you some background of my roots in Sicily with the Cavallaro family.

The Beginning

Angelo Cavallaro was born on February 12, 1867. This date is accurate; however, the year is shown differently on his military service papers. His military documents indicate he was born on February 12, but in the year 1869, two years later. This discrepancy could have occurred because he may have lied about his age in order to join the Italian Army, or they may have transcribed it incorrectly at that time. Other records documenting his date of birth have consistently been recorded as 1867; however, his actual birth certificate has been unobtainable. He was born to Alfio and Angela (Penisi) in the Province of Catania in the city of Acireale, which is just south of Giarre where he spent most of his growing up years. His father, Alfio Cavallaro, was born in Giarre where hundreds of families were named 'Cavallaro.' It is a very common name in the Province of Catania, just as the name 'Smith' is in America. Both Acireale and Giarre are on the eastern coast of Sicily. He was the second child of five living children. It is unknown how many siblings he actually had, and how many died at early ages. The family hierarchy, as his children gave it to me, is as follows:

<u>Parents:</u> Alfio Cavallaro and Angela (Penisi) Cavallaro (Neither ever left Sicily)

<u>Children:</u> 1. Rosa Cavallaro (Married Angelo Lizzio and immigrated to America)
2. Angelo Cavallaro (Made several trips between Sicily and America)
3. Salvatore Cavallaro (Never left Sicily)
4. Sebastiano Cavallaro (Yanno, never married - immigrated to America)
5. Giovanna Cavallaro (Died at the age of sixteen in Italy)

Angelo's father, Alfio, was a stonecutter and worked in the lava quarries at the southern base of Mt. Etna. As a little boy, Angelo would accompany his father to the quarries to help in any way he could; thus learning a trade that he'd have for the rest of his life. In that day, it was very common for a young boy to continue in the trade or the work of their father and grandfather before him; this training usually began at a very young age. Angelo never went to school; therefore, he never learned to read or write in Italian or English. This was not important to him because he would not have been able to cope with the daily routine that school required. He was very active and impulsive, always doing things spontaneously. While working at the lava quarry, he'd be seen working one minute, and the next time they'd look for him, he'd be gone to another area of the quarry. He would get bored very easily and was not very dependable.

His father, however, was an unusual person in a different kind of way. Alfio Cavallaro was a bully and everyone in the village was afraid of him. Because of his strength and association with the rogues of the town, other people would go to him for protection. A story related to me by my Aunt Mary will show his true characteristics:

> *There was a young married woman who lived in their village. Her husband came home drunk one night and proceeded to beat her up. The next day, she went to Alfio Cavallaro and asked for his help and protection. He went to their house, took the husband by the nape of his neck, and dragged him to the town well. He picked him up by the ankles, and he held him upside down, head first, inside the well, for a very long time. His screams aroused the remainder of the villagers and they all came out to see what was happening. Alfio didn't drop him into the well, but when he eventually lifted him out of the well, he beat him up and sent him home with the warning that he was never to hurt his wife again, because the next time, he would drop him into the well.*

Through acts like this, Alfio, and the rest of the Cavallaro men that followed him, developed quite a reputation among the townspeople. The people in that town and the small surrounding villages spoke of the Cavallaro men in awe, in fear, and of having an abrasive attitude. The word traveled around the surrounding villages that they were not to be messed with; when they passed a Cavallaro male in the street, they were to tip their hats to them as an act of respect.

Angelo wasn't responsible for doing acts like his father, but he learned to use a *bastone* well. A *bastone* was a piece of thick, rounded wood about thirty-six to forty-eight inches long and approximately three to four inches in diameter. He was good at using it as a weapon to protect himself and/or others. He was also adept at using a knife, which he carried in his pocket at all times. Even as an old man, he always had a small, pocketknife in his possession. Although it may seem unusual for men to do that today, in Sicily, it continues to be a common practice. Pocketknives were mainly used to whittle a piece of wood, peal an apple or prickly pear, or to skillfully throw into the ground, as a game played by young Sicilian boys. They were also used as a means of protection. Thus, the scene is set for the reputation of the Cavallaro men in the Province of Catania.

Rosa (Cavallaro) Lizzio

Angelo's older sister and first-born child of Alfio and Angela Cavallaro was born in the Province of Catania, as were all her siblings. It is believed that she was born in a small village near Acireale. This is located between Taormina and Catania on the east coast of Sicily. As I remember my relatives talking about the places where the Cavallaro's were born, the towns of Riposto, Mascali, and Giarre were always mentioned and any of these could be the location of her birthplace.

According to her gravestone, she was born in 1869. There is some discrepancy in her birth date. It is recorded on her brother, Angelo's, gravestone that he was born in 1867, making him two years older and the oldest in their family. However, Angelo's children assured me that Rosa was the oldest in the family. Angelo's date of birth could have been 1869 or later. There are no birth records to refer to, so their actual dates of birth are subject to the memory of their children.

Rosa Cavallaro married Angelo Lizzio in Sicily. He was a *paisano* from the same village. They had five children, in the order that follows:

1.	Mario Lizzio	1894-1962	Married to Emma (Marida) in Sicily, they had no children.
2.	Alfio Lizzio	1896-1974	Married to Maria Catena Cavallaro in 1920, They had one son, Angelo Lizzio.
3.	Josephine Lizzio	1898-1921	She died of the Spanish Influenza Pandemic; she never married.
4.	Angelina (Lizzio) LaRosa	1900-1992	Married to Philip LaRosa, they had three sons: Leo, Angelo, and Rudy.
5.	Grace (Lizzio) Trovato	1906-1999	Married to Russell Trovato, they had two children: Yolanda and Robert.

Rosa and Angelo immigrated to America with their children and located in the North Clinton Avenue area, as did the rest of the family with other *paisani*. Angelo Lizzio died in May 1946 at seventy-five years of age. Rosa died in June 1961 at ninety-two years of age.

Salvatore Cavallaro

The third child to be born of Alfio and Angela Cavallaro was Salvatore. By the time of his birth, they had moved to Randazzo, five miles west of Passopisciaro. Very little is known about Salvatore except that he was born sometime between 1870 and 1876. He never immigrated to America and lived his entire life in Sicily. He married and had at least two children that are known; Giovanna and Carmello. The family in America had little contact with him after they immigrated.

Sebastiano Cavallaro

Angelo's younger brother, Sebastiano, was the fourth child born to Alfio and Angela. Although he never married and was approximately eleven years younger than Angelo, he was very important to him and his family. As Angelo prepared to emigrate to America with his wife and six children, he approached Sebastiano for help. By this time, Sebastiano, had made other trips to America, and was currently living in Rochester, New York. He agreed to serve as a sponsor for Angelo and his family so they could make the trip, thus fulfilling all the legal requirements for immigrants.

Previously, Angelo had made other trips to America so as to make money, but he always returned to Sicily; hoping to establish a better life for him and his family there. It usually never worked for him because, before long, he'd return to America for a couple of more years to make more money. Both brothers had followed this same pattern and they were considered Birds of Passage; however, there was a significant difference between the two brothers. Sebastiano was more conservative and knew how to save his money. Angelo did not save his money and could never get ahead financially.

The ship Manifests that I researched, showed that Sebastiano made trips to America in 1903, 1906, 1909, and his last being in 1912. According to the ages he gave each time he traveled, it would indicate that he was born sometime between April and August of 1878. His voyages are recorded as follows:

Age	Ship of Travel	Port of Departure	Date of Arrival in U.S.	Cash
25	(unknown)	(unknown)	1903	?
29	Italia	Naples (Campania)	August 10, 1906	$15.00
31	Duca di Genoa	Genoa (Luguria)	February 5, 1909	$13.00
34	(Information unknown; on the 1920 Federal Census it only notes a 1912 arrival)			

It indicated further that for each trip, his destination was to the home of an American sponsor listed as his cousin, Giuseppe Sorbello, who lived at 379 North Street in Rochester, NY. In each case, it lists his last place of residence as his father's home, Alfio Cavallaro, which was located in Randazzo, Sicily. This would further indicate that his parents had moved from the area of Giarre to Randazzo, which is approximately five miles west of Passopisciaro and at the northern base of the crater of Mt. Etna.

My Aunt Mary and Uncle Roger shared that Sebastiano was in the Italian Army. At that time in Italy, you were required to serve in the Italian Army at nineteen years of age. When he reported for duty, they assigned him to the Civil Engineers, who were laborers and could not read or write. When Angelo went into the army, he served in the Infantry instead. Although Sebastiano could neither read nor write, they felt he could perform better in that branch of the service. Because they were approximately eleven years apart in age, they did not complete their military service at the same time. Although Sebastiano was illiterate, he was an intelligent man. He had good common sense and could advise others on major decisions. He was also very good at managing his financial matters. Being a conservative man, he knew how to save his money.

When it came time for Angelo and Angela to immigrate to America, they did not have the passenger fees for the two of them and their six children. Angelo approached his brother, Sebastiano, for the money needed to make the trip. Sebastiano agreed to pay for the necessary fares of eight passengers; however, he made it very clear to Angelo and Angela that it was only a loan and they were to pay him back as soon as they arrived in America. He loaned his brother Angelo the money, and they came to America. When Angelo and Angela finally immigrated to America, Sebastiano, with the help of their cousin, Giuseppe Sorbello, found sewing jobs at Adler's for Angela and her daughter Angelina. Upon arrival, they went to work immediately to earn enough money to pay Sebastiano back for his loan for their voyage.

When Sebastiano came to America, he had no trade except for stonecutting that he did in Sicily. When World War I began, he bought the farm in West Bloomfield with Angela and he moved there with her family to help run the property. Work was not easy on the farm, and sometimes he and the boys did not get along well; yet, they all worked hard and made it successful through those years. When they sold the farm, he moved back to Rochester and tried to get jobs in stonecutting or as a laborer with the City of Rochester at The Department of Public Works. He worked for them as a contractor putting in sidewalks and driveways throughout the city. His cousins, the Sorbello's, were instrumental in finding him a job with a large marble cutting company and he worked there for a while. Through perseverance and hard work, he was able to find other good jobs to better himself so he could eventually become a licensed mason by trade, and worked as a contractor for a large masonry company, which became his life's work. His cousins Giuseppe and Vincenzo Sorbello helped him in many ways, even when it came time for him to buy his homes on Albow Place. He bought two small homes, one on the front lot and the other on the back lot, and lived there his entire life. In the backyard, he took great pride in raising a quality vegetable garden, fruit trees and had an extensive grape vine overflowing with bunches of grapes that stretched along the entire width of the yard. He kept in close contact with his family; yet, he preferred his privacy. In his later years, he and Angelo led separate lives.

Giovanna Cavallaro

Giovanna Cavallaro was the fifth and final child born to Alfio and Angela Cavallaro. Very little information is available on her except that she never immigrated to America. She was born sometime after 1879 and never married. She died in Sicily of diphtheria at sixteen years of age.

Angelo Grows Up

During Angelo's early teen years, Italy found herself in many conflicts with other countries. The government was changing and many young men were going into the military to serve in the Italian Army. Angelo decided to join the military service also. It is noted by documents found in my Aunt Mary's boxes of pictures, that Angelo Cavallaro joined the Italian Army on December 19, 1887 at the age of eighteen. There are no records to show how long he was in the military service, where he served, or when he was discharged; it is only known that he was accepted and served as a soldier in the Italian Army. Specific information on his health and general identification gathered from his Induction Notice indicate that he was in very good health. The original document is in Rochester, New York with Angelo Lizzio's personal papers. This document was completely written in Italian. An English translation is provided for your information:

ORIGINAL ITALIAN	ENGLISH TRANSLATION
Nome: Angelo Cavallaro	Name: Angelo Cavallaro
Filio de: Alfio e di Pennisi Angela	Son of: Alfio and of Angela Pennisi
Nato addi: 12 Febraio 1869	Born on: 12th day of February 1869
Nel commune: di Giarre	In the community of: Giarre
Circondario de Acireale	Around the area of: Acireale
Giunto al Corpo: 19 Dec 1887	Joined the Forces: 19th of December 1887
Leggere: No	Read: No
Scrivere: No	Write: No
Capedi: Castagni	Hair: Chestnut color
Forma: lisci	Shape: Thin (smoothed down)
Occhi è Viso: Castagni è Lungo	Eyes & vision: Chestnut color & far sighted
Colorito: Bruno	Coloring: Tawny (tan to Brownish orange/tanned)
Dentaturo: Sana	Teeth: Complete and whole
Eyebrows: Castagni	Eyebrows: Chestnut color
Naso: Racciato	Nose: Racciato
Bocca: Giusta	Mouth: Normal (OK)
Fronte: Stretta	Forehead: Tightened

At some point, when he was discharged and returned home from serving in the Italian Army, he expected everything to be the same as he left it. However, he found Angela Gravagna had been living at his parent's home for a period of time. Although he was approximately twenty-four years old at this time and she was a fourteen year old teenager, a relationship began to develop between the two of them. They spent a lot of time together and would often sneak off to the countryside and take long walks and talk. It was shortly after he returned home that they decided to be wed.

His parents were not agreeable to the marriage. Although they liked Angela very much and she was an important part of their family, they didn't think it was appropriate he should marry someone from the same household. By this time, neighbors and *paisani* considered Angela to be practically related to the Cavallaro's, and there would be a lot of talk in the small community, where everyone's personal business was common knowledge. Angelo was already known for doing things impulsively, so his parents didn't know what to expect. Knowing that Angelo was as determined as he was, they made the decision to run off and get married without their parents' permission. It was recounted to me that they were married in the Court House in Giarre; however, I have no written record of that event. When they returned home, chaos prevailed at the Cavallaro home. Eventually, things subsided and life went on as usual, except that the young married couple was living together in the crowded family home.

Angelo continued to work with his father at the stone quarry at the base of Mt. Etna. He became very good at his work and they utilized his skill to do special kinds of stonecutting. In his free time, he decided to make a bench out of stone for the front of his parent's house. The bench was about four to five feet in length and about two to three feet in height. It still sits at the front door of their house to this day. When Grace Trovato (Uncle Alfred Lizzio's sister) visited Sicily, she took a picture of it and brought it back for everyone to see. I remember the excitement from all of Angelo's children, (my father, my aunts and uncles), when they saw the picture of the stone bench. The older children remembered it vividly because they had sat on it many times; they were happy to see it was still there. I remember the picture well; the bench looked like it was solid stone, very heavy, and would be difficult to move.

Angelo Moves to Another Part of Sicily

Angelo and Angela's first child, Angelina, was born in 1895 and they were still living in the vicinity of Giarre. With a new baby to care for, space in the small home was at a premium. They remained in the area until 1896. By the time Alfio was born in 1897, they had already taken up residence in Passopisciaro. At this point of their married life, Angela had assumed the responsibility of being the head of the household. This happened because Angelo worked long hours and he did not always come home after work. He had many friends and enjoyed stopping by one of their homes or at a local saloon to have a glass of wine or two. She could not depend on him, so she began to earn money on her own to make ends meet for her increasing family.

Angelo Considers a Move to America

Many of Angelo's friends and people he worked with spoke constantly of the great life there was to be had in America. *Paisani* would return from America and boast on how much money they had made there, how jobs were very plentiful and that the streets were made of gold. Sicily was experiencing a great recession at this time, jobs were lacking, and money was very scarce. Poverty was prevalent and the peasants were poorer than they had ever experienced before. Every day, people were leaving his village to find a new life in America. Just prior to 1913, there was a threat of war in Italy and hundreds of thousands of Italians were fleeing from Italy and going to America or Argentina for protection. Many of the *paisani* from Passopisciaro were fleeing the area also. Because Angelo did things spontaneously, he decided on going to America to make some money, and return to Sicily to buy a farm. Therefore, during the early years of their marriage, he made numerous trips to the United States. Each time, he would stay one to two years and then return home to Sicily for a short time until his next trip.

When he returned, he never had the amount of money he thought he would make. He'd remain in Sicily for approximately two more years, and make another trip to America. On at least two occasions, he traveled with his brother, Sebastiano, and they went to West Virginia to work in the coal mines. They worked as laborers and the work was difficult. Other times, he went to New York and worked as a laborer for various builders. Overall, he made four to five trips to America, each time returning to Sicily to live on his earnings. However, his dream and continuing desire to return to America never left his mind. Because of his absence at their house, Angela continued to work at home by sewing, washing clothes for other people and caring for her growing family. During one of Angelo's earlier trips, Sebastiano moved into the house to help with the expenses.

When Angelo made his trip to America in the spring of 1912, he worked in the Rochester area. By that time, Sebastiano had already immigrated to America in February 1912. Angelo stayed with many *paisani* and his brother, Sebastiano, during this trip. Before leaving for Sicily again, he arranged with his *paisani* and his brother to act as his sponsors so he could return with his family the following year. When he returned to Sicily in 1912, he shared with Angela that he was determined to bring their whole family to America. He had already arranged for sponsorship and for a place to stay until they secured jobs and were settled. Not being close to her natural family, Angela had no reason to remain in Sicily, and the promise of a more prosperous life intrigued her. They saved the little money they had and Sebastiano sent the major portion of the needed funds to them in Sicily with the agreement that they were to pay him back as soon as possible, once they arrived in America. He made it very clear to them that it was a loan and not a gift. Both Angelo and Angela were fine with this arrangement. They accepted the loan and planned their trip. The trip was planned for July of 1913, just prior to their youngest daughter Giovanna's fourth birthday. Eventually, the money was paid back in full to Sebastiano, as it had been agreed. Upon arriving in America, both Angela and her daughter Angelina worked very hard at sewing and washing clothes to earn the extra money in order to pay him back. Angela had a mind for business and was able to manage her finances well. She saved and conserved enough money to pay the entire loan paid back to Sebastiano within the year.

Angelo Arrives In America

It appeared that Angelo and Angela's relationship was getting better just after they had arrived in America; however, within a short time, he went back to his old ways again. In Sicily, he was a stonecutter, and in America, that kind of job was not available. He could only find work by doing part-time, handyman jobs for people in the neighborhood; therefore, his jobs were temporary. Money was not abundant, and work was difficult for him to find. He never made a smooth transition to living in America. In addition, he didn't like to stay in one place for any length of time. As was his character of doing things spontaneously, he continued his pattern of making repeated trips back and forth to Sicily, for no particular reason except to search for his dream.

From 1913, when the family arrived in America, to about 1935, he made three more trips to Sicily. His first and second trips back to Sicily were uneventful so he returned to America within two years of each of his departures. By the time he returned from his second trip to Sicily, Angela had moved to her new residence at 680 North Clinton Avenue, next door to the firehouse. Because of his irresponsible behavior, Angela would not allow him to live at their new home. Therefore, he went to live with his daughter, Mary Lizzio, on Oakman Street. Shortly after, in 1927, he returned to Sicily on his third trip. By that time, he was sixty years old. He obtained a job as a guard for a Baroness in Palermo. He remained in Palermo for approximately seven years before retuning to America; however, he was penniless again. He continued to be careless with his money, both in Sicily and America. Not having funds to support himself and being on in years, he went to live with his daughter Angelina while she still had her home on Oakman Street. By that time, Angela had sold her home on North

Clinton Avenue and was living with my Aunt Mary Lizzio, on Oakman Street as well. Her health was failing and she could not live alone at that time. Therefore, in their latter years, because of various circumstances, my grandfather and grandmother did not live together in the same house ever again. Although they did not get along very well for most of their married life, I do believe that they loved each other.

After returning from his last trip to Sicily, Angelo went to work at the Trovato farm in Hannibul, New York for a while. He didn't stay there very long because he felt there was too much work to do for the few people who were employed, and he had determined he wasn't getting paid enough for his work. Angelo was always known for having quite a temper, so one day at the farm, he became very angry over a situation. After arguing with some of the workers, he threw his tools across the field and stomped off the farm immediately. He never worked again. While working at the farm, he hurt his back, and from that time on, he walked in a bent over position. Walking hunched over, relieved the pain in his back. Shortly after, and for the remainder of his life, he used a walking cane to assist him. By that time, he was in his late sixties or early seventies and moved with his daughter, Angelina, and her family to Norton Street. He lived there until he passed away at the Monroe County Home and Infirmary.

Angelo's Final Years

One of the last memories that I have of my grandfather is when we visited him my Aunt Angie's house one evening. She lived in a big house on Norton Street and he lived with her in an upstairs bedroom. I was ten years old at the time; my parents and I went upstairs to visit with him in his bedroom. He could not come downstairs to see us. He walked with a cane and he stooped over a bit so it was difficult for him to walk the steps. When we entered his room, Aunt Angie became very angry with him because he wasn't supposed to have his clothes lying all around the room. He spoke only in Italian to my father and mother, but I noted that he had an unusual dialect. Although I could speak some Italian and understood most of it, I couldn't understand anything he said. At one point during their conversation, I asked my father what he was saying and my grandfather immediately asked me my name. Evidently, we had not seen each other for a while. I told him my name and he repeated it back to me. Then, he asked my father, "Is this your older son?" My father explained that I was the younger son. My grandfather responded by saying, "He looks like a Cavallaro." I did not know what he meant at that time; however, as I think of it now, it makes sense to me. We all called him *nannu* (nă´-new), which is the Sicilian dialect name and endearment for 'grandpa.'

During his last years, he suffered with an enlarged prostate gland. At age seventy-eight, he suffered a stroke. As reported by his granddaughter, Jennie (Lamanna) Romeo, who cared for him most of the time while he lived at the Norton Street home:

> *"He came down to breakfast one morning. He said he didn't feel well. So I made him a cup of coffee and he returned upstairs to his room; however, he never got there. While on the way upstairs, he fell down the stairs. I became frightened and called my mother, my Aunt Mary and my Uncle Al to come over. They immediately came to our house and we rushed him to the hospital where he was diagnosed as having had a stroke. He was unconscious when he was admitted to the hospital; they said there was no hope for him. He was immediately transferred to a nursing home and he stayed there for a day or two. He was then admitted to the Monroe County Home and Infirmary on Henrietta Road. This is the same hospital where my grandmother Angela was and had been a resident for a number of years. Not wanting to worry my grandmother, my Mother and my aunts and uncles asked the hospital personnel not to let my grandmother know that my grandfather was there also. The people at the County Home complied with that request and my grandparents never knew they were both in the same facility at exactly the same time."*

During his short stay at the Monroe Community Home and Infirmary, he would not eat any of the food. It was foreign to him because he was accustomed to eating only Italian cuisine. The nurses were concerned about this and shared it with the family. Jennie remembers one of her visits to the hospital very vividly:

> *"My mother and I bought him a Dixie Cup ice cream and brought it to him. He liked it and he ate the whole thing. It was like he hadn't eaten for a long time. Within a couple of days, the family was called and told that he was going in and out of a coma. We found out later, that while he was semi-conscience, he'd be calling for someone named "Jennie." The nurses ignored this, but eventually asked the family who was this person "Jennie" that he kept asking for? By the time we found this out, he was in a coma and never came out of it. Had I known that he was calling for me, naturally, I would have gone to him. It was natural for him to call for me because I*

was with him every day, fed him at home and I spent many hours talking with him prior to his stroke."

He never regained consciousness and passed away two days later on April 6, 1945. He was buried at Holy Sepulchre Cemetery in Rochester on April 10, 1945. The children chose not to tell Angela about his death because of her failing health, so the hospital personnel were told not to give her any information concerning his death. However, on one of their visits during the same week of his death, she asked my father and mother, "Your father died, didn't he!" Although Angela was in the same facility, she didn't know that he had been a patient there or that he had died; yet, she had a sense that he was gone. They did not affirm this question, but, internally, she knew something had happened to her husband. A few weeks later, on June 2, 1945, Angela suddenly died. It was a tragic time for the entire family to have both their parents die within eight weeks of each other.

Some Final Thoughts

As I said earlier, I didn't know my grandfather Angelo Cavallaro very well. I only remember seeing him a few times when I was with my parents, at Uncle Roger and Aunt Lucy's wedding, and visiting him at Aunt Angie's home. I do remember him referring to me and speaking about me in Italian, but I could not communicate with him because of the language barrier. I can recall his appearance and the sound of his voice vividly. He seemed to be a happy person and was always making jokes and laughing with those around him. His children would joke and laugh with him often. They had a close relationship.

Angelo never became an American citizen nor did he learn the English language; however, he did receive his Naturalization Papers to remain in America. When he returned to America in 1935, he never visited Sicily again; nor did he ever see his parents or other brothers again. However, he raised six fine children, my parents, aunts, and uncles. Although he was not always present in the home and Angela did most of the child rearing, he would continually counsel and instruct his children when he was home with them on their day-to-day affairs. They developed a great love for him and they desired more of his presence in their lives. They were able to fulfill this wish when they were adults and he was in America for a longer period of time. I believe that because of his absence when his children were growing up, they were determined not to have the same thing occur to them or their families. As a result, all of his children had very responsible jobs, very close family relationships with their spouses, their children, and with each other as siblings. The important issues to each of his children were, *La Famiglia* (Lă Fă-mē´-lē-ă) (The Family), and the Cavallaro name. By honoring each other, they became a close-knit family. This is the heritage that Angelo and Angela left, to be proud of the Cavallaro name and to revere the family unit above all other things in our lives.

Many families in our society today, have these same values. They understand the benefits of close family ties especially during times of joy and sorrow. The benefits of a close family allow each generation to emerge with the same strong values. These values are deep-rooted and it is the obligation of parents to pass them onto their children, and their children's children. Through this, each generation can take pride to be part of a close family unit and of their family name.

Angelo Cavallaro

Angelo Cavallaro
Formato Benetto Photographer
Taken in Sicily

Angelo Cavallaro
with Joe Cavallaro
circa 1940

Sebastiano Cavallaro
"Yanni"
Angelo's younger brother
Taken on Albow Place

Angela (Gravagna) Cavallaro

November 15, 1877 – June 2, 1945

Prologue

My grandmother, Angela (Gravagna) Cavallaro, was a very interesting woman. During my pre-adolescent and adolescent years, she lived in the Monroe County Home and Infirmary. I remember her very vividly because I would see her once a week when we visited with my father, mother, and brother. She was in the hospital because she had Parkinson's disease and needed professional nursing assistance. She had been living with my Aunt Mary Lizzio for a long time, but as the disease progressed, they found that she needed to be in a place where her specific needs could be met. She required twenty-four hour care that only a facility like the Monroe County Home could offer.

Because she was in the hospital for such a long period, her six children, not wanting to leave her alone, made it a point to take turns visiting her during the week. They each selected one evening they would be responsible to visit her, thus giving her company each night. With six children, that covered six evening visits; so on Sundays, three or four of the children would visit again.

My family selected to visit her on Thursday nights. With my mom and dad working all day, it was a struggle to drive to the other side of the city and arrive at a reasonable hour. We were usually there by 7:00 p.m. Visiting hours were over at 8:30 p.m., so it did not leave much time for us to visit with her.

Each Thursday night, we'd bring her an eggnog drink. She liked eggnogs and the doctors said that she needed them to keep up her strength. Therefore, before we left home to visit her, it was my responsibility to make her this special drink. The hospital would not provide eggnogs to the patients so the families had to provide them. The recipe was simply made. I'd measure two cups of milk and add in a heaping tablespoon of Nestlé's Chocolate Mix. To that, I'd add one raw egg and then shake it in a mixing container my parents had purchased just for the eggnogs. When thoroughly mixed, I'd pour it into a green colored bottle, seal it with a cork, and put it in a brown lunch bag. As a young boy, it was my job to carry it in the car to make sure that it remained upright so it would not leak while we drove to the Monroe County Home and Infirmary.

As soon as we parked the car in the huge parking lot, my brother and I would jump out of the car and enter through the front doors. The hospital was constructed of red brick and was massive. It sat on grounds that were meticulously kept and the green grass seemed to go on forever. Once inside the hospital, we waited for my mom and dad to join us and we would proceed up to her room. Because we visited so often, we didn't need to stop at the Information Desk to pick up a Visitor's Pass; in addition, we knew all of the nurses well. We knew exactly where her room was located.

She was in a room with about eight other patients. They called it a Ward. There was very little privacy in the Ward. Only a cotton curtain separated the patients, and it was drawn along a steel bar from the ceiling, much like a shower curtain. There was only one chair in the room for a guest and one chair for the patient in which to sit. As a young boy of about 7 years old, I have memories of running into the room to bring her the eggnog. I was the first one she would see, and she was so excited to know we had arrived. She would be sitting in her chair, next to her bed, dressed in regular clothes and waiting for someone to arrive. She was so happy to see us. I can close my eyes and still see the broad smile she always had for us. In fact, as I recall, she always had a smile on her face. She was a happy person.

Because her hands shook so much from the Parkinson's disease, she could not pour the eggnog into a cup, so my mother or father would do that for her. She'd enjoy sipping her drink through a straw and talking to us about my other aunts and uncles who had visited her earlier in the week. She didn't speak to my brother or me very much, except for greeting us.

When my parents finally arrived in the room, we stayed and enjoyed listening to her stories. She and my parents would speak only in Italian, because that was the only language she knew. During the summer, when it warm and the days were longer, my brother and I were allowed to go outside and run on the grass while my parents visited her. The hospital was near the bed of the Genesee River and sometimes, we'd walk to the edge of the hospital property to watch small boats going up and down the river.

At the end of the visiting hours, we'd give grandma a big hug and be on our way home. This was our routine every Thursday evening until the time she died in June 1945. These were the times I remember Grandma Cavallaro the most.

The stories I have to share with you about Angela were told to me by my father at various times during my life. In addition, many of them came from my aunts, Mary Lizzio and Angie Lamanna; the stories are etched into my mind. The last stories I heard about her were told in my Aunt Mary Lizzio's apartment on Fernwood Park in July 1982. She had invited my cousins Angelo and Audrey Lizzio, my Uncle Roger and Aunt Lucy Cavallaro, my Aunt Jennie Cavallaro, and me and my mother for dinner. After dinner, we had a story fest, and I wrote things down as quickly as I could to record all the information.

What I present to you at this time, are anecdotes, incidents, and accounts of her life placed in somewhat of a chronological order and they follow the years prior to and after arriving in America. These memoirs were recounted by her children as fond and real memories they had of their mother. As you read, I urge you to pictures the scenes of sunny Sicily in the late 1800s when she lived. At that time, she was located on the east coast of Sicily, in the Province of Catania, near the city of Giarre. Life was very different from from how we know it today. Sicilians had a value system they were taught by their parents and it went back many generations. They lived a very meager existence, which was the same as Sicilians who had lived many years earlier, in the tiny communities on the hillsides of Mt. Etna. These stories depict their peasant life style.

The Beginning

Angela Gravagna was born in La Provincia di Catania (The Province of Catania). From all existing records, the actual name of the town where she lived was called Piedimonte Etneo, which was often shortened to Piedimonte (Pēē-ĕd-mōn´-tā). It was approximately five miles northwest of the city of Giarre; she lived near the Cavallaro family. In those days, walking five miles was common, especially since none of them owned a mechanical vehicle or animals to provide them with travel assistance.

The Gravagna's were a large family of seven children. In the family order, Angela was the first born of the living children. Her family hierarchy is as follows:

Parents: Gaitano Gravagna
Marianna (Campagnia) Gravagna (Immigrated to Boston, Massachusetts)

Children:
1. Angela (Married to Angelo Cavallaro)
2. Alfio
3. Salvatore
4. Giovanna (Immigrated to Lodi, New Jersey - married into the Farina family and had a son Carl Farina who married Angie)
5. Name unknown
6. Name unknown
7. Sebastiano

No information is available concerning the work or trade of Angela's father; however, most men in that area earned a living by being farmers, if they owned land. They were also grape harvesters because the hillsides of the volcano were lined with vineyards. Other men worked as stonecutters in the great stone quarries and lava pits at the base of Mr. Etna. Records regarding her grandparents or any of her ancestors could not be located.

In the same locale and only one village away, Angela made the acquaintance of a woman she had met at the outdoor market one day. As Angela was walking through the vender stands in the open market area, she noticed an older woman who was shopping and very talkative with the other people. A conversation ensued and Angela accompanied the older woman while she shopped through the market and helped her with her vegetables and purchases. When she had completed gathering all her fruits and vegetables, they parted ways, but agreed to look for each other on the next shopping day later in the week. On days when the produce market was open, Angela would look for her and they would shop together and have long talks. A relationship was definitely beginning to develop. Angela did not realize how this woman would be instrumental in changing her life, because the older woman's name was Angela also....Angela Cavallaro.

After some weeks of shopping together, one day, Angela assisted Mrs. Cavallaro to her home with her purchases. She was invited to stay and help prepare the evening meal. This continued and some weeks later, Marianna Gravagna, Angela's mother, noticed that Angela was spending more and more time at Mrs. Cavallaro's home. While she was there, she would help with the chores, help cook the meals, and talk with the family. Being a very happy person, she brought a lot of joy into the home, and there was always much laughter when she visited. Mrs. Cavallaro and her family enjoyed her company. Angela, however, enjoyed spending time with Mrs. Cavallaro; she was a fine seamstress and would make new dresses and outfits for Angela often. Because of that benefit, Angela was happy to do whatever she could for Mrs. Cavallaro since she would receive a new wardrobe as a result. Mrs. Cavallaro enjoyed making clothes for her and Angela enjoyed wearing new dresses around the town.

As mentioned earlier, Angela came from a very large family with seven children. Her parents were peasants and it was difficult for them to care for all the children. Although Angela was the eldest child, she was responsible to care for her younger siblings and to complete chores at their home; she resisted that kind of responsibility. Even at a very young age, she was known to have a quick temper and had a mind of her own. No one could put anything over on her. She was always one-step ahead of what anyone was thinking and had an alternative for every request that was made of her. Angela was a very determined girl and when she did not want to do something, she would conveniently disappear from her home and could not be found for hours.

Oftentimes, this caused Angela's mother to become angry with her because it meant that she would be completing many of the household chores herself. Angela found it very convenient to appear at the home of Mrs. Cavallaro, where she wasn't expected to work; however, if she completed any of the chores, it was only because she made the choice to do them herself. She was willing to accept direction and mentoring from Mrs. Cavallaro without any debate. Mrs. Cavallaro was different from her mother. She spent a lot of time with her and Angela felt comfortable talking with her. This trait of stubbornness and of having her own way was very apparent and became more noticeable as she grew to be a mature woman.

As the Gravagna family increased with children, it became more difficult for the parents to provide for them. By that time Sebastiano Gravagna was born, her youngest brother and seventh in the Gravagna family hierarchy, and there was a lot of work to be done in the home. Having a very small home and seven children to feed, there were times when they appreciated Angela not being present. Having one less child to provide for, made it a bit easier for them.

At this time, Angela was spending most of her days and evenings at the Cavallaro home; she would only go home to sleep. As her brother Sebastiano got older and became a toddler, she completely lost her sleeping area in the home to him. Her brothers were all growing older also and needed more space, so Mrs. Cavallaro found a place for her to sleep at her house.

As was the custom practiced in that society, it was very common for one family to take in and completely care for the child of another family; this would make the child their compete responsibility. Both families agreed upon it and Angela went to live with the Cavallaro family permanently. Angela was very happy about the upcoming agreement, and decided to start living there even before her mother had set the date when this was to begin. Angela didn't realize at that time how this move would alter her life forever. She was approximately twelve years old.

A New Life for Angela

Now that she was at the Cavallaro home full-time, Mrs. Cavallaro could teach Angela the things she missed being taught in her own home. They began with sewing lessons. Angela was taught how to mend clothes; this included repairs to socks, shirts, and trousers of all the boys in the house. Mrs. Cavallaro could immediately see that Angela had an innate talent for sewing and she began teaching her more advanced methods. Before long, Angela was able to sew clothing from scratch and without any assistance from Mrs. Cavallaro. She could make shirts, trousers, and even curtains for the house without using a pattern. Of course, this was all done by hand. There were no sewing machines in the small village. This skill of sewing that she learned as a young girl would eventually have a tremendous impact on her and her future family.

As the time passed, she was a very important part of the family and enjoyed being with the Cavallaro's. She became good friends with the eldest Cavallaro daughter, Rosa. Even though she was thirteen years older than Angela was, they both enjoyed sewing. They would sit together each day with their mending and sewing projects; on the front stoop of their house and talk for hours. Rosa also taught her sewing methods and together they accomplished many projects. They became good friends and this practice continued each day for some time. Angelo, the next eldest child, was 10 years older than Angela. He was serving in the Italian Army when Angela went to live with the family. When he left the army and returned home, he paid little attention to her. Being the eldest son of the five children, each day he worked in the Sicilian stone quarries as a stonecutter with his father. However, as the days and weeks passed, Angelo seemed to have an eye for Angela and before long, it appeared that a relationship was beginning to blossom. He became enamored with her laughter and the joy she brought into the house.

At one point, Angelo being ready to marry at age twenty-four, he approached his mother and father and told them that he wanted to marry Angela. His parents were very much against it. They felt that, since she had been living in their house for quite a while, she was considered like a sister to him by the neighbors and other families they knew. Because of this, they denied his request. Angela, too, wanted to get married. She was only fourteen years old and most girls her age were already thinking about marriage or had already been promised to marry someone in the village (better known as a *paisano*). It was a common practice for parents to arrange marriages for their children; even prior to the time they were ready to make such a lasting commitment. The young lovers begged and pleaded, but there was great resistance to this union. Angelo was as determined, and as stubborn as Angela was; they were destined to have their own way. Therefore, they decided to run away and elope. They went to the Court House in Giarre, had a civil ceremony, and were married. When they returned to their home and told their parents, it created great chaos in the household. Alfio Cavallaro was very upset that his son would even consider disobeying him. He scolded them very loudly and his voice could be heard all over the town; consequently, the entire village was aware of the activities within that home.

This created another problem; Angelo and Angela had no place to live. The elder Mr. and Mrs. Cavallaro, Alfio and Angela, decided to make room for them so they could have a room to themselves in their crowded quarters. The year was 1891. Angelo was twenty-four years old and Angela was fourteen years old. There are no records to indicate the month in which they were married or the actual date. While she was still fourteen years old, her first child was born. It was a boy and he died shortly after birth. At least one or two more children were born prior to 1894, and they all died at childbirth. However, by June of the following year, 1895, their first child that lived was born, and she was named Angela, after her grandmother. This makes the name situation more confusing because, at this point, there were three Angela's in the home; Angela Cavallaro – the *mother* of Alfio, Angela (Gravagna) Cavallaro – the *wife* of Angelo the son, and Angela Cavallaro – the *daughter* of Angelo the son. To make it less confusing, they called the baby, Angelina. In Italian, adding the suffix of 'ina' to any name or word changes the meaning to indicate 'little'; thus Angelina would mean 'Little Angela.'

From that point on, all that is known about Angela is that she stayed at home and cared for her children, sewing their clothes and becoming very friendly with all the women in their small community. Her family increased as follows:

- 1891 – 1894 – Two or three children were born and died at childbirth
- 1895 – Angela (Angelina) She was named after her Grandmother Cavallaro
- 1897 – Alfio (Alfred) He was named after his Grandfather Cavallaro
- Date unknown – twin boys born and died at childbirth
- 1900 – Maria Catena (Mary)
- 1902 – Giuseppe (Joseph)
- 1905 - Orazio (Roger)
- 1907 - One child born and died at childbirth
- 1908 – One child born and died at childbirth
- 1909 - Giovanna (Giovannina, later know as Jennie and Joan)
    (She was named after Angelo's sister who died at age sixteen)
- After 1909, Angelo and Angela had no other children

The gender of the children who died is unknown, except for the twin boys; no one knows the reasons for the deaths at childbirth. In those days, pre-natal care was not available and midwives or older women in the township delivered babies. If there were any complications with the birth, doctors and hospitals were too far away and much too expensive to even consider.

Angela Moves to Another Part of Sicily

Records show that Angelo and Angela remained in the area around Giarre for about one year after Angelina had been born. Sometime in 1896, they moved northwest to the small hamlet called Passopisciaro, meaning, 'The Path of the Fisherman.' The origin of that name is unknown and does not seem to fit because the hamlet is not located close to the water where fishermen would fish. It is located at the northern edge of the volcano, Mt. Etna. They moved to that location because there were more job opportunities for Angelo. The rock and lava quarries were larger and he would be able to earn more money.

When they arrived to their new location, Angela took the position as the head of the family, which was a very easy thing for her to do. This was also necessary because Angelo was out working most of the time and she had the complete responsibility of the home. Having her own way and being as independent as she was, it was very natural for her to make major decisions for the family. It was in Passopisciaro that her second child was born in 1897. His name was Alfio, named after Angelo's father and Angelo's grandfather. The rest of the children were born in Passopisciaro as well. Her next birth was that of twin boys. It was a very difficult delivery for her and they died at childbirth. After that, she had other pregnancies and births; some of the children lived and some of them died. All her successful births were recorded at the Court House in the Commune di Castiglione di Sicilia. It is located northeast of Passopisciaro and approximately four miles away. No other pregnancies were recorded after 1909.

During these years, Angelo made repeated trips to the United States. He would be gone for a couple of years and return back home to Sicily. A short while later, he would leave for America and stay for one or two years again. She had little or no help from him, so she was solely responsible to provide for her family.

She continued her sewing for people in the community, which brought in some funds to supplement what she sometimes received from Angelo. As her children recounted, it was in Passopisciaro where she opened a business. It was a small food store; similar to a Deli that we are familiar with today. She sold items like macaroni, olives, herring and dried codfish; better known in Italian as *bacala*. This small store helped her support her children and she became well known in the community. Being a very happy, sociable, and gregarious person, she made many friends in the community who would shop in the store. They would also bring her their sewing needs and she even found time to wash clothes for other people to make more money. She was a business-minded woman, which helped her to be successful in any venture she pursued. She worked hard and required very little rest. The older children helped her, and assisted in caring for the younger children. When she needed help, advice, or extra funds for the business, she went to Angelo's younger brother, Sebastiano. He also lived in Passopisciaro, and was ready to give her assistance. He was very intelligent; she trusted his wisdom. She was truly the head of the family now and became the sole provider for her children. This was her way of life until she decided to come to the United States in 1913.

Being tired of this rigorous schedule, she felt that if she went to the United States, it would be a great relief for her. She had heard stories from other *paisani* who had returned from America that the streets were paved with gold, and that there was a lot of money to be made. Therefore, when she had the opportunity to immigrate to America, she jumped at the chance, not realizing that she would continue her same rigorous life style in the new country as well.

In the early summer of 1913, Angelo had recently returned to Sicily from America. They pooled their money to see if they could afford the trip to America. They did not have enough money for both of them and the six children, so they decided to contact Angelo's brother Sebastiano. Sebastiano had just immigrated to America in 1912. They asked him to loan them the money needed for the trip. Sebastiano agreed and they finally had enough money to purchase passage to America for the entire family. The distance they had to travel to the Port of Debarkation in Palermo, Sicily, from Passopisciaro was a long one. It was located on the west coast of Sicily, and they were located at the furthest end of Sicily, on the east coast. It was approximately two hundred kilometers away, which was very far for them to travel. The money from Sebastiano arrived and they were ready to prepare for the trip to America.

They took only the clothing they wore, a couple of small suitcases, one large trunk, a small box, and some small sacks tied with rope. They knew it would be a long trip, and with six children ages four to eighteen years of age; carrying any luggage or boxes would be difficult for them. They borrowed the suitcases from *paisani* who had returned from America and did not intend on going back. The smaller sacks were for the younger children to carry; they were tied with rope so they could sling them over their shoulders and make it easier for travel. On the day the family left Passopisciaro, they had assigned each child to a suitcase, trunk, or small sack and that would be their responsibility for the entire trip.

Angela Arrives in America

The family looked upon arriving in America with great anticipation. Once they had cleared Ellis Island, they boarded the Immigrant Train to Rochester, New York. This is where they knew they would find relatives and *paisani* waiting for them. As soon as they arrived at the house of Sebastiano, Angela began searching for work in the local dress shops to do alterations and sewing. Fortunately, the area of North Clinton Avenue was lined with various dress shops that needed seamstresses. She found a job immediately while Angelo searched for an apartment for his family. It was important for her to find work because she needed to pay her brother-in-law, Sebastiano, back for the money he loaned them to come to America. Therefore, she and her oldest daughter, Angelina immediately went to work. In a very short span of time, the loan was repaid and Angelo, Angela, and the six children moved out of Sebastiano's home.

Angela had no difficulty finding work because they could see she was capable of producing fine work. She worked at the dress shops on a part-time or evening schedule but she needed to find work that was more lucrative. She then decided to look for work at Adler's, a clothing establishment that had recently opened. She was hired, on the spot, as a finisher. She worked as a finisher on men's suit jackets, armholes, and lapels. She was making eighteen dollars a week, which was more than other finishers were making, because she was so fast in her sewing. Even though she was fast, her stitches were uniform and small; her supervisors respected her work. She became known, at the tailor shop, as the best finisher they ever had. She would even take work home from the factory so she could make more money for the family.

However, making eighteen dollars a week did not go very far with six children at home. She continued to do alterations at the dress shops but also took in other sewing jobs to complete at home. She would work on these sewing projects at night, after dinner. The house they lived in lacked appropriate lighting; there were only gas lamps that were attached to the sidewalls. She had to sit right under the light in order to see her work. Later, they had electric lighting installed into the house, which helped; however, it still did not correct the problem. In the evening, the lights were not sufficient for her to see her sewing well enough. She did a lot of fine stitching and needed enough lighting to be able to do her work. She would sew in the kitchen, which was a large room with a very high ceiling. The ceiling was metal and had a decorative design of squares and flowers on it. In the middle of the room, a cord about six-feet long came down from the ceiling with just a bulb and fixture attached to it. For that big room, sixty watts was not very bright. Therefore, when she needed to sew in the evening, she would put a chair on the kitchen table, and sit under the lone, bare bulb, to be closer to the light. She would sew until the early hours of the morning. Through these activities, she was able to run the house, support the family, and earn enough money to be able to purchase a farm in the next few years.

During this time, you may ask, "Where was Angelo?" He still lived in the same home with the family and continued to work as a laborer for local builders. He worked late, and usually, did not eat meals with the family. On Sundays, he was always out with his friends at the local saloon. He enjoyed drinking and much of his salary went to fulfilling his desire for more wine. As was related to me by my Aunt Mary, "He found out very soon how much money she was making and he wanted to take over and have all the money that she had put in the bank." By that time, Alfred (my father) had a job, was making money, and he gave it to his mother to help with the family expenses and save a portion in the bank. Angelo wanted all the money that Alfred was giving his mother. She would not let him have it. They argued over it constantly. Then, one night, he came home drunk and he wanted to hit her because she would not give the money. She took a small shovel that was next to the coal-fed stove in the kitchen, and hit him with it. She broke the wooden handle of the shovel over his back. Then, she picked up a wooden ladle from the oven and hit him with that also. From that time on, their relationship began to deteriorate.

Angela's Final Years

In 1917, she had enough money and was able to buy the farm. I discuss her life on the farm in the chapter entitled, The Farm in West Bloomfield. During these years, she lived without Angelo in the home. While he continued to make trips back and forth to Sicily, she worked hard, raised her children, bought and sold the farm, and then bought the house on North Clinton Avenue, where she lived until she became ill.

She never became a United States citizen nor did she speak English. However, she raised six fine children and was the matriarch of the family for many years. When she became ill with Parkinson's disease, she went to live with her daughter, Mary. Once she became non-ambulatory, she was placed in the Monroe County Home and Infirmary. When her husband Angelo died on April 6, 1945, the family decided not to tell her of his death. She was ill herself and they felt it would be detrimental to her health to share the sad news. Even through the days of the funeral, the children continued to visit her nightly. They made sure that they were not wearing any black clothing so she would not know what had happened. However, on one occasion, a few days after he had died, she looked at my father, Alfred, and said, "Your father died, didn't he!" She didn't say it as a question, but rather, as a statement, as though she knew what had happened. Not wanting to tell her the truth, he said, "No, Ma, he's just a little sick." She said, "No, I know he's dead." Within eight weeks, she unexpectedly died at the Monroe County Home and Infirmary on June 2, 1945.

Since I was only a young boy before her death, I can only remember bits and pieces of her mannerisms, personality, illness, and her way of speaking. There are, however, some things I shall never forget about my grandmother. The perpetual smile on her face and, her kind and loving way of speaking to my brother and me are characteristics that live on in my memory.

Although she spoke only in Italian and we responded in English, we understood each other. She had a close relationship with her children and was responsible for giving them the gift of sewing. She spent lots of time with each of her children and they all learned the craft well. At one time, my Aunt Angie shared with me how they all sat around the table sewing different projects. They helped each other sew, talked about the day's events, told little stories and jokes, and enjoyed laughing with each other. It was through activities such as these that the family members grew closer to each other, even though they were experiencing hard times. Angela was a remarkable woman. I wish I had known her better; however, my memories of her were kept alive by the stories and tales my father shared with us. As our family sat around our dinner table after the evening meal each night, he would tell us story after story of what it was like in Sicily before he came to America and of the events that helped draw his family closer together. In his way, he was repeating what his mother had done many years earlier, which helped draw his own family closer together. Little did Angela realize that these family-based activities were the key elements of developing close and loving relationships.

Angela (Gravagna) Cavallaro

Sisters:
Giovanna Farina and Angela Cavallaro (1937)

Roger Cavallaro, Angela Cavallaro
Angela's sister Giovanna Farina
and Mr. Farina.
Visiting from Lodi, NJ (1937)

Angela Cavallaro
& daughter Angelina Lamanna

Angela Cavallaro
& daughter Jennie Cavallaro

Angela (Angelina Cavallaro) Lamanna

June 2, 1895 – April 9, 1981

Prologue

Angela Cavallaro was the first-born child of Angelo and Angela Cavallaro. They had other children born to them after they eloped and prior to Angela's birth in 1895; however, none of them lived. They died at birth or just after birth because of complications with the delivery process. The year they eloped was 1891, when Angelo was twenty-four years old and Angela was fourteen years old. They were still living near the city of Giarre in the Province of Catania, at the home of Alfio and Angela Cavallaro.

The Beginning

Angela was born on June 2, 1895; her father was twenty-eight years old and her mother was seventeen years old. They were elated that they finally had a child who lived. It's important to understand that Angela's pregnancy was a special event. Being as friendly as she was, she knew many of the women in the town. Since she was so well known, the women were drawn to her naturally, and considered her as part of their own family. The birth of the new child was looked upon with great anticipation.

On the day she was born, a warm June day in sunny Sicily, all the neighbor women had gathered outside the small, stone house where Angelo and Angela Cavallaro lived. They patiently were awaiting the birth. It was recounted to me that she was a beautiful baby and, immediately after her birth, her grandmother, Angela, took much pleasure in carrying her outdoors to show her to the *paisani*. News of the impending birth traveled quickly throughout the small village. Although they lacked any means of electronic communications such as telephones, word of mouth was a very speedy means of passing information.

The women of the community, gathered outside the house in the early morning. Most of the Sicilian women who gathered were dressed in black. Sicilian custom dictates that they wore black after the passing of a loved one for one year or more after the death. By the time they were ready to shed the black attire, another relative would die, and they would continue wearing black clothing. It was such an ingrained custom in Sicily, that if they didn't have a loved one or relative who died, they wore black for a *commare, compare, paisano*, or out of respect to a friend who had lost a loved one. Therefore, wearing black was a common style for these Sicilian women.

Now, if you can picture the scene on that warm and sunny day, a crowd of black-clad women surrounding the front of the house, some prayed their rosary beads, others softly gossiped with women nearby, and some just patiently waited and listened to the activity going on inside the house. Then, the door opened and Angela Cavallaro (the grandmother) appeared with the infant in her arms. A shout arose among the crowd, loud enough to inform the rest of the villagers who were not present, indicating that the baby had been born. So when Angela Cavallaro (the grandmother) came out to show the baby to all the women, they all took pride and joy in the birth. The newborn infant was perfectly formed and a beautiful child. She had a light complexion, and in Sicily, that was a boon. The coloring of most Sicilian babies was olive-toned, so to have a baby with such a fair complexion, was quite unusual. Angela, then announced with pride, that the baby had been named Angela, meaning 'Angela' and named after her. Because she would be the third Angela in the household, they decided to call her Angelina. In Sicily, adding an 'ina' at the end of the name indicates 'small or little'. So, she immediately took on the name of 'Angelina', meaning 'Little Angela', and she used that name for the remainder of her life. Angela (the grandmother) took pride in having the new baby named after her and doted over her namesake for the short time they all lived together. Before she returned the baby into the house, Angela raised the infant up for all to see and as if to give God the thanks for a successful birth.

Angelina Grows Up

Angelina continued living near the city of Giarre for only a year or so. Early in 1897, her mother became pregnant again for her second child. Since space was extremely limited in the Cavallaro home, Angelo and Angela knew it was time to leave and move into a larger home of their own. Angelo heard of work being available in the small town of Passopisciaro. It was located about twenty-five miles northwest of the Province of Giarre, at the base of Mt. Etna. He knew there were lava quarries in the area where he could find more opportunities for employment, or work as a laborer in the grape vineyards that grew in abundance on the slopes of the volcano.

They gathered the few belonging they had, obtained a cart drawn by a mule, and proceeded to Passopisciaro. Angelina was about two years old and Angela was five months pregnant with her next child.

Angela's second child (Alfio) was born just four months later and Angelina was two years old. Now, with a toddler and an infant to care for, Angela became more focused on her domestic duties; however, she continued to sew in her home for the neighbors. Being almost twenty years old, her sewing skills became more precise and valued by the villagers and her popularity grew among the *paisani*.

Angelina remained with her parents in Passopisciaro until 1913 when the family migrated to America. Angelina, being the oldest child, needed to help her mother in caring for the younger children. She was only a young child herself; yet, she managed to be responsible for the household chores; helped her mother with her sewing jobs; and assisted in the preparation of meals. During these years, Angela passed on the sewing tradition to Angelina while she was still at a very young age. As her sewing skills became perfected during her teenage years, she helped her mother with the tailoring she was doing for all the neighbors. This was a great help to Angela and they were able to earn enough money between the two of them to provide for their growing family. Angelo could not be depended on to bring a salary home to his family, so Angela and Angelina became a team in supporting the family with their sewing.

Angelina Arrives in America

Angelina sewed for the rest of her life. After arriving in America, she worked at Levi-Adler's Clothing Factory with her mother. As a seamstress, she worked full-time sewing collars and sleeves on coats. She also continued to sew at home in the evenings to help her mother with the side-jobs she accepted.

At that time, they were renting an upstairs, three-room apartment on North Clinton Avenue. Located on the first floor was a fabric shop. The owners of the shop referred all their sewing clients upstairs to Angela and Angelina. On one particular day, the landlady was receiving a shipment of wood from a lumberyard so she could begin remodeling the store. A young man delivering the lumber noticed Angelina and a conversation ensued. The deliverer's name was Frederico Lamanna. He was a dapper gentleman from Naples, who spoke Italian as well. He returned to see her and a closer relationship developed. After a short courtship, they were married on September 11, 1915, and she began the next phase of her life.

Angelina Begins a Family of Her Own

On September 27, 1916, Angelina and Frederico's daughter, Caterina Maria Lamanna, was born. She, too, was a beautiful baby with black, wavy hair. According to my Aunt Mary Lizzio, she smiled all the time, just like her mother. She was considered a happy child, very active, and mischievous. The entire Cavallaro family embraced this first grandchild. Although her given name was Caterina Maria, the family called her *Mariuzza* (Ma rē ū´ zza). The name *Mariuzza* is a form of the name Maria, but in Sicilian dialect, when the suffix of *uzza* is added to a name, it's used to refer to the person in a comical way, to mean 'Happy Mary,' or 'Cute Little Mary.' It was an endearment for someone that was comical, active, and mischievous. Not everyone in the family agreed that she should be called Caterina; therefore, the name *Mariuzza* remained with her. As she grew into her toddler years, she became very attached to her Aunt Mary. They lived on the farm at that time and Aunt Mary cared for her while Angelina worked.

Toward the end of World War I, Angela had plans to sell the farm. Because of this, Angelina and Frederico decided to move back to the city. They moved to an apartment on North Clinton Avenue and on June 14, 1919, a second daughter was born to them. They named her Angelina Giovanna. She was a happy child, well behaved, quiet, and shy. As reported by my aunts and uncles, they said she was a very easy child to raise and quite the opposite of Caterina Maria. Although her Baptismal Record showed her given name as being Angelina Giovanna, the family called her Jennie.

During the winter of 1919 and 1920, an epidemic of Diphtheria attacked the east coast of America. The laws for required immunizations were very lax and the majority of the population was not inoculated against the disease. As a result, many children and adults died from Diphtheria. Little Caterina Maria contacted Diphtheria and was rushed to the hospital. She wasn't there for very long before the family was contacted and told that there was no hope for her to live. So on January 31, 1920, Caterina Maria died of Diphtheria at the young age of three years, four months and four days old. She was buried at Holy Sepulchre Cemetery in Rochester, New York, section O, Lot/Tier 20, and Grave 102, which marks her grave. Her burial was on February 2, 1920, and a lamb rests on top of her white headstone. This was a difficult tragedy for the family to deal with and they never fully recovered from it. Whenever it was mentioned, years later, tears came to the eyes of everyone. In those three short years, Caterina Maria had captured the hearts of the entire family.

Diphtheria is a very contagious bacterial disease and attacks the throat and nose, and sometimes the heart and nerves of its victims. At that time, it was widespread and a feared disease by all. In the 1920s, it struck about 200,000 people a year (150 cases per 100,000 people) and killed about 15,000 of them. The disease would develop in the throat and tonsils, and it would be passed to others by coughing or sneezing. It was difficult to swallow and it would cause the patient to suffocate. It also caused the lymph glands on both sides of the neck to swell to an unusually large size. It produced a poison, which would spread to other parts of the body. It was once one of the most common causes of death in children across America.

Angelina Matures into a Professional Seamstress

During the years that followed, Angelina, Frederico and Jennie moved from the apartment on North Clinton Avenue to a home on Albow Place, which was within walking distance from the same street where Angelina's Uncle Sebastiano owned two homes. From Albow Place, they moved to their home on Oakman Street, which was directly across the street from her brother and sister-in-law, Joe and Jennie Cavallaro. This was about a five-minute walk from the Albow Place home. Angelina's daughter Jennie remembers that she was six or seven years old when they moved into the Oakman Street house. It was at that residence that Angelina's father, Angelo Cavallaro, went to live with them. He had just returned from Sicily, and needed a place to live. They lived there for a long time and eventually moved to a large two-story home on Norton Street. It had a long front porch. It was a much larger house and gave them more space. Angelo also moved in with them.

Angelina's daughter, Jennie, grew up and married Joe Romeo. Apparently, much of the Cavallaro family knew the Romeo family from Sicily. They were married in a beautiful wedding on September 14, 1940. On June 1, 1943, they gave birth to a little boy. His name was Alfred Frederick Romeo. He only lived about seven days and died of a skin disease, which he contacted in the nursery at the hospital. He was buried on June 9, 1943 at Holy Sepulchre Cemetery in Rochester, New York, Section North 4, Lot/Tier 5, Grave143F.

After a few years, Jennie and Joe Romeo were expecting a child again – but this time it was twins. On November 29, 1947, Thomas Frederick and Mary Linda were born. It was an unforgettable time for the whole Cavallaro family. This was the first living set of twins in the family and quite a spectacular event. Thomas entered the world first and two minutes later, Mary joined him. From the moment of their birth, they were perfect in every way. Immediately, the entire family flocked to visit the beautiful babies. It was very exciting for everyone, especially for Angelina. She was there to help in every way she could.

Having two babies at the same time required a lot of work, care, and assistance. Jennie and Joe temporarily moved in with Angelina and Federico at their Norton Street home so they could receive some much needed help – at least until she felt well enough to care for the twins herself.

I can remember at one of our visits; I was about fifteen years old and wanted to take some pictures of the babies. They were both awake and they wanted to be held at the same time. When one was being fed, the other wanted to be fed also. Angelina was there to help Jennie with the caring of the babies and she was in her glory. She did every chore with a smile....you could feel the love in her heart with which she cared for her twin grandchildren and for Joe and Jennie also.

Angelina was a very healthy woman. The only illness reported to me occurred after her daughter Jennie was born. She had been diagnosed with some sort of cancer in her body – a woman's thing, as they used to say. Dr. Lopi diagnosed her, he sent her to Roswell Memorial Hospital in Buffalo, New York for a couple of treatments, and she was cleared of any problems after that.

In 1957, Angelina and Frederico joined their daughter and her family when they moved to California. They lived in Westminster. She wrote to my parents and literally begged them to move out West also. She told my father that the climate was just like Sicily. In a picture she sent, she wrote, 'California - *staio senza scarpi*' (I'm in California and I'm walking without any shoes.) She loved it there. However, they only stayed a few years and they moved back to Rochester because of the lack of sufficient work at that time.

Some Final Comments

Throughout her entire life, Angelina's love and passion was her sewing. Her skills were passed down to her from her mother, Angela, and from her grandmother, Angela, as well. She was employed for a few years at the Bond Clothing factory on Hand Street, as were the rest of her siblings and their spouses. She worked on flaps, and wells – the pocket parts that are used in men's suits. She was very good at her work and her supervisors respected the precision with which she sewed. She left Bond Clothing factory and continued sewing at home. Before long, she had a regular clientele for whom she sewed and started a very successful tailoring business from home.

As quoted by her daughter, Jennie,

> *"My Mother always had a smile on her face. She also had a happy personality. She never was allowed to go to school in Italy, because she was the oldest child. This did not stop her from becoming a very professional seamstress. She could not read or write, but was able to put together and sew everything from wedding dresses to women's suits. She had her very own business out of her home."*

This was a tremendous accomplishment for a woman who could not read or write in English. To be able to enter the working world, and to conduct a successful business from her home for most of her life, was not only exceptional, but the fulfillment of a passionate dream. Sewing became part of her every day life. She would share stories with us about her many influential businesswomen who would hire her to make their clothes (blouses, skirts, dresses) and complete their alterations. She also made her daughter Jennie's wedding gown, which was a focal point for the beautiful September wedding. When Angelo Lizzio was ready to marry Audrey, who had recently arrived from England, Angelina also made her wedding gown. I remember my Aunt Angie saying that she had no pattern in mind for her wedding gown but only went by what Audrey's verbal description.

It, too, was a gorgeous gown and was worn by Audrey's granddaughter when she was married, many years later.

Angelina took great pride in sharing her sewing projects. On each of our visits to her home, she would take us upstairs to her sewing room to show us her completed projects as well as those that were still in progress. Sometimes, my father would help her in pressing some of her suits or give other tailoring advice whenever he could assist.

As a young boy growing up, I recall one characteristic about my Aunt Angie. Whenever she would see me, she'd pinch my cheek with her fingers and give it a little twist and say something nice to me. She did this endearment with those she loved. She even did this on my wedding day. We had just come out of the church and all the family were gathered around me and my new wife, Aggie, kissing and congratulating us. My Aunt Angie came up to me, pinched my cheek, and said, "*Con Buona Fortuna* (With Good Luck)." I will never forget that and remember that incident with great fondness.

Her granddaughter, Mary Gray, has some very special thoughts about her grandmother. She shared the following with me:

> *"We lived with my grandmother in our early years; however I became closer to her as I became older. I remember that she enrolled me in dance classes. I'd wear my tap shoes all day long and tap all around the house. My grandmother always made me feel special when I was with her. I spent weekends with her often. I remember feeling almost like sisters with her. We would go grocery shopping together and she would buy steak and refrigerated biscuits because she knew they were some of the foods I liked very much. At other times, we would go down-town and shop and then have lunch together at Neisner's or Woolworth's Department Store. It was such a fun time for both of us. I think she enjoyed it as much as I did.*
>
> *I would often stay overnight at her house on weekends. My parents would come to pick me up on Sunday night so I could go to school on Monday morning. She also taught me how to cook by simply observing her in the kitchen. At one point, I wrote down everything she did to prepare her spaghetti sauce; I knew if I didn't, I would never remember any of it at all. My grandmother was a wonderful cook, even though she could not read or write, she remembered all the details of her recipes. At one point in her life, she did try to learn how*

to read and write. She went to a few classes at St. Michael's Church on North Clinton Avenue; I don't remember why, but she stopped going a short time later.

She was also very clean and organized. From the time she woke in the morning, she would do things in a certain order. She would exercise almost every morning with Jack LaLane who had his own TV show at the time. Then, she'd have breakfast and clean the house. Then she'd wash up for the day, and I remember her using a fresh lemon and Pond's cold cream on her face. She had a lovely complexion. By that time, we'd stop to have lunch together. After lunch, she would sit and sew for the rest of the afternoon; however, she did save some time for a short nap before she made the evening meal.

My grandparents had a young family that rented and lived above them on Wilkens Street. They would eventually have three boys of their own. My grandmother treated them like her own grandchildren. To this day, I see their mother around town, and she still talks about my grandmother and how much they loved her.

Angelina Cavallaro Lamanna left a tremendous legacy. My personal remembrances of her are as a happy person who always had a smile on her face. I never heard a cross word or any type of complaint come from her. She and my dad had a very close relationship and they'd visit often, joke with each other, and have long, confidential talks together. My father truly loved his sister. They had a lot in common and their personalities and character traits were very similar. My recollections of our visits to her home always included a lot of laughter and joyous times. She was a remarkable and talented woman with a kind and sweet spirit. All her siblings, all her relatives and neighbors, respected her including the many sewing customers she had as well. Angelina was a fine woman who embraced everyone she met in a very loving way. We love you Aunt Angie!

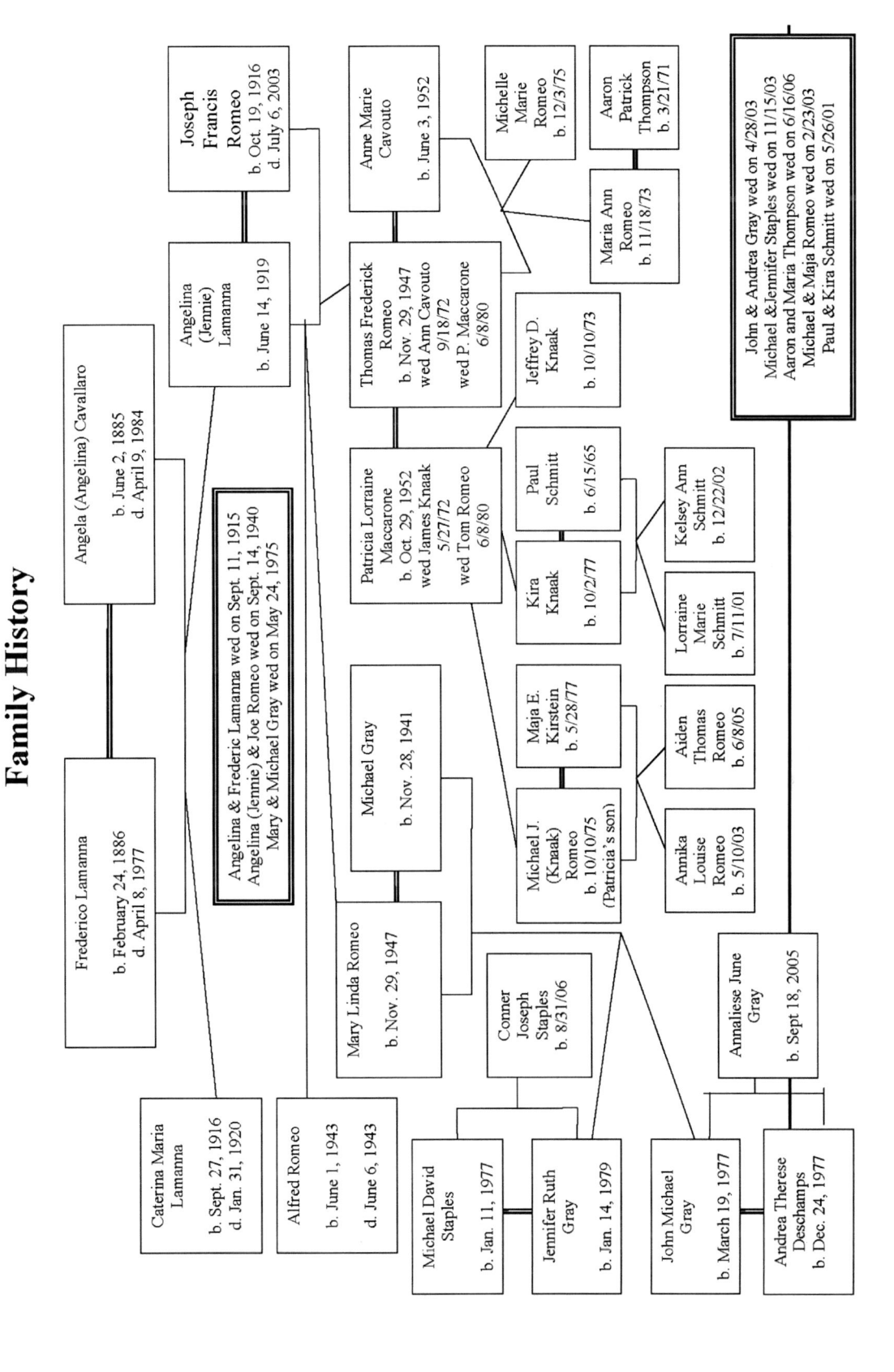

Angela (*Angelina Cavallaro*) Lamanna
Family History

Frederico Lamanna
b. February 24, 1886
d. April 8, 1977

Angela (Angelina) Cavallaro
b. June 2, 1885
d. April 9, 1984

Angelina (Jennie) Lamanna
b. June 14, 1919

Joseph Francis Romeo
b. Oct. 19, 1916
d. July 6, 2003

Caterina Maria Lamanna
b. Sept. 27, 1916
d. Jan. 31, 1920

Alfred Romeo
b. June 1, 1943
d. June 6, 1943

Mary Linda Romeo
b. Nov. 29, 1947

Michael Gray
b. Nov. 28, 1941

Thomas Frederick Romeo
b. Nov. 29, 1947
wed Ann Cavouto 9/18/72
wed P. Maccarone 6/8/80

Anne Marie Cavouto
b. June 3, 1952

Patricia Lorraine Maccarone
b. Oct. 29, 1952
wed James Knaak 5/27/72
wed Tom Romeo 6/8/80

Jeffrey D. Knaak
b. 10/10/73

Michelle Marie Romeo
b. 12/3/75

Maria Ann Romeo
b. 11/18/73

Aaron Patrick Thompson
b. 3/21/71

Angelina & Frederic Lamanna wed on Sept. 11, 1915
Angelina (Jennie) & Joe Romeo wed on Sept. 14, 1940
Mary & Michael Gray wed on May 24, 1975

Michael David Staples
b. Jan. 11, 1977

Jennifer Ruth Gray
b. Jan. 14, 1979

Conner Joseph Staples
b. 8/31/06

Michael J. (Knaak) Romeo
b. 10/10/75
(Patricia's son)

Maja E. Kirstein
b. 5/28/77

Kira Knaak
b. 10/2/77

Paul Schmitt
b. 6/15/65

Annika Louise Romeo
b. 5/10/03

Aiden Thomas Romeo
b. 6/8/05

Lorraine Marie Schmitt
b. 7/11/01

Kelsey Ann Schmitt
b. 12/22/02

John Michael Gray
b. March 19, 1977

Andrea Therese Deschamps
b. Dec. 24, 1977

Annaliese June Gray
b. Sept 18, 2005

John & Andrea Gray wed on 4/28/03
Michael & Jennifer Staples wed on 11/15/03
Aaron and Maria Thompson wed on 6/16/06
Michael & Maja Romeo wed on 2/23/03
Paul & Kira Schmitt wed on 5/26/01

Angelina (Cavallaro) Lamanna

September 11, 1915
Angelina and Frederico Lamanna
Maid of Honor: Maria Catena Cavallaro

Angelina - taken in
Westminister, California

1919
Maria Catena Cavallaro
& Caterina "Mariuzza" Lamanna
She died 3 months later at age 3

Angelina, Frederico and
Angelina (Jennie) Lamanna
At Joe & Jennie Gargano's wedding

November 1947
Angleina & Twin Grandchildren
Mary and Thomas

My Sicilian Legacy

Jennie (Lamanna) Romeo & family
Mike & Mary (Romeo) Gray
Jennie (Lamanna) Romeo
Trish and Tom Romeo

John & Andrea Gray
& Annaliese June Gray
(Born 9/18/05)

Mike & Jennifer (Gray) Staples
& Conner Joseph Staples
(Born 8/31/06)

Alfio (Alfred Michael) Cavallaro Sr.

October 12, 1897 – September 23, 1964

Prologue

Alfio Cavallaro was the second born child that lived to Angelo and Angela Cavallaro. At this point and time, Angelo was thirty years old, Angela was nineteen years old; Alfio's sister Angelina was two years old. It was just prior to 1901, that Angelo began taking his trips to America; however, it is assumed that he was in Sicily at the time of the birth of his second living child and his first son. Angela continued to do her sewing to provide enough funds to support her family, which now included two young children. Angelo continued to find whatever work he could at the stone quarries near Mt. Etna or at the grape vineyards close by.

Although Alfio always said he was born in Passopisciaro, the tiny village that is known as 'The Way of the Fisherman,' his birthplace is recorded as being in Castiglione di Sicilia, which is in the Province of Catania. It is a community in northeastern Sicily, about seven to ten miles away from Passopisciaro, and approximately two miles north of the rim of the volcano, Mt. Etna. Castiglione di Sicilia was a larger community and had a provincial building that was used to record all significant occurrences, such as births, marriages, and deaths. He and his siblings were all confident that Passopisciaro was his birthplace and the town where all the brothers and sisters that came after him were also born.

Knowing that Italians followed the tradition of naming their children after previous generations of relatives, I searched for the name of Alfio in the Cavallaro family tree and found it to be the same name as Angelo's father. So Alfio, the first-born son of Angelo and Angela Cavallaro, was named after his paternal grandfather, Alfio Cavallaro. Later in life, we find that Alfio named his first son, Alfred, to follow the same family tradition. Naming children after their ancestors or for others who came before them was a common practice for Italian families; this custom has continued to the present time. This is why many genealogical searches are so difficult to make; the same name appears in the same family, generation after generation after generation. At that time, they did not use the designation of senior, junior, I, II, or III after their names, which made it even more confusing. I'm sure, if it were possible to go back further into the Cavallaro genealogical history, we'd find many more men named Alfio Cavallaro.

The Beginning

Angelo and Angela lived in happiness with their first born, Angelina, and she brought much joy to them. However, now they had a baby son. In Sicilian families, having a son was extra-special for many reasons. Primarily, it was another opportunity for the family name to be carried on into future generations; secondly, an ancestral grandparent would be honored by having a child named after him; and thirdly and probably, most importantly, the male child would grow up to help with the family trade and assist in supporting them financially. In poorer families, this was a very important issue and sons were always revered more so than daughters. Alfio was a handsome baby and immediately after his birth, his father, Angelo, took much pleasure in carrying him outdoors to show him to the awaiting neighbors. On the day he was born, a cool October day in sunny Sicily, all the neighbor women had gathered both inside and outside the small Cavallaro home awaiting the birth. The birth occurred inside the house with the assistance of a mid-wife who lived in the town. News of the male birth traveled rapidly throughout the small village; however, Angelo was very quick to announce the birth to all the men in the town and at the quarry where he worked. It was a joyous time for everyone.

The women of the community, gathered outside the house on early mornings each day to accompany Angela as she took her children for a stroll through the town. They fussed over the baby and there were always extra hands available to assist Angela as she cared for two-year-old Angelina as they walked. If the baby began to fuss a bit, the older women would step in to give Angela, a relatively new mom, some much needed advice as to what she should do.

He was perfectly formed and a beautiful infant. He had a full head of jet-black hair, he had dark brown eyes, and his lips were like angel's wings (cupid's lips). He was a good baby and an easy child to raise. He responded to all of her training and grew very attached to his sister Angelina. Even after they grew up, and were adults in America, he was always very close to her. They were alike in so many ways.

Alfio Grows Up

Shortly after Alfio was born in 1897, Angela became pregnant again. This time she had twin boys; however, they died within three days after their birth from pneumonia. Of course, at that time, there were no remedies for pneumonia. Soon after, she became pregnant again and in March of 1900, she had her third child. Therefore, by the time Alfio was two years old, his mother had given birth to twins and to another baby girl, Maria Catena. His toddler years were very typical in that he learned to play with simple things he could find, or was entertained by his big sister Angelina.

By the time he was five years old, Alfio started to go to work with his father. Angelo took him to the quarry each day, as did the other fathers who had sons. They put him to work by having him take the drills used for stonecutting to the Blacksmiths, as they needed them. He learned very quickly, what the different sizes were and could follow their directions well. When they would ask for a particular size, he would run to get it for them, and then return the old ones back to the cabinets. In addition, they used him to carry stones and rocks in wicker baskets from one place to another. It was dirty work and it was hard work; but at a very young age, he learned to use his hands and to do all sorts of manual labor. As he grew older and stronger, they utilized him in many other facets of the stonecutting trade. Had he stayed in Sicily as an adult, he most likely would have followed his father's example to become a stonecutter or a Blacksmith. Most sons at that time followed in the same trade as their fathers and usually for their entire lifetime.

When he was approximately eight years old, he went to school and learned to read and write in Italian. I discussed this with him often and asked him how far he went through their school system. He explained to me that the schools in Sicily were different from American schools; the grades were not equated in the same way as the grades that I was used to. He told me that he went to school for about three to four years. During that time, he became totally literate and was able to read and write in Italian. This helped him a great deal when it became time for him to immigrate to the America with his family. He could read all the signs and forms for his parents and communicate with the other Italians on board the ship and at Ellis Island. It also helped him when he became naturalized in America. Having had a language base in Sicily, it assisted him as he learned to read and write English while he attended classes to qualify for his American Citizenship papers. His parents were both illiterate and never learned to read or write Italian while they lived in Sicily, nor did they learn English after they arrived in America.

During the time he was growing up, Alfio went to church with his mother on a regular basis. When he was approximately ten years old, the parish priest asked him if he'd like to be an altar boy at the Catholic church they attended. He jumped at the chance to do this. One of his good friends that he played with all the time, Nunzio Maugeri, was already an altar boy and they could do this together. Therefore, he got approval from Angela, and he started going to classes at the church to learn Latin and to learn the duties required of an altar boy. He served as an altar boy for approximately four years. The church he served at was Santa Maria del Rosario (Holy Mary of the Rosary) and was very close to their home in Passopisciaro. Occasionally, when they found themselves in Castiglione de Sicilia on a Sunday, they would attend mass at La Chiesa di Sant'Antionio Abate (the church of St. Anthony Abate) or at La Chiesa di San Benedetto e Santa Scolastica (the church of Saint Benedictine and Saint Scolastica). He enjoyed doing this, but he had to give up serving as an altar boy eventually so that he could work more hours and help take care of the family. He was the oldest son; and although this was expected of him, he did it willingly.

As a pre-teen and entering into his adolescent years, he began to work in the vineyards, which surrounded his home and covered the slopes of Mt. Etna. Since the land in that area was covered with very rich soil from the lava and magma, the grapes grew well. The hot and dry climate of Sicily added to making the growing conditions just perfect for harvesting abundant crops of grapes each year. There were many vineyards and he loved climbing the mountainside to pick grapes. When he did this, he usually went with his good friend Nunzio Maugeri. He and Nunzio were inseparable. They had been good friends since they were very young. As they were growing up, working, and going to school together, they always had a lot of time to talk. On hot afternoons, as they lay on the mountainside taking a lunch break or resting in the shade, they would talk about what the future held for them. Because they had lost so many of their *paisani,* neighbors, and other friends during the exodus to America, they thought a lot about when they, too, would go to America. It wasn't a matter of 'if' they went to America, but rather 'when' they would go. At that very young age, they made a verbal pact with each other; namely, to remain friends forever and to try to locate each other after their families arrived in America. These two young boys were so much alike. They were both very active, they both worked hard, they were both goal oriented, and they both wanted to have a better life in America. They spent a lot of time at each other's homes and they knew each other's families well. Much to their surprise and to the astonishment of their families, their fanaticizing in these pre-teen years about the future became a reality once they grew up, moved to America, and were reunited in Rochester, New York.

Alfio Arrives in America

As summer approached in 1913, Angelo and Angela decided that it was time for them to migrate to America. Alfio was very helpful in their journey to Palermo. Being the oldest son and being as strong as he was, he had the responsibility of carrying the one large trunk that contained most of their belongings. The other children were carrying their own small packages and bags. He found it best to carry the trunk on his shoulder, and whenever he had to stop, he would put it down and sit on it as a protection so no one would take it. He took care of that trunk on the trip to Palermo, on the boat to Ellis Island and on the train all the way to Rochester. Most of their clothing and simple belongings were in the trunk and he knew that they were depending on him to keep it safe.

In July of 1913, Alfio's family was ready to immigrate to America. All Alfio could understand was that they were going somewhere in New York (*Nuova Yorca*, as they would say). Nunzio and his family had no plans to leave Sicily yet, so he remained in Passopisciaro. Alfio knew that saying goodbye to his very best friend was going to be extremely difficult; however, it had to be done. Early in the morning, on the day that the Cavallaro family was leaving, Nunzio appeared at their front door to help them load the cart that would take his best friend away. When they had all their belongings loaded on the cart and all they children were in their places, Alfio and Nunzio hugged each other, not knowing when they would see each other again. Alfio climbed onto the horse-drawn cart and the boys looked at each other for the last time. As he waved to Nunzio, they both continued to say their good-byes with tears in their eyes, vowing that they would see each other again in America, *"Ci vediamo in L'America"* ("We will meet again in America"). As the cart slowly moved away, down the lane, Nunzio began to run alongside the cart. It allowed him a few extra minutes to see his best friend. From the back of the cart where my father sat, he continued waving to Nunzio. When the cart finally began to pick up speed and they drove out of sight, he could not see Nunzio any longer; however, he could still hear his voice saying, "*Ci vediamo in L'America.*" Soon, all he could hear were the sounds of the cart's wheels crossing over the rough terrain, and of the horse's hoofs trotting quickly, as they moved further from his familiar surroundings. In the stillness of that dark and cold July morning, Alfio sat in the back of the cart, crying for his friend, not knowing if he would ever see him again. From that moment on, there was no way for him to communicate with Nunzio and to tell him that they were actually going to Rochester, which was somewhere in New York. Alfio always kept the promise they made in his mind; that they would try to contact each other once they arrived in America.

Although the Manifest from the ship had him listed as Alfio Cavallaro, when they went through Ellis Island, the clerks checking on the passengers wrote his name as Alfred Cavallaro. From that time on, he was always known as Alfred. After that, he only used the name Alfio for official documents. Therefore, from now on, I too, will refer to him as Alfred.

Alfred Enters the Working World

When Alfred arrived in America in July of 1913, he was fifteen years old. For the next few years, he helped at home, took odd jobs in the community, and assisted his family each time they moved to their many residences mentioned earlier. In 1917, World War I was declared. It would only be a matter of time before Alfred would be drafted into the army. Being the oldest son, Angela really needed him at home and decided to purchase a farm in an effort to get him deferred so he would not serve in the war. Angela purchased the farm with her brother-in-law, Sebastiano, and in 1917, that became the new residence for the whole family. As a result, Alfred did not serve in the military and stayed at home to help with the family farm. After working the farm for approximately three years, Angela found that it was creating many problems for her three sons: Alfred, Joseph, and Roger. They did not get along with Sebastiano because of his demanding ways, and, as the boys grew older, they became tired of the farming life. By this time, Alfred was twenty-three years old. He and his brothers wanted to get jobs where they could make more money. There were other families nearby that owned farms; they had allowed their older children to leave and go to the city to work in the factories. When Alfred heard that they were making good money, he was determined to give it a try. His decision was not received well by Angela or by his Uncle Sebastiano. He had done some investigating and found out he could get a job at a place called Fashion Park Clothing Factory. He'd made the acquaintance of someone who was a manager there.

Alfred obtained a job at Fashion Park Clothing Factory as soon as they moved back to the city in 1921. It was then that Angelo demanded Alfred's paycheck from Angela. He was planning to return to Sicily and needed the money. Angela refused. He went back to Sicily shortly after that and did not return until 1927. Alfred continued to work at Fashion Park, but his job lasted for only a year and he was laid off. He immediately went to his sister, Angelina, and she taught him more about tailoring so he could pursue a better job at Fashion Park. In the meantime, his sister Jennie had just secured a job at a small tailor shop called Rosenberg's Tailoring. It was located on Miller Street near Clifford Avenue, in the same area as Fashion Park. She encouraged him to apply and he was hired there as well. While he was working at Rosenberg's Tailor Shop, Fashion Park bought them out and it all became one large tailor factory. After the merge took place, he happened to make the acquaintance of a young woman who just dazzled him. Her name was Theresa Siracusa. She was working in Shop #4 with his sister, Jennie Cavallaro; they were good friends. Jennie made it possible for the two of them to meet and it was love at first sight.

Alfred and Theresa's Romance Begins

Theresa was very shy and in those days; proper girls did not talk idly to young men, nor did they walk with them or were they to be seen alone with them. Therefore, for young couples who wanted to meet or become friends, it was a series of staring at each other from a distance. My mother would relate to me that if she ever looked over to where Alfred was working and she found him staring at her, she would immediately get embarrassed, look away, or drop her eyes to the floor. If my father wanted to get a message to her, he'd write her a note and pass it on to one of her girlfriends for delivery. If that didn't work, he'd give a verbal message to one of her girlfriends so they would reveal it to her during the lunch hour.

Theresa had a very domineering father and she was frightened as to what might happen to her if her father found out that she was talking to a strange young man. It was extremely difficult for her because she had fallen in love with Alfred even before she had met him. As the saying goes, he was tall, dark, and handsome and she knew many of the young girls had their eyes on him as well. Eventually, his sister Jennie saw what was happening and she began to act as the 'go-between.' Being more brave and forward, Jennie would encourage my mother to step out and talk to him and, since they all had the same lunch hour, it was a perfect place to meet and talk. She would always refuse and they would laugh and giggle about it. However, during lunch, he usually made it a point to walk by the table where she sat with her girlfriends eating lunch, and he'd throw a piece of fabric or a paper wad near her. That's about as far as he could go to get her attention.

They finally met at work and exchanged some words and each time they were together, their conversations became longer and longer. They continued their glances and eventually, my father decided to ask her to the movies. Of course, she could not go alone, so she went with her sister, Carmela or she'd go with Jennie. Naturally, Alfred would be in the theater at the same time, and they'd get to sit next to each other. In those days, they called this, 'going-out-on-the-sneak.' It was unheard of for young, single girls to date without chaperones, or without having one of their parents attending also.

As the relationship blossomed, Alfred had the desire that they should become more serious; he wanted to ask for her hand in marriage. Her father, Francesco Siracusa, who wanted to dominate the lives of all his children, played the role of the doting father who felt that there was no man good enough for either of his daughters. He refused to talk to Alfred the first time he went to his house and asked his permission to marry Theresa. When Mr. Siracusa, or *Don Ciccio (chēē-chō)* as his friends called him, found that there was a young man who was interested in his daughter, he became even more controlling and curtailed all of her social activities. He put a tremendous fear in her and she was told that she was never to speak to him again. This put a lot of pressure on Theresa and she shared these new developments with Jennie at work. Of course, Jennie shared these conversations with Alfred and he was determined not to let her father interfere with his plans for their future. He continued to pursue her attention and she ignored him for fear that her father would have his friends spy on her at the shop; then, he'd soon find out what they were doing. At this point in her life, she was twenty years old. Jennie was only fifteen years old, but she was very brave and wanted to be a part of this love adventure as it was developing. Being a young teenager, she was very enamored by this budding romance and she played a very important role in their communication. Jennie decided she would help Alfred write his letters to Theresa, and she would secretly deliver them to her since they worked together in the same shop in Fashion Park.

My mother, Theresa, saved all the letters in a very fancy box and she gave them to me because they helped to explain the love affair she had with my father. They were neatly folded and wrapped with a rose-colored, satin ribbon and tied with a bow. These letters are part of my parent's story and, although my Aunt Jennie Cavallaro wrote some of them, they give a glimpse into his heart and show what a gentleman he really was. I have only included a few letters, but as you read them, they tell a very important story of how these two lovers struggled with insurmountable adversities over a period of time; however, through determination and continual perseverance, they eventually married and lived a happy life.

After some time, Theresa's father, gave his permission for them to be married. Even though they were engaged, he never let them out of his sight so they could be alone. My father told me that during the winter and spring prior to their wedding, he would go to Theresa's house and visit on Friday and Saturday nights. They would sit in the parlor and play rolls on the player piano. My mother's fifteen-year-old sister, Carmela, was sent in the room with my grandmother to chaperone. My father said they would all gather around the piano and take turns pumping the pedals. It was a player piano that my grandfather hand-made at his work, The Aeolian Piano Factory, in East Rochester. The rolls they used had words printed on them and they would sing along and have a grand time. During this time, my grandfather sat alone in the darkened, adjoining dining room and watched from a chair where he could have full view of the activities of my mother and father. They didn't let that bother them, because my mother's sister, brothers, and her mother were in the parlor enjoying the music as well. This kind of close supervision continued until they were married.

The letters I have included begin in the year 1924 and continue into 1925; they were married on June 26, 1926. When they were married, my father was twenty-eight years old and my mother was twenty-one years old, which for that day was a bit older than usual. As you read the contents of the letters, note that my father's youngest sister Jennie, whom we all knew as Aunt Joan, wrote all the originals. They were written on plain ecru colored paper, and then folded in half. She used a black fountain pen and wrote in her usual beautiful and perfect cursive handwriting. These letters are truly a treasure. Through their contents, you will be able to understand his sincere intentions toward my mother. He always tried to do the right thing and in the right way, without ever hurting anyone's feelings. They show the patience that he was able to demonstrate under some very difficult conditions. Because of his limited English, his sister stepped in and helped him put on paper the words that were difficult for him to express. He swept my mother off her feet and, as she stated to me when I was an adult, she always knew that they would get married from the very start, but she didn't know just when that would be. In these letters, you may find a similarity to the basic story of Romeo and Juliet and the difficulty they had with their families as they tried to express their love for each other. I suggest you read them for content first, and then reread them again, concentrating on the emotions that they exude.

Love Letters Written from the Heart

<u>Letter #1:</u>

49 Moulson St.
Rochester, N.Y.

Dearest Theresa,
I'm writing this letter for my brother so that you may understand my writing more than you can his. Listen dear, why is it that you are so silent? You don't answer Alfred's letters nor mine. Are you changing lately or are you still the girl that I knew?

If you could only write a few words more often, it would cool his mind a little. Last night, my brother had a dream that your father refused him your hand. Can you tell me if this dream is true or not? Let's hope not.

In case that dream is true and <u>you</u> haven't changed your mind, with your love, he can conquer the world. All he asks is don't break that <u>sacred word</u> that you said when he gave you the ring.

Well dear, I will close with love and I will also add that he'll be waiting for an answer as quick as possible. If you haven't any spare time, **<u>make it</u>**!!
From Your Loving Friend,

Jennie Cavallaro

P.S. I forgot to tell you that Alfred sends his best regards and love and, Theresa dear, give him some kind of an answer; he acts wild lately.
x x x x x x x
o o o o o o o

Letter #2 (Written in Italian by Alfred):

Mia Deletta,

Ti scrivo queste poche righe perche mi credo che quando io vedo le tue lettere scritte dalle proprie mane tue, mi vedo rallgrare il cuore è cosí credo che sará con te. Quello che ti voglio dire io è che quando vengo alla casa a parlare con i tue genitore, come tu tieni paura, non ti fare differente cerca di fare, la risoluta lo stesso, che tu ami, non mi ai visto mai e si in coro tuo padre ti avessi domandare, non ti dimenticare della tua promessa. Salute con amore.

Alfred

Letter #2 – (Translation in English)

My Dearest,

I write these few lines because I believe that when I see your letter that's originally written by your own hand, you will see happiness in my heart and this way I will know that I am with you. That which I want to tell you is, that when I come to your house to speak with your parents, if you have fear, don't act differently except be sure that your countenance remains the same, that you love me. You have not seen me ever and in case your father were to ask, don't forget your promise to me.

Best wishes with love,

Alfred

Letter #3:

49 Moulson St.
Rochester, N.Y.
November 2, 1924

Dearest Theresa,

I received your most loving letter and Alfred and I were very glad to hear from you. I thought you had given everything up when you had not answered but fortunately Saturday, I received your letter. Did you find out your father's answer yet? When you do, please write and let me know. What makes you worry so, dear? Are you afraid you will be caught? I hope not. Listen, dear, in your last letter you wrote some words that puzzled Alfred's mind greatly.

I shall repeat them and please give the right meaning next time you write. They are: -- "If my father says "No," tell him he should not be sorry nor worry, he should forget me." Does this mean that if he says "No," that you say "No" too? Will it be all over? So your Dad has been following you lately - - Ha, Ha, trying to catch the little mouse in a trap. Be wise dear, and if he tries to get anything out of you, act innocent and don't feel alarmed. And be sure, don't spill the beans. If you catch your Dad following you again, just wait for him and say, "Hello, Dad, How are you," he won't feel so suspicious (act natural).

Today Alfred went to get an answer but didn't get any.

Listen dear, when you put your back address on, don't put your home address. Put your shop address because in case the mail man brings it back, it will go to your home and they will crown you. Well dear, I will have to close now as it is getting late.

Love and regards from all, especially Alfred.
Hoping to hear from you soon.

I remain, your loving friend,
Jennie Cavallaro

x x x x x x x x x x x x x x x x
P.S. Don't forget to answer   o o o o o o o o o o o o o o o o

Letter #4:

49 Moulson St.
Rochester, N.Y.
Nov. 9, 1924

My Dearest Theresa,

I received your most welcome letter and was very glad to hear from you. We are all in good health and hope you are the same.

Well, you were at the Strand a week ago Saturday. I'm glad you like the picture and you played a nice little joke on your father. He certainly did get fooled, Ha! Well, dear, I haven't been to Rosenberg's yet because I didn't know if the work was picking up yet or not.

*Listen, dear, you don't have to worry about my brother telling anything to your friends because he don't say anything, only that he likes you and wants you. Those people say things he has never mentioned. They just imagine them. Well, my brother got the answer from your Dad the other day and he said that you have no intentions of marriage; but, I doubt it. Don't **you**, dear? Remember your answer when he proposed dear. Now, dear, if you still keep your word, write as soon as possible and tell him how he can manage this matter.*

My brother told your friends that he's through with you but that's only so that they won't pick up any ideas and tell them to your Dad and so that your Dad will forget about this proposal.

*But Theresa dear, he **loves** you as much as ever, **even more**!*

When I receive your next letter and see about your answer, if you still keep it, he said that he will let a few months slip by and then he will come himself and speak to your Dad about it. This is just a little make-up game which he is going to be forced to play for a while so that our friends will forget about it. Otherwise, dear, your father will find out when other fellows come and propose, and you refuse them. Don't worry yourself, dear; he has a few hunches which he's going to do. Listen, dear, I've heard you are being watched. Is it true?

*He had an idea coming down Thursday or Friday at 12:30 o'clock. He will come around without stopping his car except if he sees you. If you wish to see him, be around Miller and Clifford Street; but, if you think there is danger of someone following you, **don't come**. Don't think he will get sore because he understands your situation.*

He is going to walk in front of the shop and he will just pass by and tip his hat. Have some girl friends along with you so that if he wants to let you know anything, he will call one of them and tell her what he wants to let you know.

Well dearest, I will have to close with much love and regards, especially from Alfred.

Your Dearest Friend,
X

Jennie Cavallaro
*P.S. Don't forget to answer **soon**!*

X X X X X X X X X X X X X X X X X

X X X X X X X X X X X X X X X X
X X X X X X X X X X
X X X X X X X X X

X (this is from Alfred!)

Letter #5:

49 Moulson Street
Rochester, N.Y.
February 9, 1925

My Dear Theresa,

I received your most loving letter and was more than glad to hear from you. We are all in the best of health and hope to hear the same from you.

Theresa, dear, you've wanted to know why Alfred has not written to you; well, to tell you the truth, he just don't want to get in more trouble as there has been in the past.

But, there is one thing, that he wants you to know and that is, **"Are you going to continue to be tied up in this way?"**

I know that he loves you and he worships the very ground you walk on and I know you love him too. Haven't you decided anything yet? He has been getting information about your father from friends of yours and I know that he can never come to an agreement for the very reason he went to get informed with the family which used to be his girl.

Did your father expect to get any information that was good from them? Of course not! Don't you know that? That girl still loves him and still hopes to get him back; but, her hopes are in **vain**! *Even if he's an angel from heaven, they would tell your father he was a devil from hell.*

He will try to speak to your father personally but not in your home. If he still can't persuade him to say "Yes," the only one he could depend upon for his dreams to come true is **you**!

Theresa, dear, I think you're not a baby any longer. Couldn't you tell your father that you're determined to marry him? Good God!! Get some courage, will you!! If you keep on being a sheep, the wolf will eat you up. This means, if you're going to do as your father says, you will never marry anyone whom you love. You will marry someone your father likes according to the way Alfred hears about it.

Well, dear, this letter sounds pretty blue but laugh and pick up your courage. Best regards and love from all
. Still, O O O O O O
Jennie X X X X X X
X X X X X X

P.S. Alfred has been speaking all the way through this letter to try to get an understanding. Answer as soon as you can.

P.S. Yesterday, Alfred went hunting and he got two pheasants and three rabbits and on the way coming back, he stopped over to your comare. He was trying to see about how things were getting along about that answer and they didn't seem to know anymore than he did. He wanted to go over to your house and leave some of his hunting game. But, Oh Baby, he was afraid he would be crowned King of Hallelujah! Ha! Ha! Do you blame him? Some day when everything is fixed up; he will stop in and bring something from his hunting. Bye Bye

There were more letters and notes sent during this time, too many to record here, yet they all conveyed their love for each another. Some of the postcards that my dad sent her were delivered directly to her shop at Rosenberg's, which later became Fashion Park Clothiers on Miller Street and Clifford Avenue. At that time, many of the postcards had pictures of lovers and they were sold in a series of three or four scenes. They showed couples in different scenes, in a sequence, as they were courting. On the postcards, he would note which in the series that particular card was and would relate the picture of the couple to the two of them and how it reminded him of their loving relationship. My mother kept all these letters in a little Victorian box that had little drawers in it; each drawer contained different letters from him. Only after I was in college, did my mother take the antique box out and share the letters and cards with me for the first time. I was amazed as I read them and learned more about their courtship, which was truly special. My father genuinely displayed the old adage that, 'Italians are Lovers!'

Alfred Begins a Family of His Own

For a young man who had only been in the United States for about nine years, he had already learned the English language and was working as a tailor in various shops in town. When he was twenty-four years old and living at 21 Sheridan Street, he attended classes to learn English and received his Certificate of Naturalization on June 27, 1922. By earning this certificate, he was now eligible to apply for his driver's license and vote, both of which were very important to him. During that year, he bought a car and was able to drive back and forth to work. Now, he could drive past my mother's house on Davis Street hoping to catch a chance glimpse of her in the front yard. These were good years for him. He was very happy in America.

My father made the acquaintance of some of my mother's friends and *paisani* during the time of their courtship. One of them, Nunzio Gugliuzza took a liking to my father. He had recently married a distant relative of my mother, Antoinetta Rotollo, who was related to my Grandmother Siracusa. Nunzio had been married previously and had a little boy with his first wife. His wife and son contracted the Spanish Influenza during the epidemic of 1918 and they both died, within a week of each other. The little boy was only three years old. Nunzio went back to Messina, Sicily, met Antoinetta Rotollo and they were married. During my father and mother's courtship, Nunzio tried to intercede for them with my grandfather, Francesco Siracusa, better known a *Don Cicio*. The title *'Don,'* when preceding a person's name, indicates a certain degree of importance and influence; it is only used for people who require a lot of respect. My Grandfather Siracusa demanded a lot of respect from everyone, whether he deserved it or not.

Through Nunzio's repeated efforts, he finally made it possible for my father to be received in my grandfather's home. My father's intention was to ask for my mother's hand in marriage on that evening, so he brought Nunzio with him. Nunzio's presence made all the difference in the world. He was able to speak peaceably and convincingly to my grandfather. My grandfather, however, continued to portray his symbolic and resistant posture; he sat at the dining room table, rigidly straight in his chair, arms crossed and with a stern expression on his face. He only listened and did not make any comments while my father struggled to make small talk as he approached the topic of marriage. My grandmother, my mother, and her younger sister, Carmela, sat in the adjoining room and listened to the conversation with baited breath, waiting for an affirmative confirmation to the question. After a discussion that lasted four hours, my grandfather finally relented and agreed to the marriage proposal. My father was very grateful and never forgot the role that Nunzio played in this scenario. After my parents were married, they continued a close relationship with Nunzio and Antoinetta Gugliuzza.

When Alfred's first son, Alfred Jr., was born, it was very customary in Italian families that the Best Man and Maid of Honor always baptized the first child. Therefore, when my brother was born, my father's childhood friend from Sicily and Best Man at his wedding, Nunzio Maugeri, baptized him. However, the Maid of Honor for their wedding, Rose Stella, was not asked to be his Godmother. Instead, Nunzio's sister, Grace Festa, was his Godmother. When I was ready to be baptized, my father insisted that they ask Nunzio and Antoinetta Gugliuzza to be my Godparents. Because they were somewhat older than my parents were, there was some concern that I would not have Godparents into my adult years, but they made the decision anyway. My father would say to my mother, "I can never forget how that man helped me; had it not been for him, I would have never been able to talk to your father." He never forgot people who were good to him and he treated them with the utmost respect.

After Nunzio helped him convince my grandfather to allow the marriage to take place, they eventually were married on June 26, 1926. The ceremony was held at Our Lady of Mt. Carmel Church on Woodward Street. My mother and her family attended this same church for many years. It remained my family's church home until I was grown and married.

When they married, their large wedding party consisted of ten couples, which included my parent's brothers and sisters, cousins, and very close friends. They had a large reception with approximately 250 guests at the Labor Lyceum Hall on St. Paul Street near Lowell Street. My father had made the arrangements because it was close to where his family lived. They had a live five- piece band, which played Italian music. Pizza and beer, as was typical at most weddings at that time, was served. The evening was completed with the Bridal March where the Bride and Groom led the guests around the hall to the beat of Polka music. The Bridal March ended when they made their way back to the reception table where a *Qunatera* (Quan-tĕ-ră) was waiting for them. The *Qunatera* was a large, round tray of specialty Italian cookies, arranged in circular layers that formed a high mound, with cream puffs at the very top. Then, the guests would wait in line to taste their favorite Italian cookies. They had a three-tiered wedding cake on the table, which was also served. The guest list included mostly relatives, *comares, compares, paisani*, neighbors, and their friends from work. My father told me it was one of the biggest weddings, people had seen, in a long time.

Their first apartment was on Martin Street and where my brother, Alfred, was born. The birth occurred at home with a doctor present, which was very common in those days. They resided there until 1930 and moved to an apartment on First Street for a short time. It was close to Fashion Park Tailor Factory and convenient for my father, since he had to walk to work. From there they moved to Miller Street, which is where I was born. However, by that time, they decided to go to Highland Hospital for my birth. We lived on Miller Street for a couple of years, moved to Clifford Avenue, also very close to Fashion Park, and stayed there until about 1937. At that time, my parents bought a house on Weld Street where I lived until I was married; they remained there until 1962 when they built a new home in West Webster, New York.

When I was born, we lived at 28 Miller Street and we rented an apartment from the LoPresti family. There were two houses on the lot and we lived in the house in the back of the lot. At that time, my mother was a stay-at-home mom with two young children; she was able to become friendly with the neighbors. The family across the street had four or five young girls and they loved to walk with my mother when she was out with her two young boys. They were the Altovina family and they became very good friends with my family. Next door to us, at 30 Miller Street, was the Pipitone family. Benny Pipitone had just gone to Italy to marry his second wife, Rose, who was my mother's age and could speak no English. She and my mother became instant friends and a lifelong relationship developed with the entire family. After we moved from Miller Street, the friendship continued. Benny had a daughter, Grace, with his first wife; he and Rose had a son, Sam, who was my age. A few years later, they had a daughter. Rose thought so highly of my parents that they asked them to be Godparents for their daughter. Shortly after the birth, they surprised my parents by announcing they were naming their baby girl, Theresa, after my mother. Benny had a hobby and business in his home; he raised canaries. As a result, we always had a birdcage in our home with a canary or two that would always be chirping and singing. They were good people and good friends for many years.

When my parents bought the house on Weld Street, it was a two-story home. My father, in his spare time, converted it to a two-family home. His thought was that he could have tenants living upstairs, which would help to pay for the house mortgage. We always had wonderful tenants living upstairs and we became good friends with them. At one point, my father wanted to enlarge the kitchen downstairs, but there was no cellar wall upon which to build the extension. Therefore, he decided to dig out the cellar himself. He had a lot of help and I remember my Uncle Al Lizzio and Russell Trovato assisted him. They dug the cellar out by hand, and hauled the dirt into the backyard. They built the cellar wall and installed plumbing. It became my mother's new washing area, a second bathroom, a wine cellar for my dad; it also had a storage area for the canned preserves my parents made each year at harvest time. It was a lot of work, but it allowed him to remodel the kitchen completely, build an extended breakfast nook, and increase the existing storage area for the rest of the cellar. They lived in that house for approximately thirty years and it brought them much joy. He worked hard to make it a comfortable family home and every corner of it contained memories for all of us.

Alfred's Children

My parents had two sons, Alfred Angelo Jr. and Richard Frank. We were a little more than five years difference in age. My father was very happy to have two sons and to have the opportunity to carry on the Cavallaro name. That was always very important to him. He made it a point to include both of us in everything he did; he taught us many lessons, which we were able to carry on into our adult lives and pass on to our own children.

Alfred Angelo Cavallaro Jr.
June 30, 1927 – May 25, 1986

My brother, their first-born son, was born at home when my parents lived on Martin Street in Rochester, New York. He was a large baby, and at full term, weighed over nine pounds at birth. He was named Alfred Angelo Cavallaro for a particular reason. My father wanted to name him Angelo after his father, Angelo Cavallaro; but we already had an Angelo in the family, Angelo Lizzio, which may have caused some confusion. Therefore, they decided to name him Alfred after my father, and give him the name of his paternal grandfather, Angelo, as his middle name. As my brother grew older, he always used 'Junior' after his name; but in reality, he wasn't really a junior, because my father's middle name was Michael.

During his first years, my brother was a very active child. He walked prior to age of one, in fact, my mother remembered him walking by himself at about ten months of age. My parents always said that he never really walked, he always ran to wherever he was going. His favorite game was to throw a ball and then to run and chase after it. He never grew tired of that game and played it repeatedly. He had a normal infancy and reached all the developmental milestones that children achieve during their first couple of years of childhood. Everything was on schedule for him and he was growing up to be a healthy and fine young boy.

At about twenty-two months of age, in the spring of 1929, he became ill with a fever and confined to his crib. He would just lay limp in his crib. He didn't want to eat, nor had the energy to move. This was very unlike him because he had always been such an active and energetic child. The doctors made home-visits at that time and came to examine my brother. Their doctor had difficulty diagnosing my brother's symptoms, but suggested he may be teething. He told my parents not to be concerned over it, that it was likely minor. He instructed them to call in a week and let him know how he was doing. My parents bought a large rocking chair and my mother held him all day long and rocked him to comfort him. He was so weak; he would just lie in her arms and stare into space. After a week, the fever was gone and the doctor visited again. My parents were still concerned. Although he appeared better, he was still somewhat listless and not his normal, active self. Again, the doctor said that they needed to give him time to recuperate and regain his strength. During the following month, they noticed that he wasn't running as he used to. During his playtime at the park, he tended to limp, drag his left leg a bit, and fall quite often. This was very unusual since he had never been clumsy before being ill. My aunts and uncles observed this behavior also and encouraged my parents to seek additional medical help.

They were very concerned this time so they took him directly to the doctor's office. The medical team gave him extensive tests and advised them to see two more specialists. His symptoms of limping and dragging his left leg continued to be more pronounced and it became difficult for him to walk by himself. My parents had to carry him everywhere they went.

About a month later, the Orthopedic Specialist called them in for a consultation. My parents were told the specific diagnosis for my brother, Infantile Paralysis, which was the name they used at that time for the illness we now know as Polio. The team of specialists felt he had contracted it just prior to the time he had the fever for a week; it was attacking the muscles and nerves of his left leg. The news was devastating to my parents. Just the use of those words, Infantile Paralysis were so shocking that when they heard them in the doctor's office, my mother told me she put her hands over her ears and screamed....she didn't want to hear the reality of his illness. Infantile Paralysis was a dreaded disease, which was feared by all parents because they knew it attacked young children and it was incurable. So many children throughout the community were in leg or arm braces, on crutches, or permanently confined to wheel chairs. There was no vaccine at that time and the disease ran havoc with each little body it attacked. The team of doctors also told them the disease would progress and get worse. In their prognosis, they said he would be in a full leg-brace for the rest of his life and it was doubtful if he'd ever be able to walk normally or lead an ordinary life. In fact, the team of doctors at Strong Memorial Hospital in Rochester, New York told them he would never be able to do things other children would do and that my parents had to resolve themselves to that kind of a life for him. Having received this news, they only foresaw him as an invalid for the rest of his life. Their visions of the normal, active, and happy little boy they had just a month ago, were gone. They went home and tried to adjust to this shocking reality, but all my mother could do was to hold him in her arms and rock him in their rocking chair.

Incidentally, they kept that rocking chair in their bedroom for their entire lives; my mother still had it in her bedroom when she was living in her new home in Webster, New York.

At that same time, late in 1929, a new movie was released called The Singing Fool with Al Jolson, which was a follow-up to his previous film, The Jazz Singer. My brother was about three years old. Many of my parent's friends had seen this movie and knowing the story line, they advised my parents not to see it. However, my parents liked Al Jolson and, against the advice of their friends, they went to see the movie anyway. My Aunt Carmela came over to baby-sit and they went to the movies. The film portrayed the life of a successful singer, who went on the skids after the death of his young son. It contained the first song to sell over one million copies and eventually sold over three million copies. The title of the song was, Sonny Boy. In fact, the film was best known for Al Jolson's singing performance of the song, Sonny Boy. The film was a smash hit, grossing over four million dollars, which was a lot at that time. It was the most successful film in all of Warner Brother's history. The story line of the film is about a little boy who was three years old and, as my parents shared with me, looked just like my brother....same haircut, same age, and had an incurable disease. His name was Sonny Boy. When Al Jolson sang the song, Sonny Boy, in the film, my parents related it to what they were experiencing with my brother. Al Jolson cried while he held his son on his lap and sang the touching words to his dying little boy. There wasn't a dry eye in the entire theater; people could be heard sobbing, and weeping.

At this point, I want to pause this story and let you read the words of this very sweet and tender song. As you read the words, consider the father singing it to a child whom he knew had an incurable disease.......and also consider my parents hearing it, knowing their son was in that same situation.

Sonny Boy
(Words and Music by Al Jolson, Bud DeSylva, Lew Brown and Ray Henderson)

Climb upon my knee, Sonny Boy.
Though you're only three, Sonny Boy.
You've no way of knowing, there's no way of showing,
What you mean to me, Sonny Boy.
When there are gray skies, I don't mind the gray skies,
You make them blue, Sonny Boy.
Friends may forsake me, let them all forsake me,

> I still have you, Sonny Boy.
> You're sent from Heaven, I know your worth,
> You've made a Heaven for me, right here on earth,
> When I am gray dear, promise you won't stray dear,
> I love you too, Sonny Boy.

========

> You're my dearest prize, Sonny Boy.
> Sent from other skies, Sonny Boy.
> Let me hold you nearer, one thing makes you dearer,
> Through your mother's eyes, Sonny Boy.
> When there are gray skies, I don't mind the gray skies,
> You make them blue, Sonny Boy.
> Friends may forsake me, let them all forsake me,
> You'll pull me through, Sonny Boy.
> You're sent from Heaven, and I know your worth,
> Why, you've made a Heaven for me, right here on earth,
> The angels, they don't do wrong, for they love you always,
> Now I love thee too, Sonny Boy.

In the movie, the child died, the father lost his job, and went into a deep depression. Although my parents didn't think my brother would die, they experienced similar emotions as the father in the film and had a great deal of compassion for him.

On their way home, they discussed the similarities that were in the movie to what they were experiencing in their own lives. At that point, my mother, being the determined person that she was, said, "I'll never let that happen to our son. I don't care how many doctors we have to go to or how many hospitals we have to take him to, we need to get more opinions, and more help." As they walked home from the theater in the snow, my mother said that my father was shouting so loud that people in their houses could hear him. They became crusaders during that walk home and they were going to take the situation into their own hands and get something done for their little boy who could not walk anymore.

Although they were shocked at the prognosis, and the fact that no one could give them any reason as to how he contracted the disease; nor how to correct the paralysis, they were determined to do everything in their power to find help for their child and to reverse the predictions they'd been given. From that day on, things changed for my brother and for my parents. They began to take him to doctor after doctor, specialist after specialist, treatment after treatment to find some cure or help for him. They found a team of doctors to assist them and became part of a group of parents, all of whom had children with the same disease and all who wanted to find as much help for their children as possible. The term disease is used, because, at that time, it was considered a contagious disease.

Nevertheless, that's not all that changed. After that day, my brother's name also changed. It did not change on his birth certificate or any other legal document; however, everyone began to call him Sonny. He became the Sonny Boy from the movie. It was a reminder to the whole Cavallaro family that their Sonny Boy would rise up above this disease and fight it with all his might.

Therefore, all the family knew my brother as Sonny Boy. My mother sang that song to him often. We all called him Sonny at home, including the extended family of aunts, uncles, and cousins. All his friends in the neighborhood called him Sonny, but in school, the teachers knew him as Alfred. This continued into his teen years. When he entered high school, he wanted to be called Al, which sounded a bit more grown up; but, we at home continued to call him Sonny. It was a hard transition for us to make. Because of his continual requests, when he was in his last years of high school, my parents and I started to call him Al, as difficult as it was to make the change. However, even in his adult life and after he was married, my aunts and uncles continued to call him Sonny. He took it in stride, but I know he didn't like it. As an adult, my brother would cringe whenever anyone called him Sonny…..he always felt it was a name for a little boy and not a grown adult. When I went back to Rochester recently, all my cousins still referred to him as Sonny. To some, the name never left him; he would always be Sonny Boy.

During my brother's battle with Polio, I remember several incidents that surrounded my family. Some of them were told to me, but many were observed while I was a little boy growing up in our home. By the time I was born, he was well into his treatments and already had some of his many surgeries.

As my parents were recommended to various doctors and hospitals for treatment, it was Doctor Wentworth, at Strong Memorial Hospital, that gave them the most hope. He told them that, although he could not guarantee it, he believed that if my brother had another series of operations on his left foot and leg, he could alleviate the crippling affect he was experiencing. At that point, the muscles in his left leg were pulling and contracting so much, his leg could not straighten out and was always bent backwards, which caused him to limp severely; he was not able to use the heel of his foot when he walked.

Through the years that followed, my brother was on crutches and his leg was in a metal brace to keep it straight; it gave him more support when walking. As the disease progressed and his conditioned worsened, they were concerned about where he would go to school. He couldn't function physically in a regular classroom. They recommended he go to a special school in the City School District that had an Orthopedic Wing. That was at No. 5 School located on North Plymouth Avenue. We lived on the east side of the city and the school was on the west side, which was quite a distance from where we lived. A special bus came to our house, took him to school in the morning, and then returned him home at night. When we moved to Weld Street, I was about three years old and my brother was eight years old; he was in third grade and had already started to attend the orthopedic classes at the new school. While he was there, in addition to his regular schoolwork, he received physical and water therapy two to three times daily with other children in his classroom that had Infantile Paralysis. There were nurses and therapists in each classroom all day long. As my mother explained, most of the children were far worse than he was when considering the degree of mobility they had. It was at No. 5 School, where my family met and became good friends with Joe Falvo and his wife and family. They had a son, Joseph, who also had Infantile Paralysis and was in the same class. Mr. Falvo had a funeral home located next door to the Catholic Church we attended on Woodward Street, Our Lady of Mount Carmel. That friendship continued well after the two boys became adults.

Each year, my brother attended camp for most of the summer at The Rotary Sunshine Camp that was owned by The Rotary Club of Rochester. Most of the children in his class at No. 5 School and from other locations in the city attended the camp, so he was always with many friends. It was located in Durand Eastman Park on Lakeshore Boulevard and was specifically for the use of disabled children in the city of Rochester. Most of the children who had Infantile Paralysis attended the camp. As a young boy, I remember going there every Sunday afternoon during the summer to visit him with my parents or other relatives. We would spend the entire afternoon with him and leave in the early evening. Many times, we would stay and have dinner with him and all the children in the large building that housed the cafeteria. Most of the boys and girls were in braces, wheel chairs, or on crutches. Once my brother found that his physical strength was improving, he didn't need to wear braces any longer. He found that he could walk on his own and eventually, he became an assistant counselor for the camp. His new role was to help all the others get from one place to another, to help them at game time, or to wheel them into the cafeteria at mealtime. He enjoyed the new responsibilities. When we would visit him, it was as if he owned the camp because he knew where everything was located and everyone knew him. He was quite popular with the staff and all the children. They all liked him and learned to become dependant upon him. The last year he attended, even though he was well enough not to participate, he insisted upon going because he loved being there and felt they couldn't get along without him. He was an encouragement to the other children; he was making a significant difference in their lives.

Huge pine trees surrounded the large, park-like facility. The grounds were meticulous and they were scattered with many, spacious, one-story dormitories for boys and separate dormitories for girls. There were numerous fields, playground equipment, and a large clinic on-site to provide physical therapy for all the children. My brother loved that camp. He attended Rotary Sunshine Camp until he entered the ninth grade.

When he entered seventh grade, he began attending No. 14 School in our neighborhood. Eventually, he went to East High Annex for eighth grade. He attended the old East High School on Alexander Street during his high school years. As soon as he entered eighth grade, he began leading a very busy life. He had jobs of selling newspapers on the corner of Main Street and Scio Street, delivered newspapers to about one hundred customers on his own paper-route, worked at a grocery store, and became involved with sports at school. He also became a member of the YMCA located very close to our home. He played basketball and swam in their indoor pool. He became very good at playing basketball and played on the high school team for a while. He was also very proficient at swimming and spent most of the winter months at the Y's indoor pool. He was there during most of his spare time after school and, many times, in the evening.

I have many fond memories of Rotary Sunshine Camp; however, one will remain in my mind forever. I was approximately seven years old, which would have made my brother twelve years old. On one Sunday that summer, when we arrived at the park grounds to visit my brother, he ran toward us as soon as he saw our car approach the parking lot. I noticed that he was holding something behind his back. He didn't reveal what he was hiding, but immediately took me by the hand and urged me to run with him to the large, circular pond located in the center of the grassy complex. My parents ran with us, wondering why he was displaying all the excitement. When we arrived at the pond, he and I knelt by the water's edge and he showed me what he was holding behind his back. It was a blue sailboat with a white cloth sail attached to its mast. He put it in the water and it floated perfectly along the edge of the pond. A string was tied to it and he told me to pull it so it would float further. I did exactly that and we had so much fun sailing the little boat. There were other children at the pond, also with small sailboats doing the same thing. He took it out of the water, dried it off by wiping it on his shorts, held it in both hands and, extending his arms, gave it to me saying, "It's yours, I made it for you this week." During the previous week, they had a woodshop class he attended and he made the boat, painted it blue, and put the cloth sail on it himself. I was so excited! I never had a sailboat before, and coming from the city, had never sailed one either. I took the boat home and played with it in the sink and the bathtub, but most of the time it sat on my bookshelf in my bedroom. It was so much fun, and I really loved that boat. I don't know whatever happened to it, but I do have a snapshot that was taken on that day, and I was holding that little blue sailboat in my hands. I treasure that photo and the fond memory it brings back to me. In later years, when we were adults, he would sometimes joke about the little blue sailboat he made for me, once upon a time.

From the time he contracted Infantile Paralysis through his junior high years, he had many operations on his left foot; sometimes two surgical procedures in one year. Each surgery came with more therapy and treatments for his foot and leg. I remember visiting him at the hospital after one of his surgeries; his leg was in a cast and held in traction high in the air by chains and a rope attached to a metal pipe over his bed. He must have seen the look on my face when I walked into the room because he said, "Don't worry; this won't last; I'll have it off in no time at all. I'm going to walk just like anyone else." He was an encouragement to all of us while he lay in his hospital bed.

Eleven years after he had been diagnosed with the disease, and just prior to his ninth and final surgery, we were all in the doctor's office listening to his consultation. The doctor looked at my parents and my brother and said, "I know you've had a lot of surgeries, but I believe the one I'm going to recommend now is really needed and may help you more than any of the others. I think you should do it. What do you think?" Before my parents could even answer the question, my brother stood up from his chair and said, in a very determined voice, "Let's do it, doctor. I'm going to fight this! I want to walk just like everyone else!" He had that ninth and final operation and, the doctor was right, it did more for him than any of the other surgeries had done. Nevertheless, that outrageous determination never left him. He fought it with all his might, and in the final analysis, he won over the paralysis! Nothing would keep him down ever again.

As he entered into his high school years, my parents had his shoes handmade in order to support his arches and elevate his leg a bit; regular shoes would not fit his feet. In addition, he needed his right shoe to be one size, and his left shoe to be a different size; this was because his left foot and leg did not develop as rapidly as the right leg did. You would never know this unless he was wearing a bathing suit at the beach or was wearing shorts because it wasn't very noticeable. He had to have a special mold made for the sole of his left shoe so his foot would fit properly and would elevate his leg. His left leg was a bit shorter than his right leg, but he compensated for it and the special shoes made it impossible for anyone to notice. I remember going to the shoemaker's shop and watching, as they would press the mold onto his foot. A hot cork material molded to his foot and hardened when it cooled so his foot would have a proper setting. My parents were very watchful that he took good care of those shoes since they were so costly.

At this point in my brother's story, I want to share an incident, which was very important to my brother's outlook on his life. At the time of this incident, my brother was approximately fourteen years old and I was nine years old. When we were growing up on Weld Street, we lived in the middle of the long street. There were many children in the neighborhood; 99% of whom were from Italian families. My brother had his group of friends to play with, and I had mine. Many times our friends came from the same family because they had children at both of our age levels. We both had many friends in our neighborhood. At the end of the block, there was a house with a large family, which had many children. Most of the kids on our street didn't play with these particular children in this family because they were very rough and scrappy kids who were always in trouble. Approximately six or seven of the children in that family were boys. All the children on the block called them 'The Blue Shirt' kids. They were on Public Assistance (Welfare) and they would receive free clothing from the Welfare Department. The Welfare Department only issued blue shirts to needy families, thus, the reason for their name.

On one Saturday morning during the summer, my mother was at home cleaning the house and cooking, while my father was at the lumber yard, getting some wood for a project. I was playing in front of our house with some friends. All of a sudden, I saw my brother run into our yard and into the house. This was very unusual because my brother was always the last to be in the house when he didn't need to be there. Behind him, I saw the mother of 'The Blue Shirt' kids walking in a brisk manner toward our house, followed by several of her children, along with most of the other neighborhood kids. I ran into the house to tell my mother, and in a moment, the mother of 'The Blue Shirt' kids was banging on our back porch screen door, yelling for my mother to come out. My mother opened the screen door very calmly, stood in the doorway, and held the screen door open with an extended arm, to talk with her. The mother had one of the boys standing in front of her. His shirt was ripped and he had a bloody nose with much of the blood all over his shirt. It looked bad; and I thought, "Oh, oh, my brother's really going to get it now." She began to shout at my mother and told her a tale about my brother having a fight with her son; how he ripped his shirt, and gave him a bloody nose. She wanted my mother to beat my brother so it would never happen again. My mother asked the woman to calm down and repeat the tale to her. Of course, as the story was retold, she said that her son did nothing and that my brother jumped over their fence, entered their yard, and proceeded to hit him. At that point, my mother looked sternly at my brother and said, "Is that true?" I can still see my brother, with a look of disdain on his face, and in a pleading voice, I heard him say, "But, Ma, he called me a *cripple*." My mother looked at him and very slowly repeated his words while accentuating the word, *cripple*. She said, "Are you sure he called you a *cripple*?" As he spoke to assure her what he had been called, all the other kids in our yard chimed in and said, "He's telling the truth, Mrs. Cavallaro. We heard him say it and he said Sonny was a cripple more than once."

I could see the color in my mother's face immediately turn to a bright red. At that point, she left the doorway, shut the screen door with a slam behind her, went down the two porch steps, and got right into that lady's face. She pointed her finger at her and in her loudest voice said, "My son is not a *cripple* and is as normal as any other child. I have told my son never to allow anyone to call him by that name. He has a name, his name is Sonny, and that's what you call him. I am telling him in front of you, that if your son or any of your other kids call him a *cripple* again, he has my permission to give him another bloody nose and a black eye to go with it. Now, you get out of my yard and don't you or any of your kids ever come back here again!" The woman was visibly shocked by my mother's actions, as was I. I had never seen my mother speak to anyone like that before now. As my mother continued to point her finger at the woman, telling her to get out of our yard, the woman began walking backward toward our front entrance, and then turned around in a quick manner, rapidly walking to get out to the street. My mother continued to follow her to the front of our house and watched her as she walked back home. I guess she wasn't sure what my mother would do to her. Her kids all followed her out of the yard and down the street. Then, my mother turned to all my brother's friends and said, "And don't any of you ever call him a *cripple* either. It's not nice to call people those kinds of names. He has a name and that name is Sonny; that's what I call him and that's what you're to call him too."

She went back into the house and I stayed outside with my brother and all our friends. Although he said nothing to me after that incident, I remember all the kids crowding around my brother, patting him on the back, giving him assurance of having done something good. My brother walked a little bit taller and with a little skip in his step for the rest of that day. He was the hero on Weld Street; he had beaten up one of 'The Blue Shirt' kids, something each of them had wanted to do for a long time, but were afraid to try. I think all the boys on the street were encouraged not to ever be afraid of 'The Blue Shirt' kids again.

When my father came home, my mother recounted the story to him. As I stood listening and watching my father's reactions, I could see the veins in his neck and forehead expand, and his color become more flushed as he asked more questions to get all the details. In my mind, all I could think was, is this what it's like to see a volcano erupt, or is this the beginning of World War II on Weld Street? He wanted to know where they lived because he needed to speak to them. Therefore, my brother and I led the way and my father marched down the street to their house. We opened the gate, went up the wooden porch steps, and knocked on the door. We knew they were inside, but they never answered the door and my father never got the opportunity to speak to them. When we returned home, he also told my brother the same thing my mother had told him, "Don't you ever allow anyone to call you a *cripple* again….you're as good as anyone else, if not better….remember, you're a Cavallaro…*Capish*?" (că-pēsh….meaning, do you understand?) Don't ever forget that!" And he didn't!

At the end of the summer and not long after that incident, 'The Blue Shirt' kids moved from our neighborhood and we never saw them again; however, the stories about them continued to be repeated often among all the kids of the neighborhood. The Greco family moved into that house. One of their sons, Tony Greco became a good friend of my brother in high school. They had a large family also, and my brother spent a lot of time in their home. Mrs. Greco had him over for dinner many times and Mr. Greco became a good friend of my father. I never forgot that incident with 'The Blue Shirt' kids and neither did my brother. More important than the fighting incident, the bloody nose and the encounter of the mothers, was the message that we were both taught that day. We were not allowed to call anyone else names, or to provoke others so they would call us names either….and why? Because we were Cavallaro's, this made us as good as anyone else, if not better! And we both understood!

Through all the years of surgeries and therapy, my brother's determination remained very strong. He was able to overcome what the doctors had pre-determined would be his fate as a disabled person and spend the rest of his life in braces or a wheel chair. He never wore another brace on his leg and he was able to lead a healthy and normal life. My parents related the story often of him saying, as he would lie in traction in a hospital bed, "I'm not going to be here forever. I'm going to play basketball and I'm going to fly an airplane someday.....just wait and see." As they heard a twelve year old say these words, they never expected that his determination would come to fruition. He was able to overcome all the physical obstacles and do the things normal young men could do and what he so desired to do in his lifetime. He played basketball, swam, and participated in a variety of other sports; and one day, when he was accepted in the United States Air Force, he was able to fly in planes and be the aerial photographer that he always dreamed to be.

It all began in junior high when my brother developed a liking for airplanes. He and I would ride our bikes to The Hobby Shop on University Avenue, which was not far from our house. A private home had been converted into a business. We would lay our bikes on the front lawn and go into The Hobby Shop. It was filled to capacity, floor to ceiling, with all kinds of projects, activities, kits, models to make, and all kinds of good things; a child's delight! We would browse for what seemed like hours and finally he would buy a model airplane kit. He'd bring it home, get a large piece of sturdy cardboard, and began to cut the pieces for his airplane out of balsa wood with a special X-ACTO knife. I would intently watch him; but was always cautioned never to touch any of the pieces. He'd use common pins to keep the pieces of balsa wood in place and would then glue them together. After the separate parts of the plane were completely glued, he'd carefully cover them with colored tissue paper. It was a long, tedious process and he was very neat and patient in doing this work. It usually took a couple of weeks or more to complete one plane. While he was making the plane, he'd store it and all the loose parts on the large cardboard piece, under his bed. When the plane was completed and the family had all admired it, he would hang it in our bedroom from the ceiling with thread. We shared a bedroom together and there were always numerous planes, all different varieties, and colors hanging from the ceiling, from the walls, or sitting on our dresser and bookshelves. He had a love for aviation and his ambition was to be able to fly planes. Many Sunday afternoons, after dinner was completed, my mom and dad would take us for a ride in the country, and we'd go to the Monroe County Airport, which was used for small airplanes. We would stand outside the chain link fence watching the small, private planes take off and land. Of course, my brother knew the names and details of each one. It was truly his passion.

His interest in aviation grew stronger as he became an adult. During the 1940s and 1950s, there was a mandatory draft and, at eighteen years of age, all males were required to register for the armed services. When my brother went to register and they heard he had Infantile

Paralysis as a child, he was classified as 4F; which meant that he would never be called into the U.S. Army. In a way, my parents were relieved that he would never have to go to war. However, in June of 1948, my brother went to the U.S. Air Force Recruiting Center to see about joining. He did this without my parent's knowledge. At the Recruiting Center, they gave him written tests, all of which he passed with excellence. They gave him a physical exam and said they would only allow him to go into the Air Force if he and his parents signed a waiver relieving the Air Force of any responsibilities concerning his left leg. He was so excited. When he came home, he told my parents what he had done and then handed them the papers to sign. After the initial shock of what he wanted to do had worn off, after the heated discussion had ceased, and the crying was completed, they agreed to sign the papers, which allowed him to enter into the U.S. Air Force. My brother literally jumped for joy; it was the happiest I had seen him in a long time.

He entered the Air Force during November of 1948 and he was discharged in September 1952; he served in the U.S. Air Force for four years. After he was discharged, he received a medal for heroism. In a newspaper article written about him for this deed, it stated, "Although they didn't want to take him into the Air Force in the first place because they felt he was physically unfit for military duty, he knew better and continued to try to get in. He hammered away until he convinced the military brass that he could do as good a job as anyone else and it turned out that he did just a little bit better." This is what my parents imbedded into him since he was a small child; he never forgot those words.

He served at Lackland Air Force Base in San Antonio, Texas for basic training; from there he went to Eglin Air Force Base in Pensacola, Florida, Lowery Air Force Base in Denver, Colorado, and the Air Force Academy in Colorado Springs for additional Aerial Photography training. He was sent over-seas and served in combat for more than two years in Korea. He was stationed at the Air Force base in Seoul, South Korea during the Korean Conflict. He spent some R & R in Tokyo, Japan; and finished his four-year enlistment with about six months at the Thule Air Force Base in Greenland, which is about seven hundred miles north of the Arctic Circle.

He had a tremendous experience in the Air Force; he earned various educational degrees, he was awarded many service medals, he made national news when he rescued a Korean family from a fire, and his picture was in many newspapers; he came home a hero. In an article that appeared in the Rochester Democrat and Chronicle newspaper, it featured my brother's story of the heroic event he performed in Korea. It was entitled, "Air Force Rejected Him Once…

but He's a Hero Now." The article explained how he was attached to the 8th Fighter Bomber Wing Photo Lab in South Korea. A small excerpt from that article follows:

"While riding in a jeep on a freezing day in February 1952, Airman Cavallaro was passing a hut that was engulfed in flames. Outside, a young Korean child was screaming and Airman Cavallaro saw him run back into the burning hut. Later, he found out that the boy had gone back in to try to save his mother. He leaped from the jeep while it was still moving, knocked the down the door, and ran into the house to rescue a woman and her child who were trapped inside. Inside the smoke filled room, he saw the mother on her knees, blindly groping for a few belongings as she tried to escape. She was frantically searching for her little boy also whom she heard screaming, but she couldn't see him. All she knew was that she wanted to get him, their few belongings and get to freedom from the burning hut. After he got them to safety outside, the Rochester Airman went back into the flames to salvage as many of the pitiful belongings as he could. The woman was badly burned and was blinded by the fire, but Sergeant Cavallaro saved her and her son. Despite the danger that he was in, he escaped unharmed. When it was all over, she and her little boy were safe, but the hut was totally destroyed by the fire."

For this act of bravery, my brother received the Soldier's Medal for Heroism. It is the seventh highest military decoration a man can earn in the military. He received this before a full-scale military review at Sampson Air Force Base in Geneva, New York upon his return from Korea. So on that Saturday in July, our family went to Sampson Air Force Base to attend the Medal Award Ceremony. In a full military service accompanied by the Air Force Marching Band, Major General Richard C. Lindsay, with three Colonels accompanying him, presented him the medal. They had Air Force photographers take pictures of the event and they sent them to our family the following week. The citation read in part, that...

....*"Sgt. Alfred Cavallaro Jr. distinguished himself by an act of heroism, displaying outstanding courage and complete disregard for his own personal safety. Despite over-powering heat from the flames and suffocating smoke which engulfed him, he carried the Korean woman to safety...such heroism reflected great credit upon the United States in the eyes of the Korean people."*

His picture of the incident appeared in the Rochester Democrat and Chronicle. When he was discharged from the U.S. Air Force later that year, he received a letter stating he was being recommended to receive The Korean Presidential Citation, in addition to The Soldier's Medal for Heroism.

I shall never forget that day as long as I live. Al was very proud of that award and so was the whole family. On the way back home to Rochester, we stopped by to visit and have dinner with Al's Godparents, Nunzio and Santina Maugeri in Fulton, New York, which was located very close to Sampson Air Force Base. Later that day, I found my father sitting by himself in the backyard, with Al's Certificate in his hand, reading it over and over again. At one point, I asked him why he was reading it so many times. His response to me was short, but very poignant, "This is what it means to be a Cavallaro…He was as good as everyone else and a little bit better." As the certificate had a tremendous impact upon my father that day, his answer to my question had a greater and lasting impact upon me. It was a day that was certainly a high point in our family history and it will live in infamy.

His time in the Air Force was a dream-come-true for him; something he had wanted to do since he was a young boy. He achieved his dream; he flew in many airplanes and he proved he was as good as any other airman…..if not, a lot better.

On June 19, 1954, Al married Mary Jane Pilato in a beautiful ceremony at Our Lady of Mt. Carmel Church; the same church where my parents were married some twenty-eight years earlier. Al and Mary Jane had four children: Cheryl, Darlene, Christopher, and Scott. Al worked for Eastman Kodak Company as an Inspector in their Product Quality Lab. In 1971, he transferred with Eastman Kodak to their Windsor, Colorado facility. His family relocated to Ft. Collins, Colorado and he lived there until his death on May 25, 1986.

My brother proved to the world that he was going to fight the disease that he had as a child. He did everything necessary to move from success to success, to get ahead, and to put the paralysis behind him. He was able to show the world that he capable of playing as hard as anyone could; he participated on basketball teams, swam with excellence, and eventually served his country in a heroic manner. He proved to many people, including members in our own family, that he could achieve his heart's desire and serve in the U.S. Air Force, despite all outward appearances. My brother was a survivor; he was a fighter; he was determined to achieve; and none of it was accomplished without a lot of effort, pain, and perseverance on his part. He knew that he had the support of my mom and dad in whatever he chose to do, and they stood by his side through it all. In his spirit, he kept pushing himself to move ahead successfully. I wish I had some of those qualities; I learned a lot from my older brother. I only wish he were still here so I could tell him in person, myself. My heart aches as I sit here writing about these events we both lived through. It seems like they happened only yesterday, and we took them for granted, but they were so important for both of us. He will always be

Sonny to me and to many other people, a name that means so much to our family. If I listen hard enough, I can almost hear my mother still singing that song to him again…. "Climb upon my knee Sonny Boy." In his own way, he made 'A Heaven for all he touched, right here on earth.' We all love you, Sonny!

Richard Frank Cavallaro
September 16, 1932

I am Alfred's second son, Richard, born five years after Alfred. As was Sicilian custom, the second son was named after the maternal grandfather. Since my brother had his paternal grandfather's name as his middle name, I received my maternal grandfather's name, Frank, as my middle name. There were no other children in the Cavallaro family named Richard. When I was very young, I curiously asked my mother why they chose the name, Richard, for me. Her response was they preferred not to name me after any family member. They chose my name mainly because there was a popular movie star at that time who they liked, and his name was Richard Greene. Therefore, they chose the name Richard Frank. My years in education began at Chester Dewey School No. 14 for my first through seventh grades. I went to eighth grade at the East High School Annex, which was located next door to my elementary school and I graduated from the old East High School on Alexander Street.

During my elementary years, World War II was in progress. December 7, 1941 came as a shock to many Americans. In the Cavallaro household, my dad and mom were very interested in the war in Europe. Being immigrants from Sicily, they followed the progress of the war and of the Italian involvement, especially when the war reached Sicilian shores. Having left friends and relatives behind when they emigrated, it was of special interest to them as to which areas in Sicily were coming under German control.

It all began on that infamous Sunday afternoon. We had just come home from church and I was playing outside in the backyard. My father called me indoors in an excited and urgent manner. I knew something was wrong. When I ran indoors, my father, my mom and brother were already sitting on the floor in the living room in front of our tall, Philco radio. I joined them and listened, not really understanding the impact of everything that was happening. After all, being in third grade, I didn't even know where Hawaii, then a territory of the United States, or Japan were located, both names being foreign to me. I soon knew that the Japanese Imperial Navy attacked Pearl Harbor, on the island of Oahu at 8:00 a.m. Hawaiian time.

From that time on and through 1945, we were flooded with information about the war each day at school. The teachers had maps covering the classroom walls of these new areas and before long, names such as Pearl Harbor, London, Normandy, and Anzio Beach were familiar places to all of us.

At home, we listened to the news every night with great anticipation in order to follow the progress of the war. Many times, I would start to ask questions for clarification, but the response I heard was a loud, "Shh" in return. The newspapers and Life magazines in our home were full of the events and our family discussed the issues daily. Many of the young men in our neighborhood were either drafted or enlisted into the armed forces. On my way to school each day, I would see banners hanging in our neighbor's windows with one, two, or three stars to indicate the number of sons or daughters from their family who were fighting in the war. Many women at home became part of the war effort and they took jobs in factories making weapons, ammunition, and uniforms for the soldiers. I began to see American flags waving from every house in this little Italian ghetto where I lived.

Many pleasures we had known, became scarce. Things like butter, sugar, meat, and flour could only be purchased with stamps that were in Ration Books. I became very familiar with the Ration Books because I would accompany my parents when they went grocery shopping. We always went to the same neighborhood market on Central Park. As we stood at the long counter to checkout, the grocer, Mr. Miceli, would ask for stamps for the items we had purchased. Each member of the family was issued a Ration Book and the stamps for each item of food were a different color. My dad would give me the books, and under careful guidance, I was allowed to tear out the stamps that we needed to give the grocer. Occasionally, we didn't have enough stamps for what we had purchased. When that would occur, we couldn't buy the item. Sometimes, Mr. Miceli had extra stamps that other customers didn't use; he generously shared them with my father so we could complete our purchases. He was a good man and our grocer for many years.

During the war years, we had what was known as Air Raids. These were drills that residents had to practice in the event the United States was attacked by air; we'd then have to go under cover. All our homes had to be equipped with heavy-duty shades that we'd use if the Air Raid happened at night. When the sirens would go off, we had to turn off the lights, pull the shades down in the house, and wait inside for the duration of the practice. The concept being that if all the lights were off, the planes overheard would not see the houses or lights. When the All-Clear sirens were sounded, lights could then be turned on and the window shades could be raised. Every street was assigned an Air Raid Warden. My father signed up for the job in our neighborhood. He went for training and had to be on-call to perform his duty during an Air Raid. He wore a special helmet, and when the sirens went off, he would walk up and down the street to check that everyone had their lights off and their shades pulled down. He would blow a whistle to let them know if he could see any lights through the cracks in the shades or windows. They were so determined to have complete darkness that people were told they could not even light up a cigarette during an Air Raid drill. Sometimes, my dad would let me walk with him, up and down the street to check the houses; I even blew the whistle a few times. That was exciting for me.

The schools were very involved in many ways in the war effort. One way was by selling War Bonds. With the initiation of the selling War Bonds, students could purchase Victory Stamps every Monday morning at school. They were ten cents each and could be pasted in a pocket-sized booklet. We had to buy enough stamps to make up eighteen dollars and seventy-five cents; this would increase in value and be worth a twenty-five dollar bond in ten years. The money from the War Bonds was a way in which the people could participate in helping with the war effort. I'd bring any loose change to school my parents had, (which wasn't much), to buy stamps. Some weeks, I only had enough to buy one or two stamps. If we bought stamps during four consecutive weeks, we became members of the Junior Commandos. As a Junior Commando, we received a khaki colored cap with an emblem on it, along with a membership card. This made us official participants in the Junior Commando program for elementary-age children. That was a great day when I received my cap and card with my name on it. I really felt like part of the war effort at that time and wore my hat proudly to school with all the other students.

In early 1942, my teacher told our class that if we completely filled our book of Victory Stamps, we would be able to buy a War Bond and earn a special treat in the near future. The Liberty Bell, housed in Philadelphia's Independence Hall, was touring the United States and during the month of July, it was scheduled to be in Rochester. The city was building a large walking bridge, which spanned Main Street, from one side to the other, and the Liberty Bell would be placed in the center and on top of the bridge. Anyone who purchased a War Bond, or filled their Victory Stamp Book, could cross the bridge and personally ring the Liberty Bell.

Oh, I wanted to do that so badly! Therefore, I began buying more stamps and counting the empty spaces I still had to fill prior to the end of the school year. The last Monday of school in June arrived and I still had twenty spaces to fill; I needed two dollars to complete it. I had never purchased two whole dollars worth of War Stamps before, but my parents gave me the money necessary and I was able to complete my book of stamps so I could finally buy a War Bond. I was told to go to the bridge on Main Street on a specific day in July, with my book of stamps, to ring the bell.

The big day arrived and my mother and I went to Main Street and waited in a long line to cross the bridge. I had to cross the bridge alone because we were only bought one War Bond. My mother went to the other side of the bridge to wait for me. When it was my turn to cross the bridge, I held my completed book of Victory Stamps tightly in my hands. I climbed the steps and walked toward the Liberty Bell. There were many adults waiting in the line, however, I don't remember any children being there. There were American flags waving all over Main Street and decorated the entire bridge. Below the bridge, an Army band played songs including Off They Go into the Wild Blue Yonder, and The Stars and Stripes Forever. The bridge was so high; I didn't want to look down to the street below where many people were watching. As I walked to the center of the bridge alone, I turned in my book of War Stamps to the man standing by the bell. In return, he gave me a small, metal hammer and asked me if I knew what I was about to do. I answered him with a quick response and he said to me, "You're helping our American soldiers fight for the freedom that you will have for the rest of your life." I hit the bell with all my might and it rang loudly and clearly. I walked to the other side of the bridge where my mother was waiting, wiping tears from her eyes. She knew in her heart what I had accomplished. I didn't fully understand what I had participated in for many years later. That was the first War Bond I had ever purchased but it wasn't the last. I was a Junior Commando during my elementary school years and participated in many activities with them. As I look back over the years of 1941 through 1945, I have so many memories, but one of my fondest and the one that had the most impact on my life, was to experience my part, as a nine year old, in helping to fight for our freedom by ringing the real Liberty Bell.

My elementary school years were very eventful. One year, a group of people came to our school to give a standardized music test to all fourth graders. It was called the Seashore Music Test. The famous Eastman School of Music, located just a few blocks away from my school, had many of their male students drop out because they were called into the military to fight the war. As a result, they were offering music scholarships to fourth grade students; two fourth grade children from each school in the city who passed the music test could attend The Eastman School of Music for one year, under scholarship. I took the test with all the other fourth graders in my school. Even though I had no prior musical experience, I had no difficulty following their directions. A few weeks later, they came back to announce that another girl, Eleanor DiMitri and I were the winners from our school. I was excited, but had no idea how this would change my life.

I received a scholarship for one full year, which included a one-hour group theory lesson and a thirty-minute private piano lesson at Kilburn Hall at The Eastman School of Music. For the next four years, I continued to receive the scholarship. When the war ended in 1945, all the men returned and the music school needed space for them. They told us that, should we want to continue our musical studies, we'd have to pay for the lessons privately. My mother and father discussed this option for a long time. Lessons were not cheap and money was scarce; however, they decided that I should continue with my piano lessons. They paid for my lessons through my senior year of high school. I was always so thankful for the sacrifice my parents made for me. My music affected the entire family. Whenever we had a gathering, they would ask me to play; my mother came to all my recitals, and my father loved it when I began to learn all the Italian songs that he knew so well. When I played at home, he would sing along with me. Many times, he would teach me the melody of songs or buy the sheet music for me. When I went to college, I stopped taking lessons but the love of music continued to be an important part of my life.

Upon high school graduation, I attended Brockport State Teacher's College to obtain my teaching degree. Having never been away from home, living on campus was a new adjustment. At that time, Brockport had dormitories only for women; therefore, men had to live in private homes. I was fortunate to live directly across the street from the college in an upstairs apartment that housed ten college students; three friends from my high school and the other six were upper-classmen from the college. I really enjoyed my four years at Brockport. I made friends early that first week of school; they are still friends of mine to this day. I was involved in many organizations: a member of Delta Psi Omega which included my participation in a drama production each year, a member of the mixed chorus and the Men's Glee Club, a student writer for the school newspaper all four years, and the Layout Editor for The Saga - my senior yearbook, to name a few. I loved going to college and taking classes was so natural for me. Enjoying the school as much as I did, I decided shortly after arriving that I would declare a second major. Therefore, in addition to Elementary Education, I completed a second major in English. I graduated with a B.S. in Education in 1955.

Upon graduation, I was required to serve in the U.S. Army because the mandatory draft law was in existence. While I was attending college, I was deferred from serving in the military as long as I maintained a B+ average each semester. Although I was the first senior in my graduating class to be offered a teaching contract, I had to decline the offer because I was required to fulfill my military duty obligation first. Although this was not my priority, I entered the Army, went into the Signal Corps, and I was trained to be a high-speed radio operator, taking Morse code at more than sixty words a minute. I was sent overseas to a Signal Battalion in Darmstadt, Germany for twenty months. When I arrived, my records indicated I was a teacher; they immediately put me in a classroom, teaching Non-Commissioned Officers. It was a great opportunity because during my non-duty time, I was able to travel throughout Germany and other parts of Europe. I was very fortunate to visit Paris many times, various parts of France, Spain, Italy, Switzerland, and Austria. Because of my service in the military, I had the chance to visit and experience many different cultures. Thankfully, this was peacetime Europe and we traveled with no fear of war.

After my tour of duty with the U.S. Army in Europe, I returned to the United States and married my fiancée, Agatha Desio. My career in Education began by teaching in the City School District at No. 14 School; the same elementary school I attended as a youngster. It was a thrill to return to my former childhood school and to be part of the staff. During my first two years, my own second grade teacher was still on staff. A few years later, I returned to Brockport and received my Master's Degree in Educational Administration. I became a Testing Consultant at the City School District's main office. I was responsible for the standardized testing program for grades K-12 throughout the city of Rochester. The following year, I was appointed as Vice-Principal at No. 37 School on Carter Street. After one year, I became the Elementary Principal at No. 1 School on Hillside Avenue. In 1970, my family moved to Southern California and I accepted positions as principal at schools in both Orange and Los Angeles counties. During a short move to Colorado, I served as a principal in Loveland, Colorado, returned to California, and continued in administration of elementary schools in Orange County. My wife, Agatha, and I have four children: Richard Jr., Lisa, Cathy, and Andrea. We currently live in San Diego County in Southern California.

Alfred's Many Interests

Like his brothers and sisters, my father was a man who was never idle. He always had a project he was working on in the garage. He was continually remodeling our house, constructing room additions, painting, wallpapering, putting in new windows, or re-landscaping the entire back yard. No project was too big for him. One project had him mixing concrete and laying a complete sidewalk from the front of the house to the furthest point in the backyard. He created flowerbeds that produced the most beautiful roses on the block. His roses were his pride and joy. It was very important for him to have healthy roses; for that reason, he insisted on purchasing Jackson and Perkins rose bushes only. He said they were the best. I remember when he'd cut a budding rose, bring it in to my mother, and explain to her how it was perfectly formed. He would work on wood projects in the garage in the cold of winter and late at night, just to get them completed. He designed and created fancy wood cornices for our living and dining room picture windows. On his fancy table saw, he also cut crown moldings that he installed in every room in the house. As delicate and detailed as he was with his sewing, those traits carried over in his work with wood.

Another passion my father had was a love for hunting. Each fall, he would go hunting with his brothers, Al Lizzio, Russell Trovato and other relatives and *paisani*. He wore a fancy, beige colored hunting jacket and a matching vest. The vest had spaces on the two front panels to store all the shells, one by one, that he'd use in his guns. His jacket was equipped with two large pockets under each arm that open into the full back of the jacket where he could store the game that was caught. He would always say they were going to hunt on the farm. Later, I found out this was the same farm, which his family owned when he was a young man. In the back areas of the farm, there were large fields and wooded areas where they would hunt for all kinds of game. He would check with the new owners for permission to go into the fields to hunt. We always had a pet dog at home that my father trained to be a hunting companion. We had either beagles or cocker spaniels, both of which were hunting dogs. He would tell us how the dogs really helped them as they hunted. The dogs would come home dirty and full of burrs; we would have to wash them before nighttime. He always came home with something he had caught. It ranged from pheasants and woodchucks to rabbits. Whatever it was, he would bring them home, and my mother would prepare a nice meal with them. She usually cooked them in Italian tomato sauce. On one occasion, I tasted the rabbit my mother had cooked in the tomato sauce; I remember that I didn't like it. It was hard for me to eat any of the game after I had seen it being unloaded from their cars when they returned. He had three or four guns he used for hunting. One of them was a shotgun and later, my mother bought him a Browning Automatic, which he really wanted. He was so excited that Christmas when he opened his box. It had a beautiful wood-grained stock; it was a true work of art. He was very meticulous in cleaning his guns; he spent hours taking them apart, cleaning and oiling all their little parts, and replacing them in their separate cases. He was careful to store the guns away safely and securely in the attic of the garage. We knew we were not allowed to touch the guns once they were stored away.

My father also loved to fish. Our neighbor who lived across the street from us, Ralph Simolo, was an avid fisherman. We knew his family quite well because his wife, Mary, and my mother grew up together, and their son, Ralph, went to school with my brother. My father went fishing with Ralph at the local fishing areas around Rochester. Before long, my father was buying large tackle boxes, a variety of hooks, and different types of fishing poles with special reels. Every time we were in a hardware store, we would spend, what I felt was hours, looking at the many varieties of fishing lures. We usually left with one or two that he just had to have and would help him catch certain types of fish. He and Ralph, along with other friends would go fishing on a regular basis each summer. Sometimes, my Uncle Roger would join them, and he soon became part of the fishing group.

My father learned that Ralph went fishing with other friends to Fairhaven Beach State Park, where the fishing in Lake Ontario was supposed to be the best. He joined them and camped for a couple of weekends that summer; they came home with many fish. Now my father felt that our family also had to go camping the following summer. Therefore, he began buying camping gear and storing it in the garage. That winter, he bought a Coleman camping stove, gas lanterns, individual army cots, sleeping bags, and all the other equipment needed for the family to go camping. Now that he had this new equipment, he needed to determine how he was going to transport it to a park about sixty miles away. Therefore, he decided to build his own trailer. He bought all the pieces at the junkyard, and began building a trailer with two wheels and an 'A' frame hitch. It had twenty-four inch wooden sides all around. When he finished, it looked like a brand new trailer. He painted the sides blue, the hitch black, and attached a spare tire on the tailgate in the back. By that time, he bought at the Army-Navy Surplus store, a sixteen-man navy tent with mosquito netting around the sides and with roll-up flaps. It was covered with a thick coating of weatherproofing making it very heavy to lift. He even made special wooden boxes for the Coleman stove and lanterns, bought extra poles and stakes for the tarpaulin we'd use over the picnic tables, and an extra tarp to cover the equipment that covered the trailer as we traveled. We were set.

In the meantime, my mother would prepare things in the house; she would pack extra dishes, pots and pans, blankets, pillows, sheets; and all the things she'd need to prepare meals for the time we'd be camping. Then, the big day would come to pack the trailer. My brother and I would help him. He was so organized that he'd have us pack the things at the bottom of the trailer that we would need to use last, and things like the tent that we'd need as soon as we arrived, were packed on top. His fishing poles and gear had a special place in the trunk of the car so he could get to them at any given time. When the car and trailer were fully packed, he covered the trailer with the tarp, tied it down with ropes that were secured by anchors at various points around the trailer, and we pushed it into the ally behind our house. After he attached the trailer to the car, he could hardly see over it from his rear view mirror when he got in to drive. We would pile into the car and prepare for an exciting drive to Fairhaven Beach State Park.

Once we arrived, we would set up camp and had all the conveniences of home. Our friends and neighbors would camp close by; each of us separated by patches of wooded areas. Each night at dusk and in the early morning before dawn, my father, and the other men could be found by the lake or out in boats fishing to their hearts content. They would catch many fish and the women would cook them that evening for supper. After dinner, we'd all gather at one of the campsites, build a fire, roast marshmallows, and sing the usual campfire songs. We had a great time; we enjoyed each other's company. Each year, we would invite friends or relatives to camp with us. Sometimes I would invite my school friends for the week. Other times, friends and relatives came to visit us just for the day and then drove back to the city. After we had gone camping for a few years, I made a wooden sign that we'd nail to a tree in front of our campsite that read, 'The Cavallaro Clan.' In each of the four corners of the sign, I painted our names, Al, Theresa, Al Jr., and Dick. It gave us some family identity even when we were out in the woods.

We brought some our traditions with us to the campground. One of the things we could depend upon was that my mother would have all the ingredients to cook a large pot of tomato sauce and we would have pasta every Sunday and Wednesday, just as we did when we were at home. She learned how to bake cakes in a covered fry pan on our propane Coleman stove. She would say they were lighter than the cakes that she made in our oven at home. We camped each year from the time I was eight years old, through the years that I was in college. Camping became a very important part of my life and I have many fond memories of our weeks at Fairhaven Beach State Park. I remember the mosquitoes, putting up the tent at dusk, the campfires, the stillness of the forest nights, the days at the beach, and trips into the little town of Fairhaven to get supplies or things we forgot to bring; but most of all, I remember my father and his fishing trips. He loved going to Fairhaven. Each year, Bond's would close shop in July and everyone would go on vacation. There was no doubt where our family would be going; we always looked forward to it with great anticipation.

Another great interest of my father was his love of winemaking. I think this was something that all the Cavallaro's brought to America with them from Sicily. Having lived in the wine country, and sometimes working in the vineyards picking grapes, they were very knowledgeable of the winemaking industry. My father would only make two barrels of wine each year. Each fall, we would prepare the barrels for the new grapes. He would empty any remaining wine from the barrels into bottles and he'd store them in our wine cellar. He removed the ends of the barrels, lay them on their side in the backyard and my brother and I had the job of crawling inside to clean them. We had to scrape off any residue that was on the inside of the barrels. If it remained, he said, it would make the wine taste sour. Afterwards, he'd reseal the barrels and take them back to the cellar. Then, we'd go to the Public Market on North Union Street and buy crates of grapes to make the wine. He would make a Zinfandel wine that required a certain variety of white grapes. We would buy approximately twenty-five crates of the white grapes and about five crates of the purple grapes; these were used to give the wine a slight rosé color.

In addition to having his own barrels, he also had a large winepress and grape-grinder. We would grind the grapes and the juice would flow into the barrels. It was my job, during the grinding phase, to pull out all the stems. These would make the wine taste acidy. When the grapes were pressed and all the juice was squeezed into the barrels, they were positioned in the wine cellar on racks that my father built so they would be off the ground. He put a fermenting tube in a hole at the top of the barrel and surrounded it with hot wax to create an airtight seal. Then, the waiting period began. My father would put his ear next to each barrel every so often during the winter months and listen. He'd always say, "Shh, It's boiling really well." That meant that the wine was fermenting.

In the spring of the year and usually around the Easter season my father would listen to the barrel again and say, "It's now time to taste the new wine." He would hammer a wooden spigot into the front side of the barrel and draw the first glass of wine. This all seems very simple to do, but to my father, this was like a religious experience. The whole family was called down to the cellar to watch him draw the first glass of wine. It had to be drawn into a clear glass container, the size of a juice glass. The first thing he'd do was to hold the glass up to a light bulb located just over the barrels, to check for its clarity. He'd say, "Look how clear this is. Look at the beautiful color. It is just perfect." Then, we each took a sip of the wine from the juice glass and smacked our lips to show how good it was. We would give our confirmation of the delicious taste and he would smile and draw another glass so we could each take another sip.

He was proud of his wine and it gave him great pleasure to share it with his brothers and sisters, close friends, and neighbors. We had a small liter of wine on the table at every meal. Each night, he would have a small glass of wine with his evening meal. When my brother and I were older, we were also allowed to have wine with our meals. As young adults, my brother and I preferred to have the wine cold, rather than at room temperature and we would put a couple of ice cubes in the glass with the wine. My father would become irritated. He would say that wine was meant to be drunk cool from the wine cellar or at room temperature, and ice would ruin the flavor. Of course, he was right. Therefore, for his sake, we learned not to put ice in our wine drinks.

Some Fond Memories

One of my first memories of my father happened at our dinner table. As a young child of five or six years old, I found it easier to eat my meals with a fork or a tablespoon. When my mother made pasta, she would ask what variety I preferred. My response was usually large shells that I could eat with a tablespoon, or *rigatoni*, *mostaccioli* or *ziti*, all of which could be eaten with a fork. When she made *spaghetti*, *linguini* or *macarongelli*, or any long macaroni, it was more difficult for me to eat. My mother would have to cut it in smaller, bite-sized pieces so I could eat it with a spoon. I noticed that whenever we had pasta, my father, my mother, and my brother always used a fork in their right hand and a tablespoon in their left hand in order to twirl the *spaghetti* before they ate it. I carefully watched my father eat his pasta in that way but I couldn't figure out how he accomplished it. I tried to imitate the twirling motion using two utensils, but my spoon was not comfortable in my left hand and it would fall onto the table; it never worked for me. Then one day while we were eating pasta, my father stood behind my chair. He took the tablespoon and positioned it in my left hand letting it rest on the plate for stability. Then with my right hand, he helped me twirl the spaghetti in my spoon before eating it. He said, "Now, this is how they eat pasta in Sicily and you need to learn how to eat it this way because you are Italian." Therefore, every time we ate *spaghetti*, *linguini*, or any other long macaroni, everyone used spoons and forks to help twirl the macaroni before we ate it. I worked hard at mastering this skill and soon it became easy for me to do. When I had children of my own, I taught them, at a very young age, how to eat their pasta with a fork and spoon exactly how my father taught me; and they all did it well. To this day, none of us can eat *spaghetti* without a spoon. When I'm eating pasta in a restaurant and I need to ask for a tablespoon, I explain to the server, "This is how they eat *spaghetti* in Sicily."

Being a normal young boy growing up in my family, I sometimes needed to be reminded to complete my chores. My brother and I had our individual responsibilities and one of mine was to throw out the trash every night as my mother finished washing the dishes. Our trash barrels were in the furthest corner of the yard and in a shed that my father had built; it housed about seven trashcans. The door in front was kept closed, making it dark inside. The usual time for me to throw the trash in the evening was after dark. I didn't like going outside at night. We had no lights in the backyard and the huge apricot and pear trees cast all kinds of eerie shadows across the entire area. The only lighting in the backyard and near the shed came from a tall street light that was in the alleyway behind our house and by our back gate. It didn't help my attitude about going out there because, whenever I needed to throw the trash during the day, I would sometimes see mice running in and out of the shed. My father would set mousetraps and catch the mice, but it still frightened me to go in, especially in the dark. Each evening, my mother would repeatedly remind me to take out the trash. I procrastinated and usually waited until the last minute before following through with her request or I'd really be in trouble. Taking the trash bag in hand, I would run to the shed, shake the door to scare anything that was inside, throw the trash in the closest barrel, and run back as fast as I could. I bring this up, because, although I sometimes had to be told to do things more than once, I never remember my mother or father having to spank me for not doing something. They didn't need to resort to spanking because the only thing it took for me to shape up was 'the look.' My father was a man of few words and when he said them, they meant something. Sometimes, he didn't have to speak to me, but only gave me 'the look.' That special stern look in my father's eyes told me I had better do what I was told. He never raised his voice; however, his eyes spoke louder than words. This showed me what a patient and loving father he was. The look he gave was not used often, so I knew when I saw it, he was serious. I'd immediately comply with any request that was being made of me.

My father loved gardening. As a result, he always had a Victory Garden, where he grew vegetables, during the war years. It was located in the immediate rear of our house on Weld Street. Not only did he have a green thumb for growing vegetables, he also developed a passion for roses. On the opposite side of the backyard, he planted his infamous rose garden. It was a long rose bed that separated our yard from our next-door neighbor. It measured four feet wide and was at least thirty feet long. He enriched the garden soil by adding used coffee grounds, eggshells, peelings from fruits and vegetables, and any other nutrients he could find. He bought a few roses each year and planted them in two long rows, the length of the yard. He was very particular about the roses he purchased. At that time, the Jackson and Perkins nursery was located in Newark, New York and, according to my dad, anyone who wanted healthy and hearty rose bushes only bought that brand. He was so protective of his roses and he wouldn't allow my brother or me to till the soil or water the rose bed. He insisted on doing it himself. One day when I became a teenager, he gave me a hoe and careful instructions on how to cultivate, properly water, and prune the roses. Only then was I allowed to work in the rose bed. At the beginning, I only did it under his direct supervision. I was always cautioned not to dig too deeply into the soil because I would disturb the roots and kill the rose bush. His roses thrived. After they had been planted for a couple of years and were more mature, he experimented in grafting small branches from one rose onto the bush of another rose. He was very meticulous how he did this and covered up the splice with melted wax to keep it airtight. He would check it daily to be sure that it survived and hadn't died. The next spring, we would have roses in a variety of colors and shapes because his grafting process usually was successful. Then in the fall of the year, he would plant a rose sprig or two in the ground and cover them with a Ball or Mason jar for the winter. In the spring, we would have a new rose bush again. Whenever he found a perfectly shaped rosebud, he'd cut it and bring it to my mom, which she loved. When my parents moved to their new home in West Webster, he brought a few of his favorite rose bushes with him. Again, he was very successful in obtaining some of the most beautiful blossoms that I had ever seen. He loved his roses, and of course, he had the best in the neighborhood. As a result, I developed a love for roses and I, too, have numerous rose bushes in my yard. Whenever I see one of my bushes display a perfectly formed rose blossom, I think of my dad. He would have been pleased to see that I had roses as lovely as his.

When he passed away in 1964, my mother picked out the stone monument for the gravesite. She wanted the monument to depict something of my father's life and passions. She chose one with the statue of Jesus that had an urn on each side. Clumps of grapes are engraved into the granite, on the main part of the monument, and on each urn. In addition, rose blossoms are entwined among the grapevines. He would like that.

When my mother left Bond Clothing and started to work at Sibley's Department store in downtown Rochester, our lives changed a bit. She worked on Saturdays so I was home alone with my father. My brother was either working or at the YMCA, which left the two of us alone for the day. Wherever my father went, he took me with him. He would make many trips to the LaPlaca Wrecking Yard on Portland Avenue and I would accompany him. If he was working on a project, we would go to the 'junkyard' as he called it, and rummage through layers of wooden doors and other remnants from houses that had been torn down. He would look for brass hinges for cabinets, pieces of wood for cornices, window sashes, or pieces of pipe. After he brought his treasures home and worked on them, they looked like new. On one occasion, he brought home a long piece of twelve-inch wood that had been painted and looked old and neglected. He knew he had found a goldmine. After he burned off the paint with his blowtorch and sanded the wood to see the grain, he uncovered a piece of solid mahogany, which he used to make cornices in our dining and living rooms. He said that had he bought the piece of wood new, he would have paid at least five times more. He always liked a bargain.

We spent Saturday mornings working together in the garage. He taught me all I know about woodworking and tools, gardening and names of different plants, painting, and wallpapering. I helped him in everything he did. We would eat lunch together and then go out to the garage to continue with our projects. Everything I learned as a small boy, I learned from my father. The simple lessons he taught me are as sharp in my mind as though I heard them yesterday.

One of the highlights each Saturday was listening to the Texaco Opera of the Air on the radio. Operas were broadcast from the Metropolitan Opera House in New York City each week. Without fail, we'd listen to the opera each Saturday afternoon. He'd interpret the stories and sing the arias with the opera stars. He knew the words and the music by heart. My father loved the opera. Each season, he and my mother went to the Eastman Theater on a regular basis with some of their friends. They'd attend the opera, and usually the group of friends returned to our house for coffee and dessert. I could hear them coming into the yard, singing as a group; they sounded great.

The following day, my parents discussed the performance. I sat and listened as they retold the interesting stories they had seen. They bought the Libretto and followed the story, word for word. Then, the best part happened when they sang some of the famous arias that were still fresh in their minds. One of their favorite operas was La Traviata by Giuseppe Verdi. I think it was a favorite of theirs, because of not only the beautiful music and touching story, but the lead tenor's name was Alfredo, just like my father's name. At one point in the opera, Violetta is alone on stage and sings an aria to Alfredo to express her love for him because she knows that she will be leaving him soon. My mother often sang, with much expression, to my father, the beautiful aria that Violetta sang to Alfredo in Italian:

> Alfredo, Alfredo, di questo core
> Non puoi comprendere tutto l'amore!
> Tu non conosci che fino a prezzo
> Del tuo disprezzo – provato io l'ho.
> Ma verrà giorno in che il saprai
> Com'io t'amassi confesserai.
> Dio dai rimorsi ti salvi allora,
> Io spenta ancora, – pur t'amerò.

English Translation:
Alfred, Alfred, who can impart
The love I bear you within my heart!
You'll never know your scorn I drew
To prove how great my love for you.
Some day you'll know and you will bow
Your head, and my true love avow.
May God from your remorse then save you,
For even in death, I'll ever love you.

Knowing the words from memory, my mother would begin singing the aria; then they'd sing it together, always ending it with a kiss. It was very special for them. It became special to me also and has held many memories for me over the years. It has become my favorite opera and I try to see it whenever it's being performed near my community. When I hear that aria, I can still hear my mother and father singing it to each other with such love and sincerity.

Because of this, my interest in opera deepened and I enrolled in some graduate courses to study it more intently. I've often thought how difficult it must be for opera stars to learn all the words and music for each performance. In Italy and Sicily, people absorb opera and music like a sponge. It is all around them, in everything they do, and they love the music; they sing the songs as part of their everyday lives. In the same manner, children in Brooklyn play baseball everyday; they assimilate the skills and it becomes a way of life for them. Similarly, as Italians and Sicilians, we approach music and opera in the same way. It is our way of life, something inside us that is part of our being, a part of our culture, a part of our rich heritage, and our legacy to pass on to future generations.

Another fond memory I have of my father, is our discussions around the dinner table each night. During the years while my mother was still employed at Bond Clothing Factory, both my mother and father worked in Shop #1 where they could see each other from their work stations. At the dinner table each night, they sat across from each other and my brother and I sat at the other two ends. We usually ate our dinner talking about their day at Bond's. There was always something going on. My father would mention the names of Mr. Ciacia, Dominic Fuino, Mr. Guzzetta, Mr. Laudisi, and Jacob, Isaac, and Abe. My mother would mention the names of Anna Fuino, Rose Giordano, Anna Weigand, Mickey Bellini, and Anna Marzanno. Although I never met some of these people, I felt I knew them well, as if they were actual members of our family. Their discussions always started with, "Guess what Anna did today?"

or "Abe came in the middle of my work and put me on another job." They continued with a "Can you top this" discussion of the day's events. They really liked these people and seemed to enjoy working with them. Then we heard about my father's lunch hour where he played a card game called pinochle with his friends. They were interesting discussions and we listened intently.

After dinner, while my parents had their coffee and we all had dessert, my father would look at my brother and me and ask, "Now, what did you do today?" He would wait for a response from each of us. After a while, I knew that the question would be asked, so I prepared myself with something to say. My brother usually had a comment about a basketball game or his part-time job. My comments usually centered on my experiences at school and my friends. Whatever we discussed, my father always brought it back to two topics, which were his favorites.

His first topic was about education. He had a keen respect for earning a good education as the key to self-improvement. After he and my mother would finish talking about their jobs that day, he looked at us, point his finger to each of us, and end with, "That's why it's important for you to get a good education. I don't ever want either of you to have to go and work in a tailor shop or a 'sweat shop' like I do. With a good education, you can have a job with some special skills so you don't have to work as hard as me and make nothing in return." He always brought up the education issue and told us he wanted us to have a better life than he did; he knew education was important in order to gain better employment, which led to a better life.

The second topic he brought up was to be proud of our Italian heritage, our family, and of the Cavallaro name. Every opportunity he had, he told us to be proud of our name. He said that when people heard the name, Cavallaro, they would look at us with respect and honor. If people mispronounced our name in any way, he encouraged us to pronounce it correctly for them. The Cavallaro's worked so hard to bring pride to the family name and it was important to him that we carry on that same tradition; that it would not vanish with him and his brothers and sisters. He reminded us how people in the past made fun of our name or our Italian heritage; we must never let that happen again. His experiences made him believe that this kind of prejudice would continue into the next generation. Then he shared stories about when he arrived in America; for the first time in his life, he was exposed to incidents where he was called derogatory names, such as, 'Wop, Dago, and Guinea.' These slang words were used against Italian immigrants in general. He experienced them as a young immigrant, and as an adult in the tailor shops. One day, when we were in the garage together, he told me a story of how these names affected him through an incident that happened when the family lived on the farm; my Uncle Roger related this same story to me in 1982.

My father said that, once on a hot summer night, he, Uncle Joe, and Uncle Roger went to a local saloon, not far away from the farm. It was the only place in that part of the county where young people could gather to hear music, eat, or have a beer. Many of the other farmers, with their older sons, were there as well. Also present that night, was another family who owned a farm just down the road from the Cavallaro farm. They had young boys the same ages as my father and his brothers. They never got along with this family and there was a lot of competition with them. While they were in the saloon, the other boys repeatedly called my father and his brothers some derogatory names including, 'Dago and Wop.' My father had heard enough and in one leap, he was on top of the oldest son who was also twenty years old. They were immediately on the floor, punching each other bitterly. In the next moment, Uncle Roger was fighting with the younger brother; they were both fifteen. In the midst of the fighting, Uncle Roger looked over and saw my father holding the oldest son in a headlock; he couldn't move his head and it looked like he couldn't breathe either. Uncle Roger ran over and jumped on my father's back. With the help of Uncle Joe and others, they retrained my father and left the saloon. Uncle Roger said, from that time on, those boys always kept their distance. They never called them names or bothered the Cavallaro boys again.

This was very unusual behavior for my father, but it showed how angry he became when he was called any names that were degrading to his Italian culture. When my father related this story to us at the dinner table, I was very young and really didn't understand the magnitude of it. However, when I heard the story as an adult from my Uncle Roger, it certainly showed me the strong emotional affect it had on my father and his brothers. It spoke volumes of his intense respect for his Italian heritage and of his desire to keep it honorable.

I believe that he was successful in achieving this. To this day, I've had an intense esteem for my Italian culture and my Italian name. I have tried, with my wife, to pass these values on to our children. They have grown up in a home where we have carried on many of the Italian traditions that have become our way of life. Because of my father's sincerity and true dedication to his Italian culture, I can honestly say I caught that pride of being an Italian. Yes, I was born in America and I am proud to be an American; however, my roots, my personality, my inner character, and my temperament are truly Italian; it gives me great joy to be able to say, "I love being an Italian."

Another discussion we would have at the dinner table centered on my parent's experiences of what life was like during The Great Depression. Having been born during the depression, I don't remember very much about it except from what they told us. They told stories of how neighbors and close friends lost their jobs, had no money, and sometimes lost their homes during the depression. They shared how hard it was to find employment and how my father searched, wherever he could, to find work. He advised us that when we had a job, we should be very thankful, to arrive early and stay late if necessary. He taught us to have good work ethics. He emphasized on always doing our best so our supervisors could depend upon us. It was important to gain a lot of experience and to strive for promotion to higher levels in our careers.

During the Great Depression, money was hard to come by and my parents had to watch what they bought; they spent their money on necessities first. My father told of events when I was a baby and how he waited in long lines at the grocery store just to buy a quart of milk for me, or a loaf of bread for the family. At that time, it was common for storekeepers to keep a running bill for known customers in the neighborhood. They knew that people were paid each Friday and they would come in that evening to buy more groceries and pay their bills from the previous week. At this point in the story, my father spoke in a very proud manner. He would speak slowly and clearly and look right into our eyes. He would say to us, "All our neighbors had a running bill at the store, but not us. Whatever we bought, we paid in cash. The storekeeper would ask me to put it on my slip and run up an account; but I would say, No! I have the money; I want to pay in cash." I didn't realize it then, but he was teaching us a lesson that was very loud and clear. He emphasized how we should spend our money wisely, and explained the benefits of not having to owe money to anybody at any time. We heard these types of stories about the depression many times. Sometimes they would change a bit by waiting in line for butter, meat or in zero degree temperature; but they always depicted the sacrifices that were made to provide for the family. My parents didn't have a lot of money; however, through their experience of living through the depression, they spent their hard-earned money wisely. They managed to save, dress well, and enjoyed fun family events.

Another memory I have of my father was his love for dancing and music. Because of my parent's many friends and *paisani*, we were invited to many weddings. In a given summer, we'd probably attend five or more weddings; it seemed as if we were going to weddings all the time. Naturally, they were mostly Italian weddings and, at these joyful events, there was always music and dancing. My father and mother would dance all evening. They danced very well. My father held himself in a straight position and was very smooth and graceful;

he always looked very suave as he moved across the dance floor. If it was a wedding where the other Cavallaro families were invited also, he could be seen dancing with his sisters and sisters-in-law. He said that his sister Angie danced the waltz the very best and he loved to dance the polka with my Aunt Lucy; but when he danced with my mother, they exhibited perfect precision and grace. When we grew older, he found great pleasure to be able to dance with both of his daughters-in-law also. I often wished that I could dance as well as him.

Of all the remembrances I have of my father, one in particular stands out from the rest. He spent hours at the sewing machine. We had an old Singer sewing machine that was a trundle model. It sat in the corner of our large kitchen on Weld Street. Although he worked as an armhole presser at Bond's for most of his life, he learned to sew at a very young age, just like his brothers and sisters. Since both my parent's sewed on the same machine, he made sure that it ran like a charm. He was always adjusting it, oiling it, and checking that my mother was using it the correct way. And what do you think he was he doing all those hours on the sewing machine? He was making clothes for my brother and me.

Until I was in my early teens, I don't ever recall going to the clothing stores to buy trousers, suits, or winter coats for myself. My father made those for us at home. After he bought the material from Bond's, he would cut the patterns on the kitchen table and then my mother would begin basting and getting the pieces ready for stitching. After he sewed for a while, I'd be called in to try it on for size. He would make some adjustments, maybe rip a seam or two, and continue with the sewing process. Then my mother would take over. While she completed the project, he would start another. They worked as a team. If he had difficulty with part of the sewing project, his sister Angelina would assist him. She would look at it in a very discerning manner. Her first comments would always be about the quality of the fabric. They had a way of holding the material between their thumb and forefinger and rubbing the fabric in between. An expression would come over their faces as if they were sipping fine wine. She would say, "*Mischa*, (Mēē-skă) this is good material." She would spread the pants or jacket on her big sewing table and examined the area in question. It didn't take her very long to find the problem and they began to discuss its solution. Sometimes, she would perform the necessary stitches and adjustments right there in her sewing room so he could continue on the project on his own at home.

When the item of clothing was completed, I tried it on for the last fitting; I felt like I was modeling it for one of the top Italian clothing designers. I had to walk back and forth; and standing very straight, he would pull up the back of the jacket by the collar so it would look better. Then it was put into the closet on a strong, wooden hanger with his words of caution, "Now, take good care of this and don't ruin it. We worked a long time to make it. If you had to buy that in the store, do you know how much you would have to pay?" I was very appreciative of these clothes and they seemed to last forever. They never wore out. When I outgrew them, they were passed to my cousins, on my mother's side of the family, who were a couple of years younger. It was a normal practice in our house that when I came home from school, I was instructed to take off my good school clothes, hang them up on a hanger, and then put on my play clothes, especially if they were clothes my parents had made for me.

The clothes did look a bit different from my friend's clothes, mainly because mine were made with heavier material. The other kids at school didn't have clothes like mine that were made out of worsteds, tweeds, and woolen fabrics. Occasionally, I would admit to my mother that sometimes the material was itchy and bothered me; however, I was always reminded that my clothes were much better and would last longer. And that was true.

While all this going on, my brother, being older and in high school, was already purchasing his own clothes at the department stores. My father continued making my clothes until I was in junior high school. I convinced him that the other kids wore pants and coats that were different from mine and I, too, wanted to purchase my clothes at the department store. Reluctantly, he conceded and, from then on, I was able to go shopping for clothes downtown. However, during my high school years, many of my friends had a particular style of corduroy sport coat that had a belt sewn into the back of it. Of course, I wanted one; but we couldn't find one in the color I wanted in any of the stores. Therefore, my father and my mother decided to make it for me and, of course, it was wonderful and exactly what I wanted; I wore it with a lot of pride.

While I was in high school and college, whenever I needed pants, winter coats, or suits, my father insisted I shop at the Bond Clothing Department store in downtown Rochester. He would accompany me and, although the sales clerk would try to fit me into the correct article of clothing, my father always took over, told the clerk to stand back, and said, "I make these in my shop and I know exactly what material to get and how I want it to fit him." Buying a suit with him was his pride and joy. He'd check the tickets attached to the arm of the suit to see which shop made it and who completed the inspection. If it came from the wrong shop, he'd throw it aside and say, "You don't want that one." When we would finally find one that fit and in the material that we all liked, he began his own fitting process He used his own personal piece of white chalk in hand and helped the person in charge of alterations and made additional marks so the pants were the correct length and the sleeves on the jacket hung perfectly. An important part of the fitting process was that the back and collar fit perfectly, with no wrinkles, pulling, or puffy lumps in the material. When we brought it home, we had to put it on a special wooden hanger that was made especially for suits. It hung in the closet, next to my father's suits, with a plastic bag over it to keep it from collecting any dust.

His interest for everything we bought at Bond's continued even after we got home. I found, that every time I'd wear the suit or trousers and I was ready to go out, he'd stop me and say, "Let me see how that looks. Now, turn around so I can see the back." I'd have to be sure that I was wearing it well and according to his liking. Then, he would remind me not to throw my jacket around and to take good care of it because it was a good suit and made with fine material. I would leave the house knowing that he was concerned on how we looked and how we were dressed. He took a lot of pride in seeing us wear our suits, coats, and trousers well. I saw that same kind of pride when he would dress up in a suit to go to a wedding or special event himself. He would stand in front of the mirror and look at how the trousers fit, look at the suit jacket to be sure that it was fitting just perfectly. Then, he would check how it looked from the back also. I believe that this perfectionist attitude came from his working in the tailor factories. He would often tell us, that although he was an armhole presser, his supervisors occasionally asked him to model a particular suit jacket for the designers. It usually one made from a new fabric or one that was a newer design for the company. He wore a perfect size 40-Regular, which was the same as their sample products for the models. He would model for them while they made the chalk markings for the alterations. When the suit was finished, they would call him in to try it on for a final fitting. Then, they would bring all the new samples to him for the final ironing. I could tell that he enjoyed this part of his job very much. It involved precision and the suits had to be perfect when he finished the steam pressing and they were presented to the supervisors of the department. Because he was able to preview all the new designs and fabrics being used, it gave him the opportunity to purchase fabrics he especially liked so he could make suits for himself at home.

When I returned home from the service, I discussed my up-coming wedding with him. We were in the garage and he was working on a project. As he stood at his workbench, I told him I was planning to get married soon. I also wanted to know his opinion about Aggie, the girl that I was going to marry. He knew her well because we had dated for about four years prior to my entering the service, and had been engaged during the two years I was in the service; she had spent much time with my parents while I was away. They took her to family events, weddings, and often had Sunday dinners together. As my father worked on his project, I asked him, "Well, Dad, what do you think?" He continued to work at the workbench and without looking at me, he said, "You know what I told you in the past. You have to look at a girl as to how she treats her mother and her father to help you know how she will be in your home and as your wife someday. That's how I decided to marry your mother." Then, he faced me and looked directly into my eyes very clearly, as only he could do, leaned on the bench with one elbow, and said, "And, from what I have seen of her, she treats her mother and father very well and she comes from a respectable family. This is how you have been raised also. You have made a good choice. She will make you a good wife." I knew he would be honest with me, and he knew I would always respect his comments and suggestions. At that point, he gave me a hug and a kiss and we shifted our conversation to the possible dates we had in mind for the wedding and other plans we had made for the event.

When we returned from our honeymoon, and made our first visit to my parent's home, he asked me to join him in the garage. I thought he had something to tell me privately. As we walked into the garage, he had a box of things he wanted me to have. Looking in, I saw an assortment of his own personal tools; I recognized them because I had seen him use them many times before. I found pliers, hammers, two saws for wood, a hacksaw, an electric drill in a metal case, various sized screwdrivers, wrenches, chisels, and a variety of other tools. Although some of them were tools from his own collection, many of them were new tools that he had purchased. He also included boxes of assorted nails, screws, nuts/bolts, brads, and other hardware. Most of the tools were labeled with the Craftsman brand, which he bought at the Sears and Roebuck Department Store; he insisted they were the only brand I should buy in the future because they were the best. I still have all of those tools that he gave me many years ago. Some, I have replaced with newer models; however, the original tools he gave me, still hang on a pegboard attached to my workbench in my garage. I think of him each time I use any one of them.

These are only a few of the special memories that I personally have of my father. I could continue with many other memories, words of wisdom, and activities in which he was involved in my life. I think I can best express this by saying; a day does not go by that I don't think about him. It could be because of a song I hear, something I see around my house, a tool I may be using in the garage, or just when I shave in the morning. When I look in the mirror, I see our family resemblance. His words of advice and wisdom still echo in my mind; I remember the special events in which he played an important part in my life. He left me with many memories I shall never forget.

Other Memories

My Dad was very close to his grandchildren and he took every opportunity to spend time with them. He'd play with them, talk with them, and teach them new things they could use later in life. My niece, Cheryl Cavallaro has some special memories of him.

"Some of my fondest memories are of family get-togethers on the holidays at Grandma and Grandpa Cavallaro's house, or just going on picnics, camping, playing cards, singing...or even putting on plays for our parents and grandparents. The funny part about all of us Cavallaro kids being together, is that we never fought....we may have been loud, but we always got along well together.

Grandma and Grandpa loved having us all together, especially when we put on plays for them. One of my earliest memories of Grandpa was when he used to come to our house on Sullivan Street every Saturday morning after he drove Grandma to work at Sibley's Department Store. My sister, Darlene, and I loved spending time with him. Sometimes, he would ask me to check in his pockets and I'd find that he would have a small bag of dried Italian Garbanzo beans (he would call them ci-ci beans) for us to eat. Grandpa also bought me my first bamboo-fishing pole when I was two years old. Although I don't ever remember catching any fish on it, there are pictures of me with a sunfish on my line.

He and Grandma would have us over to spend the night, and we would play games or watch TV before we went to bed. In the morning, we would always have prunes for breakfast. Then, we would help Grandpa in his garden, picking vegetables or flowers in Grandma's flower garden. Sometimes, we even watched as he worked at his workbench making things like birdhouses. In the evening, we would watch The Lawrence Welk Show because that was their favorite program. Grandpa made his own wine. It was so much fun on Sunday when our parents would come to pick us up; we would have a spaghetti dinner and he'd give us a little wine mixed in with Hawaiian Punch. We felt so grown up."

My niece, Darlene Bahr, had some special memories of my father also.

"My Grandpa Cavallaro called me his "Diavolita" (Dē-ă-vō-lē´-tă). In Sicilian, it's an endearment meaning "little devil." It was because I was so rambunctious as a child. I remember him laughing a lot at me and the things I would do. Many times, as a small child, when we went to Grandma and Grandpa's house, Grandpa would steal me away to the small grocery store that was right across the street from their house to buy something for Grandma. I remember him holding my hand because we had to cross a very busy road, Bay Road, to get to the store. We would take a short cut through his back yard to get there faster and it was just across the street. I remember holding hands with him very tightly, (I can still tell you exactly how his hands looked) and I'd skip all the way to the store. When we got there, we'd get whatever we went for; however, each time we went, I got a purple bubblegum. He'd say, "Let's get one for Cheryl and one for Ricky, too." I would hold one in each hand and by the time I'd get back home, both hands were purple, and he'd laugh while he washed my hands in the big kitchen sink.

He was a very special man to me. He was the first one in my life to really validate me, someone who stuck up for me. I still miss him terribly today. Some of the specific things I vividly remember about him are:

- *He ate his cereal in the morning in a giant cup with coffee and milk.*

- *He was always fixing something. He had lots of tools and lots of paint.*

- *He napped in the afternoon with only his undershirt on and I remember that he had a hairy chest.*

- *Every Saturday morning, he'd come to our house to paste his work stamps on his cards. He always brought a bag of peanuts with him, that he would cut in half with his pocketknife for my sister and me.*

- *I remember singing or dancing for him and his eyes would light up; he would throw his head back in laughter.*

- *He had a great garden. He'd show me all the plants in his garden and explain how they grew and what they were called. Many had Italian names and I couldn't pronounce them. He showed me what to pick and what not to pick; then, he'd let me pick the ripe ones and bring them into Grandma so she could cook them or put them in the refrigerator.*

I have many fond memories of my Grandpa, and I still miss him to this day."

Alfred's Final Years

My father's final years came quickly for him. In 1962, he and my mother sold the family home they had lived in for twenty-seven years. They remodeled it many times to make it the attractive home it became. It was the home where they had spent most of their married life and raised two sons until they, too, were married. It was very special and it held many memories for the whole family. When they began to search for a new home, they looked in various Rochester suburbs and found a development in West Webster they liked very much. It just so happened, their former tenants, Tony and Mary Gianuso had just moved to West Webster on Bay Road; they encouraged my mother and father to look at the homes in that area. They went to investigate the neighborhood, and found one just down the street from where his sister and brother-in-law, Alfred and Mary Lizzio lived. My father established a close relationship with the builder who was developing the tract. He was very happy with the quality products they used to produce such fine homes. Therefore, they decided to build a new, one story home on a half-acre lot.

They loved that house and it was just perfect for the two of them. It had an unfinished, walkout basement, so my father began remodeling it immediately. He covered all the walls with walnut paneling, put in a separate workshop for all his tools, and a complete kitchen for my mother. This is where they put their old kitchen set, along with a stove, sink, countertop, pantry, cupboards, washer, and dryer. They loved it because they had all the conveniences in their finished basement for whatever they wanted to do. Whether they were canning peaches and tomatoes in Mason jars, summertime cooking so as not to heat the kitchen upstairs or when preparing any type of fried food, they could use the kitchen area. It was such a convenience for them. In addition, they could walk outside to the backyard from the basement and that made it very easy for my father when he gardened.

As soon as they were completely moved in, my father immediately planted the front and back lawns and put in all the shrubs in the front yard. Without wasting a day, he proceeded to plant a large vegetable garden in the backyard. It had the richest soil of all the gardens in the area. There, he was able to plant at least a couple dozen tomato plants, corn, squash (*cucuza*, as he would call it), and bitter greens (which he called *cicoria* or *broccoli rapi)* that were cooked with olive oil and garlic. He also planted bell peppers, onions, garlic, eggplant, and of course, a large plot was reserved for our favorite oregano and Italian basil for all the seasonings my mother needed for her cooking. He grew more than he and my mother could consume, so each time my brother's family or my family would visit, we would go home with baskets full of the best specimens of vegetables he had grown. He took a lot of pride in his garden and worked in it every day. Whenever I would visit them, he insisted I go out to the garden in the backyard to see how it was growing, even before going into the house to see my mother. He would point out that his vegetables were bigger and better than what I could buy at Wegman's Grocery Store down the street; and he was absolutely right. As I would examine his plants and garden, he would also show me there weren't any weeds to be found in the entire garden. It was truly a work of art, his passion. Because he worked at it every day, his garden had a full array of healthy vegetables and our family ate well all summer long.

Shortly after they moved in, my father retired from Bonds. My mother was still working in Rochester for Sibley, Lindsey & Curr Company. Therefore, each day he drove her to work, returned home to work in his garden or on other projects he had started, rested in mid-afternoon and then returned into the city to pick her up when she finished work. Many times on Saturdays, after he left my mother off to work, he would stop by my brother's house on Sullivan Street or at my house on Abby Lane to see his grandchildren and visit for a while. The children always loved to see him. I remember him picking up my daughter, Lisa, and calling her "figlia bedda" (beautiful child). He played ball with my son, Rick, who was about four at the time, and pitched the ball to him so he could hit it with a plastic bat. When Rick missed hitting it, my father would say, "Managgia l'America" and run after to ball. He loved being around the family and enjoyed his grandchildren so very much.

In the spring of 1964, he began to complain of pain in his neck and shoulder. He went to the doctor and they decided he needed surgery to have a ruptured disk removed. In early September, he went to Rochester General Hospital for the procedure. The surgery was successful; however, in the early morning hours the day before he was to be released, we were all called to go to the hospital because he became seriously ill. Immediately, the entire Cavallaro family rushed to his side. By the time I drove in from the suburbs, they were all at the hospital, waiting to find out what had happened. As soon as I arrived, he was placed in the

Intensive Care Unit and allowed only two relatives at a time to visit; one of those was always my mother. Each time I went in to see him, he expressed that he was in a tremendous amount of pain and couldn't endure it anymore. He was yelling so loud, he could be heard all the way down the hall; the pain was very severe and the medication was not helping him. The very last time I saw him that day, I entered the ICU with my mother. I thought he was sleeping, but he had gone into a coma. My mother was holding his hand trying to comfort him. There was a nurse in the room and, as I glanced at her, our eyes met. I quietly asked her how he was doing. She didn't answer me. She only looked at me and shook her head from side to side, as if to say "No." I did not realize what she was trying to tell me. That was about 9:00 a.m. After our ten minute visit, I immediately went back to the waiting room to sit with my mother, my brother, and all my other relatives. Every hour, two more people went up to see him for their ten-minute visit. Strangely, I would see them return to the waiting room, crying and wiping their eyes; I didn't understand what was happening.

When noontime arrived, my aunts told my brother, his wife Mary Jane, my wife Aggie, and me to go to the hospital cafeteria to get something to eat; then we could go up to see him again after lunch. We took their advice. In the midst of our lunch, I noticed my uncles and some of my aunts by the window, motioning for us to go out. I immediately ran over to them and my Aunt Joan was the first person I saw. She came to me and said, "Dick, your father has expired." I looked at her in a daze. She hugged me for a long time, as did my other aunts and uncles. I did not understand. I didn't realize he was so sick that he would die. He was supposed to come home the following day. I wasn't prepared for a shock like this. I felt I wanted to have the opportunity to say my final good-bye to him and that never happened. He died alone with neither of his sons nor his wife by his side. I wanted to have a quiet time with him, to hold his hand and say, "I will always love you, Dad." Now, it wasn't possible. He was gone forever. A feeling of complete emptiness and hopelessness filled me.

Once he was gone, life changed for our whole family. His was the first death of all the Cavallaro brothers and sisters. It was felt deeply by everyone. My niece, Cheryl Cavallaro, who was seven years old at the time, shares these memories of the incident:

"Even as young as I was, I can still remember the day that Grandpa died. We were at my Aunt Francis' house and my Dad was standing in the corner with his back to us so we couldn't see him crying as he explained that Grandpa was in heaven and wouldn't be here with us anymore. I was

so confused and so incredibly sad that he was gone; I think I was even mad at God because He took him away. After that, I felt that life for me and for the rest of our family wasn't ever quite the same again…everyone acted so differently. I spent many nights awake, thinking about him and all the fun that we used to have. Even to this day, if I close my eyes and think hard enough, I can almost smell the tobacco that he smoked in his pipe; that familiar smoky-orange odor that was always present on his red checkered hunting jacket; and the comforting feeling I had as I sat on his lap while he hugged me………I miss my Grandpa!"

I have often felt that the memories we have of those that leave us are imbedded in the love we have experienced with them in life. I have found that I have so many fond memories of my father as I reflect upon his life; my father is still very much alive in my remembrances of him. In my mind's eyes, I can still see him in the backyard working in the garden and watering his plants; I can see him fishing in a rowboat just off shore at Fair Haven State Beach Park on a cool, summer afternoon; or I can see him working on a project and hammering nails in a board. I can picture him in Sicily, in Rochester, at my wedding, and at the christenings of my children. He is with me wherever I go.

I have so much to be thankful for having a father like him. He showed me how to care about other people; he challenged me to educate myself and to enjoy learning; he opened up the world of music for me; and he modeled how to be a good husband and a kind father. However, more than these things, he taught me the importance of family. He loved his family, his wife, his sons and their families, his brothers and sisters, cousins, nieces, and nephews. They were all very important to him. He never sat down with us and insisted that we were to do something this way or that, but instead, he modeled the kind of behavior he wanted his boys to emulate and we followed it.

Because of the deep love I have for my father, I may be guilty of being somewhat oblivious to his faults. I'm aware that he had imperfections, as we all do; however, they were overpowered and hidden by the positive qualities of his character. He was neither dishonest nor vindictive, but a selfless and patient person. He was naturally intelligent, a perfectionist, and a true craftsman with his hands. He approached his marriage with passion and his role as a father with total commitment. No matter what he was doing, or what he had or didn't have, his care and attitude toward his family was unfaltering. This made all the difference in the lives of my mother, my brother and his family, and in my family and me. What more could anyone ask of any man?

In the days that followed his death, my sadness mounted because I never had the opportunity to have those few, final moments with him before he died. He was taken away from us so suddenly. All through the days of the funeral, I was in shock from his loss. I busied myself in trying to take care of the arrangements for the funeral and caring for my mother who needed a lot of comfort and attention. I never thought to focus on the loss that had occurred to me, personally; I only knew I had an emptiness within me and was filled with extreme sadness. In the years that followed, I always felt a void in my spirit; I never had closure with him. I didn't have the chance to give him one last hug or one last kiss, to tell him how much he meant to me, or just to hold his hand for one last time……it is a chasm deep within me that I have always felt.

After all the years of research and digging deeper into his life, I have found a new relationship with my father. I have been able to relive all the great experiences we had in our home. As I went through the old family photo albums, it brought to mind many scenes and activities of when he was with his siblings and my family over the years. I reminisced about the special events and holidays in our home, our vacations, and the quiet times I shared with him. It helped me to focus on his life as a young man who was adjusting to a new world…..America, and to view his total involvement with his family at the many stages of his life. While I was growing up, much of this was taken for granted, that these were just normal events in my life with my father; however, I was now able to uncover all the little things that I had forgotten about him….and they mean so much more to me now.

Writing this book has given me a renewed time of fellowship with my father and his family. I truly believe that this has given me closure; it is my way of saying,

> *"Thank you, Dad, for all you did for me. You molded my life and made me into the man I am today. I miss you very much. I will always love you. I will never forget you…..and as I did when I was a little boy, I will always be looking to you and holding on to your hand."*

Alfio (Alfred Michael) Cavallaro Sr. Family Tree

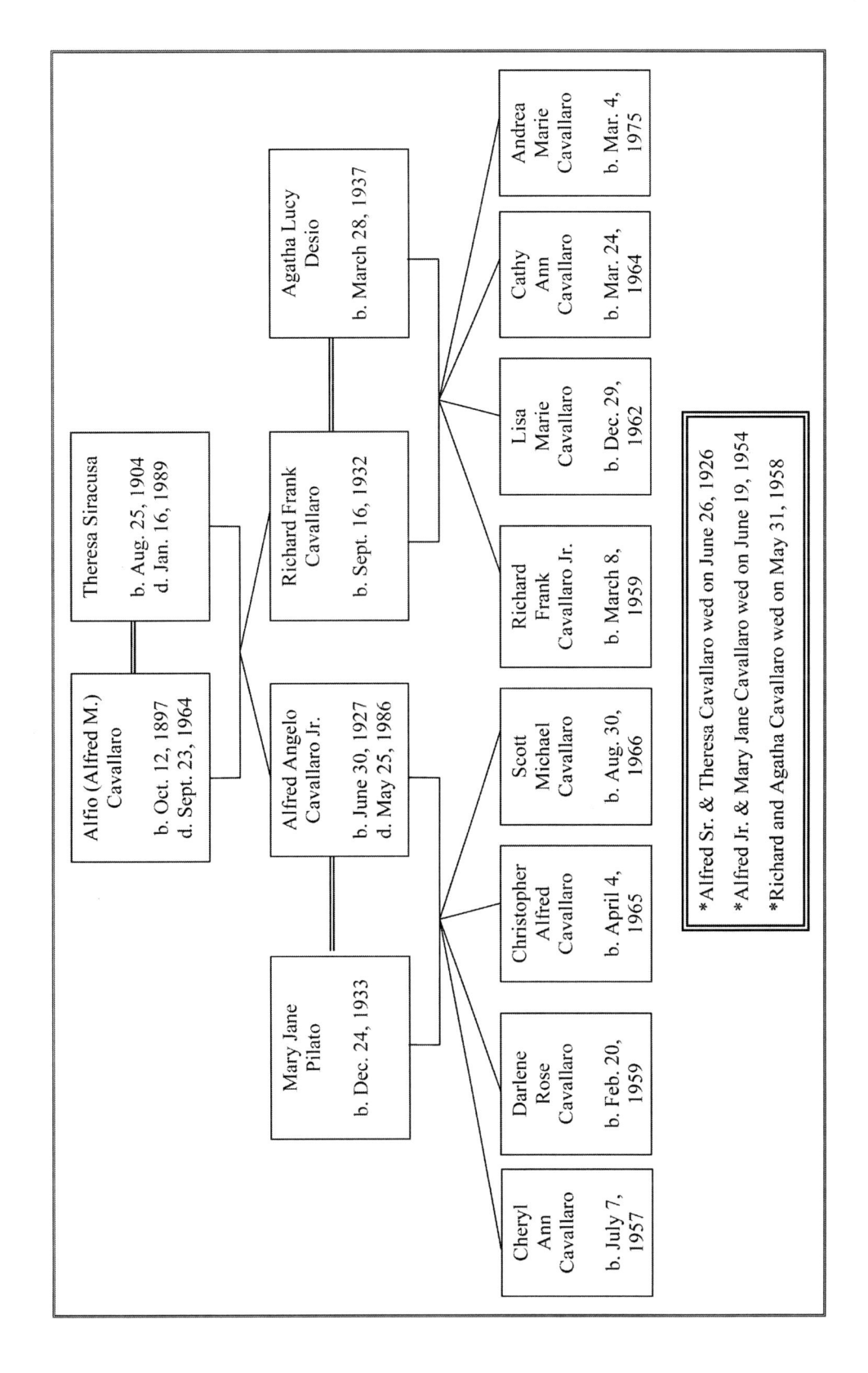

Alfio (Alfred M.) Cavallaro
b. Oct. 12, 1897
d. Sept. 23, 1964

Theresa Siracusa
b. Aug. 25, 1904
d. Jan. 16, 1989

Mary Jane Pilato
b. Dec. 24, 1933

Alfred Angelo Cavallaro Jr.
b. June 30, 1927
d. May 25, 1986

Richard Frank Cavallaro
b. Sept. 16, 1932

Agatha Lucy Desio
b. March 28, 1937

Cheryl Ann Cavallaro
b. July 7, 1957

Darlene Rose Cavallaro
b. Feb. 20, 1959

Christopher Alfred Cavallaro
b. April 4, 1965

Scott Michael Cavallaro
b. Aug. 30, 1966

Richard Frank Cavallaro Jr.
b. March 8, 1959

Lisa Marie Cavallaro
b. Dec. 29, 1962

Cathy Ann Cavallaro
b. Mar. 24, 1964

Andrea Marie Cavallaro
b. Mar. 4, 1975

* Alfred Sr. & Theresa Cavallaro wed on June 26, 1926
* Alfred Jr. & Mary Jane Cavallaro wed on June 19, 1954
* Richard and Agatha Cavallaro wed on May 31, 1958

Alfred Angelo Cavallaro Jr. Family Tree

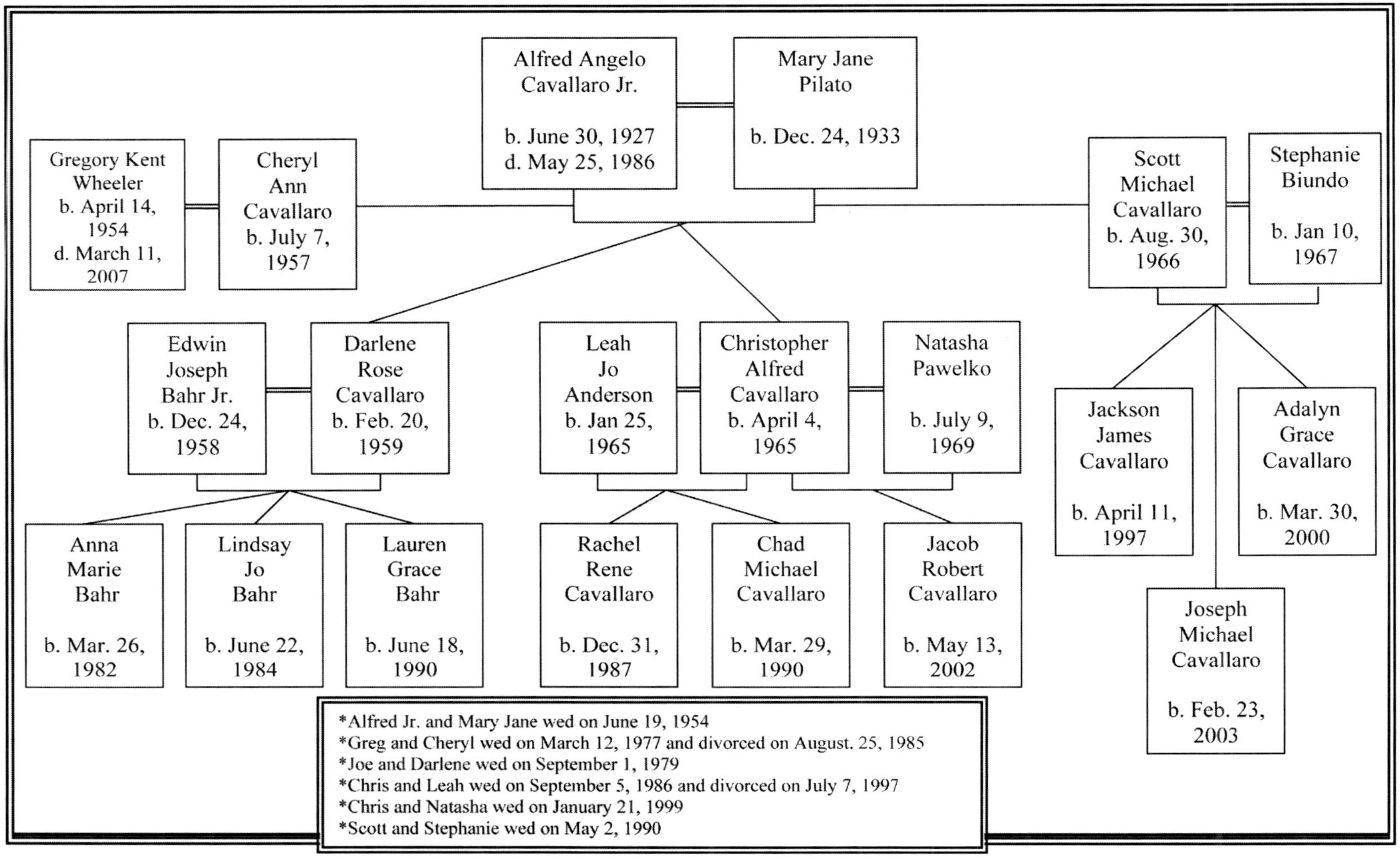

- **Alfred Angelo Cavallaro Jr.** b. June 30, 1927; d. May 25, 1986
- **Mary Jane Pilato** b. Dec. 24, 1933

Children of Alfred Jr. and Mary Jane:

- **Cheryl Ann Cavallaro** b. July 7, 1957
  - married **Gregory Kent Wheeler** b. April 14, 1954; d. March 11, 2007

- **Darlene Rose Cavallaro** b. Feb. 20, 1959
  - married **Edwin Joseph Bahr Jr.** b. Dec. 24, 1958
  - Children:
    - **Anna Marie Bahr** b. Mar. 26, 1982
    - **Lindsay Jo Bahr** b. June 22, 1984
    - **Lauren Grace Bahr** b. June 18, 1990

- **Christopher Alfred Cavallaro** b. April 4, 1965
  - married **Leah Jo Anderson** b. Jan 25, 1965
    - **Rachel Rene Cavallaro** b. Dec. 31, 1987
    - **Chad Michael Cavallaro** b. Mar. 29, 1990
  - married **Natasha Pawelko** b. July 9, 1969
    - **Jacob Robert Cavallaro** b. May 13, 2002

- **Scott Michael Cavallaro** b. Aug. 30, 1966
  - married **Stephanie Biundo** b. Jan 10, 1967
  - Children:
    - **Jackson James Cavallaro** b. April 11, 1997
    - **Adalyn Grace Cavallaro** b. Mar. 30, 2000
    - **Joseph Michael Cavallaro** b. Feb. 23, 2003

- *Alfred Jr. and Mary Jane wed on June 19, 1954
- *Greg and Cheryl wed on March 12, 1977 and divorced on August. 25, 1985
- *Joe and Darlene wed on September 1, 1979
- *Chris and Leah wed on September 5, 1986 and divorced on July 7, 1997
- *Chris and Natasha wed on January 21, 1999
- *Scott and Stephanie wed on May 2, 1990

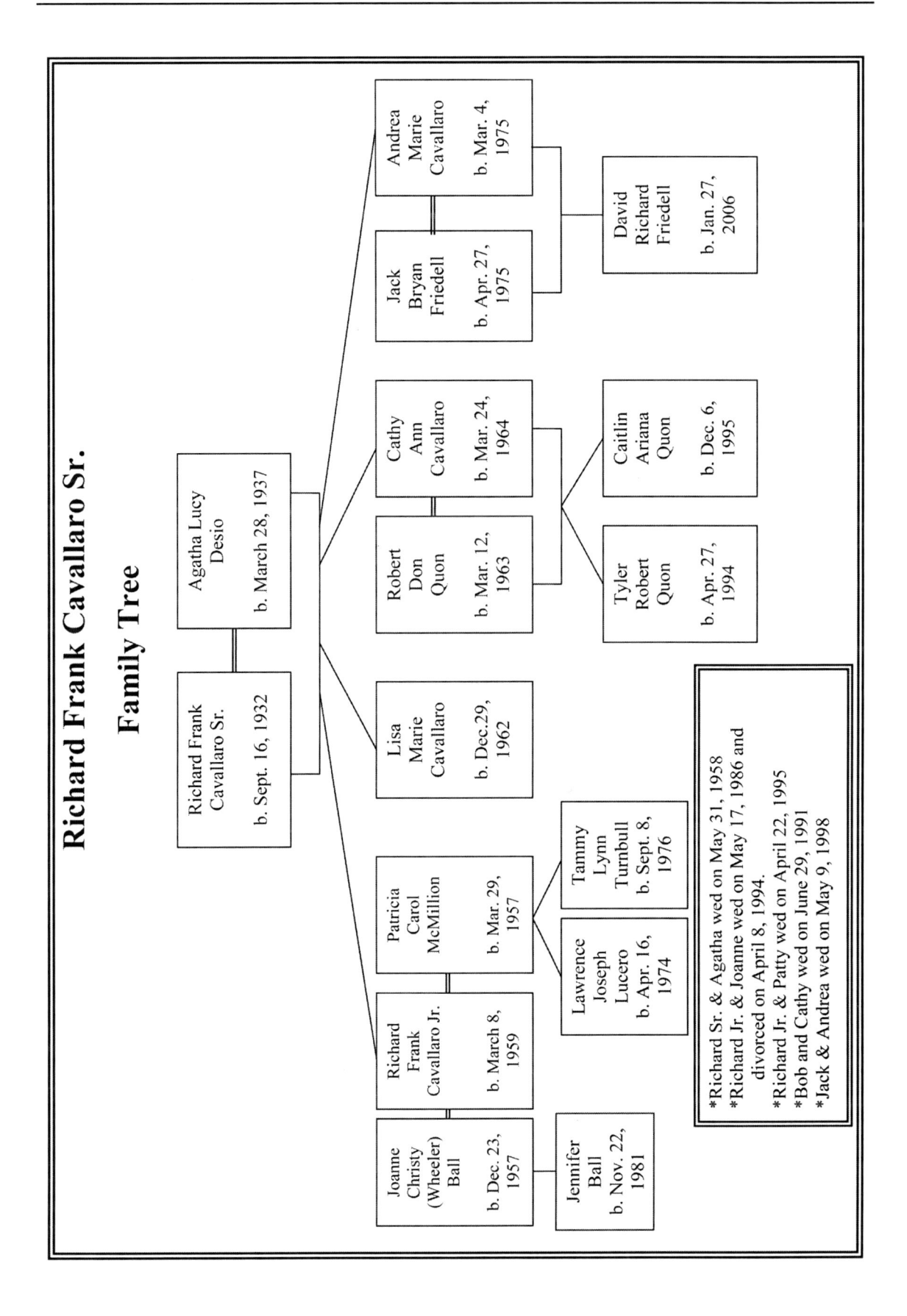

Richard Frank Cavallaro Sr.
Family Tree

Richard Frank Cavallaro Sr.
b. Sept. 16, 1932

Agatha Lucy Desio
b. March 28, 1937

Children of Richard Sr. and Agatha:

- **Richard Frank Cavallaro Jr.** — b. March 8, 1959
  - m. **Joanne Christy (Wheeler) Ball** — b. Dec. 23, 1957
    - **Jennifer Ball** — b. Nov. 22, 1981
  - m. **Patricia Carol McMillion** — b. Mar. 29, 1957
    - **Lawrence Joseph Lucero** — b. Apr. 16, 1974
    - **Tammy Lynn Turnbull** — b. Sept. 8, 1976

- **Lisa Marie Cavallaro** — b. Dec. 29, 1962

- **Cathy Ann Cavallaro** — b. Mar. 24, 1964
  - m. **Robert Don Quon** — b. Mar. 12, 1963
    - **Tyler Robert Quon** — b. Apr. 27, 1994
    - **Caitlin Ariana Quon** — b. Dec. 6, 1995

- **Andrea Marie Cavallaro** — b. Mar. 4, 1975
  - m. **Jack Bryan Friedell** — b. Apr. 27, 1975
    - **David Richard Friedell** — b. Jan. 27, 2006

*Richard Sr. & Agatha wed on May 31, 1958
*Richard Jr. & Joanne wed on May 17, 1986 and divorced on April 8, 1994.
*Richard Jr. & Patty wed on April 22, 1995
*Bob and Cathy wed on June 29, 1991
*Jack & Andrea wed on May 9, 1998

Alfred M. Cavallaro

Certificate of Naturalization

June 27, 1922

Alfred Michael (Alfio) Cavallaro

June 26, 1926
Alfred & Theresa (Siracusa) Cavallaro

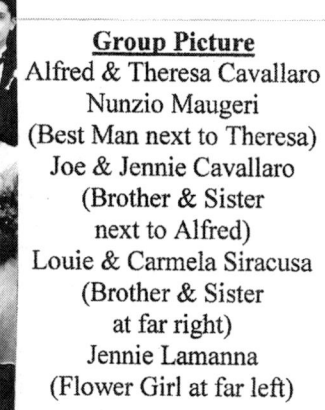

Alfred at Age 18

Group Picture
Alfred & Theresa Cavallaro
Nunzio Maugeri
(Best Man next to Theresa)
Joe & Jennie Cavallaro
(Brother & Sister
next to Alfred)
Louie & Carmela Siracusa
(Brother & Sister
at far right)
Jennie Lamanna
(Flower Girl at far left)

My Sicilian Legacy

1928
Alfred & Theresa Cavallaro
(at Joe & Jennie Gargana's wedding

Rotary Sunshine Camp
Al & Theresa
Al (Sonny) & Richard
The day he gave me the
sail boat he made

Alfred Cavallaro
(Best Man at a wedding)
1925

Al & Theresa Cavallaro
(At Chuck & Mary Palumbo's Wedding)
September 1948

Alfred's Hobbies

Although Alfred was a tailor, his hobbies were hunting and fishing.

Easter (circa 1939)

Alfred and his two sons, Alfred Jr. & Richard.
Alfred made both suits the boys are wearing.

Alfred Cavallaro
U.S. Air Force
(Circa 1947)

Richard Cavallaro
Senior at NY State Univ.
1955

Alfred with Grandchildren
Rick, Cheryl, Darlene
Easter 1962 at Webster, NY home

Alfred & Theresa
At Joe Cavallaro's wedding
May 1963

Alfred
(May 1926)

Alfred & Theresa
At Pinochle Club Picnic
1931

Alfred & Theresa
Carmella Siracusa in back
Al (Sonny) on ground
1930

Al Cavallaro Jr. Family
Darlene & Cheryl
Chris, Scott,
Mary Jane & Al Jr.
(Circa 1970)

Richard Cavallaro Family
Andrea, Cathy, Lisa, & Rick
Aggie & Richard
(February 2003)

Side Yard on Weld Street
Al (Sonny) wearing Scout uniform,
Alfred & Richard
(Circa 1940)

Easter 1953
Al & Theresa
At Weld Street side yard

The Bike Ride

My Grandfather took me bike riding
Before I was the age of two.
My feet didn't even reach the pedals
Of the red trike that was shiny and new.

The bike came equipped with features
Of everything I would need,
Handlebar streamers for fashion
And Grandpa's hand for speed.

Dad captured the two of us on camera,
The moment was etched in time.
An insignificant little event
That I wouldn't trade for even a dime.

A look of joy and happiness
Was present on Grandpa's face,
As he watched his grandchild playing
With his pipe correctly in place.

I wish I had the memory
Of how I felt that day,
When spending time with Grandpa
Just me and him at play!

Poem written by granddaughter, Lisa Cavallaro in June, 2006.

Lisa and Grandpa Cavallaro at Abby Lane, August 1964.

Maria Catena (Mary Cavallaro) Lizzio

March 12, 1900 – December 9, 2002

Prologue

Maria Catena (her given birth name) was the third born, living child of Angelo and Angela Cavallaro. According to existing records that I have seen, they were living in Passopisciaro, Sicily. When she was born, her sister Angelina was four years old and Alfio was two years old. According to the age-spacing pattern of children of being born about every two to three years apart, it is obvious that Angelo was a 'Bird of Passage' and had already started making his trips to America. With three children under the age of five years old, Angela continued to provide the necessary funds for her family through her sewing and alterations work for friends and neighbors in their small town.

The Beginning

Mary, as I will refer to her from now on because it is the name most of us know her by, was an easy child to raise. She was well behaved and followed the guidance of her big sister Angelina, who many times, was responsible to care for Mary because of her mother's work. She played well with other children and busied herself with simple playthings. However, as calm and well behaved as she was, as she grew older, she developed an occasional display of stubbornness – especially when she wanted her own way. As a young adult, she began to voice her opinions openly when something needed to be corrected or she needed to give counsel to someone.

This was always done in a proper and calm manner, but because of this personality trait, she became known as the 'Mother Hen' of the family. She tried to take care of everything. Whenever anyone needed assistance, she was there to provide any help in terms of service, meals, money, or counsel. She was a caregiver to others and she knew how to give excellent advice when needed.

Mary Grows Up

Mary's childhood years were very ordinary as compared with other children growing up in rural Sicily; except that she spent most of her days and nights learning the family craft of sewing from her mother and her older sister, Angelina. By the time she was a teenager, she was as proficient in sewing as Angelina. The two of them assisted their mother greatly in all the projects Angela brought home for them to complete. This extra work meant more money for the family. Mary also branched off and learned to embroider, crochet, and knit, which she continued for her entire life. Her embroidery projects were very elaborate, colorful, and carefully completed. It was through these projects that she learned to perfect her ability to sew very precisely. Her sewing was evenly spaced and her delicate stitches were painstakingly made. Eventually, these skills would be used as she became a professional seamstress.

Her crocheting and knitting projects were equally as intricate and attractive. She would sometimes follow patterns from books and manuals; in addition, she had the ability to look at a finished product that was commercially manufactured or made by another person, and duplicate it perfectly with no personal instruction. She would examine it closely, look at the stitches very carefully, and know exactly how to make it. Usually, her finished product was better than the original because it contained embellishments and decorations that she would create to make the project more attractive. They were truly works of art. She literally taught herself how to accomplish many of the more advanced skills necessary and she had the perseverance to complete each project to its completion. Being a very generous person, many of her projects were given away to other family members and close friends; however, her own home was decorated with much of her handiwork (blankets, doilies, sofa throws, bedspreads, coverlets, or towels) that were all completed in unique designs and brought much beauty to her home.

Mary Arrives in America

When the Cavallaro family and their cousins, the Lizzio's, migrated to the United States, they all settled in the same area of Rochester, New York. It was very common for new immigrants to settle in areas within the city that were close to other relatives and *paisani*. Similarly, other ethnic groups lived together in small neighborhoods such as, the Irish, German, Polish and Jewish families. The Cavallaro and Lizzio families settled in the area of North Clinton Avenue, just south of Clifford Avenue. Living in close proximity to each other brought, not only the comfort, protection, and security they all desired, but it gave them a sense of continuity in recreating the lifestyle they had left in Sicily. They strengthened their family relationships and replicated their ethnic way of life in Rochester. That tendency became a tradition and continued into the next generation.

When Angela decided to buy the farm in West Bloomfield, Mary moved with the family and helped with the daily chores. She did everything, which included feeding the chickens and cattle, milking the cows, and preparing meals for the family. While living on the farm, she also went to work at the local canning factory. It was a seasonal job and she worked there when they were canning fresh peas. She walked to the factory and back home again each day, which was approximately three miles one-way. She would bring her entire paycheck home to her mother for her to use as needed. She never complained about it and did it willingly as a help to the family.

Although she lived on the farm, her name does not appear on the 1920 census, which was enumerated on January 12, 1920. Since this was just prior to her marriage, there could be many reasons for this. She may have been busy on the farm and unavailable to answer questions from the census taker; she could have been in Rochester for a few days with relatives; or she could have already moved from the farm to live with her sister Angelina in preparation for her wedding, which was only four months away. Not having any accurate information at this time, any of these reasons are possibilities.

Mary Begins a Family of Her Own

The Lizzio family had a major impact on her life. Mary's father, Angelo, had an older sister, Rosa. She was Mary's Aunt Rosa. Rosa married a young man named Angelo Lizzio, who was a *paisano* and the Cavallaro's knew the family well. Angelo and Rosa Lizzio had five children; Mario, Alfio, Josephine, Angelina, and Grace. These children were first cousins to the Cavallaro children and they all grew up together in the Passopisciaro area as relatives, friends, and neighbors. They were a close-knit family.

The Lizzio family lived around the corner from the Cavallaro family. They visited each other often, and the siblings shared many activities together. Alfio Lizzio, known as Alfred, spent much time at the Cavallaro home. His attention focused on Mary and they would spend long hours in each other's company. At this point in her life, his presence in the Cavallaro family became very prominent and had life-long effects on her future.

It was reported to me that in 1921, Alfred Lizzio entered the U.S. Army. There are numerous photographs throughout the family albums of him in his army uniform. In speaking to other relatives, it was confirmed to me that he was in the military during World War I. As we know, the United States declared war on Germany on April 6, 1917; the Armistice was declared on November 11, 1918; and the Treaty of Versailles was signed on June 28, 1919. With all this information in mind, it can be determined that he served sometime during those dates. Therefore, the date of 1921 cannot be accurate since his dates of service had to be between 1917 and 1918. This was confirmed because, while he was in the U.S. Army, he was sent overseas to France to fight in the American attack on Germany. While he was there, he was exposed to nerve gas and had to be returned immediately to the United States. He spent time in the Veteran's Hospital to recover. This occurred prior to 1918. At the end of the war, he was rehabilitated and returned home to Rochester.

Before long, many friends and both families became aware that Mary Cavallaro and Alfred Lizzio were developing an attraction toward each other. He was three years older and was a very handsome, intelligent young man. He spent a lot of time with his cousins, the Cavallaro boys, which caused him to be near Mary often. Although he always made the excuse to visit with the boys, he usually spent more time watching and flirting with Mary.

Through much discussion and some concern from both families and their siblings, Mary and Alfred decided to be married. From this point on, Alfred Lizzio will be referred to by the name I called him, Uncle Al Lizzio. They were married on April 10, 1920 in Rochester, New York. Mary's two sisters, Angelina and Jennie, were bridesmaids for the wedding. Angelina made the wedding gown for Mary; it was beautiful and sewn with precision to fit her delicate frame. She also made the dresses that she and Jennie wore that day.

Three years after her marriage to my Uncle Al, Aunt Mary gave birth to a baby boy on April 30, 1923; he was named Angelo. It was the Italian custom that the first-born child was named after the paternal grandmother or grandfather. Since both the maternal and paternal grandfathers were named Angelo, this was the ideal and proper name for their new son. Angelo Lizzio was the only child born to them.

Mary and Alfred Lizzio Venture Out

In 1924, my Uncle Al and Aunt Mary Lizzio began to think about farming again. They searched for available farms and found one in Rush, New York. Therefore, together with Russell and Grace (Lizzio) Trovato, and Angelo and Rosa (Cavallaro) Lizzio, they purchased the farm. The farm was approximately fifty acres and they maintained it from 1924 to 1926, when it was sold. They all continued to live in Rochester during this time and took the train back and forth to the farm each day. Oftentimes, instead of taking the train, my Uncle Al drove his Model "T" Ford. The farm mainly produced dairy products so there was an abundance of cows. They milked the cows by hand, twice a day, and sold the milk. They also farmed acres of grain with which to feed the cows. My Uncle Al joined The Dairyman's League and he attended all the meetings in his efforts to stay abreast of the new laws and regulations they needed to follow to be in compliance. Through his membership, he made many contacts with other farmers and buyers who would purchase the milk they produced. They were constantly inspected by the New York State Health Department and the Dairyman's League to be sure they were following all the legal regulations. They were very successful at the farm, but it became too much work for just the six of them to work the fifty acres. Therefore, within two years, the farm was sold and they all obtained jobs in the city. Bond Clothing factory had recently opened a large factory in their neighborhood and they decided to return to their family-given talent of sewing and put it to good use in the Tailoring Industry. Working at Bond Clothing was much more convenient because it was within walking distance of their homes and many of their siblings were already working there full-time; this brought much comfort and security to them.

My Aunt Mary worked at Bond's as a finisher on armholes of men's suits. All of a finisher's work is completed by hand; with very fine, even stitches. She stitched the hems where the sleeves would eventually be attached to men's suit coats. Later, they put her to work on machines. Then, she made the flaps that were placed on the side pockets of the suit coat. She also made the pocket that was on the front of the suit. It was located at the top, by the lapel, and was called the welt pocket. She enjoyed this job because it paid more money; however, her supervisors preferred that she remained as a finisher on the armholes because her stitches were so fine and precise, exactly what they needed. There were few in her shop that could sew as well and do such a neat job. My Uncle Al's job at Bond's was as a pocket maker and general tailor of men and women's suits. In the evenings, he completed a number of special courses on tailoring; he eventually became a suit designer for Bonds.

During this time, they were able to purchase a home at 41 Oakman Street. It was within walking distance to Bond Clothing, which was on Martin Street, so it was perfect for them. The 1930 census indicated that they owned the house in the rear of the lot. There was another home located in the front of the lot. It belonged to Angelina and Federico Lamanna (my Aunt Mary's sister). Again, living close to family brought comfort and security. It was while they were living on Oakman Street, that Angelo and Angela Cavallaro were getting on in years and needed assisted care. Angela sold her house on North Clinton Avenue because she couldn't care for it any longer. In that day, it was unheard of to put older parents in an assisted living home or care unit unless they were very sick and no one could care for them. Therefore, Angelina took Angelo into her home and Mary arranged for her mother and her brother, Roger (who was still un-married at the time), to move into her home to care for them. This arrangement worked out well until Angela developed Parkinson's disease and Mary could not care for her any longer. Eventually, Angela was admitted into the Monroe County Home and Infirmary on West Henrietta Road in Rochester, New York.

Through this and other difficulties that occurred over the years, my Aunt Mary was always very helpful to the family and never complained about anything that had to be done. Even when others in the family were ill or needed care, she was always the first relative to assist. Whether it was in the middle of the night or during the day, it made no difference to her. She was the guiding hand for everyone. She not only gave physical assistance in the help she rendered, but also good, sound advice, a strong trait of hers that continued throughout her life.

A few years later, my Uncle Al and Aunt Mary purchased the two-family home down the street at 35 Oakman Street. They lived downstairs and rented the upstairs apartment to tenants. When they bought their next home, their son and daughter-in-law, Angelo and Audrey, moved into the downstairs apartment they had just vacated. They rented to upstairs apartment to my Uncle Roger and Aunt Lucy Cavallaro. Their new home at 20 Almira Street was on a double, side-by-side lot. It gave them added space for a large lawn in the front and the side. My Uncle Al filled the yard with numerous flowerbeds and it was very neat and attractive. A four-foot chain link fence extended across the entire front yard; neighbors and people walking down the street were attracted to the beautiful and unusual flowers he had planted in the front planters. On any given day, my Aunt Mary could be seen, working in the garden, weeding, loosening soil, and planting new flowers; she loved gardening and reaping the harvest of her hard work.

In their front yard, my Uncle Al erected a huge flagpole in a concrete base from where he flew the American flag during World War II. Daily, he raised the flag to commemorate his son's European service in the U.S. Army as he fought for many American freedoms. In their backyard, they had a large Victory Garden containing all kinds of vegetables including, tomatoes, cucumbers, peas, green beans, eggplants, and green peppers. They also grew many herbs such as, Italian basil, Italian oregano, rosemary, and dill. A large grapevine predominated the back fence. Since they had such a large harvest from their garden, they preserved many of the vegetables in Mason and Ball jars for use in the winter. My Uncle Al used some of the grapes from his yard along with others he purchased from the Public Market to make his own wine each year. Their yard was large enough to hold many family gatherings. I specifically remember some that included the reception for my Uncle Roger and Aunt Lucy's wedding; the Cavallaro-Lizzio Family Reunion for the Gravagna relatives visiting from Lodi, New Jersey; and the large homecoming party for Angelo when he returned from serving in World War II.

It was during this time that my Uncle Al and Aunt Mary began to purchase other real estate property. They bought other homes in the area, rented them out, and eventually resold them. They did this all in the same neighborhood where they lived, making it easy for them to manage the property and check on their tenants. They were always on the lookout for available properties they could fix-up and rent out to tenants. They were very successful at this endeavor. In their senior years, they eventually sold all the properties and moved to a new home on Creek Street in West Webster, New York.

Angelo Lizzio

Angelo Lizzio was born April 30, 1923. He attended Number 20 School for his elementary grades, Benjamin Franklin High School, continued his education at the Rochester Institute of Technology while majoring in Tool and Dye Engineering. He worked for Alliance Tool until his retirement as a Division Manager. In his earlier years, he served in the U.S. Army during World War II in the 3rd Army ETO (European Theater of Operation) which was under the direction of General George S. Patton. He was attached to the Antiaircraft Command in Europe. To commemorate his active duty, my Aunt Mary and Uncle Al hung a silk, red, white, and blue banner with one star, in the front window of their home. It showed they had a son serving in the military. Toward the end of his tour of duty, he reflected on his experience with the first jets being sent over the combat areas. His comment was, "They were going so fast we could never hit a one of them. Our antiaircraft weapons were not effective on the new jet flyers."

At that time of the war, General Patton was a Three Star General and had already developed quite a reputation for himself among the American people, the Europeans, and other commanders in the war. He was gruff, non-compensating, and a relentless driving force behind the major battles in Europe. General Patton's 3rd Army forces liberated France, Belgium, Germany, Bavaria, Austria, and Czechoslovakia. He and his troops traveled faster across battlefields, killing and wounding more and more enemy everyday, seizing more land and capturing more prisoners than any other army in history. He was considered the best commander of armored and infantry troops, even by the German High Command. Despite the worst winter in years, on December 20, 1944, General Patton diverted the 3rd Army from eastward attacks, turning ninety degrees to the north and attacked the Germans in the Ardennes Mountains. Most historians agree that no other commander and no other army could have accomplished this incredible feat. Angelo Lizzio was a part of this activity during his service in Europe.

During his years in the war, Angelo wrote to his family of his experiences. Letters from the military were being screened at that time, so he had to be very careful about discussing anything specific to his location or to the war in general. When anyone received a letter, his news was shared with all the family. My Aunt Mary and Uncle Al did the same with all the news they received. We listened to the radio broadcasts daily during the war years, following the activities of the 3rd Army, as they moved through Europe. Since we had no television, we had to depend on the newspapers and radio as our only media to receive our current war up-dates. Each evening, we listened as a family to see if they would give the exact location of the 3rd Army. We were hopeful it would give us some information of where Angelo was located or what battle was ensuing at that time. It was a very intense time for the entire family since Angelo was our only relative who was on the front lines during the war. It became very personal for each of us. As a pre-teen, I would boast to my friends at school that my cousin, Angelo, was at the front lines in the Antiaircraft Division in Europe. I was very proud to be able to say that, not realizing the jeopardy he was facing each moment he was there. My friends asked endless questions about the war because they thought I knew more about what was happening since I had a relative on the front lines. They didn't realize I knew very little about the war; everything I gleaned was from my parent's conversations after they had finished listening to the radio broadcast of the news. Suddenly, one day we received notification that Angelo had been wounded in battle.

My Aunt Mary and Uncle Al received a telegram and passed the information on to the remainder of the family. We didn't know the extent of the wounds, but we understood they were not life threatening. He was sent behind enemy lines to a hospital in England.

While Angelo was in the hospital located near London, he met an attractive, English Nurse's Aide who cared for him by the name of Audrey Herbert. A strong relationship developed between them. While he was recovering, he wasn't required to return to the frontlines in France, so he remained in England for a time. He continued his relationship with Audrey and met her parents and siblings. When it was time for him to return to the United States, he and Audrey had already made a commitment to one another that they would marry in the United States. The war ended and he returned home alone, leaving Audrey behind in England.

On the day the war ended in Europe, an incident occurred that I recall very clearly. The news came over the radio just after suppertime. All the neighbors on my street were outdoors shouting, "The war is over…the war is over….the war is over!" I could hear fireworks and people outdoors banging pots and pans together along with the metal covers of trashcans to make loud noises. It was a time to celebrate and many of the neighbors passed our house in groups to go to the downtown area and see the celebrations, which would occur on Main Street. My mother and father drove to my grandparent's home to give them the good news. My grandparents didn't have a phone and this was the only way for them to find out what was happening. I was at home with my brother and they told us to stay at home and wait for their return. It was just about dusk and my brother and I went to sit on our large front porch to talk to our neighbors and watch the procession of people going downtown. As we sat there, a large truck came by. It was an open truck with no top, but it had slotted panels on the side. It was filled with teenagers, many of whom were my brother's friends from high school. They were all waving American flags and shouting, "The war is over…the war is over….V for Victory…..V for Victory!" As the truck passed in front of my house, it stopped and my brother ran out to the street. He jumped onto the back of the truck with his friends. When I saw this, I ran out after him because I wanted to get on the truck also. He said, "No, you need to stay home. This is only for the kids in high school. We are going downtown to see the parade. Tell mom and dad that I'll be home soon." Therefore, I went back on the porch, sat alone, and waited. By this time, it became dark and I continued to sit outdoors, waiting. It was a hot August evening and I, too, wanted to watch the activities going on in our neighborhood.

All of a sudden, a car pulled up in front of our house. It was my Uncle Al and Aunt Mary. They had come to share the good news with my mother and father. They were excited and tremendously elated. They wanted to know where the family was. I recounted what had transpired that evening and they said, "You're coming home with us. We'll leave a note for your mother and father and you're coming to our house for the night." Of course, I agreed, locked the doors, and went to their home. When we arrived, my Aunt Mary gave me a snack and all they could talk about was what they were going to do when Angelo came home from the war. I slept overnight at their house. I slept in Angelo's bedroom, which was just off their large kitchen. The next morning over breakfast, my Aunt Mary said she had never allowed anyone to sleep in Angelo's bed while he was gone. She also said that when she got up in the morning, she checked on me. I must have been asleep and all she could see was my dark hair showing from under the blanket. She said it looked just like Angelo sleeping there, and that made her even more excited in anticipating his return. The next day, my parents came to pick me up and they visited a long time, just talking about the end of the war and of Angelo's eventual return. I shall never forget how my Uncle Al and Aunt Mary 'rescued' me that evening and took me to their home, as if I were their own child and at a time, which was very special for them.

Angelo returned home from the war and they gave a huge party in his honor. It was at their Almira Street home. The yard was full of relatives and close friends. It was such an exciting time for all of us. I can still picture, in my mind, the joy and relief in my Aunt Mary on that day. She wouldn't leave Angelo's side, continually hanging onto his arm, always looking up at him with her beaming smiles of pride and contentment. He was home. He was safe. He was with family again.

Shortly afterward and prior to Christmas 1946, Audrey arrived from England to the United States. She fit in with the family perfectly. One of the first things she concentrated on was learning all the family names. She was cordial to everyone, had a very sweet personality, and was very much in love with Angelo. Because of her strong English accent, that everyone enjoyed listening to, we all encouraged her to talk more.

In talking with Audrey in November 1997, she gave me some information about her background. She was born in West Bromwich in Staffordshire, England. It is located near Birmingham and Wolverhampton. Her family later moved to Wolverhampton, England to live. A few years later, they moved to Gloucestershire, which is near Gloucester and Cheltenham, all of which are about an hour drive from London. When she came to the United States, she came from Gloucestershire.

The first Christmas Audrey was in America, my Aunt Mary and Uncle Al invited my family to their home for Christmas dinner. We had a wonderful time and became somewhat better acquainted with Audrey. For the New Year holiday, my parents invited my Aunt Mary, Uncle Al, Angelo, and Audrey to our home for dinner. My mother had prepared a complete Italian meal and they really enjoyed it. After dinner, we decided to play cards around the dining room table. Audrey had a very difficult time understanding the American money system. She hadn't been here long enough to know how to use American money. She couldn't distinguish the difference between a quarter and a nickel, so she referred to the quarter as the 'big one' and the nickel as the 'little one.' Again, we had a great time.

A few months after her arrival to America, she asked me if I would be interested in writing to her sister, Pauline, in England. We were both about the same age and she thought it would be nice to have a pen pal in another country. I agreed and we began to correspond. I wrote to Pauline in Wolverhampton and we began communicating on a regular basis. We exchanged photos of each other and post cards with scenes of our cities. We wrote mainly about our schools and friends. It was an enjoyable time and I felt I really learned a lot about her and her country through our letter writing, which lasted all through my high school and college years.

Audrey and Angelo were married on a cold, winter morning. It was January 25, 1947 at St. Luke's Church on Fitzhugh Street. She asked my Aunt Angie to make her gown and chose a heavy, white-on-white, brocaded material. It was a beautiful gown with yards and yards of material. My brother, Al, was asked to be one of the ushers. A few days prior to the wedding, Audrey approached my mother and asked, "Since my own mother is not here in America and won't be at the wedding, would you, Aunt Theresa, please sit in the seat at the church my own mother would normally sit in?" My mother was reduced to tears because of the great honor Audrey bestowed on her. On the morning of the wedding, my mother gave Audrey a special white embroidered handkerchief, edged in lace, as a remembrance of her wedding day. It was embroidered by hand and the edging was hand-tatted lace, which made it very delicate; she carried it with her down the aisle on that special day. It was an important time for both of them. It was the beginning of a close relationship; besides being related to each other, they were good friends for their entire lives.

A couple of years later, Audrey and Angelo had their first child, Pauline, named after Audrey's sister in England. Pauline was born on December 1, 1949. Audrey always dressed her in the latest of little girl fashions and other beautiful outfits that my Aunt Mary handmade for her. Being as well behaved as she was, she always conducted herself as a 'lady' and never looked wrinkled or messy. Aunt Mary prided herself with Pauline and loved her so much; she was the little girl that she never had. She made countless dresses, sweaters, blankets, and other clothing for her. She couldn't do enough for her. She treated her like a little princess. A few years later, Angelo and Audrey were expecting again. This time it was twins - Twin Boys! Wow, this was the first set of twins for the Lizzio family, but it was the second set of twins for the Cavallaro family. What a joyous event. The entire Cavallaro family celebrated again at the news of another set of twins. On September 1, 1955, Mark Edward and John Christopher were born. They looked somewhat alike and were perfect in every way. My Aunt Mary gave Audrey much assistance during the first year, especially to care for the twins and help with all the necessary chores. She found herself giving the same grandparent assistance as her sister Angelina did when she had her first set of twin grandchildren. The boys grew up to be fine, young men and completed the family for Audrey and Angelo.

Mary's Final Years

My Aunt Mary and Uncle Al had a happy life together. They enjoyed spending most of their time with family, close friends, and *paisani*. In April of 1970, they celebrated their 50th wedding anniversary with a large party for the whole family. There was good food, music, and dancing; everyone had a grand time. A few years prior to that, they decided to move from their Almira Street home, which had been home for them for many years. My Uncle Al, with his designing skills, created a home they wanted to build in a suburb of Rochester. They found a large piece of property in West Webster that suited their needs and started building their new home on Creek Street. It was a one-story home with a finished basement. The design was unusual and a one-of-a kind house, in the shape of a wide letter 'U.' The backyard allowed them a lot of room for planting gardens and vegetables, which gave them a lot of pleasure. They moved into their new home and shared it often for many family gatherings and events. During the summers, they were in their glory working in the yard, in their gardens, and harvesting healthy vegetables and fruit.

Just after they moved to West Webster, my parents decided to sell their home on Weld Street in Rochester, which had been home to them for more than twenty-five years. They began looking for a home in West Webster also. They built a new home on Brookwood Drive in West Webster, which was only five minutes away from my Uncle Al and Aunt Mary and they visited each other often. During the winters, my Uncle Al and Aunt Mary traveled to Homestead Park, Florida, where they had a winter home. This allowed them to enjoy the summer weather in the south, during the same time that Rochester was experiencing cold, winter weather. Many members of the family, including my mother, visited them in Florida. Of course, as soon as they arrived in Florida each year, they immediately planted their gardens and harvested new and different crops. They looked forward to those trips during the winters.

In September 1974, my Uncle Al became ill and passed away at the age of seventy-eight. They had been married for fifty-four years. My Aunt Mary sold their beautiful home in Webster and moved to an apartment in the city limits of Rochester, on Fernwood Park. She brought much of her furniture with her and set up housekeeping again. It was a very difficult time for my Aunt Mary because she depended on my uncle for so much. He was very handy around the house and did everything for her. The entire family missed him greatly.

After I moved to California in 1970, I didn't see my Aunt Mary as often, except on my yearly trips when I went to Rochester to visit my mother. However, I made it a point to send her notes, cards, and pictures of my family throughout the year, especially on holidays and on her birthdays. It was during one of my visits to Rochester that I actually began my research on this genealogical quest. Each trip I made, she would invite me over for dinner along with the rest of the family. It was in 1980, when we were visiting her home on Fernwood Park that we began talking about the family history and I started gathering much of my information for my book. Her mind was so sharp and accurate; she never forgot a detail, many of which I have included in this book.

Earlier, I shared what took place at those eventful dinners when we discussed *cose di lungo fa* or *cose antiche* (things of long ago). Now, I want to take this time to express my heartfelt thanks to my Aunt Mary for providing me the opportunity to embark on this glorious journey. Without her encouragement and candid information, this project would have never happened. I am very disappointed she is not here to see this completed book and to enjoy its contents.

Many years passed and my Aunt Mary finally needed to be placed in a nursing home where she could be cared for and monitored continually. On one of my trips to Rochester, I visited her at the nursing home and found her to be in the very best of spirits. As I walked toward her from a distance, she immediately recognized me and began waving. We sat in her room and talked for a long time. Later, we took a walk outside in the gardens and had a wonderful afternoon visit. She was so happy to see me. At one point, my wife, Aggie and I were sitting on a park bench near the entrance of the building and she was holding my hand. She put her other arm around my shoulder, moved her head close to mine, looked directly into my eyes and said, "You remind me so much of my brother, Al. I look at you and I see him. You look just like him." I could see tears in her eyes as she continued, "I miss him so much." It was a very tender moment that I shall treasure forever. I looked at her and said, "Aunt Mary, my father loved you very much too. And I want you to know that I love you very much also." She gave me one of her famous 'Aunt Mary smiles' and a big, strong hug. When it was time for us to leave, she wanted to say goodbye to us outside, so we left her by the front door with one of the Nurse's Aides at her side. She was standing with her walker and continued to wave at us as we walked out to the parking lot to our car. Before we drove away, I looked back and saw her waving to us with that perpetual smile on her face. That scene continues to live on in my memory.

Aunt Mary had an unusual and very long life. I received word on December 9, 2002, that my Aunt Mary had passed away at 9:30 a.m. at the age of one hundred and two years old. On her one hundred and first birthday, she was featured in an article in the Rochester Democrat and Chronicle, published on July 10, 2001, to be one of the two hundred and thirteen centurions in Rochester, New York at that time. I called her, at the nursing home, on the afternoon of her one hundredth birthday. Her entire family was there to celebrate the big event. When we spoke, her mind was clear and sharp and we talked like old times. She was happy and very coherent. However, at one point in the conversation, she invited me to go over to have a piece of birthday cake. I told her I would love to but I was in California and couldn't attend. I think she had forgotten that piece of information for the moment. To the very end of her days, Angelo and Audrey were continually at her side and cared for her every need. She was a friend to all and was the part of the family that held everyone else together. My greatest memory of her is the smile she always had on her face. She was very happy, uplifting, and one of the most pleasant people I have ever known. She loved the family. She loved her brothers and sisters and helped them in many ways; and they all loved her in return. She was the tiniest built of all her siblings, yet she outlived them all. In her own way, she left a very strong legacy with many memories of her own. They were all important pieces of the puzzle that make up the Cavallaro and Lizzio families. We all love you Aunt Mary and you shall continue to live on in our memories.

Personal Comments

My Aunt Mary's granddaughter, Pauline, shared the following comments:

"Mary Catena Cavallaro Lizzio was the best grandma anyone could have. She baked the best bread, and made the best Italian tomato sauce. She could sew anything. She was always making clothes for her grandchildren and great-grandchildren; many of which were saved and passed on to her great-great grandchildren. She was filled with love and she was blessed with an unending amount of energy. She was always happy and with a sweet smile on her face. She had a tough life growing up. She wasn't allowed to go to school. She had to clean, cook and bake for the family from an early age. She learned to read and write from her wonderful husband."

With much love,
Granddaughter:
Pauline (Lizzio) Mitelli

Maria Catena *(Mary Cavallaro)* Lizzio
Family Tree

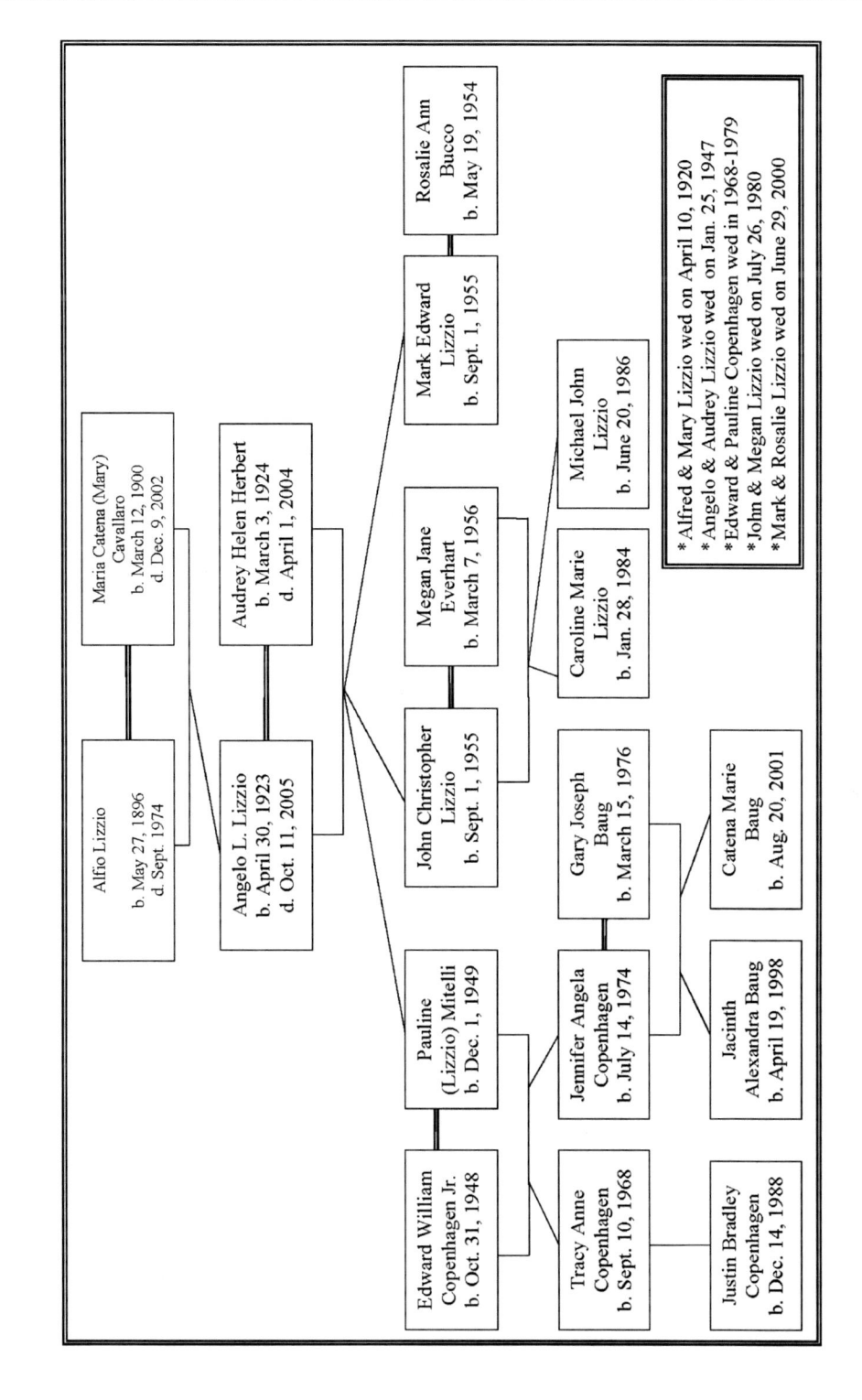

- Alfio Lizzio
  b. May 27, 1896
  d. Sept. 1974

- Maria Catena (Mary) Cavallaro
  b. March 12, 1900
  d. Dec. 9, 2002

- Angelo L. Lizzio
  b. April 30, 1923
  d. Oct. 11, 2005

- Audrey Helen Herbert
  b. March 3, 1924
  d. April 1, 2004

- Pauline (Lizzio) Mitelli
  b. Dec. 1, 1949

- Edward William Copenhagen Jr.
  b. Oct. 31, 1948

- John Christopher Lizzio
  b. Sept. 1, 1955

- Megan Jane Everhart
  b. March 7, 1956

- Mark Edward Lizzio
  b. Sept. 1, 1955

- Rosalie Ann Bucco
  b. May 19, 1954

- Tracy Anne Copenhagen
  b. Sept. 10, 1968

- Jennifer Angela Copenhagen
  b. July 14, 1974

- Gary Joseph Baug
  b. March 15, 1976

- Caroline Marie Lizzio
  b. Jan. 28, 1984

- Michael John Lizzio
  b. June 20, 1986

- Justin Bradley Copenhagen
  b. Dec. 14, 1988

- Jacinth Alexandra Baug
  b. April 19, 1998

- Catena Marie Baug
  b. Aug. 20, 2001

*Alfred & Mary Lizzio wed on April 10, 1920
*Angelo & Audrey Lizzio wed on Jan. 25, 1947
*Edward & Pauline Copenhagen wed in 1968-1979
*John & Megan Lizzio wed on July 26, 1980
*Mark & Rosalie Lizzio wed on June 29, 2000

Mary (Maria Catena Cavallaro) Lizzio

April 10, 1920
Alfred and Mary Lizzio
Angelina Lamanna & Jennie Cavallaro
(Bridesmaids at right)

50th Wedding Anniversary
Mary & Alfred Lizzio
(1970)

Mary Lizzio & Angelo Lizzio
(He'd just returned from WWII duty)

Angela and Maria Catena Cavallaro

Mary Lizzio & Richard Cavallaro
(At Penfield Place Nursing Home 1995)

Cousins
Alfred Lizzio & Alfred Cavallaro
(circa 1919)

Cousins
Alfred Lizzio & Alfred Cavallaro

(Alfred Cavallaro put on Alfred Lizzio's
uniform just to take the picture.
Only Alfred Lizzio had served
in the Army – taken circa 1919)

Maria Catena Cavallaro
Alfred Lizzio
(March 1920 – just prior to their wedding)

Early 1920s
Rosa (Cavallaro) Lizzio
Angelo Lizzio
In Rochester, New York

Angelo & Mary Lizzio
(1995 at Penfield Place Nursing Home)

Mary & Angelo Lizzio
Audrey and Alfred Lizzio
(At the Lizzio 50th Anniversary Party)

November 1928
Mary, Alfred, & Angelo Lizzio
(At Joe and Jennie Gargano's wedding)

Christmas 1946
We celebrated Christmas with
Audrey who just arrived from England

Angelo & Audrey Lizzio & Family
Audrey (Herbert) Lizzio with Mark
Pauline
Angelo Lizzio with John

Mary With her Brothers & Sisters
Roger, Joan, Mary, Angelina & Joe

Giuseppe (Joseph P.) Cavallaro

October 21, 1902 – February 5, 1983

Prologue

Giuseppe Cavallaro was the fourth living child who was born to Angelo and Angela Cavallaro. At this point and time, Angelo was thirty-five years old, Angela was twenty-five years old, and the ages of Giuseppe's sisters and brothers were as follows: Angelina (seven), Alfred (five), and Mary (two) years old. It was just prior to 1901 that Angelo began his many trips to America. It is unknown whether he was in Sicily at the time of Giuseppe's birth, but we find Angela at age twenty-four with four children under the age of seven to support. She continued her sewing at home in order to earn enough funds to provide for her family.

Giuseppe's birthplace is recorded as being in Castiglione di Sicilia, which is in the Province of Catania. It is a community in northeastern Sicily, approximately eight miles away from the infamous Passopisciaro, the town where most of my relatives were born. It is located about two miles North of the rim of the active volcano, Mt. Etna. Knowing that Italians followed the tradition of naming their children after previous generations of relatives, I searched for other Giuseppe's in the Cavallaro family tree. The only other Giuseppe I could find was a son, born to Salvatore Cavallaro, Angelo's younger brother. Other than Angelo's nephew Giuseppe, there was no other person in the family with that same name prior to his birth.

The Beginning

Joseph (as I will refer to him from now on, since it is the name he used in America) was a relatively easy child to raise. He was even tempered, patient, and was a well-behaved child…. all traits he continued to have into his adult life. He grew up with much care from his older sisters, Angelina and Mary. As young as they were, they brought Joseph everywhere they went. He was like a new toy for them and they played with him constantly. As he grew older, he wanted to do everything with his brother Alfred. Alfred, being five years older, spent much time teaching him many things. When his father, Angelo returned to Sicily from his trip to America, he would bring Alfred and Joseph with him to work at the stone quarries. It was hard work for little boys, but many of the men brought their young sons there to learn the trade of stonecutting and to help in earning more money for the family. When Angelo wasn't working at the quarries, Joseph remained at home with the other children and his mother. As he grew older, his mother started to teach him to sew; he began to learn all the basic stitches of sewing and practiced them often. The three older children were learning to sew as well and they helped him learn the trade. In later years when he grew older and was in America, he refined his sewing skills by learning more about tailoring from his sister Angelina. By this time, she was very skilled at sewing and helped him perfect his techniques so he could work in a tailor factory.

Joseph Arrives in America

When Angelo and Angela made the decision to sail to America, it was in the year 1913 and Joseph was ten years old. Along with the other children, he was very excited about going to a new country. By that time, Angelo and Angela had six children to transport, the youngest being three years old. Joseph was strong and could assist his parents in a number of chores that needed to be accomplished with the move. He was old enough to care for his younger siblings, but more importantly, he was strong enough to carry bags, luggage, or any packages the family needed. When they left Passopisciaro for their trip to Palermo, he was responsible for two large canvas bags of clothes along with a medium-sized suitcase. It was more than a child his age could carry, but he managed it well. The two canvas bags were tied with rope and he was able to strap them on his shoulders like a backpack and still manage the piece of luggage. He transported those same pieces all the way to Palermo. He was responsible for them on the boat for twenty-three days, and when he walked down North Clinton Avenue from the train, he was still holding onto them. Sometimes, when they became too heavy, he would have to drag them on the ground and his brother, Roger, would help lift them as much as he could.

While they walked down North Clinton Avenue, they began to see many *paisani* from Passopisciaro. He recognized a few of them and it gave Joseph a feeling of security in knowing they had some friends in this new country. They spoke the same dialect and he felt everything would be fine now. They walked to the home of his Uncle Sebastiano (known later as Uncle Yanno) who had sponsored the family and had offered them a temporary place to live at his home on Albow Place.

After the family moved into their first home on Lowell Street, Joseph found it lacked a central heating system. There was only a stove in the kitchen; half of it had been converted to burn wood or coal, which would provide heat in the cold winters of upstate New York. Wood and coal were expensive to purchase. It was the responsibility of the boys in the family to go into the neighborhood to find wooden scraps from trees or old houses. They would bring them home to burn. That worked for a while, but since wood does not burn for very long, the house would get cold again. The following is shared by Joe Cavallaro, Joseph's son:

> *"The only things I remember my dad telling me about his early years (before marriage) was that as a young boy he gathered coal (for heating) that fell from the trains."*

Gathering coal that fell from trains was a very common practice among immigrants. Since coal was at a premium, they had to be at the train tracks early in the morning before others would beat them to this treasure. If they didn't find coal where the trains were, they would walk down the tracks to find it elsewhere. At that time, coal was transported in open boxcars and when the train would go over a bump where the tracks were connected, some pieces of coal would fall to the ground. Many of the immigrants could be seen at the tracks collecting coal; sometimes, whole families would be there. They would carry sacks or bring wagons in which to carry the coal. Coal was very important to have during the cold winter months in Rochester. It would burn slowly and heat their living quarters much better and for a longer period than using wood as their fuel.

At every opportunity, Joseph continued to accompany his father and brothers to collect coal, which became a daily chore. As reported by his son, Joe Cavallaro:

> *"On some of the trips, they were collecting something else. My dad told me he remembers his father bringing home bottles of wine in a wagon across the Smith Street Bridge. He said that on one occasion, a bottle fell from the wagon and broke. My grandfather sat on the curb drinking as much wine as he could recover from the broken bottle. I believe dad was trying to tell me that grandfather Cavallaro really liked his wine or had a drinking problem."*

This occurrence confirms what was recorded earlier in the life of Angelo Cavallaro. On occasion, he was known for enjoying a good glass of wine. Of course, since he couldn't afford this indulgence very often, when the opportunity arose, he wouldn't waste a drop of it, even if the bottle had broken.

Joseph found that life in America was not as he had envisioned. While in Sicily, he was told that he could pick up gold from the streets in America, but in reality, he was picking up coal with his father and brothers, which turned out to be a hard and dirty job. This activity of collecting coal scraps continued throughout the long winters in Rochester. Coming from Sicily, where the weather was considerably warmer and similar to the climate in California, long winters with a lot of snow was a new life-style for the entire family. However, they were home now and had to deal with the elements the best they could. This meant working hard to make a new life for themselves. As he grew older, Joseph was determined that he would not continue that kind of existence as an adult. He worked hard to provide a comfortable life for him and his family.

Joseph Begins a Family of His Own

When the United States became involved in World War I on April 6, 1917 and declared war on Germany, Angela decided to purchase the farm in West Bloomfield. At that time, Joseph was about fifteen years old. He worked with his brothers, Alfred and Roger, and with his Uncle Sebastiano to run the farm. It was hard work, but they made it a success as a family. When the farm was sold in 1920, Joseph went to live with his sister and brother-in-law, Angelina and Frederico Lamanna on Albow Place. While he was living there, Angelina helped him to refine his sewing skills. He wanted to apply for a job in a tailor factory and she helped him break into the clothing industry. As reported by his son, Joe Cavallaro:

> *"He eventually was employed by Bond Clothing as a pocket maker. My Uncle Roger was soon to follow as a pocket maker also. Two other uncles and my mother worked at Bond Clothing also. My Uncle Alfred was a presser and my Uncle Al Lizzio worked on vests. I remember working as a rush boy at Bond's. During the two summers I worked at Bonds, I was able to visit each of them and observe what they did."*

During his early years of working at Bond Clothing and while he was still living with his sister Angelina, he brought his paycheck home to her and she helped him budget his money. He felt very comfortable in having his older sister do that for him. He continued to work at Bond Clothing factory, in Shops #1, #17, and #18 until his retirement. His wife, Jennie, worked as an edge-baster on collars of men's suit jackets in Shop #17. My Uncle Roger also worked in Shop #17 with them. It was a real joy for him to see his brothers and sisters every day at work.

As he began to work and have money of his own, he used it to buy clothes for himself. He always prided himself in being neatly and smartly dressed. It was very unusual for him to be out with his friends or to see him on a Sunday afternoon when he wasn't dressed in a suit, shirt, and tie. Most of the photographs I have of him were taken in his late teens and early twenties. They show he was always well dressed and had excellent taste in selecting his clothing. He had many friends; some were *paisani* that he knew from Sicily. They went out on the weekends, mostly just to walk the neighborhood and to be together. His son, Joe Cavallaro reports the following:

> *"I also remember when my dad brought me to buy clothing and we ran into one of his old friends. He commented on the fact that my dad was a great dancer and the girls liked him. However, dad talked the story down. To him it was more important for me to study than to go dancing with girls."*

To write about one brother without commenting on the other two, Alfred and Roger, is not easily done. My Uncle Joe, Uncle Roger, and my father were all great dancers. I remember attending many family weddings and functions where they would always be on the dance floor, dancing with their wives, sisters, sister-in-laws or other relatives and friends. Each one had perfected the steps to the popular dances of the time. They could waltz, foxtrot, or polka to perfection. They could be picked out from a room full of dancers as being the most graceful and rhythmic on the dance floor.

Moving ahead a few years to 1954, I remember watching them dance at my brother, Al's, wedding. The wedding reception was held at the Seneca Hotel in downtown Rochester, New York, and there was a five-piece live orchestra playing. They played all the popular Italian songs. At one time that evening, all three brothers were on the dance floor with their wives. All of a sudden, my Uncle Joe switched partners and began dancing with my mother, my father went to dance with my Aunt Lucy, and my Uncle Roger went to dance with my Aunt Jennie. It happened so quickly, it appeared to be pre-planned. Maybe it was, but I think they did this often whenever they were all present at a wedding where the whole family was invited. They laughed and laughed and had a grand time. They were playing a polka during that dance set and a lot of the family was on the dance floor. I watched them from the edge of the dance floor with many other spectators who stopped dancing just to watch them. We all began clapping our hands, and shouting comments from the sidelines to them. I stood there in amazement and marveled at how they all danced with other partners and never missed a beat of the music. When the dance ended, a shout went forth with clapping from all the guests around the dance floor. In response, my Uncle Joe, my Uncle Roger and my father all bowed to their partners; my Aunt Jennie Cavallaro stretched her skirt at both sides and did a courtesy, which I can remember her doing often. We don't have any pictures of that scene, but I will never forget the memory of my uncles, aunts, and my parents dancing together. It truly showed how much they enjoyed each other's company, how they appreciated the same things in life, and how much they loved each other.

It is simply impossible to discuss Joseph Cavallaro without discussing his wife, Vincenzina; my Aunt Jennie, as we all knew her. When I first began collecting information on the Cavallaro genealogy, my Aunt Jennie was also at my Aunt Mary's house and she, too, shared her early background with me. Because of the strong role she played in the Cavallaro family, I feel it is important to include her information also; it being somewhat different from Joseph's experience in coming to America.

My Aunt Jennie's parents, John and Agatina Samperi were from San Giovanni, a very small town that bordered Passopisciaro, where the Cavallaro family lived. It, too, was located in the foothills of Mt. Etna. Aunt Jennie's birth was registered in Castiglione di Sicilia, which is the same community where most of the Cavallaro children's births were registered. Therefore, the Samperi family, *paisani* of the Cavallaro family, knew each other prior to their immigration to the United States. She and her family immigrated to Argentina in 1908, when she was nine months old. They settled in Buenos Aires and lived there until she was ten years old. In 1918, which was during World War I, they returned to Sicily until she was fourteen years old. Then in 1922, she immigrated to the United States. Her father, John Samperi, came to America six months earlier to settle in Rochester, New York in preparation for his family's arrival; then, he sent for the rest of the family. My Aunt Jennie came to America with her mother, Agatina, known to us as *'Donna Tina'*, along with her brothers Frank and Pat.

When the Samperi family settled in Rochester, they, like the Cavallaro family, chose to live in the same area of North Clinton Avenue, where the rest of the *paisani* from the Mt. Etna area were living. It gave them a sense of security and helped them to feel more at home in a new country.

When Father J. Winterroth married twenty-seven year old Joseph and twenty-two year old Jennie at St. Michael's Church on North Clinton Avenue, on February 15, 1930, little did they realize it would be their parish church for most of their lives. According to the Marriage Certificate, Joseph had been living with his mother at 680 North Clinton Avenue and Jennie was living with her parents at 42 Oakman Street prior to their marriage. Their honor attendants were Betty Nielfe as Maid of Honor, and Andrew Prisciullo as Best Man. It is not known what relationship either of these people had to my Uncle Joe or Aunt Jennie.

According to the United States Federal Census, which was taken on April 11, 1930, it indicated that, after their marriage, Joe and Jennie were living with my Grandmother Cavallaro at the 680 North Clinton Avenue address. In addition, it showed that Joseph was working in the clothing manufacturing industry as a brusher and Jennie was working as a coat feller. A few years later, they had a son but he died at birth. Then, on August 7, 1937, their son Joseph A. Cavallaro was born. They had no other children after Joseph. By that time, they were living in the house in the rear of the Samperi family home at 42 Oakman Street, and lived there until after Joseph retired.

In later years, Joseph became involved in the political scene in the 5th Ward. He worked at the voting booths in the November elections and for other special elections that were held. On November 7, 1969, he ran and was elected to the position of Constable of the 5th Ward. He had many contacts with other politicians within the community through this position and he took his work very seriously in fulfilling his duties and responsibilities.

In a brief synopsis of his life up to this point, his son, Joe writes:

> *"Where he came from and where he lived: I believe my dad came to the United States from a small town in Sicily called 'The Way of the Fisherman' in the Province of Catania. They lived in the North Clinton Avenue/Oakman Street area of the city of Rochester for approximately fifty years. When my dad and mom were married, they lived the first few years of their marriage with my Grandfather and Grandmother Cavallaro at their North Clinton Avenue home, which was next to the old firehouse. After that, they lived at the 42 Oakman Street address with my Grandfather and Grandmother Samperi. An interesting note about where this family lived, is that also living on Oakman Street, at one time or another, were the following: my dad's father, my mother's father and mother, my dad's brother Roger and his wife Lucy, his sister Mary and her husband Al Lizzio, his sister Angelina and her husband Fritz, and niece Jennie and her husband Joe Romeo. My Aunt Joan lived on Oakman Street also with my dad and mom after her first marriage to Joe Gargana. After living on Oakman Street for many years, my dad and mom moved to an apartment in the Lake Avenue/Charlotte area of Rochester, which was within walking distance from where I lived. Dad lived there until his death in 1983."*

Trips to Old Forge, New York

As Joe Cavallaro, his son, shares:

> *"My Mom and Dad managed to spend five weeks in the Adirondack Mountains each year during the latter part of August and the early part of September."*

As I was growing older, I remember the family talking about my Aunt Jennie having something called Hay Fever. I had never heard of it before; however, I knew when she had it, she was very uncomfortable. She couldn't breathe well, her eyes watered, her nose became reddened, and her voice sounded like she had a very bad cold. This always happened during the fall of each year. My Uncle Joe decided that she needed to be away from the pollen in the city during that time of year and took her to the Adirondack Mountains where she could breathe cleaner air. During the years they went to the mountains, they stayed at various locations. At first, my Uncle Joe found a place in White Lake. They stayed there a couple of seasons. Joe, their son, was about four years old. Then, they found a cabin at Otter Lake they enjoyed for a few years. From there, they found a place at Old Forge called The Heimer Cabins. They returned to Old Forge for many years until those cabins were sold. The following fall and for a few years after, they went to Inlet; this was approximately ten miles from Old Forge. When my Aunt Jennie went to the mountains, she had significant relief from her allergies; she'd return home when the pollen season was over and it had stopped polluting the air. I remember, on at least two occasions, when the whole family went to visit her in the mountains.

One of those times was in the fall of 1941. It was just one year after Joe and Jennie Romeo had been married. Most of the Cavallaro family decided to take their vacations at the same time and visit Aunt Jennie together. My Uncle Joe and Aunt Jennie were able to rent a large house for us, which was in the same area where they were staying. The house only had two or three bedrooms and a long front porch. One of the bedrooms was reserved for Joe and Jennie Romeo because everyone referred to them as the 'honeymooners,' and they needed a room of their own. The other two were shared by the adults. Any remaining adults and all the younger children slept on the floor in the large living room.

An incident occurred on that particular trip that most of the family remembers well. It happened on the first night of arrival and after everyone had retired for the evening. Nighttime in the mountains are very dark; there are no streetlights and the only light that can be seen is the moonlight that shines between the trees. Therefore, there is practically total darkness. In the middle of the night, my Uncle Fritz had to use the restroom. He decided not to turn on any of the lights because he knew the general location where the bathroom was located. However, he had to go from his bedroom, through the living room where some of the adults and all the children were sleeping on the floor, and then to the bathroom on the other side of the house. Well, before he got very far on his quest, we began to hear shrieks from some of the people on the floor. There was yelling and screaming heard from many as they were being stepped on by my Uncle Fritz. I think he stepped on each one of us, one at a time. This aroused everyone in the entire house to see what was happening. All the lights went on and there stood my Uncle Fritz, in his shorts, trying to get to the bathroom. We all erupted in total laughter. We relived that scene many times before we left the mountains and for many years later. Whenever we gathered together as a family, it was very common for someone to say, "Hey, Frederico, so you remember the night you were trying to go to the bathroom in the dark in the mountains?" It would go on from there, to reliving the whole incident with a lot of laughter again and again. We had a great time and when we left the mountains, I always looked forward to returning someday soon. We did go back a few years later and we had a very enjoyable time. We went on hikes, played baseball, had picnics everyday, and the family did a lot of eating and laughing together.

As you can see from the pictures at the end of this chapter, those in my family who attended were as follows: Uncle Fritz and Aunt Angie; Joe and Jennie Romeo; my mother, father, brother, and me; Aunt Mary, Uncle Al Lizzio, and their son Angelo; and Uncle Joe, Aunt Jennie Cavallaro and their son Joe. The others in the pictures were not from the family, but people who lived at the White Lake property.

Those were wonderful outings for the Cavallaro family and, again it was another occasion to spend quality time together, drawing us closer to each other. Many years later, when I was married and had a family of my own, my wife and I and our three children went to Old Forge a few times to vacation – it was a great time to reminisce and relive all those great memories we had as a family long ago.

The Sport of Hunting

One hobby the Cavallaro brothers enjoyed was the sport of hunting. When the family owned the farm in West Bloomfield, they often went hunting for rabbits, pheasants, and woodchucks in the woods. After they were all married, they continued to hunt there, either together or separately. Each time they returned to hunt at the farm, they would always ask permission from the new owners before entering the property. As recounted by my cousin, Joe, in his memories of hunting, he states:

> *"I remember the time dad brought me and Uncle Yanno to the West Henrietta farm to hunt woodchucks. We cooked steaks on a campfire and toasted wheat shafts on the fire also. We rolled the shafts in our hands to break out the kernels which we ate, followed by the steaks and some bread. And the men always had a glass of wine with their steaks."*

Sometimes the hunting party included all three brothers; yet, depending upon their schedules, there were times when only two of them would spend the day hunting. There were other times that the hunting party included other friends, *paisani,* or relatives; such as, Russell Trovato, my Uncle Al Lizzio, Uncle Yanno, Frank Samperi, Phillip LaRosa, Sam LaRocca and in later years, my brother Al. Invariably, they always came back with some type of game for the women to cook.

If the day was ending and they hadn't caught any game, they might choose to stay a bit longer until they shot something to bring home to show their day had been well spent. Over the years, they would reminisce about those special hunting excursions, the great times they had on the farm, and how it had changed over the years; there was always some discussion as to who shot the most game, which usually ended in a lot of laughter by all of them.

The Early Years Through Retirement

In sharing information about his dad, Joe Cavallaro shares the following memories:

> *"The average week for our family consisted of Dad going to work, coming home, and having dinner. Dad would read the paper, mom would clean the dishes, and I would study and listen to the radio. On Saturdays, you would see Dad working on a house he owned on Oakman Street, and the house we lived in (owned by Grandma and Grandpa Samperi) and eventually Uncle Yanno's home on Albow Place. Dad would often go to the Public Market on Saturday to buy fruit and vegetables, pick up a live chicken or two on Joseph Avenue (which he killed and cleaned himself), and would stop by The Mazza Meat Market for two Porterhouse steaks, which were split between my father, mother, grandmother, and me. Grandma and I would always get the best part of the steaks."*

> *"In the latter years and after retiring, Dad would garden behind my house on Valley Street. He especially liked Italian flat beans. My mother would prepare them in tomato sauce and freeze the flat beans for the winter. He also enjoyed reading and liked to watch soap operas, baseball, football, and western movies. At the Adirondack Mountains, he enjoyed walking, reading, picking berries, and a little fishing. He would often bring his granddaughter Patricia, and later followed by my daughter,*

Denise, to the Adirondack Mountains. He would tutor Patricia in any subjects she may have had problems with. He was a loving grandfather. Dad and Mom visited Sicily after retiring. As far as I know, he did not know of, or visit any Cavallaro's in Sicily. Dad and Mom did visit my mother's sister and spent several weeks touring Sicily and the peninsula of Italy. Dad and Mom also visited Aunt Mary Lizzio in Florida."

Cavallaro Traditions

It was a tradition that all the Cavallaro brothers made wine each year. My Uncle Al Lizzio did the same. This must have some connection to winemaking that goes back to Sicily. After all, they lived in the highest wine producing area of Italy and Sicily combined. In addition to that, they worked in the vineyards as young boys and grew up with wine always being served on the dinner table. Therefore, when the brothers were all married, one by one, they decided to make wine. They made it in their own homes; however, they used different methods of winemaking each had perfected. Since they all worked at Bond Clothing, many times they would discuss their winemaking while they ate lunch together. They shared their ideas and received suggestions from other Italians who worked with them. In contemporary times, it is very common for men to gather together and discuss lawns, gardening, or cars. In that day, among Italian immigrants, it was very common for the men to discuss winemaking skills. Each year, they changed their recipes a little bit until they perfected the process, the taste, and the color of their wine. Although the wine was made in their own homes and the process discussed extensively, they each made it a bit differently. My cousin, Joe, remembers the annual event as follows:

> *"The fall of the year was the time for winemaking. Dad would buy grapes on Jay Street. He and I would press the grapes. After that, he would place the crushed grapes in the barrel and allow the grapes to ferment. A few months later, the wine would be ready for drinking. It was usually around Easter, which was also the time for cooking a baby lamb; however, at Christmas, we would make homemade sausage, macaroni, and cookies."*

Each year, my father visited his brothers and my Uncle Al Lizzio and they exchanged bottles of wine with each other. It was comical to see their reactions when they tasted each other's wine. Each brother thought their wine was the best. Comments went around the table that one wine was too sweet, one was too weak, one didn't have the correct color, or one may not have been dry enough. They were probably all very good wines, each with their own unique flavors, but their comments were like an annual ritual to prove that each brother's wine was the best.

As a young boy growing up, I looked forward to one special event. It was always on Christmas Day. My mother was busy preparing the Christmas dinner for our family and any guests we invited, and my father would tell her that he was going to visit his brothers and sisters for Christmas. Each year, I would accompany him on these Christmas morning visits. My mother sent along some Italian cookies she had made for each family; in addition, my father brought a bottle of wine for them. I looked forward to this and it was a lot of fun for me. Even if we didn't have enough time to visit all of them, he always made sure to stop by his brother's homes, Joe and Roger. They lived diagonally across the street from each other so it was very convenient, especially if the weather was bad and there was a lot of snow and ice on the ground.

I can vividly remember going to my Uncle Joe and Aunt Jennie's house on Christmas morning. They would be busily preparing for the Christmas meal also, but as soon as we arrived, we'd sit at the kitchen table and my Aunt Jennie would have a large plate of homemade Italian cookies for us to sample. They would have coffee or wine for the adults and a glass of milk for me. *Donna Tina* was there and sat next to me, encouraging me taste each variety of cookie they had made. We always went home with some to share with the rest of the family. Then my cousin Joe would invite me into the living room to see their tree and some of the gifts he had received for Christmas. We didn't stay very long because we had other family to visit. However, because most of them lived close by, either on Oakman Street or around the corner on Almira Street, our travel time was minimal. We walked across the street to my Uncle Roger and Aunt Lucy's house, and then drove around the corner to my Aunt Mary and Uncle Al Lizzio's house on Almira Street. Our last stop was usually at my Aunt Angie and Uncle Fritz's home. They lived on Norton Street and it took us a little longer to get there. Sometimes when the weather was bad, we would only visit my Uncle Joe and Aunt Jennie, as well as my Uncle Roger and Aunt Lucy. We were only gone from home for a couple of hours on Christmas morning, but it was a tradition I shall never forget; I know my father really enjoyed doing it as well. It was a special tradition, and one that brought him closer with his family.

Final Comments

I have many happy memories about my Uncle Joe and vivid recollections of my times with him and his family. Along with the other Cavallaro children, he worked hard for what he had. From having no trade at all, he became an excellent tailor at Bond Clothing Company; his work was well done and his supervisors always requested him to do certain jobs that needed special attention. He was an intelligent man; taught himself to read and write in a second language, became naturalized, and was successful in community affairs. He always looked neat and well dressed. He carried himself straight and tall and his clothes were stylish and well cared for. He was never in a hurry and had time to talk to each of us. At various family gatherings, he spent time with my brother and me, just the three of us. I remember the time when he had a party for his son, Joe, just prior to his wedding. He invited all the Cavallaro and Samperi men along with all the ushers in the wedding. It was a proud moment for my Uncle Joe. He cooked steaks outside in the backyard and he was a perfect host. I don't recall him ever being angry or cross with anyone; in fact, he always had a smile on his face. As you've probably noticed, I've used this phrase many times in this book because I think it was a strong and dominant characteristic of all the Cavallaro children; each one was very happy, contented, always smiling and laughing with each other and their families.

A major character trait of my Uncle Joe I feel dominates all others was his love for family – his personal family of my Aunt Jennie, Joe and his Samperi in-laws and, his extended family of brothers and sisters. Being an immigrant and having to struggle and survive in a new country as he did, he understood the value of education. He had a strong belief that receiving a good education was very important and would make life easier and more fruitful for the next generation. Therefore, when it came time for his son, Joe, to go to college, he sacrificed greatly and made it possible for him to attend a four-year university; both the University of Buffalo and the University of Rochester. Joe began to study in the field of Pharmacy and then changed his major to the field of Accounting. This helped him to pursue his life's work in the field of Finance, which led to his eventual position of being the Treasurer for the City of Rochester for approximately thirty years until his retirement. My Uncle Joe and Aunt Jennie were very proud of their son. I remember one summer when I was visiting in Rochester, my Aunt Jennie had already moved into her apartment on Hudson Avenue on the eleventh floor. She brought me out to the balcony, pointed to the tall buildings in the center of the city, and said, "Do you see that building over there? That's where my Joey works. I can look over there and almost see him every day." What a blessing for her to be able to say in her later years. I am confident that it brought her much comfort and security to know that he was so close to her.

Uncle Joe and Aunt Jennie were always faithful in supporting the family. Whenever there was a family emergency, they would drop everything and run to give support or assistance wherever they could. When my father was dying in the hospital in 1964, my Uncle Joe and Aunt Jennie waited at the hospital with us into the late hours of the night and the early morning. They were there to give support and help us grieve when we received word that my father had died. I shall never forget that.

Uncle Joe was a fine man. He loved his family. As stated very aptly by his son Joe:

> *"My father was a caring man. His family came first over his personal needs or wants. He was a good grandfather, too."*

Joseph Cavallaro was a very important part of the Cavallaro family and brought much tradition and stability to our heritage. We all appreciated and respected him very much. He was a very dear man, important in all our individual lives, and we all loved him. To this day, we sincerely miss him, his comforting words and, most importantly, his smile. We love you Uncle Joe!

Giuseppe *(Joseph P.)* Cavallaro
Family Tree

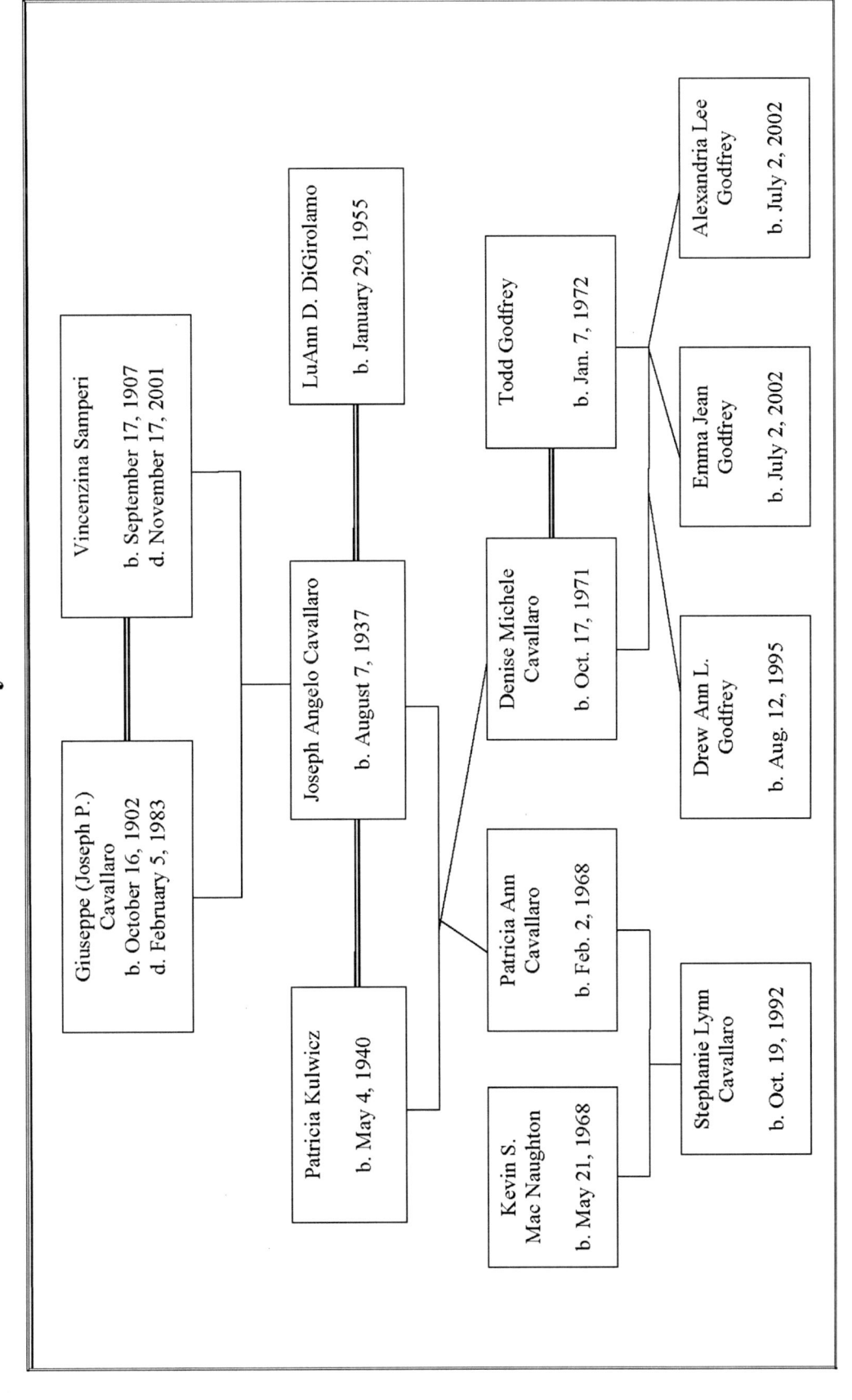

- Giuseppe (Joseph P.) Cavallaro
  b. October 16, 1902
  d. February 5, 1983
- Vincenzina Samperi
  b. September 17, 1907
  d. November 17, 2001

- Joseph Angelo Cavallaro
  b. August 7, 1937
- Patricia Kulwicz
  b. May 4, 1940
- LuAnn D. DiGirolamo
  b. January 29, 1955

- Denise Michele Cavallaro
  b. Oct. 17, 1971
- Todd Godfrey
  b. Jan. 7, 1972
- Patricia Ann Cavallaro
  b. Feb. 2, 1968
- Kevin S. Mac Naughton
  b. May 21, 1968

- Drew Ann L. Godfrey
  b. Aug. 12, 1995
- Emma Jean Godfrey
  b. July 2, 2002
- Alexandria Lee Godfrey
  b. July 2, 2002
- Stephanie Lynn Cavallaro
  b. Oct. 19, 1992

Joseph P. Cavallaro
Certificate of Naturalization
September 28, 1926

Joseph P. Cavallaro
Certificate of Birth
October 21, 1902

COMUNE DI CASTIGLIONE DI SICILIA
Provincia di Catania

CERTIFICATO DI NASCITA

L'Ufficiale dello Stato Civile
Visti gli Atti d'Ufficio

C E R T I F I C A

che....Cavallaro Giuseppe di Angelo e di Gravagno Angela

é nat° nel Comune di....Castiglione di Sicilia........

il giorno....ventuno....dem mese di....ottobre........

DELL'anno mille....novecentodue....................

Così risulta dal Registro degli Atti di nascita

di questo Comune dell'anno....1902..................

Parte....I....Serie....U....Numero....286..........

Il presente si rilascia a....Cavallaro..............

per....uso pensione....AI SENSI DELL'ART. 3 DEL D. P. R.
                      DEL 2-5-1957 - N. 432 -

Castiglione di Sicilia lì....16/5/1967..............

L'impiegato responsabile

L'UFFICIALE DELLO STATO CIVILE

Joseph P. (Giuseppe) Cavallaro

February 15, 1930
Joseph & Vincenzina (Jennie Samperi) Cavallaro

Joe and Jennie Cavallaro
(At his birthday party)

LuAnn, Jennie, & Joe Cavallaro
(1995)

ELECT
JOSEPH CAVALLERO
CONSTABLE
5th WARD
Vote Democratic—Vote Row B

A flyer used during the campaign when Joe Cavallaro ran for 5th Ward Constable in Rochester, NY

Roger & Joe Cavallaro
Picking grapes in Naples, NY

Joseph & Jennie Cavallaro
With Joe Cavallaro

Jennie Samperi & Joe Cavallaro
With Angelo Lizzio (1929)

The family visits Joe and Jennie at the Adirondack Mountains
September 1941

Jennie Romeo,
Angelina Lamanna,
Theresa Cavallaro,
Mary Lizzio
Jennie Cavallaro

Al & Mary Lizzio,
Theresa Cavallaro,
Angelina Lamanna,
Jennie & Joe Romeo

Jennie, Joe & Joe Cavallaro

Joe & Jennie Romeo,
Al & Theresa Cavallaro

Joe Romeo (behind sign)
Alfred Lizzio

Early Morning in the Mountains
Angelo, Alfred & Mary Lizzio, Theresa, Alfred &
Richard Cavallaro, Angelina & Frederick Lamanna,
Jennie and Joe Romeo

White Lake, New York
Theresa Cavallaro, Mary Lizzio
Joe & Jennie Romeo

Going Home
Back Row: Alfred & Theresa Cavallaro, Angelina
Lamanna, Joe & Jennie Romeo, Joe and Jennie
Cavallaro, Frederick Lamanna
Front Row: Al Cavallaro Jr., Mary & Alfred Lizzio,
Joe Cavallaro, Richard Cavallaro,
(Boy in front & man at right own the property)

Rowing a Fallen Log Boat
Joe Cavallaro
Joey & Jennie Cavallaro
Mary Lizzio
Theresa Cavallaro
Joe & Jennie Romeo
Angelina & Frederico Lamanna

Orazio (Roger Joseph) Cavallaro

November 30, 1905 – January 6, 2000

Prologue

Orazio Cavallaro was the fifth living child that was born to Angelo and Angela Cavallaro. At the time of his birth, Angelo was thirty-eight years old, Angela was twenty-eight years old, and the ages of Orazio's sisters and brothers were as follows: Angelina – ten years old, Alfred – eight years old, Mary – five years old, and Joe – three years old. It was just prior to 1901 when Angelo began his trips to America; joining other Sicilian men, he was known as a Bird of Passage. It is unknown if he was in Sicily at the time of Orazio's birth, but we find Angela at age twenty-eight with five children under the age of ten to care for and support. She continued her sewing at home to earn enough to provide for her family.

Orazio's birthplace is recorded as being in Castiglione di Sicilia, which is in the Province of Catania. It is a community in northeastern Sicily, which is approximately two miles north of the rim of the volcano Mt. Etna, and about eight miles away from the infamous town of Passopisciaro; the town my relatives talked about endlessly. Although his birth is recorded at the Municipal Hall in Castiglione di Sicilia, he was actually born in Passopisciaro and they traveled to Castiglione di Sicilia to have it documented. Having it registered there only meant it was the closest place in the province where births in the local villages were recorded – Passopisciaro was such a small town that the closest Municipal Hall was in Castiglione di Sicilia.

Knowing that Italians followed the tradition of naming their children after someone in previous generations, I searched for other Orazio's in the Cavallaro family tree. With all the information I was able to gather, I found no other child named Orazio over the previous four generations. It was very unusual not to name a child for someone in a previous generation; however, this was the case for Orazio Cavallaro. I can only assume they had a good friend or close neighbor in town named Orazio, which led them to name one of their children after him. All of his siblings had names or a derivation of the name of someone in the family in the genealogical line of relatives. In Italian, Orazio is translated to Horatio; however, once he arrived in America, he was always known as Roger. This could have happened at Ellis Island where they were noted for changing people's names because immigrant agents didn't know how to spell them or how to translate them into English. I did notice that when my grandmother spoke to him in Italian, she always used his Italian name, Orazio, as did his own brothers and sisters. Many times, it was shortened just to 'Razio.'

The Beginning

Roger Cavallaro (as I will refer to him from now on in this book; it is the name by which we all knew him) was a very easy child to raise. With his mother, being very busy with her sewing business at home, his sister Angelina, at age ten, took over much of the responsibility of caring for him. Economically, things were difficult in Sicily at that time. Money was scarce and, as a result, food was difficult to attain for their home. It was related to me by my Uncle Roger, that at one time, he almost died. He was not receiving the correct amount of food as a toddler and became weaker and weaker by the day. He would lay in bed, listless and weak; no one knew exactly what to do for him. Then one day, some older women in the town, came to Angela's house carefully cradling fresh eggs in their aprons. They started to feed him raw eggs every day, and in no time at all, he started to get better and regained his strength again. In the weeks that followed, the whole family continued to show much concern for him because he was so weak. They thought they would lose him since they couldn't provide enough food to eat on a daily basis.

In other stories that were told to me, his sisters and brothers remembered him as a child who was always happy and laughing. He played well with other children and was very friendly with others in the town. Just prior to the family immigrating to America, Roger attended school in Sicily for a short time. However, before starting school, he helped his brothers whenever they worked with their father in the vineyards on the slopes of Mt. Etna. Being as young as he was, he could only pick the smaller bunches of grapes that grew on the lower vines closer to the ground; then, he'd carefully lay them into large, hand-woven baskets. The older boys carried the baskets to a central location to be dumped into the large horse-drawn carts that eventually took them to the large wine press machines. As he was growing up, Angela continued to be concerned that he was smaller built than the other children his age, yet he seemed as normal as anyone else. She blamed it on the time when he almost died and she became resolved that he would always be smaller than her other children. As he grew older, this never appeared to be a problem for him.

Roger Arrives in America

When Angelo and Angela decided to make their trip to America, their main concern was bringing enough clothing for each of their six children along with enough clothing for themselves. Whether they brought any other belongings is not known. As they packed their one large trunk, small canvas bags, and sacks that contained their clothes, they were tied up with pieces of rope. When they started off on their journey, each child was given their own bag or sack of clothes to carry. With Roger being only seven years old, they couldn't depend upon him to carry anything too heavy, so he was given a canvas bag to carry over his shoulder. Since it was tied with rope, he carried it over one shoulder at first and, when he grew tired, he would move it to the other shoulder. However, whenever he could, he helped the others lift and carry their bags. He was very responsible in caring for his sack of clothes and never let it out of his sight. He kept it near him always while they were on the boat for the entire twenty-three day voyage. One incident he shared with me was concerning the ship's arrival in New York and their debarking from the ship. He rushed to keep up with the rest of the family and proceeded to walk down the gangplank. He had to drag his sack all the way down because the pitch of the gangplank was very steep. He felt he could easily lose his balance and, since there were no side rails, fall into the water. He had to hold onto the railing with both hands. He made it down the gangplank without ever letting go of his sack of clothes and quickly ran to catch up with the rest of the family.

He traveled the remainder of the trip with his parents and siblings, always within close view and not falling far behind them. After the incident on Ellis Island where my Uncle Roger created a small scene at the Health Inspection Center, (as discussed in the <u>Ellis Island</u> chapter), he never moved far away from his family. Because of this incident, he developed a fear that he would be left alone in this new and strange country; that some unknown circumstance would occur to prevent him from remaining together with them.

He carried his original sack all through Ellis Island and on the Immigrant Train that went to Rochester, New York. By the time they arrived in Rochester, the canvas bag was beginning to show signs of wear and tear and the bottom was soiled from being stored in a variety of unclean places throughout their trip. He told me when they arrived at Uncle Sebastiano's house, his sack was one of the first things they threw into the trash.

Upon leaving Ellis Island to get on a ferry, the family waited in a long line that never seemed to move. Finally, they were allowed to board the ferry. My Uncle Roger remembered standing at the railing. He was searching to see the Statue of Liberty, which was to the south. All of a sudden, there was a shout from the passengers and everyone began pointing. He could see her standing in the middle of the water, with her hand held up, holding the torch. The people were shouting, *"La donna con la luce"* (The lady with the lamp). As he looked north, he saw the skyline of New York. He was awed to see such large buildings. The trip was a short one across the bay. They disembarked at the dock, which was near 44th Street on Manhattan Island.

Immediately, they were corralled with others to begin their long walk to the train station area; however, there were no trains to be seen. All they saw was an unending series of train tracks going into a maze of different directions. The special Immigrant Trains brought immigrants to various cites using these train tracks. They would be transported to all areas of New York State, Chicago, New Orleans, or Philadelphia. As they walked past the maze of tracks, they eventually came to where the Immigrant Trains were waiting. They walked among the trains and showed their tickets to the men in uniform who were positioned in front of each passenger car. They directed the family to the correct train, which would take them to Rochester, New York. Having been there before, Angelo knew the general area where they were to go. When they reached the correct area, they found their train had not arrived yet; they had to wait until the next morning to board the train. That night, they huddled together on the platform with their bags and luggage tucked in around them and slept. They were not alone. Many other families were going to Rochester and had to spend the night on the platform as well. It was not pleasant for them, but there were other benefits; it was a warm evening in early August, they were finally on solid ground, the Ellis Island experience was over, and they were on their way to their new home. Early the next morning, they were awakened by the whistle blasts from the train engine as it slowed to a stop in front of them. They waited in a long line again, had the tags checked that were still attached to their coats, and rendered their tickets. As they boarded the train to begin the next phase of their trip, they were filled with renewed excitement.

Upon arrival at the station in Rochester, the family quickly disembarked from the train. As my Uncle Roger approached the exit door, he proceeded to help my Uncle Joe with his bags from behind. In doing so, he fell down the steps of the train and onto the wooden landing platform. He immediately scrambled to his feet because the others were all ahead of him already and walking toward the exit door of the train station. With the station being located on Court Street, they had another long walk ahead of them and my Uncle Roger didn't want to be left behind.

Leaving the train station, the family walked the city streets until they arrived at the intersection of Central Avenue and North Clinton Avenue. My Uncle Roger remembered walking down North Clinton Avenue in the middle of the street because there were no sidewalks. There were other immigrants walking with them, but the Cavallaro family walked as a complete family, the older ones holding the hands of the younger ones. Some of the other immigrants had family and friends meet them at the train station, but there was no one to meet the Cavallaro family. My Uncle Roger shared with me that he had such a lonely feeling being in a new country. Everything looked so different. The houses were made of wood; there were some sidewalks in certain areas; there were stores with signs in the windows that he couldn't read; and there were many people involved in various activities. The streets were at least three times as wide as the streets he had known in Sicily. These were strange sights for him. As he walked down the street, he was amazed at all the new sights.

My Uncle Roger was accustomed to living in a rural area where the houses were made of stone and had very small windows. The shops were mainly located in the center of town in the *Piazza*. Storefronts did not have signs in the windows because everyone already knew what they sold; one store sold bread, while another only sold vegetables. The streets were very narrow, so narrow that a horse-drawn cart could not travel down them. He also remembered it was relatively quiet during the day; the men were off in the quarries or in the vineyards working, while the women were in their homes cooking and sewing, or sitting in front of their houses on stone benches talking with other women in the neighborhood. As he walked down North Clinton Avenue, no one was there to explain why this new country was so different. Filled with complete awe and wonder, he just didn't understand.

As they continued to walk, he remembered experiencing a great deal of joy when friends ran out from one of the shops to greet them. My Uncle Roger recognized them as being *paisani*. When this occurred, my Uncle Roger felt free from fear. His family was finally with people who spoke their same Sicilian dialect, who were from their own hometown, and whom they had known as neighbors. He was home at last!

North Clinton Avenue was a long street. As they continued to walk, they searched for familiar faces and the street sign that read, Albow Place. They continued to see many *paisani* who gave them a warm welcome to America. My Uncle Roger was feeling less fearful the longer they were there. Finally, when they reached the home of Uncle Sebastiano on Albow Place, he felt confident they had finally arrived safely. He remembered Uncle Sebastiano from Sicily, especially since his name was mentioned throughout the entire trip. He always heard his father say, "When we get to the house of Uncle Sebastiano, we'll…" Now that they had finally arrived, he thought their lives could continue from where they left off some thirty days prior in Sicily. Although he didn't realize it at the time, life would be different for Roger and the others from how they had ever known it in Passopisciaro.

Once my Uncle Roger arrived in America, he learned a lot of information in a very short amount of time and he acclimated well to the change. He was the first child, along with his sister Jennie, to become more accustomed to life in America. He learned the language quickly and, as time passed, he and Jennie spoke English more than they spoke Italian. Although they were fluent in English, they still spoke Italian to their mother and older siblings, making them truly bi-lingual. By the time he was a teen, he had no accent at all.

His son, Roger, shared the following:

> *"My Dad told me many things about himself growing up in Italy and coming to Rochester. I know he lived in the general neighborhood of Clinton Avenue and Oakman Street for a lot of his life. He told me of the days when he was working on Uncle Sebastiano's farm with Uncle Joe. He was ten or twelve years old at that time and things weren't very easy on his farm. Also, the Cavallaro family had a farm in West Bloomfield. I think that was around the time of World War I. He always spoke well of his Uncle Sebastiano. I guess our grandfather wasn't around that much during those years."*

When my Uncle Roger wasn't working on Uncle Sebastiano's farm, he would return to the family home in the North Clinton Avenue area. He noticed that all the other children his age were attending school, so he enrolled at No. 20 School on Oakman Street. He was well liked by his teachers. He made many friends very quickly. He enjoyed learning and being a part of the school setting. He did well in his studies and was an excellent student. In addition, being in school helped him perfect his use of the English language and his penmanship skills; those were very important to him. As he told me, "It was important for me to be like all the other kids I knew. I wanted to speak and write good English or at least better English than I was using at that time. I knew school was the place where I could accomplish that and get all the help I needed."

As his son, Roger shared with me:

> *"During the time, he attended No. 20 School on Oakman Street, I know he did well there. He skipped the fifth grade, going from the fourth grade and directly into the sixth grade. I think that was it for his formal education. I know he worked many jobs after that."*

No. 20 School provided a good, basic education for my Uncle Roger and he reluctantly left the place he loved at the end of sixth grade. At that time, boys of his age could go to work and help earn money to support their family. When he left No. 20 School with sadness in his heart, little did he realize what a huge impact it would have on his life in later years. After he was married, he lived and eventually owned a house at 35 Oakman Street, which was diagonally across the street from No. 20 School. When his son, Roger, became school-aged, he also attended No. 20 School. This gave my Uncle Roger the opportunity to return to the school of his youth. It was a pleasure for him to see his son attend his old Alma Mater. It brought back many memories and gave him a sense of confidence and security knowing that his son was receiving a great education … just as he had many years ago.

Roger Enters the American Working World

Once my Uncle Roger started to look for work, he found employment wherever he could. Funds at home were scarce and he knew he had to help with the expenses. By this time, some of his older brothers and sisters were married and not living in the family home; others, were already working and helping with the upkeep of the house. He had many friends and he tried to get jobs wherever they worked. He worked for many years at Bond Clothing like the rest of the Cavallaro family, but prior to that, he worked in a variety of other places. In 1984, when I discussed this with him at my Aunt Mary's house, he said,

> *"In 1929, I worked at the Cameo Radio shop for $80.00 a week. My job was to change tubes in the radios and to test for all the wire connections in the back of them as they were brought in for repair. It was here that I obtained much of my training and experience in working with electrical circuits and mechanical devices. This job didn't last long because of The Great Depression and jobs became very scarce. During the Depression, I worked for Simpson and Weller for $5.00 a week and I worked 50 hours each week. Jobs were hard to find then, and when you made $5.00 a week, that was <u>good</u> money. I would work anywhere I could find a job."*

It is unknown what type of job he had at the Simpson and Weller Company, but I know he was there for a long time because they liked his work; he enjoyed what he did, and the money was good.

As shared by his son, Roger:

> *"In addition to working on the farm, he worked at the Rochester Box and Lumber Company, Colonial Radio, on the WPA, and other places before working at Bond Clothes. I know he liked it there (at Bond's) because he had a skilled job and he worked with just about the whole Cavallaro family."*

My Uncle Roger worked in Shop #17 at Bonds as a pocket-maker. He worked on men's suit coats, making the flaps for the two side pockets, as well as, the wells pocket (the top pocket where the handkerchief was displayed). His brother Joe worked in the same shop and they enjoyed seeing each other everyday. In fact, since his older brother Alfred, his brother-in-law Al Lizzio, and his sisters and sisters-in-law also worked at Bond Clothing, he was able to see his family daily.

His future wife, Lucy Squilla, worked there also. As his son, Roger writes:

> *"It was at Bond's where he met my mother around 1938 or 1939. They married on June 13, 1942. He worked there until he retired in 1969."*

As the Cavallaro and Lizzio families increased through marriages and their children became old enough to work during summer vacations, they became a well-known family at Bond Clothing and a very important entity to the clothing industry in Rochester.

Roger Begins a Family of His Own

Roger married Lucy Squilla on June 13, 1942, at St. Andrew's Catholic Church located on Portland Avenue in Rochester, New York. I remember their wedding well. When the family heard that my Uncle Roger was getting married, they were very excited. My mother and father were close to my Uncle Roger and he made it a point to spend a lot of time with my brother and me. Prior to the wedding, he brought the future Lucy Cavallaro to our home often, so we could get to know her better. One evening, just a few weeks before the wedding, my Uncle Roger was at our home visiting with his future bride. The invitations had been sent out and naturally, the discussion centered on the wedding and the preparations that were being made. I don't remember how it came up, but my parents shared, in passing, that my brother and I would not be attending the wedding. My brother was almost fifteen years old, and I was nine years old; we had never been to a wedding before. Most people did not bring their children to weddings; usually, they were considered adult functions. When I heard that we would not be attending, I was disappointed because I had planned to be part of the wedding festivities with my parents. My Uncle Roger became very indignant and said, "Oh, no! I want your boys to be there. They are my nephews and they are part of this family. I want all my nieces and nephews there." They discussed this issue in great depth; they brought up reasons why we should or should not attend. It was finally decided that my brother and I would accompany them on that day. It was so exciting to hear the decision. I ran to my Uncle Roger and gave him a hug around the waist. He said, "I wouldn't think of not having your boys at my wedding; they're very important to me." The feeling was mutual and the closeness with my Uncle Roger continued throughout our adult lives.

I was so excited. I was going to my first wedding ever. It made a fantastic impression on me. On that day, I tried to remember everything that occurred around me and to make sense of it all. The only understanding I had about weddings was what I had heard from my parents when they shared the details of others they had attended in the past. My father immediately made us new suits to wear; we all wore our finest and took part in each of the events that day.

The church was beautiful with a huge sanctuary and very high ceilings. It was decorated with many bouquets of white flowers. After the wedding ceremony, we hurried outside to the front of the church. There were many people milling around and waiting for the happy couple to emerge from the church. As soon as they appeared, rice and rose-petals showered the bride and groom, which celebrated their union. There were shouts of *"Buona Fortuna"* (Congratulations) and *"Che Bellezza"* (How Beautiful) all around me. I knew some of the people there, including my aunts, uncles, cousins, and grandparents. I didn't know many of the other guests. As I observed this unified expression of joy, it appeared to me that everyone knew each other well. There was hugging and kissing among them all. The guests were like a close-knit family as they greeted each other. As I think of it now, the ironic thing about this was that all of them worked together at the same place everyday; even the extended family who attended. They acted as if they hadn't seen each other for a long time. They enjoyed being in the company of the family and close friends and always showed so much affection toward one another.

The reception was held in my Uncle Al and Aunt Mary Lizzio's yard. It was a beautiful, sunny day so we enjoyed the event outdoors. Folding chairs surrounded the yard for the guests and everyone was taking snapshots. It was such a happy occasion and the family had a wonderful time being together. It had been a long time since there was a wedding in the family and they were making the most of the special day. It was a memory-making experience for us all.

My Uncle Roger and Aunt Lucy lived just around the corner from Bond Clothing in the upstairs apartment of the house at 35 Oakman Street that belonged to my Uncle Al and Aunt Mary Lizzio. They walked to work and life was good for them. Then in 1946, life became even better when they found out they were expecting their first child. Everyone was excited for the new addition to the family. Being the youngest male of the Cavallaro clan, everyone showered my Uncle Roger and Aunt Lucy with much attention as the whole family anxiously anticipated the birth of the next Cavallaro to enter *La Famaglia*. Then, on August 9, 1946, my Aunt Lucy gave birth to a son, Roger. He was referred to as "Roggie." There was great elation to have another boy in the family, someone who would carry the Cavallaro family name onto the next generation.

At every possible opportunity, the Cavallaro brothers and sisters visited my Uncle Roger and Aunt Lucy so they could ogle over the new baby. On one of those visits, as my family was going upstairs to their apartment, my Aunt Lucy stuck her head out of the doorway at the top of the steps and said, "Shhh, I just put him down for a nap and he'll wake up very easily."

After a while, my mother begged to see him in their bedroom. We all followed. There he was, asleep in the crib, situated close to their bed. Before we left that evening, the baby woke up for a feeding and we all had an opportunity to hold and play with him for a short time.

Uncle Roger always had his camera ready to take pictures of Roggie with each of the relatives who visited. My brother, Al, was also interested in photography and together, they took numerous pictures of him. As a result, we have many snapshots of Roggie growing up.

My Uncle Roger loved to go camping, hunting, and fishing. Each year, he knew my parents spent a week or two camping at Fairhaven Beach State Park with a group of other friends and neighbors. When his son, Roggie, was about one-year old, my father convinced his brother to join us on our annual camping vacation. We always went during July when Bond Clothing factory was closed and everyone went on vacation at the same time. My Uncle Roger and Aunt Lucy packed their camping equipment and one-year old toddler for the two-week escapade. They brought a small tent for the family. When they arrived at Fairhaven Beach State Park, my family had already been there since early morning; we saved a camping space for them right next to our camping area. They arrived at dusk and hurriedly unpacked their equipment and rushed to put up their tent before dark. All the men in our large group helped them set up camp while the women proceeded to assist my aunt with the baby and all his special needs.

The park provided raised, wooded platforms for each campsite upon which to pitch tents in order to keep them off the ground. My Uncle Roger's tent was set on top of two, wooden platforms. They were exposed on the inside of the tent because it lacked a sewn-in canvas floor. Because they pitched the tent in such a hurry, they never cleared away the dead leaves that were under the platform. They set up their sleeping bags and other equipment on the platforms and joined the other families for a sing-along. My Uncle Roger brought his guitar and while he played, we all sang around the huge campfire my father had built in a fire pit. The combination of our family group, along with our neighbors and friends, was a crowd. Before long, other campers joined us and we sang together into the evening. What fun!

When darkness arrived in the wooded campground, all the mosquitoes arrived as well. During the day, they hid in stagnant pools of water, under dry leaves that covered the entire wooded area and in dark places. At night, they started to fly around and search for people to bite. Although we came prepared with repellent and mosquito-netting hats that covered our entire heads, it was difficult to get through the night without a few bites here and there.

Then it happened! When my Uncle Roger and Aunt Lucy entered their tent to put Roggie down to sleep for the evening, some uninvited visitors greeted them. Unexpected as it was, they walked into a wall of mosquitoes waiting to get out. They opened the side and front flaps of the tent to allow them to fly outside and all the other campers proceeded to spray the area with various types of repellants. There was so much spray in the air that a gray cloud covered the whole camping space. Even the people spraying were having a difficult time breathing clean air; however, it did not affect the mosquitoes very much. They seemed to disappear for a while and finally their tent was cleared of them. The family entered the tent to sleep for the remainder of the evening; however, that didn't last very long. They spent the entire night, shooing the mosquitoes away. Early the next morning, they began packing their gear. They were going to return home to Rochester. We were all up by then and everyone was trying to help them with the problem. By the time they were ready to leave, they were both covered with numerous mosquito bites. Aunt Lucy said she had counted at least forty bites on Roggie; none of them had slept during the night and they couldn't see staying another day under those difficult conditions.

A couple of years later when Roger was older, they joined us again at Fairhaven. They never experienced the same mosquito problem after that first year because they came prepared with sufficient repellant to remove the threat of those annoying mosquitoes. They also brought mosquito-netting hats and remembered to rake the leaves away from under the platforms before they set up their tent. This helped a great deal. In later years, we were informed that the New York State Parks Department made a concerted effort to spray all wooded areas in the state parks more thoroughly so campers could enjoy their outdoor experience more. After that, they came camping with us on a regular basis.

As Roger grew older, the family continued to visit often and we always attended his birthday parties. Because his birthday was in the month of August, many of the family parties were held in their backyard on Oakman Street. The Cavallaro and Squilla families attended in great numbers and the two families grew very close with each other.

As Roger states about his childhood years:

> *"I lived at 35 Oakman Street until I got married in 1969. I moved to a house at 40 Barberry Terrace from 1969 to 1973, at which time I moved to my present address on Selkirk Drive. My younger years living on Oakman Street are filled with fond memories. I remember walking on Clinton Avenue in the early 1950s with my*

parents shopping, and I would get to see Uncle Joe and Aunt Jennie doing the same thing. Every once in a while, we would get to see Uncle Sebastiano who lived around the corner on Albow Place. Holidays were always great when we would get together on Weld Street with Uncle Al, Aunt Theresa, and their boys for Christmas or New Years. My Uncle Al and Aunt Theresa and their family were always very special to me. I had a great childhood with many fond memories. It's too bad that kids today can't experience those times we had in the 1950s."

Roger's Many Interests

My Uncle Roger was a man who was never idle. He was always working on a project or involved in one of his many leisure activities. He was interested in almost everything and usually found someone in the family or a close friend to participate with him. He was a very gregarious kind of person who enjoyed being around people and, by the same token, people enjoyed being with him as well. He was very responsible and someone who could be trusted and depended upon; he was a true friend.

Hunting and fishing were pastimes he enjoyed with my father and uncles. They met at my house early in the morning and prepared to go to the farm to hunt. They took our dog, a beagle named Queenie, with them. When I was younger, I didn't know anything about the farm they referred to, and I thought it was just a farm somewhere in the country. Living in the city, I had never been on a farm and I could only relate it to pictures I had seen in books. In later years, I understood they would hunt on the farm they once owned in West Bloomfield during World War I. They always asked permission of the owners before going onto the property and into the wooded areas to hunt. They spent the day together hunting various types of game. They came home with pheasants, woodchucks, and/or rabbits.

They had guns (I think they were some sort of rifles) and all the equipment that goes along with being able to hunt, including hunting pants, hats, and jackets. The jackets were made with large, side-pockets under each arm where they stored the game they caught. When they returned home, they displayed all the game on a table in the backyard and then proceed to prepare the animals for cooking. They skinned the rabbits and saved the feet for the children. When they dried out, the rabbit's foot would be used as a good luck charm. They cleaned the pheasants and then the women cooked them in a homemade tomato sauce. I did not like eating the game; it gave me a queasy and uncomfortable feeling to see it in our plates, but it was a treat for everyone else.

At every opportunity, my Uncle Roger went hunting or fishing. As stated by his son, Roger:

> *"After he retired, he bought the cottage on Seneca Lake. I loved it there and so did he. We had a boat and did a lot of fishing from 1970 until he sold it in 1983. We would go there with my children on weekends; it was a great time of his life. He loved to fish; to go to stock-car races and boat races; to go hunting with his friends and family. In the mid 1930s, he was in a rifle club with Uncle Joe. It was called the Indiana Rifle Club. They were the Monroe County Champions in 1935 or 1936. He was always proud of accomplishments like that."*

His granddaughter, Karen Cavallaro Ricotta, remembers the cottage well. They were special times for her and her brothers. As she remembers:

> *"The Cottage! These were some of the best times our family had together when I was growing up. As we drove out to Seneca Lake each summer, we'd talk about all the things that we would do once we got to the cottage. Once we got there, we'd spend our time between fishing, catching salamanders, skipping stones across the lake, and walking on the railroad tracks. I will always remember one summer in particular. Papa tried to remove a bee's nest under the steps. He put a net over his head and he covered himself all up with long pants and long-sleeved jacket. When he came out dressed like that in the middle of a hot summer's day, we all just laughed and laughed. We just thought this was hilarious. But, after all was said and done, he got the bees out from under the steps. Papa could do anything!"*

My Uncle Roger's story would not be complete without mentioning his love for Photography. For as long as I can remember, I would see my uncle with a camera in his hands and talking about some great shots he had just taken. I think he owned the best and newest editions of cameras along with a variety of filters and lenses to help him take the best pictures. He had all kinds of attachment for his cameras; he had special flash attachments, spring shutter connections, tripods, and splicers. The entire family depended upon him to be the official photographer for every family event. He enjoyed taking group shots of people, portraits, and scenery. He took much pride in sharing close-up pictures he had taken of his rose blossoms or of water scenes with the reflections of clouds in the water. Although this hobby was self-taught, he was very professional at it and achieved fantastic results. He spent hours in camera stores and reading photography magazines.

He not only took still pictures in black and white, but also began to experiment in color processing. He also had a movie camera and took movies, both on 16 mm and 8 mm film. Of course, when it came time for me to get married, he took my wedding movies and gave them to me all spliced onto one reel when we returned from our honeymoon. I cherish those movies to this day. At any family wedding, baptism, or shower, you could expect to see my Uncle Roger all set up with his equipment and taking the pictures. He took movies at our annual Cavallaro family picnics each year, family anniversaries, and all the family events. When he went to the World's Fair in New York City, he also took his cameras to capture all the magnificent buildings. He went to the World's Fair with my father and mother, Uncle Al, Aunt Mary and Angelo Lizzio. They went in September of 1939 and had a wonderful time. Because he was always behind the camera taking pictures, he wasn't in many of the shots himself; however, my Aunt Lucy tried to have someone take over for him so he would be in at least a small segment of the photographs and movies.

His enthusiasm was so great for photography that his son and all his nephews became fond of photography also. He and my brother, Al, would have long conversations together and spend hours in his basement talking about photography. My brother became so addicted to it that he, too, had to have the best cameras and equipment available. He and I decided to continue with our study of photography by taking courses at East High School. During those high school years, my father helped us build a darkroom in the basement of our house. With the help of my Uncle Roger, we purchased all the necessary darkroom equipment so we could develop our own film and print black and white pictures. Soon after, my brother bought an enlarger and he was able to make enlargements of the pictures we were printing. My aunt and uncle came over often to see the developments of what was taking place in our darkroom. When my brother entered the U.S. Air Force, he chose to go into the field of Aerial Photography and was a photographer during the Korean Conflict. He eventually spent his entire adult career in this field because of my Uncle Roger's influence. My Uncle Roger's love for photography deeply enriched the lives of each one of us in my family.

Growing up, watching home movies was a common occurrence. Whenever we visited my uncle's home, he'd frequently ask, "Would you like to see some movies of the family?" We were excited to see them. As a young boy, I positioned myself on the floor in front of the portable screen he set up in the living room. I waited patiently while he prepared the table and camera, took out the boxes with reels of film, and began to select which events he would show that evening. I watched with much interest and great anticipation of what the next reel would bring. There was always a lot of laughter especially at times when he had forgotten that the camera was still running and had inadvertently shot a scene of the grass or sky. He eventually spliced those parts out of the final copy. There were repeated "ooh's" and "aah's" at some of the many scenery shots that he so creatively captured. The time passed by so quickly while we watched the movies and slide shows. Driving home after the evening, I recall how much I wanted to return to visit them again very soon so we could see more home movies.

Many years later when he had grandchildren, that 'theater scene' didn't change very much. His granddaughter, Karen remembers:

> *"I loved watching movies on the movie projector at Papa's house. This was always a special treat for me and my brothers. We would get very excited when Papa would take out all his movie equipment and boxes of movies so we could have an evening of looking at old films."*

As I grew older and had children of my own, I remember reenacting that same familiar scene in my family room. My children would get so excited to see the movies and slides of the family or from one of our vacations. When my Uncle Roger and Aunt Lucy visited our home, I sometimes showed movies and slides of the family. I would remind him, "Do you remember when we used to do this at your house, Uncle Roger?" With a very knowing and understanding look, he'd nod and say, "Yes, I remember. Those were the good old days, weren't they?" Yes, they certainly were the good old days. Though it was his hobby at first, it later became his passion; his interest in photography left many memories for the family and for generations to come. Through it, he influenced the lives of those around him. We have so much to be thankful for, Uncle Roger; we appreciate how you shared your love with us.

Some Fond Memories

Growing up in the Cavallaro family was a unique experience because of the different people who affected our lives. As first generation Italian Americans, we had the privilege of being brought up in the American way of life, but always having it supplemented with the Italian ways of our parents and relatives. As a result, many of the fond memories I have of my Uncle

Roger are because he seemed to be the one who brought himself down to our level. He was younger than the rest of the siblings and he had many interests that spurred the attention of the rest of us to become more closely attached to him.

One of my earliest memories of him was when I was about seven years old in 1939. We were at my Grandma Cavallaro's house on North Clinton Avenue, which was next door to the brick covered firehouse. While we were visiting, a couple of my Uncle Roger's friends came to the house. They entered with a burst of laughter and excitement; the room was soon filled with much conversation. It was a Sunday afternoon and my Uncle Roger announced to his friends, "Let's go for a ride in the country." We all ran out to the car and my brother asked to go with them. Uncle Roger agreed and said, "We don't have room in the front, but you can ride in the rumble seat." He had a small coupe that fit three people in the front seat and two people snuggly in the rumble seat, which opened in the back. My brother jumped on the chrome bumper and flew into the seat. I begged my uncle to go also. I had never had the opportunity to ride in a rumble seat before and wanted to go too. Naturally, he agreed, picked me up, and seated me next to my brother. I was so excited. As he drove through the country roads, I felt the cool air rushing past my face. It was like riding in a convertible. I felt so privileged. When we returned, I rushed in to tell the family about my adventure. This was a big deal for me. As you can tell, that ride meant a lot to me; it was a thrill and has been a memory that has lasted a lifetime. I shall never forget it.

Another fond memory I have of my uncle is watching him play his guitar. I never knew anyone who played a musical instrument so I was fascinated with his ability. While he played at various family occasions, my mother sang with him as he harmonized. He'd played some favorite songs and one, in particular, was Mexicali Rose. I can still hear him strumming his guitar and singing:

> Mexicali Rose, stop crying;
> I'll come back to you some sunny day.
> Every night you'll know that I'll be pining,
> Every hour a year while I'm away.
>
> Dry those big, brown eyes and smile, dear,
> Banish all those tears and please don't sigh.
> Kiss me once again and hold me;
> Mexicali Rose good-bye.

Some of his other favorites were Red River Valley, Little Brown Jug, and Home on the Range. He had the whole family singing once he sang the first line of any song. He brought his guitar whenever we camped and we sang around the campfire or he'd take it out at his house and we'd sing in his backyard on hot summer evenings. Can you just imagine all these Italians gathered around him and singing Country Western songs? I don't think they even knew who cowboys were or where the prairie was located. However, none of that really mattered; it was more important that the family had gathered to sing, and have a happy time together.

There were many years when my Uncle Roger, Aunt Lucy, and Cousin Roger celebrated the holidays with us at our home on Weld Street; sometimes for Christmas and/or New Year's Day. Whatever the holiday, we were always sure to have a great time. It took my mother a full day to prepare for the family feast. Sometimes, I didn't know they were invited until the day of the holiday. I was so excited because I knew we would have a fun time. She would set the big dining room table with her finest china for all the invited guests.

As the years passed, guests may have included my roommate from college, my grandfather Siracusa, along with my brother and sister-in-law, Mary Jane, and later my wife, Aggie, and me. When my Uncle Roger, Aunt Lucy, and Roger arrived, my parents always had gifts for Roger under the Christmas tree. After he opened them, we spent time on the floor teaching him how to play the game or show him how to use the toy he had just received. My Aunt Lucy would bring one of her favorite dishes or a dessert she had made. My father would be sure a bottle of his best wine was on the table that had just been drawn from the barrel that day. We would sit down to a feast and eat with a lot of conversation and laughs in between.

After dinner, I would sheepishly ask my Uncle Roger if he brought his guitar with him. He'd answer with, "Yes, you know I wouldn't leave it at home," I became so excited because I knew we were about to enter into the best part of the day. I prepared the music on our piano while he went out to get his guitar. Occasionally, I would accompany him with chords on the piano and we'd have a great time playing and singing songs together. We didn't sing very many Christmas Carols, but we sang many of his favorites and some old Italian songs as well. My father loved to sing them because he knew all the words in Italian. My Aunt Lucy occasionally corrected him; he knew the words in the Sicilian dialect and she knew the words in the Calabrese dialect, and they differed a bit. They laughed over this a lot and the music filled every corner of our house. As we sang, we'd eat nuts, figs, homemade cookies, and of course, *cucidati* (coo-chē-dă´-tē), the fig-filled cookies that my mother made each year. The *cucidati* cookies were a Sicilian tradition we enjoyed each year, only at Christmastime. We took them for granted, but these times were filled with warm and lasting memories.

As his granddaughter, Karen reminisces:

> *"Christmas! I remember all our Christmas holidays so well. I loved spending the day over Papa's house. I can remember the silver Christmas tree with all the pretty ornaments, the brightly wrapped presents under the tree, and the great dinner we had sitting around the big table. Since my Papa has gone, Christmas has never been the same."*

Another remembrance I have of my Uncle Roger and Aunt Lucy took place somewhere between 1964 and 1970. My wife, Aggie, and I had recently built our new home on Abby Lane in Gates, New York. It was in the fall of the year and they had called to tell us they were coming to visit. It was on a cool October evening and the sun had just set. As soon as I heard their car in the driveway, my Uncle Roger called us to come outside to the front yard. We all ran outside to see what was wrong. He pointed toward the northern sky and said, "Look up there. We just saw the Aurora Borealis in the sky." At that moment, the sky was completely dark except for the many stars that were shining above. We waited a few minutes and all of a sudden, we saw the dark sky light up with colored lights in flashing intervals. It lasted for only fifteen seconds at a time, and then it was repeated every two to three minutes. It was a beautiful sight. My children, all being very young, were outside with us also to see the spectacular sight. Some of our neighbors, who were sitting in their front yards, joined us to watch the colorful light show. This display in the sky didn't occur often and I have only seen it one other time after that night.

Through my uncle's watchful eye, we all able to experience and enjoy a wonderful viewing of the Aurora Borealis, also known as the Northern Lights, which are radiated in the sky in the northern areas of the United States, Canada, and the Arctic regions. It was an exciting experience for all of us. Had he not called us outside to view this spectacular scene on that cool October evening, it would have gone unnoticed.

My Uncle Roger was a great dancer. In my mind's eye, I can still see him and my Aunt Lucy dancing at many of the relative's weddings and people would comment on his gracefulness. At my Uncle Al and Aunt Mary Lizzio's 50th wedding anniversary dinner, he and my Aunt Lucy danced a polka like no one else. Their feet moved so quickly; it was a marvel to watch them. He could dance the waltz, the fox trot, the tango, and the polka (which was one of his favorites). They could be seen dancing the Italian Tarantella that was usually played at Italian functions; he was good!

As his granddaughter, Karen, states:

> *"Papa used to teach me how to dance. He liked to teach me the waltz because he liked the music the best. I would try to follow him, but I'd always step on his feet while we danced; we had to stop because we'd be laughing so hard."*

He had record albums of the best Italian music and played them on his record player whenever we visited. Of the many albums he owned, his favorites were the songs sung by Jerry Vale. He played them with such pride; he had memorized every word of each of his songs. While Jerry Vale sang, he'd point out how clear his voice was. He also taught us to listen carefully for the high notes that occurred in certain sections of the song; he knew exactly where they'd come up. Through this, I became interested in the music of Jerry Vale also, so much so, that I have many of his record albums, tape cassettes, and CDs to this day in my personal collection of music. Whenever I play one of his CDs and hear songs like <u>Inamorata</u> or <u>A Di La</u>, I think of my Uncle Roger and Aunt Lucy, sitting in their living room and enjoying the music. As he grew older, his love for music never waned.

His granddaughter, Karen fondly remembers:

> *"Playing his records on his record player was always something to look forward to when we visited him. All his records would be labeled with numbers. In fact, I think he would label everything he had. He was very organized. Whenever he asked me which record I'd like to hear, I'd always ask him to play <u>The Chipmunks</u>."*

Another fond memory I have of my Uncle Roger, occurred in years that are more recent. When my mother suffered a stroke in 1984, I had many occasions to return to Rochester to care for my mother's needs. A few of those times, my Uncle Roger and Aunt Lucy invited me to stay at their home. Although I was at St. Anne's Nursing Home every day with my mother, I'd return after visiting hours, and my aunt would have dinner waiting for me. We sat around the table for hours afterwards and have long talks about various topics. That was such a special time for me. My father was gone and my Uncle Roger gave me a lot of needed and sound advice. He counseled me in many areas that helped me a great deal.

Many times, we reminisced about past family events and shared many laughs. He had numerous stories to share with me, some of which I have included in this book. He had a very sharp mind and a vivid memory; he could remember all the details of stories that had happened many years before. It was during one of these times, that my aunt and uncle brought to my attention the severity of my brother's illness when he was first diagnosed with Hepatitis. They walked me through some very difficult times in my life when my mother was ill and I shall forever be indebted to them for spending so much time with me. His granddaughter, Karen, treasured his skill in telling stories full of excitement and charm.

As she states:

"I remember Papa best for all his stories. I could just sit with him in his brown chair and listen to all his stories forever. No one else ever sat on that chair but him, so I felt really special to sit in it with him. I miss those special times, when I'd be nestled in his lap, with his arms around me and completely lost in the stores he'd be weaving."

As I finish this chapter on my Uncle Roger's life, I want to add a couple more incidents that were shared with me by his granddaughter Karen.

"Whenever I'd sleep over to Papa's house, we'd always go out to lunch the next day. I'd always look forward to that because it was such fun. We would either go to McDonald's or to Shaller's. That was always a special treat for me. When we'd arrive at Shaller's by 11:30 a.m., he didn't even have to look at the menu. He knew exactly what he wanted; a Shaller's Soft Roll was his favorite."

"Playing with the train set in the basement was one of my favorite things to do at Papa's house. We just loved it when Papa would take us down-stairs to play with it. He'd crawl underneath the train table that he had built for my dad when he was young; he'd sit in the middle just like a conductor and would operate all the switches that activated the trains. As if in a trance, we would stare at the trains as they moved all around the tracks, through miniature towns, over bridges and mountains, and around small lakes. It was always a special treat for me and my brothers."

"Papa would play catch with me and my brothers all the time. We had mitts and so did he. As we threw the ball to him or when we'd try to catch it, he would always

give us tips on how to improve our game. We usually had a lot of laughs when we were out in the backyard or in the driveway playing catch with him."

The events that have lived in the memory of Karen are just a snippet of all the things he did with his grandchildren. He loved them dearly and found great pleasure in giving them quality time whenever he was in their presence, the same he had done for years with his own son and with all his nephews. He always had time to give; time to talk, time to instruct, time to play, and time to laugh. It was never rushed, but it was given in love.

I have so many memories of my Uncle Roger and Aunt Lucy that I could go on forever. They both played a very important part in my life and in the lives of my family and all the other Cavallaro's.

He was a good and caring man. As stated by his son, Roger:

"He was always there for anyone who needed help. He led a good and honest life. He drove until the day he died. He was very proud of that."

I don't recall him ever being upset or having an unkind word to say about anyone. He was 'happy-go-lucky' and walked around as if he didn't have a care in the world. In fact, when he walked, he had a little bounce in his step that, I felt, portrayed his happiness and joy in life. He took care of his family well, worked hard, spread his love to everyone he met, and led a calm and peaceful life. I will always remember him with a smile on his face.

As has been stated in previous chapters, you have read this last statement often; *he/she always had a smile on their face.* This was a major trait of all the Cavallaro children. They were happy people and their happiness was passed on to others in a very positive way. My Uncle Roger was a very special person; his family, relatives, and neighbors loved him; we all loved him for who he was, what he did, and for enriching each of our lives. We are all different people because of how he touched us. He has a special place in all our hearts forever. We love you Uncle Roger!

Orazio *(Roger Joseph)* Cavallaro
Family History

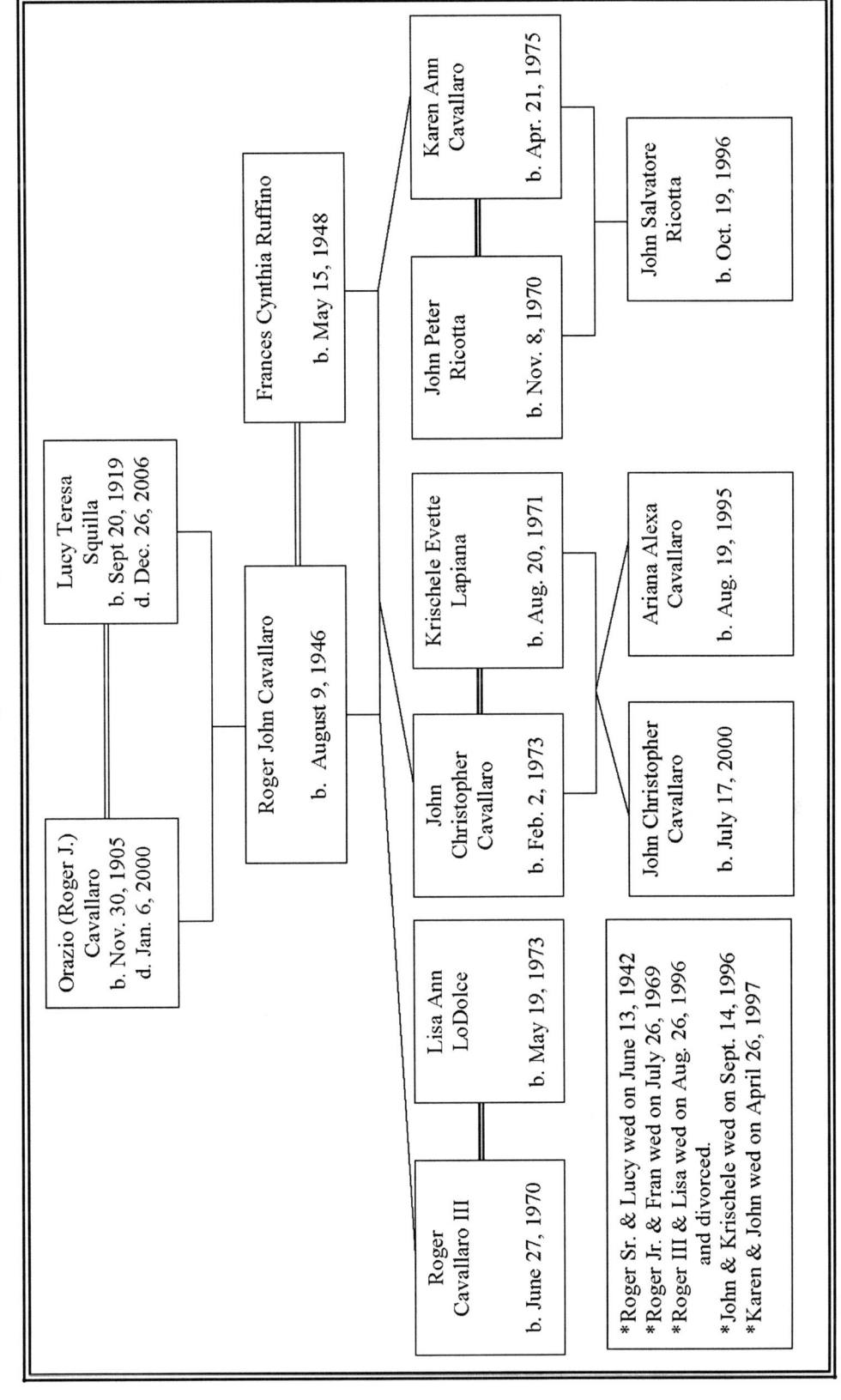

Orazio (Roger J.) Cavallaro
b. Nov. 30, 1905
d. Jan. 6, 2000

Lucy Teresa Squilla
b. Sept 20, 1919
d. Dec. 26, 2006

Roger John Cavallaro
b. August 9, 1946

Frances Cynthia Ruffino
b. May 15, 1948

Roger Cavallaro III
b. June 27, 1970

Lisa Ann LoDolce
b. May 19, 1973

John Christopher Cavallaro
b. Feb. 2, 1973

Krischele Evette Lapiana
b. Aug. 20, 1971

Karen Ann Cavallaro
b. Apr. 21, 1975

John Peter Ricotta
b. Nov. 8, 1970

John Christopher Cavallaro
b. July 17, 2000

Ariana Alexa Cavallaro
b. Aug. 19, 1995

John Salvatore Ricotta
b. Oct. 19, 1996

* Roger Sr. & Lucy wed on June 13, 1942
* Roger Jr. & Fran wed on July 26, 1969
* Roger III & Lisa wed on Aug. 26, 1996 and divorced.
* John & Krischele wed on Sept. 14, 1996
* Karen & John wed on April 26, 1997

Roger (Orazio) Cavallaro

June 16, 1942
Roger & Lucy (Squilla) Cavallaro

Roger with Frank Samperi

Mary Lizzio, Roger, & Lucy Cavallaro

Roger & Lucy's Wedding
(Far left: Mr. Squilla, Joe Cavallaro is behind Roger, Angelo Cavallaro & Alfred Lizzio are on the right, Jennie Cavallaro with son, Joe, is on front right)

Roger at the cottage in NYC
During the 1939 World's Fair

Lucy & Roger Cavallaro at home
On Oakman Street

New Year's Eve 1984
At Roger & Fran's house
With grandchildren Roger III, John & Karen

Lucy, Roger, & Roger Cavallaro
(Sept 1995)

Roger's Hobbies (Hunting, Fishing & Playing Guitar)

Roger hunting at the farm property
West Bloomfield, New York

Roger hunting rabbit at the farm

Roger loved to fish at Seneca Lake, NY

Roger played guitar at the party when
Richard & Aggie Cavallaro went to California

Giovanna (Jennie / Joan Cavallaro) D'Amanda

July 15, 1909 – June 26, 1996

Prologue

Giovanna (her given birth name) was the sixth born and final living child of Angelo and Angela Cavallaro. At the time of her birth, their ages were forty-two and thirty-one years old respectfully. According to existing records, they were still living in Passopisciaro in the year 1909, when she was born. At the time of her birth, the ages of her siblings were as follows: Angelina was fourteen years old, Alfred was eleven years old, Mary was nine years old, Joseph was six years old, and Roger was three years old. According to the age spans of the children being born at about every two to three years apart, it is obvious that Angelo continued to be a Bird of Passage through all these years, making several trips to America and back to Sicily. Now, with six children under the age of fourteen years old, Angela continued to provide the necessary support for her family through her sewing, making alterations, and washing clothes for friends and neighbors. When the new baby girl was born, Angelina and Mary took over her care, thus relieving their mother so she could concentrate on the other chores for the family.

The Beginning

As could be expected from two young girls, ages fourteen and ten, they treated Giovanna as their own, personal baby-doll. Daily, she was dressed in new outfits they each handmade for her. They took much joy in sharing her with all the neighbors and friends in the *paese* (town). Giovanna was a beautiful child. She was light skinned, had curly, red hair, had perfectly formed features, and smiled at everyone. In Sicily, it was not common for children to be fair skinned or to have curly, red hair. Although her brothers, Giuseppe and Orazio, were both fair complected and had red hair also, her three oldest siblings were olive-skinned and had dark hair as most Sicilian children. Therefore, when the *paisani* saw Giovanna, they marveled at the beauty of this child. Giovanna's personality complimented her features. She loved being dressed in cute and frilly outfits and took great care to always keep herself neat and clean. Her sister, Mary, remembered that as a very young toddler, Giovanna always wanted to have her hands washed. It was very difficult to stay clean all the time while living in the dusty and arid community of Passopisciaro at the base of Mt. Etna, where there was very little grass. "Therefore," as my Aunt Mary said, "we were constantly washing her hands at the fountains in the center of town. It gave us another opportunity to bring her to where all the people gathered so they could fuss over her."

Giovanna Grows Up In America

Giovanna or Giovannina, as she was also known in Sicily, traveled to America under the care and supervision of her older siblings. Being almost four years old, she could not carry any of the bags or luggage that the older children toted with them, nor could she assist with any of the last minute chores that had to be completed prior to their departure date. She only knew she was going to a new home in America; she was going to travel on a big ship. As they prepared for the trip, she was told that her fourth birthday would be celebrated on the ship. She didn't remember anything about the trip to Palermo or about the voyage on the ship except that they had celebrated her birthday while on board. As mentioned earlier, the ship docked in New York Harbor on July 23, 1913. Since the trip was twenty-three days in length, her birthday on July 15th occurred when they were a little more than half way across the Atlantic Ocean. On the day of her birthday, someone she didn't know shared a small piece of cake with her at mealtime in celebration of her birthday. This was always a special memory for her.

When the family settled in the North Clinton Avenue area, Giovanna entered No. 20 School with my Uncle Roger. Once she was in school, the other children began calling her Jennie and that name remained with her for some years until she was an adult. While she was growing up, it was very obvious that she was a bit different from the rest of the family. She busied herself with reading books, practiced her handwriting daily, and was always interested in wearing nice clothes. She carried herself well, walked very straight and tall, and had a very graceful manner. In fact, she was the tallest child in the family. She grew into a beautiful young lady. She maintained a clear complexion and her red hair was always styled perfectly; heads would turn whenever she took a walk in her predominantly Italian neighborhood.

Like her sisters and brothers, she was also taught the family trade of sewing. She learned it well and immediately began sewing her own dresses. Often, she asked for assistance from her older sisters whenever she became confused while making an outfit. She dropped out of school in her later junior high years and went to work at a very early age. North Clinton Avenue was lined with dress shops and she constantly window-shopped as she took her walks. She fantasized wearing all the lovely fashions displayed in the store windows. When she entered the working world, it was very natural for her to seek employment as a sales clerk in one of the dress shops that were close to her home. She loved working in that environment and it was such a pleasure for her to do what she enjoyed best; over the years, she was very successful at it and was elevated to higher positions in the fashion industry in Rochester.

Jennie Marries and Begins a New Life

In her later teen years, Jennie had many friends and they often went to the local drug store to have a soft drink and talk with other teenagers who congregated at the soda fountain. In those days, drug stores were a combination of pharmacies, health product stores, and gift shops. All drug stores, as did this one, had soda fountains that were very popular with teenagers. It consisted of a long, white marble countertop and had stools, covered in red leather, that were tucked underneath. The counters were usually the full length of the store and could seat at least twenty people. There were always small tables and booths available for the overflow of customers. They served all kinds of sodas, ice cream sundaes, banana splits, milk shakes, and other such fountain drinks. The most popular drink of the teens at that time was the milkshake; it was made in a tall stainless steel container. There were usually five or more milkshake machines lined up on the back counter under a mirrored wall. When they were all turned on, it became a very noisy place. She and her friends went there often to talk and have fun. This particular drug store was on the corner of Lowell Street and North Clinton Avenue and was owned by the Gargana family. It was here where she met Joe Gargana, who eventually became her first husband.

He was two years older than she was; he was handsome, debonair and swept her off her feet. He made a fuss over her every time she came into the store and treated her like a queen. They began dating and became a popular couple in the neighborhood. He, like she, always dressed in the latest fashions that caused heads to turn no matter where they went. They complemented each other in both appearance and personality. In 1928, they were married, the year she turned nineteen years old. They had a beautiful wedding. My Uncle Joe Cavallaro was the best man and Joe Gargana's brother, Charlie, was one of the ushers. The other usher and the three bridesmaids in the group picture are unknown. Naturally, my Aunt Jennie made a beautiful bride, wearing a gown of lace and frills; and, of course, it was the latest style of the day. Their wedding picture captures the style of the day along with the precision she took in planning the wedding; it is a jewel to view.

After the wedding, they took up residence at the home of Joe Gargana's parents. According to the information from the National Archives for the 1930 United States Federal Census, taken on April 7, 1930, it indicates that Joe and Jennie Gargana were living at the residence listed as 2 Barry Road in the town of Irondequoit, New York. The entire record of all residents at that address is as follows:

Head of Household:	Thomas Gargana	age 43	Occupation: clerk in drug store
Wife:	Carrie Gargana	age 43	Occupation: none
Son:	Charles Gargana	age 23	Occupation: clerk in drug store
Daughter-in-law:	Natalie Gargana	age 21	Occupation: camera measurer
Son:	Joseph Gargana	age 22	Occupation: professional, drug store
Daughter-in-law	Jennie Gargana	age 20	Occupation: saleslady, dress shop

The census identifies the oldest son of Mr. and Mrs. Thomas Gargana, Charlie Gargana, was also living at the residence with his wife, Natalie. It further indicates that the father and two sons were working at the drug store they owned, and my Aunt Jennie was working as a saleslady in a dress shop. The move to Irondequoit must have been a huge adjustment for my Aunt Jennie for many reasons. First of all, Irondequoit, at that time, was considered to be out in the country and far away from the city. Secondly, she didn't live in the area of North Clinton Avenue, which had been her home since she had immigrated to America.

Thirdly, she was living very far away from her family and siblings, while they all chose to live near each other and the other *paisani*. This initial experience of living away from her family, which occurred at the beginning of her married life, set a pattern for the remainder of her future. From then on, she was somewhat distant from the family both in relationships and in locations of where she chose to live. She visited and kept in touch with the family, but not as regularly as the other siblings.

Jennie's Life Takes a Turn

As mentioned earlier, the Gargana family was in the drug store business. They owned two stores that were called 'People's Drugs.' Joe worked at the store on the corner of Lowell Street and North Clinton Avenue. There is no record where the second store was located. It is important to mention here that Aunt Jennie frequented the drug store prior to and after her marriage to Joe Gargana. A few years after her marriage, her father-in-law, Tom Gargana, hired another young man to work as a pharmacist. His name was Angelo D'Amanda. It was at this location that my Aunt Jennie first met Angelo D'Amanda and their friendship was initiated.

Her first year of marriage was fine, yet living in a house with her in-laws and another married couple gave little or no privacy to the newlyweds. She wanted to move to their own apartment, but Joe insisted they remain with his parents. After the first year, things began to decline and they each became very busy with their jobs. With much more responsibility and longer hours, she became very successful in the fashion industry. She moved to larger and more exclusive dress shops in the Rochester area. Besides selling women's fashions, she was also called upon to model dresses at fashion shows that were put on by the dress shops in other parts of the city. She was in high demand because of her demeanor, her perfect dress size, and her overall appearance. When the fashion designers from New York City visited Rochester, they called her to assist them in suggestions for creating new styles and outfits they'd be designing for the next season's fashions. She was very aware of what was in vogue at the time and they highly valued her opinions and suggestions.

In the meantime, she noticed that her husband, Joe, was spending less and less time at home or with her. She did some investigating on her own and found that he was seeing other women. When she finally caught him with another woman, she left him and went to live with my Aunt Mary and Uncle Al Lizzio, who were living on Oakman Street. After a while, she went back to Joe and they tried to reconcile their marriage one more time. Shortly after, Joe's old patterns of infidelity resurfaced and it all happened again. She went to live with my Aunt Mary and Uncle Al each time it occurred; this went on for a period of approximately five to six years. Finally, it came to the attention of her brothers. My father told me, that one night he, along with Uncle Joe and Uncle Roger, went out to look for Joe Gargana. They found him with another woman in a local bar. After watching him through the window showering his girlfriend with all kinds of attention, they went into the bar and the three of them beat him up. It caused quite a commotion at the bar, but no one stopped them because they knew of Joe Gargana's tendencies toward other women; also, the patrons knew the Cavallaro boys and held them in high esteem. My father said that the owner called the police, but he and his brothers left before they arrived. After that incident, my Aunt Jennie never went back to him again and they finally divorced in 1934. She could not trust him any longer because of his infidelity during their married life. My Aunt Jennie continued to live with my Aunt Mary and Uncle Al Lizzio for a few more years. She then rented her own apartment on Evergreen Street, which was located about five streets north of Oakman Street and near the intersection of Clifford Avenue and North Clinton Avenue. This was the closest she had ever lived to the rest of the family.

She continued to work in the garment industry. By this time, she was well known in her field and was offered positions in the better dress shops downtown where she was able to mingle with people who were in the fashion industry. She worked at Kroll's Dress Shop on North Clinton Avenue, one of the largest and most fashionable dress shops in the area. She sold and modeled dresses for them. She also worked for I. Malley Fashions and David's Dress Shop in the Rochester downtown area located on East Avenue. These shops catered to very exclusive clientele and sold original and expensive designs. They featured all types of eveningwear and professional outfits for women in business. She not only sold these expensive dresses but also continued modeling for all three dress shops. Through her interaction with people in the fashion industry and in the field of design, using the name 'Jennie' didn't seem quite professional enough for her. It was at this time, she began referring to herself as 'Joan,' and her family and friends complied with her request. Occasionally, some of us would forget and call her Jennie. She was usually very gracious about it and reminded us that she was now known as Joan.

In the meantime, Angelo D'Amanda continued to work as the pharmacist at People's Drug Store with the Gargana family. Then, in 1940, he left the store and moved west to El Paso, Texas. He worked as a pharmacist while also attending school to receive advanced training.

In 1943, he contacted Joan, and asked her to move to El Paso. She complied with his request and they were married in 1943 or 1944. Shortly afterward, they moved back to Rochester and bought their home located at 465 Laurelton Road, which was on the corner of Shelford and Laurelton Roads in the town of Irondequoit. She lived in that home until after my Uncle Angelo D'Amanda passed away.

Memories of Aunt Joan and Uncle Angelo

Prior to her moving to El Paso, Texas, my Aunt Joan needed surgery. Since she had no one at home to care for her while she was recuperating, my parents invited her to stay at our house during that time. The planned surgery was during the summer and I was home on vacation from school. I was ten years old. I spent a lot of time with her and we'd have long talks while sitting in the backyard. She had beautiful penmanship and she helped me to improve my handwriting skills. We sat in the backyard and read, or she would crochet, and/or needlepoint. I think it was the longest time I had ever spent with her; I really enjoyed her company. She and my mother talked a lot also; I sat and listened to their conversations. She and my mother had been good friends since they were both young girls at the Fashion Park Clothing Factory; and during the time of my parent's courtship. That was a great summer with many fond memories.

When my Aunt Joan and Uncle Angelo moved back to Rochester, my uncle opened his own drug store. It was called, Parsells Pharmacy, located on the corner of Parsells and Webster Avenues in Rochester. It was a large store and he was the pharmacist. He had some part-time help occasionally, during busy seasons, but he usually took care of all the business in the store himself; which included ordering, pricing, stocking shelves, sales, and filling prescriptions. He worked hard at the store and it was successful. When I became a senior in high school, he asked me to work for him on a part-time basis. I didn't have a car for transportation so I took the Rochester Transit Company bus in front of East High School on Main and Alexander Streets to the corner of Parsells and Webster Avenues where the drug store was located. I worked some afternoons and all day Saturday. Saturdays were very busy so my Aunt Joan came in to help us occasionally. This gave me an opportunity to see her more often than normally. I enjoyed working there. In addition to learning a lot about the operation of a drug store, I was able to get to know my Uncle Angelo better. He taught me to do all kinds of jobs at the store and he trusted me implicitly. We had long talks and he gave me very helpful counsel just prior to selecting the college I was going to attend; he also helped me in identifying some long-term goals for my career. Although I only worked there in the summer and during my senior year in high school, I developed a close relationship with him before I left. A few years later, my cousin, Joe Cavallaro, also went to work for him part-time and that proved to be a very positive experience for him as well.

After I was married, I visited my Uncle Angelo and Aunt Joan with my family often. My wife, Aggie, knew the area where they lived well because her family resided in the same neighborhood in Irondequoit. It was very convenient to stop by and visit them while we were visiting her parents. Their home was a new, one-story model and they had decorated it beautifully. My mother called it a 'Doll House'. Their living room and dining room were exquisite. They were decorated with French provincial furniture and the accessories they selected were in different shades of the color blue. Everything matched perfectly. When we built our new home on Abby Lane in Gates, we chose to follow suit and decorate with French provincial furniture and with the same monochromatic blue theme. It looked beautiful. When they visited our home, they were very pleased as they admired all our blue accessories.

My Aunt Joan became an expert gardener and loved to work outdoors. She hired a professional gardener to get her started, but then, she continued to work on her own to keep her garden in perfect shape. She was very proud of her rhododendrons, tulips, and daffodils; they were gorgeous. She grew gladiolas that were perfectly formed and roses of every variety. She also had some azalea and lilac bushes that blossomed profusely. In fact, one time when we visited, I commented on the beauty of her white, double blossom lilac bushes. She went outside, dug up a small section of one of them, and gave it to me to take home. We planted it in the yard of our first home we had just bought on Cabot Road in Greece. It took very well, and each year when it blossomed, I thought of her. When we moved to our home on Abby Lane in Gates, I dug out a 'sucker' of it and took it with me; again, it rooted well and blossomed profusely each year. Its sweet aroma scented the entire garden.

When our first child, Rick, was born, my Aunt Joan and Uncle Angelo came to visit us and brought us a gift. It was a little suit that had dark gray, flannel, short pants with suspenders, a white shirt with a bow tie, and a red-velvet jacket with a black-velvet collar. It was too large for him to wear immediately, but he grew into it eventually. By the time he was one, we dressed him in the outfit for his one-year-old portrait. It looked great on him and the portrait was perfect. We had an enlargement made and it currently hangs on the wall in our home to this very day. I think of my Aunt Joan and Uncle Angelo every time I look at that picture, remembering the day they brought us the suit with the red-velvet jacket for Rick. The enjoyment they expressed in giving it to us still lives on in my memory.

Her nephew, Roger Cavallaro, wrote his memories of her as follows:

> *"I don't have too much information about Aunt Joan. I do remember she ived on Shelford Road in Irondequoit from the 1950s until she went into the hospital. She had several cats throughout those years and they were all named "Dukie." I remember Uncle Angelo at his pharmacy on Parsells Avenue. He was a great guy. I remember tuning up his 1965 Buick in the later 1960s and he wanted to pay me way too much for the job I did. She didn't attend many of the family functions or get together with us often. After Uncle Angelo died, she did spend a few Christmas and New Year holidays with us at Uncle Joe's house on Oakman Street."*

Aunt Joan's Final Years

Aunt Joan lived alone for many years at her Laurelton Road address. She had some contacts with the family, but not on a regular basis. Approximately ten years after her husband Angelo's death, it came to the attention of the family that she was not well. To confirm this, Angelo Lizzio related the following instance to me. As he remembered, my Aunt Joan called him one day because she needed some help. She said she needed twenty-five pounds of kitty litter from the grocery store. The grocery store was located just across the street from her house, but she could not walk to it, nor would she leave the house. He bought the kitty litter and brought it to her home; however, she wouldn't allow him inside. She paid him what she owed and told him she had evil spirits in the house and didn't want them to attack him. Upon hearing this, he contacted my Uncle Joe and Uncle Roger and they convinced her to be admitted into the Monroe County Hospital on South Avenue. After running some tests, they contacted the family to say she would need to be confined to the regular part of the hospital and could not return to her home. It was determined she had been suffering from Alzheimer's disease and it was progressing rapidly. After a couple of years in the hospital, her condition had stabilized and she no longer needed close supervision. She was transferred to the Monroe County Home and Infirmary on East Henrietta Road. She remained at that facility for approximately five years, until 1986, where she received assisted care in addition to having more personal freedom.

In the summer of 1984, I made one of my trips to Rochester and planned to visit her at the hospital. My Uncle Roger and Aunt Lucy arranged with the hospital staff to be sure it was a good day for her to receive visitors; and it was. Therefore, my uncle and aunt, my mother and I went to visit her on that sunny afternoon. Up to that point, I had heard all kinds of stories about my Aunt Joan, and I didn't know what to expect when I saw her. Would she be bed-ridden, too ill to walk, or would she recognize me when I entered her room? When we arrived at the main entrance of the hospital, I saw her at the end of the hall and began walking toward her. She was standing with some people and she saw me immediately. Much to my surprise, she instantly recognized me, called my name out loud, and rushed over to meet me. She hugged and kissed me numerous times, telling me how she had missed seeing me for so long. We decided to take a walk outside and found a bench on the beautiful hospital grounds where we could sit and talk. We had a long visit and caught up on the past five years that I hadn't seen her. I found her to be completely coherent, very verbal, and so excited to see us. As I sat there, I thought, "She looks great. Her hair is beautifully styled, her make-up is perfect, and she's wearing a very fashionable outfit. She looks like she usually does and I don't understand why she needs to be in the hospital." Later, I found out her medication was masking the symptoms of her illness and she could never live alone again. When it came time for us to leave, she grabbed my hand and held it tightly, telling me how much she loved me and that she wanted me to visit her again. We said our 'good-byes' at the edge of the parking lot and walked to our car. As we drove off, she remained there with a nurse at her side, a broad smile on her face, as she continued to wave to us. I shall never forget that scene, mainly because it was the last time I ever saw her alive.

During the next few years, she began to succumb to the disease. She underwent more tests and it was determined she needed to be in a facility where she could receive constant care and supervision. She was transferred to the Thompson Memorial Hospital in the city of Bath, New York in approximately 1988. Through necessity, she had to be more heavily medicated, confined to her bed, and fed intravenously.

I checked on her condition with various family members whenever I phoned them in Rochester. My Uncle Roger shared with me that she was not getting better. Whenever they visited her at the hospital, they tried talking to her, but she was totally unresponsive as she stared at them. Her brothers visited her on a regular basis, but she never improved. While she was at Thompson Memorial Hospital, her personal funds were entirely exhausted. She remained on feeding tubes for approximately eight years until she had another stroke. She died in June 1996 at the age of eighty-six years old. She would have celebrated her eighty-seventh birthday just a few weeks later. She is buried with her husband Angelo D'Amanda at Holy Sepulchre Cemetery in Rochester, New York.

Some Final Comments

Aunt Joan was an unusual woman. Because she was the youngest of six children, it put her in a place of being catered to by her other siblings during her childhood years. She preferred the nicer things in life, and enjoyed dressing up in new and stylish clothes. She was one of the first Cavallaro's to become totally americanized. She left the family traditions behind her and moved on beyond the Italian neighborhood and into unknown areas in the working world, intermingling with non-Italians and other ethnic groups. She always kept in touch with the family and attended all their major events, but she preferred being considered as an American rather than as an Italian-American. Of all the children, she was the only one who didn't work at Bond Clothing or any other tailor shop. Her sewing skills were not perfected as well as the other children, yet she did some sewing for herself, usually under the supervision of her sisters Angelina and Mary. She was personable, attractive, and very pleasant at social functions. I am proud to have known her as I did, and I cherish the fond memories that I have. She was a fine person, a beautiful woman with a lot of class, and an asset to the Cavallaro family. We love you Aunt Joan!

Giovanna *(Jennie / Joan Cavallaro)* D'Amanda

Family History

Joseph Gargana	Giovanna (Jennie / Joan) Cavallaro	Angelo D'Amanda
b. 1911	b. July 15, 1909	b. 1903
	d. June 27, 1996	d. March 17, 1969

Joan wed Joe Gargana in 1928. They were married for approximately 10 years. The marriage ended in divorce.

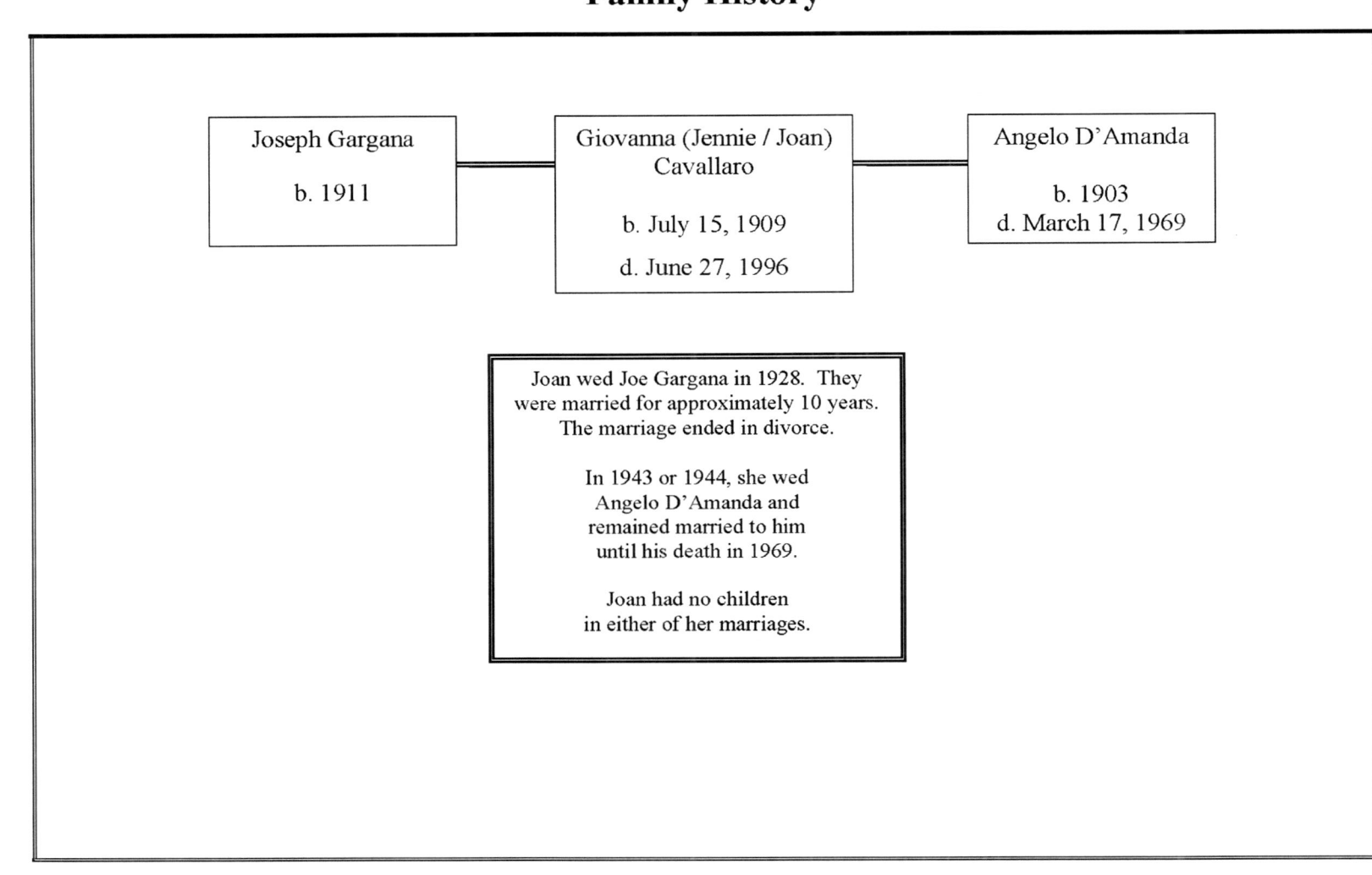

In 1943 or 1944, she wed Angelo D'Amanda and remained married to him until his death in 1969.

Joan had no children in either of her marriages.

Joan (Giovanna Cavallaro) D'Amanda

November 1928
Joe & Jennie (Cavallaro) Gargana
Joe Cavallaro (Usher in center)
Charlie Gargana (Usher behind groom)

Roger & Jennie Cavallaro
(At Clinton Ave. home)

Theresa Siracusa
Jennie Cavallaro
(circa 1925)

Jennie Cavallaro, age 7,
wearing a dress made by
her sister Angelina

Jennie Cavallaro
Angelo Lizzio

Angelo & Joan D'Amanda
At Highland Park
On Lilac Sunday

Joan Cavallaro
Modeling a new coat

Joan D'Amanda at
Monroe County Home & Infirmary
June 1984

Richard Cavallaro, Lucy Cavallaro,
Joan D'Amanda, and Theresa Cavallaro
Visiting Joan in June 1984
at Monroe County Home & Infirmary

Life on the Farm

World War I Moves the Family to the Farm

Italy emerged as an independent state after a long struggle for unification that started with the revolution of 1848. By 1911, Italy had an increased population of 34.7 million people. The southern kingdoms of Sardinia and Sicily, both agricultural economies, joined forces to help provide the crops needed throughout the mainland of Italy. Although there was considerable industry in the northern areas of Italy, they could not provide the quantity of food needed for the country. To feed its growing population, Italy needed to import some foods, notably grain, from Russia and Germany. By 1914, only the Vatican and San Marino retained independence within the recently unified Italy.

In July 1914, a year after the Cavallaro family had emigrated from Sicily to America, General Luigi Cadorna became Chief of Staff of the Italian Army. Although the Italian government declared its intentions to be neutral at the outbreak of World War I, he expected a war ensuing, and began building up his army. However, as weak as his forces were, he decided to concentrate the army on the Italian borders that were close to the Austria-Hungary regions, since a large part of the Italian population remained within the Austria-Hungary and Trieste regions.

It was because of the threat of war in Europe that hundreds of thousands of Italians fled from Italy and went to America or to Argentina for protection. The Cavallaro family was part of that exodus in 1913. There was great turmoil in Sicily and their decision to move was an easy one to make.

Once they were in America, the war in Europe was beginning to rage during 1915 and 1916; there was word it would only be a matter of time before the United States entered into the war effort. In 1917, that word came to pass. As with any world war, the United States established the mandatory draft so as to increase the numbers in their armed forces. Alfred was nineteen years old at that time and was sure to be drafted into the U.S. Army. Angela, being very frightened of what the war might do to her family, decided that she had to take whatever steps necessary to prevent her son from going to war. By this time, Angelo was back in Sicily and not available to assist her, so she discussed the matter with her brother-in-law, Sebastiano. They found out the young men of draft age could be exempt from going into the armed forces if they were working on farms that were producing food crops. Farm workers were important because they were growing food for the nation, in addition to, providing food for the service members over-seas. Therefore, Angela and Sebastiano decided to look into purchasing a farm.

They found a farm that was perfect for them, which was located in West Bloomfield and they bought it together; each paid fifty percent of the purchase price. Angela, the children who were still at home, and Sebastiano all moved to the farm property and made it their home for three years until the war ended. When they moved to the farm in 1917, her oldest daughter, Angelina, was already married to Frederico and they were living in the city; however, they went to the farm daily to help the family with some of the necessary chores. Her son, Joseph, was living with Angelina in the city and also traveled to the farm to work with the family.

While they were on the farm, Alfred, being the oldest son and the oldest sibling at home, had the majority of the responsibilities; however, he was very content while working on the farm. He enjoyed the planting, the harvesting, and caring for the animals; he liked working outdoors. He worked hard, grew stronger, and remained out of the armed forces during the entire time the United States was at war in Europe.

The Spanish Influenza

Shortly after they had purchased the farm and moved the family to West Bloomfield, the newspapers were full of articles and pictures of how World War I was ravaging all of Europe. At this same time, they were experiencing another war across Europe, the Spanish Influenza. It was a devastating disease and took the lives of more people in Asia and Europe than those that were killed in the war. Although the Spanish Influenza had developed in Asia prior to 1918, it extended into and infected people on all continents rapidly. It had three waves of infection as it spread during 1917 through 1919. It was brought across the Atlantic Ocean as our troops retuned to American and Canadian ports; it quickly traveled across the North American continent. It was estimated that one-third of the world's population was infected between the years of 1918 and 1919. As it festered throughout America, the Spanish

Influenza developed into an exceptionally severe disease and it was considered a pandemic, the first of three during the 20th century.

With one-third of the population dying from the disease, my relatives in Rochester became very concerned and did everything they could to prevent contracting the illness. One of the preventative measures people were advised to follow, was to avoid crowds or large numbers of people in the cities. Upon hearing this information, many of my extended relatives and *paisani*, joined the Cavallaro family on the farm. They knew that being away from the city crowds and staying in the country for a while would help keep them well. Breathing fresh air was a sure way to prevent contracting the disease. As a result, they had many visitors during those years. This was beneficial to Angela and Sebastiano because the guests helped with the chores on the farm. They stayed with them for a week or so at a time. Whether or not, this is what prevented them from being infected with the Spanish Influenza is unknown. A few of them did become ill with the disease, but fortunately, no deaths were realized in my family because of the devastating contagion. Rochester was reported as having seventy percent of its population infected with the disease, with thirty percent of them perishing in a premature death.

When one group of cousins, extended family, and *paisani* left the farm in West Bloomfield after their extended stay, a new group would arrive for another couple of weeks. The Lizzio and Trovato families visited more often, but there were visits from other *paisani:* the LaRocca, Maccarone, and Quagliata families. When they came to the farm, they arrived with their children, clothing for the extent of their stay, and food for everyone to eat. From being an emergency health situation, it turned out to be a festive time when they all gathered together. The men helped the family with the chores on the farm, and on some days, went hunting in the wooded areas for game that could be eaten. The women helped with the chores on the farm also. In the afternoon, they congregated with Angela on the front lawn of the farmhouse to work on various sewing projects while catching up on the news from the city. Later, everyone gathered inside to feast on the meals the women had prepared. They ate as a large family, drank wine, and sang all the Sicilian songs they knew from the old country. It was a time reminiscent of their days in Sicily, prior to leaving their beloved Passopisciaro.

After the first frost in the fall, all the company finally returned to the city and the family went back to their individual chores. They had many laying chickens that roosted in a large chicken coop. My Aunt Mary was responsible for their care. She fed them, gathered eggs every day, cleaned the coop, and selected the chickens they would have for dinner occasionally.

In the coop, they had an incubation section, and as the eggs hatched, she cared for the young brood also. My father was responsible for the livestock, the horses, cows, lambs, and goats. In addition, he worked the horse-drawn plows in the fields, tilling, planting, and sowing all their crops. They grew wheat, corn, potatoes, and cabbage. They also grew peas and the entire crop was sold to the local canning factory. In the rear of the farm, they had a large apple orchard. In the fall, many of the crops were sold to the local canning factory. Although the apple trees were never cut down, they were constantly pruned so they would produce a good crop of apples each year. The farm was fifty-four acres and every bit of the property was used for raising crops or livestock. Sebastiano, being half owner of the farm, lived on the premises full-time. He was out in the fields each day with the boys. Although he was very strong, he worked more as the supervisor of his nephews. He was very hard on the boys and required them to increase their workload each day. He expected them to do more work than he was doing and the boys resented him immensely for the way they were being treated. Angela never supported the boys and allowed him to supervise them in whatever way he wanted. He was especially hard on my father, being the oldest son, he demanded more from him. This created hard feelings and altered their relationship from that point forward.

My Uncle Roger shared the following incident with me concerning the farm. When Angela and Sebastiano purchased the farm, Angelo was on one of his trips to Sicily. When he returned and found they had moved to the farm at West Bloomfield, he went to stay with them. As has been mentioned earlier, Angelo enjoyed a glass or two of wine, and each evening he'd relax with his favorite beverage. Late one night, because of the amount of wine he had consumed, Angelo was unable to get out of his chair and pour another glass for himself. Therefore, he asked my Uncle Roger to do the task for him. At the time, my Uncle Roger, who was only a young teen, went into the dark wine cellar, and poured what he thought, was a glass of wine. Little did he realize that he poured kerosene into the glass instead. He gave it to Angelo to drink. Angelo didn't drink all of it, but drank enough to make him very sick. The next morning, my uncle was in a lot of trouble.

While Angelo was still on the farm during this visit, he began to urge Angela to sell the property. He wanted the money so they could return to live in Sicily. By this time, the farm was producing well, they had established procedures for all the chores, and they were making money from the crops. Angela vehemently refused. She wanted to keep the farm; however, she was more intent in not giving him any of the money because she knew she would never see it again. Sebastiano agreed with Angela. Angelo became very angry and left the farm. Within a week, he was on the boat again to return to Sicily. A few years later when he returned to

Rochester, the farm had been sold. He had nowhere to live so his daughter, Mary who had just married Alfred Lizzio, offered to house him in her home. Years later, when Angela sold the home on North Clinton Avenue, she went to live with Mary, making it necessary for Angelo to live with their daughter Angelina and Frederico.

World War I Ends

When the war ended in 1920, they continued working the farm as usual. No one working at the farm received wages and all the money that was made went for its upkeep. Because of the problems between her sons and Sebastiano, Angela saw that there was dissention among the family members. There were daily disagreements that had to be resolved. She needed to make a decision about whether or not to remain on the farm. She knew her sons wanted to begin working in tailor factories and to continue with the skills that she had taught them many years previously. Even though she had discussed this with Sebastiano, she had already decided to get out of the farming life herself. Angela began to seek ways in which she could make this happen and found someone that was willing to trade a house in the city on Electric Avenue for the farm. They made the deal quickly, Angela and the children moved to the new home, and Sebastiano moved back to his home on Albow Place.

The Farm in Later Years

The few years they lived on the farm were very significant to the Cavallaro family. They only owned it for a little over three years, yet they talked about it at almost every family gathering for many years to follow. They had fond memories of it and of the family's activities there. After the farm had been sold, they remained in close contact with the new owners long afterward. Every fall, my father, Uncle Roger, and Uncle Joe hunted on the farm grounds. On many occasions, others joined them including, my Uncle Al Lizzio, Russell Trovato, Frank Samperi, my brother Al, Sebastiano, *paisani,* and other farmers from the area. They always asked permission of the owner before they entered the wooded area to hunt for rabbits, pheasants, woodchucks, and other game. One or two of them brought their dogs to help stir up the game. Whatever they caught was brought home and my mother and aunts would cook it for dinner. The hunting days on the farm were always special times for the Cavallaro men. They brought large lunches to share, walked through the woods of their youth, and talked about the good old days. I don't think that hunting game was as important to them as the quality time they had with each other to renew their family ties. If they were fortunate enough to catch something that day, it was like icing on the cake.

On one of my trips to Rochester, my cousin Angelo Lizzio took me for a ride to see the farm as it currently looked. I was amazed to see that the original barn was still there, yet barely standing…..it leaned to one side significantly. The original house they lived in had been remodeled. All this could be seen from the road. It looked well maintained and cared for. With the invention of automobiles and improved roads, West Bloomfield is not far away from the city of Rochester; we arrived in about twenty minutes. However, in 1917, when people mentioned West Bloomfield it was as if they were talking about a community halfway around the state; it was only out in the country. As a young boy growing up in the city, I remember my father taking us for a Sunday afternoon ride in the summer. He would say, "Let's go see the farm." We piled into the car and off we'd go. He drove by it numerous times to absorb everything he saw. Many times, he stopped the car and pointed out some significant features he didn't want us to miss. While we drove around it a few more times, he never stopped telling us stories of all the incidents that happened on the farm. As I listened to the stories, the farm became as real to me as it was to him. I felt like I had actually lived there myself. However, since I was a 'city-boy,' I had never experienced that, but I dreamed about it many times. He helped us relive his three short years on the farm, which seemed like a lifetime to him, and I never forgot it.

Directions to the 'Cavallaro' Farm

West Bloomfield, New York

Size of Farm: 54 Acres

1. Take **Route 390 South** to **Route 251**.
2. Go east on **Route 251** toward Rush, New York.
3. At **Route 65 South**, go south toward Honeoye Falls, New York.
4. Go south at the Four Corners of Honeoye Falls to **Route 65 South**.
5. Pass the cemetery and corn fields on the right.
6. Pass **Hickory Lane**.
7. Pass **County Road #14**.
8. Pass **Amann Road**.
9. It is on the southeast corner (Left) of **House Road** and **Route 65 South**.
10. The house number on the mailbox is **#2101**

Directions to the 'Lizzio' Farm

Avon, New York

Size of Farm: 40 – 50 Acres

1. Take **Route 5 and 20** to the town of West Bloomfield and to Avon, New York.
2. The Lizzio farm is on the corner of **Route 253** and **Erie Station Road**.
3. It is on the right side.
4. Turn on to **River Road** (Rochester Street is another name for it).

Life on the Farm

The family on the farm
Back: Jennie Cavallaro, Angelina Lamanna holding Caterina, Mary Cavallaro, Angelina Lizzio
Front: Roger, Alfred & Joe Cavallaro
Rover, the family dog

Alfred with Rover

Alfred with two of the horses used for plowing

Mary Cavallaro feeding the large brood of laying chickens

Back: Mr. Trovato, Josephine Trovato holding Grace, another Trovato brother, unknown man, Grace & Russell Trovato, Alfred Cavallaro, Angelo Cavallaro
Front: Emma Lizzio, Mary & Angelo Lizzio, Joe Cavallaro, Roger Cavallaro, Theresa and Alfred (Sonny) Cavallaro

The Hunting Party
Alfred Cavallaro, Angelo Lizzio, Mr. Trovato, Alfred Lizzio, Joe Cavallaro, another Trovato brother, Roger Cavallaro, Sebastiano Cavallaro, Russell Trovato, Angelo Cavallaro holding Alfred (Sonny) Cavallaro on his shoulders.

A new farm house has been Built next to the old house (1995)

The Original Barn 1995 (With an overhead door)

Getting Ready for the Hunt
Russell Trovato, Roger Cavallaro, Frederico
Lamanna (in back), Joe Cavallaro, (next 2
men and child on ground are unknown)
Alfred Cavallaro, man standing next to him
is unknown, Sebastiano Cavallaro (sitting)

Farm House 1918

Back of Farm House 1995
(Notice the same roof line)

The Annual Cavallaro Family Picnics

As a child growing up in Rochester, I have some very vivid memories of my family, which I have shared with you throughout this book. Some of my favorites are memories of the Annual Cavallaro Family Picnics. Each year in July, Bond Clothing closed down for two weeks and everyone went on vacation at the same time. Since most of my family worked at Bond Clothing, it was a perfect time for us to have our annual family picnic. It was usually held at Ellison Park on Blossom Road and my Uncle Roger, Uncle Joe, or my father went to the park early in the morning to move tables so the entire family could sit together for our meals. When the next generation became old enough, they sent my cousin, Angelo Lizzio and/or my brother, Al, early in the morning and they moved the tables to our usual spot. When we arrived, we found them sitting on the tables to be sure that no one else took them. The tables were placed next to a running stream, which was Irondequoit Creek and just across the road from the baseball fields.

The menu was always the same. My father, Uncle Joe, and Uncle Roger grilled steaks on the park barbecues near our tables. We had huge tossed salads, Sicilian style, made with Italian greens, olives, and plum tomatoes. Everyone brought casseroles, vegetables, and their favorite desserts to share. Some of the dishes that graced the table included baked pasta and meat sauce (a must at any Italian gathering); eggplant *parmigiana*; baked Italian sausage and bell peppers; and Italian potato salad. On the other side of the table were bowls of Italian bean salad (with olives, *ci-ci*, *fave*, and lima beans) and baked spinach with *ricotta* (Aunt Mary's specialty). Scattered throughout were platters of stuffed zucchini and bowls of black, Greek olives. Large green olives that had been marinating for days in olive oil, vinegar, capers, onions, and celery were a favorite also. After dinner, all the Italian desserts were brought out and they covered the entire table. Of course, they included rum-flavored *Cassata* cake, anise-flavored *biscotti*, pies, and a large platter of freshly filled *canoli* with Italian *ricotta* cheese and chocolate chips. They were so fresh that each bite would melt in your mouth. The feast was a banquet fit for a king; that is, an Italian King.

The tossed salads that were placed on the table were prepared alike except for the tossed salad my Aunt Angie brought. It had extra vinegar added to it because she liked its flavor more than the rest of the family. She received a lot of kidding because of the amount of vinegar she put into the salad. In my opinion, it was tastier. I still tend to enjoy more vinegar in my salads to this day, and so did my father and Aunt Mary as well.

While the men were grilling the steaks at the over-sized barbeque nearby, the women prepared the tables with all the special treats. Each time a new casserole, bowl, or platter was uncovered, we heard the oohs and aahs from the women setting the table. The person who brought that particular casserole would proceed to tell the others all the ingredients and the details of how it was made. My mother, my aunts, and my cousins were buzzing around the table, exchanging recipes, and sharing their own personal methods of making that same dish. As they took the platters out of the coolers, their discussions centered on how best to display the food and to make sure there were enough places set for everyone in attendance. There was a lot of talking, laughter, and joking as they worked together.

Just prior to taking the steaks off the grill, my father, Uncle Joe, Uncle Roger, and Uncle Al Lizzio, each brought their personal bottles of wine to the table. They were not chilled and all agreed that the wine should be enjoyed at room temperature and not diluted with ice. The wines were different varieties and, of course, the men had to taste each of them before the meal and talk about the attributes of each one. My father and each of my uncles took great pride in their wine making skills and they defended their own wine as being the best on the table. When, the steaks were finally cooked to medium-well, they were put on large platters, and brought to the tables. There was so much food, enough for at least two or three more families. When you think of six brothers and sisters and all their families gathered, along with any extended family that were invited, we were a very large crowd. There was laughter and joking among everyone. Through it all, the men continued to critique each other as to who cooked the best steaks; it was always a very happy time. It was truly a wonderful feast for all of us.

My Uncle Roger always took movies and snapshots to capture the day's events. He was notorious for taking candid pictures of people when they least expected it. At one time, I remember my Aunt Angie throwing a piece of bread at him when she caught him taking pictures of her trying to cut into a tough piece of steak.....and everyone laughed.

After lunch was finished and the tables were cleared, we could always expect my cousin, Joe Romeo, to get a softball game going. This was another fun activity for the family. He usually brought most of the equipment; some of us brought extra bats and mitts to use also. Joe played on a baseball team in town and knew how to organize a group into two teams and get the game started. It was easy to get the men involved but he tried to persuade all of my aunts to play as well. This wasn't always easy, but he had a very convincing way and once he rallied one of them to participate, the others would follow suit. He would even-off the teams so there were an equal number of men, women, and children.

I remember one game in particular. While the game was in process, it was my mother's turn to bat. Approaching home plate, she announced that she was going to hit a homerun. After many tries, she finally hit the ball. She stood there in amazement, not believing that she had hit the ball. Everyone was yelling at her, "Run, Theresa, run!" She finally realized she had to run to first base. As she was making her way to first base, Joe ran along side her, yelling loudly, "Run faster, Aunt Theresa! Run faster! You can make it." She had forgotten and was still carrying the bat with her as she ran. Joe yelled, "Throw the bat, Aunt Theresa," which she did and it landed in the middle of the field. When she finally arrived at the base safely, she was completely out of breath from running. In the midst of all the laughter, everyone clapped and cheered for her. At that point, Joe ran back to home plate and went through the same encouraging prompts with my Aunt Jennie……and then again, with my Aunt Mary, Aunt Angie……and all the others. He was the energizing force that ushered everyone into the spirit of the game and made it a lot of fun for us. Whenever Joe was up to bat, it was usually a home run or a triple; as a result, everyone on the opposite team moved further out into the field. He encouraged a lot of cheering throughout the game. We had so much fun that it drew people from other picnics to sit on the sidelines surrounding the baseball field, watch the game, and cheer along with our family.

Our family picnics were an annual event for many years, and we always looked forward to them. My parents and my aunts and uncles planned for months in advance for this celebration. Once the date was selected, everyone made it a point to be there. There were some years when our extended families were invited also. They included my Uncle Al Lizzio's sisters, brother, and their families, namely, his brother, Mario and Marida Lizzio; his sister, Grace and Russell Trovato; and his sisters Angelina and Josephine and their families. The Lizzio's kept in close contact with the Cavallaro family and, when we got together, we were one big, happy family.

After the baseball game, there was time for the women to sit around a talk. They would sit in lawn chairs under the shade of the huge elm trees by our tables. The men usually gathered around the tables and played a few hands of Pinochle or one of the Italian card games, either *Briscula* or *Scupa*. Sometimes, they would take a walk around the park. All the kids, regardless of age, spent a lot of time playing nearby in Irondequoit Creek. We walked on the rocks that were at the waters edge, collected frogs and tadpoles, and then competed to see who could throw stones the furthest into the water. Usually, someone had an unexpected dunking when playing too close to the water or trying to cross the creek. Living in the city did not allow us to be near water very often; therefore, we thoroughly enjoyed the experience.

Overall, the annual Cavallaro Family Picnics were a pleasurable time for everyone. When the evening dusk approached and all the cars were loaded with our personal belongings, we began to go from family to family so our good-byes could be exchanged. This usually took a long time because we had to hug and kiss everyone and there were a large number of people present. As we drove back into the city toward home, I remember sitting in the back seat of our car with my brother. We reminisced with my parents about the highlights during the day, which brought about more laughter. We went home tired, completely content with food and snacks, and with many memories that we knew would last a lifetime; and they have. As I sit here writing this account of our annual picnics, I can vividly picture my parents and the whole family as though it happened only yesterday. Events like these are a part of the rich legacy that was left by my father's family of six brothers and sisters. These family picnics continued each year, even until I was married and had children of my own. Tears come to my eyes as I remember these dear, dear people, and the wonderful things we did together. My heart longs to experience the kind of love they gave us – the next generation - as we were in those formidable, growing up years. Little did we realize then, how those picnics would live on in our memories as highlights of our family's closeness, and how they were used to show the strong bonds of love between the Cavallaro brothers and sisters and their children. It was a simple activity, yet they left a huge imprint upon each one of us.

The Annual Cavallaro Family Picnics

July 1932
Back row: Al Cavallaro, Frederico Lamanna, Roger Cavallaro, Joe Cavallaro

Front row: Jennie Lamanna, Carmella Siracusa, Theresa Cavallaro, Angelina Lamanna, Angela Cavallaro, Mary Lizzio, Jennie Cavallaro

On ground: Al (Sonny) Cavallaro, Angelo Lizzio

(Theresa was 8 months pregnant for Richard)

July 1932
Back row: Frederico Lamanna

Front row: Sonny Cavallaro, Jennie Cavallaro, Mary Lizzio, Theresa Cavallaro, Jennie Lamanna, Carmella Siracusa, Angelina Lamanna, Angela Cavallaro

July 1954
Far Left:
Mary & Audrey Lizzio talking, Jennie Cavallaro leaning over table giving something to Angelo & Joan D'Amanda
Far right:
Al Cavallaro (with hat) sitting at table

July 1959
Left: Jennie & Joe Cavallaro, Aggie Cavallaro, Joe Cavallaro, Angelo & Pauline Lizzio
Right: Roger Cavallaro, Mary Jane Cavallaro, Theresa Cavallaro, Audrey Lizzio, Alfred Cavallaro, Al Cavallaro

July 1960
Cheryl & Al Cavallaro, Al, Angelo & Mary Lizzio, Jennie Cavallaro in front

The Legacy They Left Us

We all have our own definitions of what a 'legacy' is or what it means. According to The American Heritage Dictionary, the word 'legacy' is defined as follows:

Legacy: leg-a-cy (lĕg´-ə-sē) n.
1. Money or property bequeathed to someone by a will.
2. Something handed down from an ancestor or predecessor from the past.

Synonym: Bequest, inheritance, estate.

My family ancestors handed down a rich legacy to me, my cousins, and onto the next generations. Some of them are included in the stories I have related in this book. However, I could not include everything because they were not just events, relics, or tangible items. Much of what they handed down were characteristic traits, likes and dislikes, opinions, mannerisms, ways of speaking, and gestures; all of which my cousins and I possess. They gave us their emotions, their talents, their religious beliefs, and most of all, their dedication in raising a family in love and harmony. They instilled in each of us the importance of strong family ties through love and honor, our commitment to exemplary work ethics as a means to being successful in our jobs and careers, and in having the genuine pride in our surname with satisfaction and respect for our roots and in being Sicilian..

These brave Cavallaro men and women made many sacrifices in order to establish a new life for themselves and their families in an unknown country. They worked hard at everything they did, and we have much for which to thank them. They helped each one of us grow to our potential, taught us how to be committed to our work, and passed on their individual skills and talents to us. They did all this in a loving and determined manner without ever losing sight that, in all they were doing and in all the struggles they had to overcome, there was nothing more important than their family. As demonstrated in the various chapters in this book, they loved and respected one another and devoted quality time with each other. They were willing to help whenever there was a need and in the midst of every get-together, there was much laughter, happiness, and music, which was topped off with a glass of wine; usually a dry zinfandel that one of them had made.

Most Italian families are close and have wonderful memories of their ancestors. My Cavallaro family is no different; in fact, they excelled in creating memories, which each of us carry in our hearts. I cannot help but feel the pride they taught us which makes me forever dedicated to my family. Of course, there were imperfections and I don't want you to think that I'm blinded to their faults; however, through my eyes, those were minor and incidental. The qualities they passed onto their children were strengths that have helped each of us live a better life. Those, which stand out in my mind, are listed below:

- Be honest with the people you meet and always practice the utmost integrity.
- Be straightforward, and if you make a promise, keep it.
- Have a committed work ethic and be dedicated to your job; always give your best.
- It is good to have many friends, but select them wisely.
- You need self-respect in your life in order to succeed.
- Love everyone in your family and express this to them often.
- It's important to socialize with your family often and break bread together. It warms the heart to sit at the table with family or friends over a plate of pasta and sauce made with fresh tomatoes that were grown in the back yard. It's flavor is enhanced with large springs of fresh basil, picked from the garden, and sprinkled with the best Parmesan or Romano cheese. Add a couple of meatballs or sausage, some fresh Italian bread, a good glass of wine and you've got a meal. Now that's Italian! It's at our dinner tables that many memories are created.
- Music (Italian music, of course) is like bread and a staple of life.
- Keep busy and active; always doing something that satisfies you.
- Don't allow others to belittle you or make fun of you, your name, or your family.
- Keep your name clean and be proud of it. When others hear your name mentioned, they'll think good things about you.
- And most of all, be proud to be an Italian….better yet, to be a Sicilian. Don't ever forget your roots, where your family came from, and the history of your beginnings.

What more can a first generation Italian-American ask for? As I was growing up, I took all that my family gave me for granted; but it was rooted deep in my heart. I thought all families were like mine until I grew older and began to understand how privileged I was to have parents who cared for their family so lovingly, and to have aunts and uncles who always treated me as if I was their own child. I tried to raise my family with the same qualities and the wonderful things my ancestors had given to me so I could pass them onto my children. I could never begin to compare what they gave me and what I was able to do with my family. They were my mentors and I learned so much from them. Each had a part in making me the person who I am today.

An old Italian proverb sums it up:

*"La vita del bambino è come pezzo de carta
su cui ogni persona lascia un contrassegno."*

"A child's life is like a piece of paper
on which every person leaves a mark."

My piece of paper (my life) is covered with the fingerprints of each of my relatives; they are all memorable, unforgettable, and are indelible in my being.

Thank you to my Grandfather Angelo and Grandmother Angela, Aunt Angie, Aunt Mary, Uncle Joe, Uncle Roger, and Aunt Joan. I especially thank my father, Alfred Cavallaro, who was my mentor, my guide, and who lovingly, taught me so much about life and how to live it. They left my cousins and me a rich legacy, which has been passed down to future generations. It will continue to be passed onto the next generations of Cavallaro's and to their descendents. Their lives continue to live on through us as we share with our children the memories they left and the love they gave each of our families. Let us embrace this legacy and keep it alive; let it live on through our children and grandchildren as we serve as ambassadors to the next generations and connect them to the heritage they deserve to know.

"But you must continue in the things
which you have learned and been assured of,
knowing from whom you have learned them,
and that from childhood you have known....."
2 Timothy 3:14, 15 (NKJ)

"Finally, all of you be of one mind,
having compassion for one another;
love as brothers, be tenderhearted, be courteous;
not returning evil for evil or reviling for reviling,
but on the contrary, blessing,
knowing that you were called to this,
that you may inherit a blessing."
1 Peter 3:8, 9 (NKJ)

.....and so it is with the Cavallaro's as our story continues into future generations.

Appendix

The Cavallaro Surname

During my research of the Cavallaro family, I became interested in knowing where other families in my ancestral history were located in Italy and Sicily. I have included charts, which show the general locations of others named Cavallaro and Gravagna. The migration trail spans into Italy, Sicily, and America.

When searching for Italian surnames, I found the origin of the names gave specific identities to individual families. The surname could be linked to their occupation, location where they lived, father's name, and/or personal characteristics. The surname, Cavallaro, appears to be occupational in origin, and it is believed to be associated with the Spaniard's, meaning 'one who grooms horses or one who is a professional horse rider'. It can also mean 'horse dealer' or 'horse keeper'.

There are different spellings of the name for a variety of reasons. The most common were because the people could not spell very well and they wrote the name as it was pronounced (how it sounded). Secondly, they spelled it differently depending on which dialect they used, or from what part of Italy/Sicily they originated. Some variations of the name Cavallaro include Cavallero, Caballero, Cavalieri, Cavaliere, Cavalleri, Cavallo and the list goes on.

Available census records indicate there are approximately 1,000 heads of households in the United States with the old and distinguished Cavallaro name. This research was completed using the exact spelling that is used by my family. This equates to approximately 4,000 people in the United States named Cavallaro. Although the figure seems relatively low, it does not signify the many important contributions that individuals bearing the Cavallaro name have made to history and to our society. A notable bearer of the name is Lena Cavalieri, the Italian operatic soprano who sang at La Scala di Milano in numerous concerts and operas. Another is Pietro Francesco Cavalli, the Italian composer, whose music is still being enjoyed by Italians and others throughout the European continent. Finally, another related to the Cavallaro heritage is Pietro Cavallini, the Italian painter, whose exquisite paintings currently grace churches in Rome, Naples, and many others throughout Sicily. Cavallini's colorful mosaics are located in *piazzas*, fountains, and churches in Palermo, Catania, and Siracusa in Sicily. They are on permanent display in various churches in Naples and Calabria on the mainland.

This list does not include, of course, the noted Sicilians who are closer at home; among them are my parents, aunts and uncles, cousins and their children who have made, and continue to make significant contributions to the American society. During the 20th and 21st centuries, my Cavallaro family name has been prominent in the clothing industry, technology, photography, education, city government, automotive industry, business world, medical fields, music, and in many other areas too numerous to mention. It is my prediction, that in future years they will continue to aspire to greater fame as the next generations of these young Sicilian-Americans continue to immerse themselves into the American society and utilize the talents they have been given.

Although I have focused on the Cavallaro family who lived and worked on the eastern coast of Sicily, at the present time, one can find someone named Cavallaro in all the provinces on the island of Sicily. To give you a glimpse of where they are located, I have made a basic genealogical search of the heads of households with the names Gravagna and Cavallaro. They are listed by province, not city, only because the list is quite lengthy as we look at the names, city by city. The numbers listed on the charts indicate the heads of household for each city. It is estimated that each household contains approximately four people. In order to determine the approximate number of Cavallaro's or Gravagna's within a city, you must multiply the head of household number by four. Therefore, this rough figure can be significantly higher since many families had more than four individuals living in the home. The current population of the island of Sicily is listed as 5.1 million and growing. The map of Contemporary Italy and Sicily list the provinces by name and number where all the Cavallaro's are located.

Location of Heads of Household in Sicily with the 'Gravagna' Surname

Name	Province	Number
Gravagna	Caltanissetta	27
	Catania	269
	Enna	74
	Messina	17
	Palermo	75
	Ragusa	20
Total		**482**

Location of Heads of Household in Sicily with the 'Cavallaro' Surname

Name	Province	Number
Cavallaro	Agrigento	229
	Caltanissetta	134
	Catania	5748
	Enna	188
	Messina	518
	Palermo	1087
	Ragusa	49
	Siracusa	217
	Trapani	20
Total		**8190**

As you review these charts, please keep in mind that this search only includes the spellings of Gravagna and Cavallaro as we know them; had I changed one letter on either name, such as making Gravagna into Gravagno, or Cavallaro into Cavallero, the numbers would change significantly. As we look at these charts, they show I have family covering the entire island of Sicily. When I was in Italy, I was told the name 'Cavallaro' was as common in Sicily as the name 'Smith' is in America.

I made another search of the Cavallaro name; specifically, where it appears in larger numbers on the mainland of Italy. The chart shown and the maps of Italy and Sicily that follow, have each city listed within the province where they are located. You can trace the cities that have heads of household named Cavallaro in Italy. These charts indicate how Cavallaro's have migrated throughout Italy also. The provinces for each numeric category are listed from the south and then move northward.

Location of Heads of Household in Italy with the 'Cavallaro' Surname

Number	Province	City/Town
5,000+	Calabria	Reggio
	Campania	Salerno Napoli
	Lazio	Roma
	Veneto	Rovigo Verona
	Piemonte	Torino
	Lombardia	Milano

Number	Province	City/Town
1,000+	Calabria	Catanzaro Crotone
	Abruzzo	L'Squila
	Toscana	Firenze
	Liguria	Savona
	Piedmonte	Alessandria
	Lombardia	Como Brescia
	Veneto	Vicenza
	Trentino	Bolzano

Number	Province	City/Town
100+	Calabria	Vibo Valentia
	Liguria	Genova

	Lombardia	Pavia
		Varese
	Veneto	Venezia
		Padova
Number	**Province**	**City/Town**
None	Basilicata	Matera
		(Near Bari)
	Molise	Iserna
		(Near Abruzzo)
	Marche	Ascoli Piceno
		(Near Umbria)
Total		**6,100+**

The island of Sardinia is mainly populated by people from Spain, Italy, France, Tunisia, and Morocco. However, some Cavallaro families made their way to the island in the following numbers:

Heads of Household in Sardinia with the 'Cavallaro' Surname

Number	**Province**
25+	Caligiari
	Oristano
Number	**Province**
5+	Sassari
Number	**Province**
0	Nuoro
Total	**30+**

Provinces and Cities where Cavallaro Families are Located in Italy and Sicily

(Each province is listed in italics and underlined)
(Individual cities, located within each province, are numbered)
(Only provinces shown are where Cavallaro Heads of Households are located)

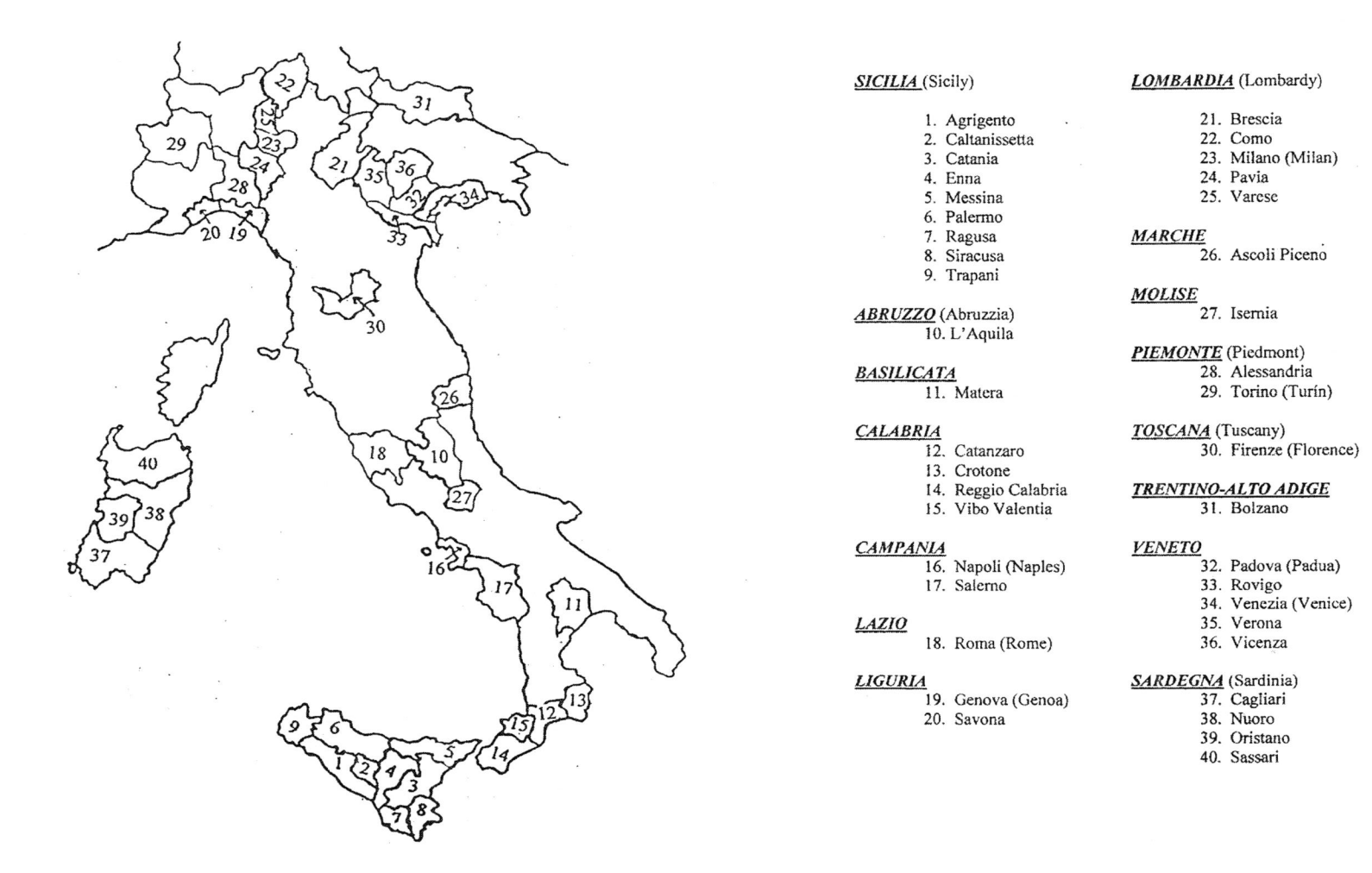

SICILIA (Sicily)
1. Agrigento
2. Caltanissetta
3. Catania
4. Enna
5. Messina
6. Palermo
7. Ragusa
8. Siracusa
9. Trapani

ABRUZZO (Abruzzia)
10. L'Aquila

BASILICATA
11. Matera

CALABRIA
12. Catanzaro
13. Crotone
14. Reggio Calabria
15. Vibo Valentia

CAMPANIA
16. Napoli (Naples)
17. Salerno

LAZIO
18. Roma (Rome)

LIGURIA
19. Genova (Genoa)
20. Savona

LOMBARDIA (Lombardy)
21. Brescia
22. Como
23. Milano (Milan)
24. Pavia
25. Varese

MARCHE
26. Ascoli Piceno

MOLISE
27. Isernia

PIEMONTE (Piedmont)
28. Alessandria
29. Torino (Turin)

TOSCANA (Tuscany)
30. Firenze (Florence)

TRENTINO-ALTO ADIGE
31. Bolzano

VENETO
32. Padova (Padua)
33. Rovigo
34. Venezia (Venice)
35. Verona
36. Vicenza

SARDEGNA (Sardinia)
37. Cagliari
38. Nuoro
39. Oristano
40. Sassari

Italian Influence on American Life

Few ethnic groups have ever had as much influence on Americans and the American way of life as the Italians. Italians have helped to advance the quality of life in America since colonial times. This can be attributed, in part, to the unusually large number of Italian immigrants who entered this country from the early 1800s and into the first quarter of the 1900s. Immigrants who never became citizens also made significant contributions. The immigrants found many opportunities here and saw the values this country offered to their children. As a result, they made many sacrifices to enable their children to gain prominence in their new home. To this day, many generations of Italian-Americans continue to enrich and augment this country. Those influences can easily be researched in encyclopedias, general references books, and on the Internet. By reading magazines and the daily newspaper, it is apparent how Italian-Americans are involved in American life today. It is a rich heritage they have given that continues to increase.

The 1930 United States Federal Census reported there were almost two million Italian-born residents in America. It was determined seventy-five percent had emigrated from southern Italy (Naples, Abruzzi, Puglia, and Calabria) and the islands of Sicily and Sardinia. In fifty years, that number changed considerably. The 1980 United States Federal Census reported there were over twelve million Americans who indicated they were of Italian ancestry. At that time, it would imply that one in every twenty people in America was a descendent of an Italian immigrant. Undeniably, this influx has had a definite affect on current American culture.

Upon arrival in America, the Italian immigrants established residence with their relatives or known *paisani*. As a result, neighborhoods that were referred to as 'Little Italy' began to spring up in many of the larger cities across America; Mulberry Street in New York City is a classic example. Many immigrants were drawn to Mulberry Street because of the encouragement they received from other Italians and their *paisani*, whose opinions and suggestions they valued. The vitality of that camaraderie was, and continues to be, a most enduring quality of the Italian heritage. The new immigrants were able to overcome many obstacles and adjust to the many challenges that American life offered them by always seeking the direction and assistance from their *paisani*.

I grew up in a neighborhood on the east side of Rochester, New York that was considered a 'Little Italy'. For many city blocks, from one end of the street to the other, practically every family living there was Italian. On the street where I lived, only a couple of families were not Italian and they were referred to as the 'non-Italians,' or as *l'americani*. They were different than we were and we didn't have a lot in common; however, we were always cordial and greeted them politely when we passed each other on the street. You never walked by their house and smelled the rich, distinctive aromas you often inhaled as you passed one of the Italian homes. Walking by my Italian neighbor's homes, I could identify the scents of Italian spaghetti sauce cooking over a low flame; eggs, sausage, and peppers frying in pure olive oil; or *verdura* and *cicoria* cooking on the stove in a large soup pot. In fact, walking down my street was filled with a series of Italian aromas as we passed all the homes just before dinnertime. I am not sure what the 'non-Italians' ate because we could never smell anything coming from their house. As my parents would say, they were *rifridate* (very cold people).

I believe the rich Italian heritage I received first came from my family. My father always spoke of what an honor it was to be Italian and how their influence had shaped our world. As a young boy, I listened to him, but I didn't fully understand what he was trying to teach me. However, while I was doing the research for this book, a light appeared and I began to see the meaning in what he was talking about all those years. As I buried myself in many books and read the research, I kept saying to myself, "I don't believe it" or "I didn't know they were from Italy," or "Wow, they were really Sicilian, weren't they." I believe I have been given a rich heritage and it brings me great pride to be able to say, "I'm a Sicilian!"

What follows is a compilation of Italians, some who immigrated from Italy and Sicily, along with the names of the next generation of Italian-Americans who have enriched the American culture. There are names on this list that you may not recognize, but I included them because of the importance of their many different contributions to our culture. Some of the names chronicled are Italian-Americas who became notorious because of their illegal actions. This is common with any ethnic group that emigrated from a foreign country. The names I have included are just a small sample from numerous classifications that are available. They are here for you because it is always helpful to see Italian names in writing so we may better identify their ethnicity and their contributions to the American culture. As other Italian-Americans read the names of these people along with what they have accomplished, I hope the pride of being of Italian decent will well-up within them, as it did with me. Italian-Americans have a distinguished heritage to be proud of, one that has known no bounds, and one that continues to be esteemed by the entire world.

Name	Born/Died	Immigr.	Contributions to America
Charles Atlas (Angelo Siciliano)	1893-1972	1903	Body Builder from Calabria, Italy. Known as the "Perfectly Developed Man" with a 53" chest and a 30" waist.
Frank Capra (Francesco Capra)	1897-1991	1900	Movie Director – Born in Bisaquino, Sicily – his first big hit was It Happened One Night with Clark Gable and Claudette Colbert. His films stood out against crime and corruption.
Frank Costello (Francesco Castiglia)	1891-1973	1895	Born in Calabria, Italy. A gangster involved in organized crime and controlled a vast gambling empire with the Luciano and Genevese families.
Charles (Lucky) Luciano (Salvatore Lucania)	1897-1962	1907	A gangster involved in the Cosa Nostra and the mastermind behind organized crime and drug trade.
Al Capone (Alfonso Capone)	1899-1947		A gangster and bootlegger – involved in the St. Valentine Day Massacre in 1929. He was declared Public Enemy #1 in Chicago and a symbol of the Mafia. Born in Brooklyn, NY. The movie Scarface was based on his life.
Nicola Sacco

Bartolomeo Vanzetti | 1891-1927

1888-1927 | 1908

1911 | Sentenced to death on 8/23/27 for the murder of a shoe factory paymaster. Thirty years later, the Governor of Massachusetts, Michael Dukakis declared them innocent, stating that the trial was permeated by prejudice against foreigners. |

Name	Dates	Year	Description
Arturo Toscanini	1867-1957	1909	Musician, Conductor at Metropolitan Opera House in New York City 1909-1913; born in Parma, Italy.
Armadeo Peter Giannini	1870-1949		Opened the Bank of Italy – It was so successful, it became the Bank of America. He provided most of the funding for the movie, <u>Gone With the Wind</u>.
Andrew Sbaroro	1870	1879	Established <u>Swiss Colony Wine Company.</u>
Hector Boiardi	1897-1985	1914	He was born in Piacenza, Italy; he started an Italian Restaurant and canned the tomato sauce under the name <u>Chef Boy-ar-dee.</u>
Armadeo Obici	1877-1947	1889	Pushcart Peddler who started <u>Planter's Peanuts</u>.
Joseph Di Giorgio Rosario Di Giorgio	1874-1951 1876-1955	1890	They were born in Cefalu, Sicily; They developed fruit orchards in California and canned them under the <u>S & W</u> Label.
Ernest Gallo Julio Gallo	1909-2007 1910-1993		Born in northern California, their family was from the Piedmonte region of Italy. <u>Gallo Wines</u> produces almost half of all California wines.
Marco J. Fontana Antonio Cerruti		1859	Established the <u>Del Monte Canning Company</u>

Frank Biondi	1945		CEO of Universal Studios (1987-1996) Member of Board of Harrah's Entertainment (2002- present).
Frank Mancuso Sr.	1927		Born in the Bronx, NYC. He was the CEO of Paramount Pictures.
Frank Mancuso Jr.	1958		Born in Buffalo, NY. He was the President of Paramount Pictures.
Richard Grasso	1946		CEO of New York Stock Exchange (1995-2003).
Phil Guarascio	Circa 1942		Former General Manager & Vice President of Advertising for General Motors Corp. Current member of Board of Directors of Papa John's Pizza.
Tommy Mottola	1949		President & CEO of CBS Records and SONY Music Entertainment (1988-2003).
Lucio A. Noto	1938		CEO of Mobile Corporation (1994-1999).
			- POLITICAL INFLUENCE -
Fiorello H. LaGuardia	1882-1947	1923	Interpreter at Ellis Island, New York Congressman, Mayor of NYC in 1934 for 12 years, NYC airport named for him.
Angelo Rossi	1878-1948		Mayor of San Francisco 1931-1944.

Anthony Celebrezze	1910-1998		First Italian-American appointed to a presidential cabinet in 1962 as Secretary of Health, Education, and Welfare. He served under Presidents Kennedy and Johnson.
John Pastore	1907-2000		First Italian-American to be a governor (R.I.) 1946-1950. First Italian-American Senator 1950-1977.
Joseph Alioto	1916-1998		Mayor of San Francisco 1968-1976
Alphonse D'Amato	1937		Senator from New York 1981-1999.
Pete Domenici	1932		Senator from New Mexico 1973 – present.
Mike Enzi	1944		Senator from Wyoming 1997 – present.
James Florio	1937		First Italian-American Governor of New Jersey 1990-1994.
Rudolph Giuliani	1944		Mayor of New York City 1994-2001.
Romano Mazzoli	1932		Congressman from Kentucky 1971-1995.
Susan Molinari	1958		Congresswoman from New York City 1990-1997. In 1990, the youngest member of Congress.
Leon Panetta	1938		Chief of Staff under President Clinton 1994-1997.
John Podesta	1949		Chief of Staff under President Clinton 1998-2001.

Robert Torricelli	1951		House of Representatives 1983-1997. Senator from New Jersey 1997-2003.
John Volpe	1908-1994		Governor of Massachusetts 1961-1963 and 1965-1969.
Mario Cuomo	1932		Secretary of State, Lt. Governor, and Governor with the longest tenure of any Democratic governor in the history of New York State 1983-1994.
Antonio Scalia	1936		The only Italian-American Justice in the U.S. Supreme Court. Appointed by President Reagan in 1986.
Peter Rodino	1909-2005		From New Jersey – Chairman of House Judiciary Committee during the Watergate Hearings.
John Sirica	1904-1992		Judge who presided over the Watergate Hearings.
Ella Grasso	1919-1981		Governor of Connecticut 1975-1980.
Geraldine Ferraro	1935		House of Representatives from New York. 1979-1985. The first and only woman, to date, who was nominated to run for Vice-President of the U.S., chosen by Walter Mondale in 1984.
			-SPORTS INFLUENCE-
Tony DeFate	1895		1917 Detroit Tiger First Italian-American in Major League Sports.

Ping Bodie	1887-1961		Chicago White Sox, Philadelphia A's, and New York Yankees. He was the roommate of Babe Ruth. He nicknamed Babe Ruth as 'The Bambino.'
Tony Lazzeri	1903-1946		NY Yankees Hall of Fame in 1991.
Ernie Orsatti	1902-1968		St. Louis Cardinals.
Gus Mancuso	1905-1984		New York Giants.
Joe Cicero	1910-1983		Boston Red Sox and Philadelphia Athletics.
Frankie Crosetti	1910-2002		New York Yankees, player and coach.
Lawrence Berra 'Yogi Berra'	1925		New York Yankees and New York Mets. Inducted into Baseball Hall of Fame. Son of Pietro Berra who emigrated in 1923.
Roy Campanella	1921-1993		Brooklyn Dodgers.
Phil Rizutto	1917		National Baseball Hall of Fame 1994. Played for New York Yankees.
Ernie Lombardi	1908-1997		National Baseball Hall of Fame.

Joe DiMaggio (Giuseppe Paolo) DiMaggio)	1914-1999		National Baseball Hall of Fame 1955. He played for the New York Yankees. Married to actress Marilyn Monroe. Both of his parents were Sicilian.
Johnny Antonelli Rocky Colovito Tony Conigliaro Vic Lombardi Mike Mussina Mike Piazza Dave Righetti Frank Torre Robin Ventura	1930 1933 1945-1990 1922-1997 1968 1968 1958 1931 1967		Johnny Antonelli is from Rochester, New York. All others are baseball players and/or coaches on various teams.
Babe Pinelli Steve Palermo	1895-1984 1949		Baseball Umpires
Tommy Lasorda	1927		Manager, Brooklyn & Los Angeles Dodgers Inducted into Hall of Fame 1997.
Joe Torre Jim Fregosi Tony La Russa	1940 1942 1944		Baseball Managers
Angelo B. Giamatti	1938-1989		Former President of Yale University In 1986, 7th Commissioner of National Major League Baseball.

Dolph Camilli Dom DiMaggio Sam Mele Carl Furillo Vic Raschi Sal Maglie	1907-1997 1917 1923 1922-1989 1919-1988 1917-1992		**Baseball Dream Team** Dodger's Hall of Fame; Dom DiMaggio was brother to Joe and Vince DiMaggio.
Luigi Piccolo	1893-1978		Coached at Columbia University 1930-1956. Known by the name of Lou Little.
Sammy Urzetta Gene Sarazen (Eugene Saraceni)	 1902-1999		1950 National Amateur Golf Championship; 'Outstanding Athlete' in NYS in 1950. Won all four major Golf Tournaments of the U.S. Open in 1922 and 1932; PGA Championship in 1922, 1923, 1933; British Open in 1932; Masters in 1935.
Dan Marino	1961		Miami Dolphins Football All-Star Quarterback in NFL. Pro Football Hall of Fame 2005.
Eddie Arcaro	1916-1997		Jockey with a career of thirty years; First Italian-American jockey to win in horseracing. Only jockey to win the Triple Crown twice, in 1941 and 1948. Inducted in Racing Hall of Fame 1958.
Joe Montana	1956		Pro Football Hall of Fame 2000.
Alan Ameche	1933-1988	Late 1930s	College Hall of Fame.

Franco Harris (½ Italian)	1950		Pittsburgh Steelers All- Star. Pro Football Hall of Fame 1990.
Joe Paterno	1926		Penn State Football Coach since 1966.
Vince Lombardi	1913-1970		Played for Fordham University, and New York Giants. Head Coach of Green Bay Packers. The Super Bowl Trophy is now called 'The Vince Lombardi Trophy.'
Pete Rozelle	1926-1996		<u>Commissioners of National Football League</u> 1960-1989
Paul Tagliabue	1940		1989-2006
Jake LaMotta	1921		World Middleweight Championship Boxer 1949-1951. Movie <u>Raging Bull</u> was his based on his life.
Rocky Graziano (Thomas Rocco Barbella)	1922-1990		World Middleweight Boxing Champion 1947-1948.
Carmen Basilio	1927		World Welterweight Champion 1955-1957. World Middleweight Champion 1957-1958.
Rocky Marciano (Rocco Frances Marchigiano)	1923-1969		World Heavyweight Championship in 1952-1956, he remains the only champion to retire undefeated in all boxing history He had 43 KOs in 49 fights. He knocked out Joe Lewis, Jersey Joe Wolcott, Ezzard Charles, and others.

Al Cervi Tom Gola Hank Luisetti Lou Carnesecca Jim Valvano Rick Pitino	1917 1933 1916- 2002 1925 1946- 1993 1952		<u>Basketball Hall of Fame</u> Basketball players and coaches.
Mary Lou Retton	1968		The first and youngest Italian-American woman to win the Olympics Gold Medal in Gymnastics in 1994; youngest inductee into the USOC Olympic Hall of Fame; also entered into the Italian-American Sports Hall of Fame.
Mario Andretti	1940		The only race driver in history to ever win the Indianapolis 500 (1969), the Daytona 500 (1967), and the Formula One World championship.
			- THE ARTS -
Antonio Stradivari	1644-1737		Born near Cremora, Italy, he was a crafter of the finest stringed instruments ever made; to include, violins, violas, cellos and harps in the field. He made over 1,100 instruments, 650 of which are still in use today; the Stradivarius violin, being the most famous.
Dario Soria	1912-1980	1939	Founder of Angel Records and Founder of the Metropolitan Opera Guild in New York City

Rudolph Valentino (Rodolfo Alfonzo Raffaelo Pierre Filibert Bublielmi di Valentina D'Antonguolla)	1895-1926	1913	Dramatic Actor and Tango Dancer. His famous quote in 1923 was "Live and Let Live."
Joseph Volpe	1940		General Manager of the Metropolitan Opera. He started at the Met as a Carpenter, advanced to Master Carpenter and on to Technical Director, and has been the General Manager of the Met from 1990-present.
Pietro Mascagni	1863-1945		Composer: In 1890, wrote *Cavalleria Rusticana*, his most famous opera that was set in Sicily. It was featured in the movie, Godfather III. He was born in Livorno, Italy and died in Rome.
Giacomo Puccini	1859-1924		Composer: He was best known for his operas *La Bohème* and *Tosca*.
Giuseppe Verdi	1813-1901		Composer: He was best known for his operas *Aida* and *La Traviata*. Born in Parma, Italy.
Gioacchino Rossini	1792-1868		Composer: He was best known for his opera *The Barber of Seville*.
Gaetano Donizetti	1797-1848		Composer: He was best known for his opera *Lucia di Lammermoor*.

Benlamino Gigli	1890-1957		Famous Italian Tenor
Ruggeo Leoncavallo	1857-1919		Composer: Born in Naples, his most famous opera, *I Pagliacci*, was a short opera and a favorite of Enrico Caruso.
Enrico Caruso	1873-1921	1904	Sang at the Metropolitan Opera House for eighteen years; his most famous was *I Pagliacci*. Considered the 'Greatest Tenor ever known.'
Luciano Pavarotti	1935		Born in Medena, Italy Contemporary Italian Tenor singing in all the major opera houses of the world.
Andrea Bocelli	1958		Born in Tuscany, Italy. Contemporary Italian Tenor who has gained notoriety in America, Europe and the world over.
Ferruccio Tagliavini	1913-1995		Born in Reggio, Italy, he was the finest Tenor, second only to Caruso, who sang throughout the world. He debuted at La Scala in 1942 and at the NY Metropolitan Opera House in 1946, both times singing the role of Rodolfo in *La Bohème*, his most frequently sung role. He was known as 'The Tenor with the Velvet Voice.'
Licia Albanese	1913	1945	Born in Bari, Italy, she is one of the most beloved Italian Coloratura Sopranos of the 20th Century; known the world over for her roles in *La Traviata*, *La Bohème*, *Madame Butterfly*, *Lucia de Lammermoor*, and *Aida*.

Renata Tebaldi	1922-2004		Born in Pesaro, Italy. 20th Century Soprano who sang at The Met.
Rosa Ponselle (Rose Melba Ponzillo)	1897-1981		19th Century Soprano.
Carlo Buti	1902-1963		Born near Florence, Italy. He became most popular singing familiar Neapolitan songs. (*Santa Lucia*, *Come Back to Sorrento*, etc.) He was known as the Frank Sinatra of Italy.
Mario Lanza (Alfredo "Freddie" Arnold Cocozza)	1921-1959		One of the greatest Tenors of the 20th Century. Born in So. Philadelphia, he was discovered at age twenty-one. He sang in many operas: *La Bohème*, *Madame Butterfly*, and others; he appeared in seven movies: *The Great Caruso*, *Serenade*, *Toast to New Orleans* and others.
Anna Moffo	1932-2006		Operatic singer making 220 performances at The Met in eighteen different operas. She was known as, 'One of the most beautiful women ever to grace the stage of any opera house'.
Sonny Bono (Salvatore Phillip Bono)	1935-1998		Singing partner with Cher; He was former Mayor of Palm Springs, CA.
Perry Como (Pierino Ronald Como)	1912-2001		Born in Canonsburg, PA, he was a crooner that was also known as… 'The Singer Most Watched on TV'. A former barber, he was the seventh of thirteen children.

Emile Pandolfi	1946		Born in NYC, raised in Greenville, SC. Contemporary Pianist.
Guy Lombardo (Gaetano Lombardo)	1902-1977		Big Band Leader of The Royal Canadians from the 1940s to the 1970s He was best known as the band that played <u>Auld Lang Syne</u> at the Waldorf Astoria on New Years Eve each year until 1976. Born in London, Ontario, he had the longest running act in show business history.
Vic Damone (Vito Rocco Farinola)	1928		**<u>Popular Contemporary Singers</u>** Born in Brooklyn, NY
Bobby Darin (Waldon Robert Cassotto)	1936-1973		Born in the Bronx, NY
Connie Francis (Concetta Franconero)	1938		Born in Newark, NJ
Al Martino (Alfred Cini)	1927		Born in Philadelphia, PA
Frankie Valle (Francis Stephen Costelluccio)	1937		Born in Newark, NJ
Russ Columbo (Ruggiero Eugenio di Rudolpho Columbo)	1908-1934		Born in Camden, NJ

Jon Bon Jovi (John Francis Bongiovi)	1962		Born in Perth Amboy, NJ
Madonna (Madonna Louise Ciccone)	1958		Born in Bay City, MI
Bernadette Peters (Bernadette Lazzara)	1948		Born in Queens, NY
Anna Maria Alberghetti	1936		Born in Pensaro, Italy, she was discovered at age twelve in Italy and immigrated to the United States to star in movies as a singer and actress throughout her adult years.
Louie Prima	1910-1978		His parents were immigrants from Sicily. He was born in New Orleans, LA, and was an accomplished drummer. His raspy voice was famous as he sang with Keely Smith.
Frank Sinatra (Francis Albert Sinatra)	1915-1998		Born in Hoboken, NJ, he was discovered by Harry James in 1939; his first recording was at age twenty-three; he also sang with the Tommy Dorsey Orchestra from 1940-1942; he had a career of over fifty years; 'He sang with meaning'.
Tony Bennett (Anthony Dominick Benedetto)	1926		Born in Queens, NY, he is a top singer in the U.S. and also an accomplished artist.

Julius La Rosa	1930		Born in Brooklyn, NY; Italian singer during the 1950s-60s. He made the song, _E Cumpare_, a household word.
Jerry Vale (Gennaro Luigi Vitaliano)	1932		Born in the Bronx, NY; currently resides in Las Vegas, NV; top Italian singer in US. Known the world over for his clear Tenor voice. He said, "I sing from the heart; people understand that."
Carol Lawrence (Carolina Maria Larria)	1932		Born in Melrose Park, IL; a contemporary singer/actress on stage and screen. She appeared on Broadway in musicals and she is currently on the road singing and dancing in many plays and musicals.
Fabian (Fabian Forte)	1943		Discovered at fourteen years old in Philadelphia, PA, he appeared in thirty movies and has three Gold Records to his credit. Known as 'The Most Promising Male Vocalist of 1958'.
Frankie Avalon (Francis Thomas Avallone)	1940		Born in South Philadelphia, PA, his biggest hit was _Venus_, selling one million+ copies. He had three other songs selling one-million+ copies. He starred in many movies with actress Annette Funicello.
Jimmy Durante (James Francesco Durante)	1893-1980		He was a Singer, Comedian, Actor, and Pianist. Both parents were from Salerno, Italy.
Nick La Rocca	1889-1961		Born of Sicilian parents, he founded the first Dixieland Jazz Band in New Orleans, LA.

Don Ameche (Dominick Felix Ameche)	1908-1993		Singer/Actor of the 1930s-40s. His original name was spelled 'Amici'.
Frankie Laine (Francisco Paolo LoVecchio)	1913-2007		Singer: Born in Chicago, IL. His parents emigrated from Monreale, Sicily.
Johnny Desmond (Giovanni Alfredo DeSimone)	1919-1985		Singer in 1940s to 1950s. Born in Detroit, MI.
Danny DeVito (Daniel Michael DeVito)	1944		**Movie/Television Stars** Actor: Born in Neptune, NJ.
Joe Pesci (Joseph Eliot Pesci)	1943		Actor: Born in Newark, NJ.
Anne Bancroft (Anna Marie Louisa Italiano)	1931-2005		Actress: Born in the Bronx, NY.
Leonardo DiCaprio	1974		Actor: Born in Hollywood, CA.
Alan Alda (son) (Alphonso Joseph D'Abruzzo)	1936		Actor: Born in New York City

Robert Alda (dad) (Alphonso Giuseppe Giovanni Roberto) D'Abruzzo)	1914-1986		
Tony Danza (Antonio Salvatore Iadanza)	1951		Actor: Born in Brooklyn, NY; his grandparents were from Corleone, Sicily.
Anthony (Tony) Franciosa (Anthony George Papaleo Jr.)	1928-2006		Actor: Franciosa was his mother's maiden name.
Ben Gazzara (Biagio Anthony Gazzara)	1930		Actor: Born in New York City.
Al Pacino (Alfrerdo James Pacino)	1940		Actor: Born in Manhattan, NY; his grandparents were from Corleone, Sicily.
Ida Lupino	1918-1995		Actress: Born in London, England.
Jay Leno (James Douglas Muir-Leno)	1950		Talk Host/Comedian: Born in Farmington, MA.
Robert Loggia	1930		Actor: Born in Staten Island, NY; his family emigrated from Sicily.
Mira Sorvino	1967		Actress: Born in Tenafly, NJ.

Name	Year		Description
Paul Anthony Sorvino	1939		Actor: Born in Brooklyn, NY.
Penny Marshall (Carole Penny Marsciarelli)	1942		Actress/Director: Born in the Bronx, NY.
Garry Marshall	1934		Director: Born in New York City.
Sylvester Stallone	1946		Actor: Born in New York City; His father is from Castellammare del Golfo, Sicily.
Connie Stevens (Concetta Rosalie Anna Ingoglia)	1938		Actress/Singer: Born in Brooklyn, NY.
John Joseph Travolta	1954		Actor/Dancer/Singer: Born in Englewood, NJ.
John Michael Turturro	1957		Actor/Director: His father is from Bari, Italy and his mother is from Sicily.
Talia Shire (Talia Rose Coppola)	1946		Actress: Born in Lake Success, NY; she is the sister of Francis Ford Coppola.
Robert Mario De Niro Jr.	1943		Actor; Born in Manhattan, NY; his grandfather lives in Syracuse, NY.
Sal Mineo (Salvatore Mineo)	1936-1976		Actor: Born in the Bronx, NY; both of his parents were born in Sicily.
Kaye Ballard (Caterina Gloria Balotta)	1925		Actress/Comedienne: Born in Cleveland, OH.

Lou Costello (Louis Francis Cristillo)	1906-1959		Actor: Born in Patterson, NJ, he acted in the Bud Abbot-Lou Costello team and made numerous comedy movies.
Annette Joanne Funicello	1942		Actress/singer: Born in Utica, NY, she began as a Mouseketeer on the Walt Disney Show and The Mickey Mouse Club.
Isabella Rossellini (Isabella Fiorella Elettra Giovanna Rossellini)	1952		Actress/Model: Born in Rome, Italy, she is one of the twin daughters of Ingrid Bergman and Roberto Rossellini. She spent much of her young life between living in Rome and the island of Stromboli, off the Italian coast. She is the recipient of many awards.
Henry Fonda	1905-1982		The family all lived in New York City. Their ancestors are originally from a valley in the Apennine Mountains in Italy, about twelve miles outside of Genoa. In the 14th Century, the Marquis de Fonda fled to Amsterdam. The first Fonda to immigrate to America was Jellis Douw, a Dutch/Italian who came in the 1600s. He traveled up the Mohawk River to Caughnawaga. When all the Indians left the area, it was called Fonda, NY. It is located near Albany, NY.
Peter Fonda	1940		
Jane Fonda (Lady Jayne Seymour Fonda)	1937		
Henry Mancini (Enrico Nicola Mancini	1924-1994		Composer/orchestra leader: Born in Cleveland, OH. His parents emigrated from Abruzzi, Italy.
Dean Martin (Dino Paul Crocetti)	1917-1995		Singer/Actor/TV star: Born in Steubenville, OH, he was part of the original 'Rat Pack' in Las Vegas. He's most famous for That's Amore and other songs. He spoke only Italian until five years of age.

Liza Minelli	1946		Singer/Actress/Las Vegas headliner: Born in Los Angeles, CA, she is the daughter of Director, Vincent Minelli, and singer/actress, Judy Garland.
Lennie Tristano	1919-1978		Jazz Pianist: Born in Chicago, IL, he was blind from birth.
Liberace (Wladziu Valentino Liberace)	1919-1987		Concert Pianist/ TV/ movie star/ Las Vegas performer. His father was an immigrant from Formia, Italy. He had a twin brother who died at birth.
Pat Martino (Pat Azzara)	1944		Musician: Born in So. Philadelphia, PA.
Tony Mottola	1918-2004		Musician: Born in Kearney, NJ, he worked exclusively with Frank Sinatra and Perry Como. He also played with the Doc Severinsen orchestra on the Tonight Show Both Pat Martino and Tony Mottola were Jazz guitarists.
Chuck Mangione	1940		Born in Rochester, NY, he is a Jazz Trumpeter and professor of music at The Eastman School of Music.
Gap Mangione (Gapspare Mangione)	1938		Born in Rochester, NY, he is a renowned professional pianist.
Jack Valenti	1921-2007		Born in Houston, TX, he was the President and CEO of The Motion Picture Assoc. of America; Current movie ratings are the results of his efforts.

Vincent Minelli (Lester Anthony Minelli)	1903-1986		Born in Chicago, IL, he is a Movie Director and best known for directing <u>An American in Paris</u>. Both of his grandparents were from Sicily.
Francis Ford Coppola	1939		Born in Detroit, MI; he is best known for directing The Godfather series: <u>Godfather I</u> in 1972, <u>Godfather II</u> in 1974, and <u>Godfather III</u> in 1990; although he completed them amidst public controversy, he became one of the most successful directors in Hollywood. His father played flute with Arturo Toscanini. His parents were from near Naples, Italy.
Martin Scorsese (Martin Luciano Scorsese)	1942		Born in Flushing, NY, he is an award winning Movie Director.
Brian DePalma (James Giacinto DePalma)	1940		Born in Newark, NJ; director of many films that include: <u>Scarface</u>, <u>The Untouchables</u>, and <u>Mission Impossible</u>.
Michael Cimino	1939		Born in New York City, he directed many films that include, <u>The Deer Hunter</u>.
Quentin Tarantino	1963		Born in Knoxville, TN; an actor/director/screenwriter.
Joseph Stella	1877-1946	1896	Artist from near Naples, Italy.
Beniamino Bufano	1898-1970	1901	Sculptor: Born in San Fele, Italy. He designed the statue of St. Francis of Assisi which towers over San Francisco, CA.

Robert De Niro Sr.	1922-1993		Artist: Born in Syracuse, NY, he's the father of actor, Robert De Niro.
Danny Aiello	1933		Actor: Born in New York City.
Anthony LaPaglia	1959		Actor: <u>Without a Trace</u>, TV series.
Al Molinaro	1919		Feature actor, 'Al', who owned Arnold's Restaurant on <u>Happy Days</u>.
The Sopranos Cast			**Character Played** (Ninety percent of the cast of The Soprano's is Italian-American)
James Gandolfini	1961		Tony Soprano; born in Westwood, NJ.
Edie Falco	1963		Carmela Soprano; born in Brooklyn, NY.
Lorraine Bracco	1955		Dr. Jennifer Melfi; born in Brooklyn, NY.
Michael Imperioli	1966		Christopher Moltisanti; born in Mt. Vernon, NY.
Aida Turturro	1962		Janice Soprano; born in New York City.
Hill Street Blues			**Hill Street Blues**
Daniel Travanti (Danielo Giovanni Travanti)	1940		Capt. Frank Furillo Best Dramatic Actor in a TV Series, 1981; born in Kenosha, WI.
Joe Spano	1946		Officer Harry Goldblume; born in San Francisco, CA.
Ed Marinaro	1950		Officer Joe Coffey; born in New York City.

David Caruso	1956		Actor: NYPD Blue, CSI: Miami; born in Queens, NY.
Ray Romano	1957		Actor/Comedian: Appeared on Comedy Central and had the notable role of Raymond on TV series, Everybody Loves Raymond; born in Queens, NY. David Caruso and Ray Romano attended the same elementary, middle, and high schools during the same years.
			- SCIENCE AND MEDICINE -
Salvadore E. Lauria	1912-1991	1939	Born in Torino, Italy, he won the Nobel Prize for Medicine in 1969.
Enrico Fermi	1901-1954	1939	Born in Rome, Italy, he won the Nobel Prize for Physics in 1938. Was involved in the 'Manhattan Project' and his work in the development of the first Atomic Bomb which ended WWII in 1945.
Renato Dulbecco	1914		Born in Catanzaro, Italy, he was the Nobel Prize winner in Physiology or Medicine. He was President of the Salk Institute 1988-1992. He retired in La Jolla, CA in 2006.
Guglielmo Marconi	1874-1937		Born in Bologna, Italy, he is credited with the development of the wireless telegraph – the forerunner of the radio in 1895. In 1909, he received the Nobel Prize for physics. His company, The Marconi Wireless Company, developed into The Radio Corporation of America…. known today as *RCA*.

			- LITERATURE -
Mario Puzo	1920-1999		Born in Manhattan, NY; he was the writer of many books with Sicilian themes, but he was best known for <u>The Godfather</u> series and <u>The Godfather</u> screenplays, series I, II, III. His parents were born in Sicily.
Paul Gallico	1897-1976		Born in New York City, he was a successful novelist, best known for writing <u>The Snow Goose</u> and <u>The Poseiden Adventure.</u>
John Ciardi	1916-1986		Born in Boston, MA; he was an Italian American poet who wrote twenty-one books of poetry (many for children), translated Dante's <u>Divine Comedy</u>, and by the time of his death, was the best known poet in America.
Gay Talese	1932		Born in Ocean City, NJ, he wrote many novels including <u>Honor Thy Father</u> and <u>Unto the Son</u>.
Tomie dePaolo	1934		Born in Meriden, CN, he is an author Illustrator of more than 170 books for children. He's received numerous awards for his books. <u>Strega Nona</u> is one of his most popular books. In 1976, he received the Caldecott Honor Award for his illustrations, and the Smithsonian Literature Medal.
Don DeLillo	1936		Born in the Bronx, NY, he received the Jerusalem Prize for his books on the themes of freedom; he was also nominated for the National Book Award for his novels.

Dante Alighieri	1265-1312		Born in Florence, Italy. His masterpiece, <u>The Divine Comedy</u> is unparalleled in world literature.
			- MISCELLANEOUS -
Mother Frances Cabrini (Maria Francesca Cabrini)	1850-1917		Born in Sant'Angelo Lodigiano, Italy, she was the first Italian-American saint canonized by the Catholic Church on July 7, 1946.
Amerigo Vespucci	1454-1506		**<u>Explorers</u>** Born in Florence, Italy, he was an Italian merchant and cartographer. The Americas were named for him.
Christopher Columbus (Cristoforo Columbo)	1451-1506		Born in Genoa, Italy, he was a navigator and maritime explorer; he is credited with discovering the Americas.
John Cabot (Giovanni Caboto)	1450-1499		Born in Genoa, Italy, he was a merchant, expert mariner, navigator, and explorer; he helped the British claim Canada.
Gioranni da Verrazzano	1485-1528		Born near Florence, Italy; first European to explore the Atlantic coast of N. America, New York Harbor where the Verrazano-Narrows Bridge in Brooklyn is named in his honor.
Marco Polo	1254-1324		Born in Venice, Italy, he is best known as a Venetian trader/explorer. He gained fame for his travels to China.
Maria Montessori	1870-1952		Born in Ancona, Italy, she opened *Casa dei Bambini* in Rome in 1907. In 1912, she wrote her book, <u>The Montessori Method</u> and it's still being used to this day. There are thousands of Montessori Schools worldwide using her highly successful methods of educating young children.

A Famous Cavallaro

Salvatore John Cavallaro is a name that many people don't know; however, it is someone with my same family name who became quite famous in the Naval Reserve. I do not know where his family originated from in Italy or the exact location of his home in the United States. However, it is important to include him in this list with other Italians who bring pride to the Cavallaro name.

He was born on September 6, 1920 in New York City. When he was twenty-one years of age, he enlisted in the Naval Reserve on January 6, 1942. This was just after the United States was attacked at Pearl Harbor on December 7, 1941. In the year following his enlistment, on January 28, 1943, he was commissioned with the rank of an Ensign. He received training in landing crafts and eventually joined the crew of the Lyon (AP-71). This prepared him to be a guide in the landing of the waves of assault boats in the invasion of Sicily during World War II. He did this with great skill, courage, and while under repeated bombing attacks that were carried on throughout the night and early daylight hours on July 10, 1943. At the invasion of the Gulf of Salerno on September 9, 1943, he was killed in action when his LCT was struck by shellfire. As a result of his courage, bravery, and gallant service in Sicily, the Untied States Navy awarded him the Navy Cross posthumously.

In 1944, the U.S. Navy chose to name a ship in honor of him. They called it 'The USS Cavallaro'. It was originally a DE-712, but on July 17, 1944, it was later reclassified as an APD128. At the time of construction, it was converted to a high-speed transport. Officially named The USS Cavallaro, she was eventually launched on June 15, 1944 by Defoe Shipbuilding Co. in Bay City Michigan, and Mrs. A. Cavallaro sponsored her. The ship was commissioned on May 13, 1945 with Lieutenant Commander E.P. Adams, USNR, in command.

The USS Cavallaro arrived for training at Pearl Harbor on May 20, 1945 and sailed shortly after on June 13, 1945, for convoy escort duty out of Ulithi. Ulithi, located about 360 miles southwest of Guam and about 850 miles east of the Philippines, was the U.S. Navy's Secret Weapon. As Admiral Nimitz recalled, "Ulithi was used to devise a miraculous mobile service force that made it possible for the U.S. Navy to move toward Japan in great jumps instead of taking the slow and costly alternative of capturing the whole series of islands on which to build a string of land bases."

Ulithi was made up of three dozen little islands that rose slightly above the sea and the largest only being about a one half square mile in area. At that time, Ulithi was the biggest and most active naval base in the world and was a tremendous asset to the U.S. Navy command, yet, it was unknown to the rest of the military. Many civilians had never heard of it. It provided the Navy with an ideal protected anchorage as the U.S. Fleet fought its way ever closer to Tokyo Bay.

Within a month of its occupation by the U.S., the entire floating base was in operation. Six thousand ship fitters, welders, carpenters, and electricians arrived aboard repair ships, destroyers, floating dry docks, and anchored throughout the bays of Ulithi. Smaller ships in the battles at the front needed a multitude of services; ships and tankers from Ulithi rushed to the strike areas bringing men, mail, and medical supplies along with spare parts and technicians to repair the ships in need. The USS Cavallaro was one of these ships and played a very important role in the battles in the Philippine Islands. She made repeated trips from Ulithi to the Philippines and Okinawa until September 20, 1945.

She was then sent to Sasebo, Japan and carried men between the many Japanese ports. On October 12, 1945 she departed Tokyo Bay and was bound for San Francisco. After operating for a few months along the west coast, she was decommissioned and placed in reserve at San Diego on May 17, 1946. The USS Cavallaro was re-commissioned on September 4, 1953 and after intensive training, she sailed for Japan on March 12, 1954. At that time, she served as a primary control ship in several large amphibious exercises for that tour of duty in the Far East. She was used to transport underwater demolition teams in day and night practice reconnaissance missions. In the fall of 1954, she was stationed at Haiphong and Saigon, in Vietnam and she became the headquarters for those supervising the debarkation of refugees from Communist North Vietnam. She carried them in safety to the south in the U.S. Navy Operation, 'Passage to Freedom'. On November 23, 1954, she returned to be docked in San Diego, California once more.

From March 1955, The USS Cavallaro was home-ported at Long Beach, California and conducted operations along the entire California coastline while participating in exercises with Marines. She was deployed again from January 12, 1956 through October 4, 1956 and she served once more in the Far East when she joined in a reenactment of the assault on Iwo Jima made for training purposes. She also visited ports in Japan and the Philippines as well as in Hong Kong. Her final cruise to the Orient was between February 10, 1959 and May 23, 1959 when she was involved in exercises with both Korean and American Marines.

The USS Cavallaro returned to Long Beach, California once more to prepare for transfer to the Republic of Korea where she was decommissioned. She was finally transferred to Korea on October 15, 1959. She currently serves under the Korean flag in the Korean Navy; she is known as The Kyung-Nam (APD 81).

Morreale, Ben & Carola, Robert, (2000). Italian Americans: *The Immigrant Experience*. China: Hugh Lauter Levin Associates, Inc.

Spangler, G., March 1998, *Ulithi. (Online)*, July 27, 2005. http://www.laffey.org/ulityi/Page%201/Ulithi.ht

A Lifetime of Memories

A Potpourri of Cavallaro Family Memories

680 N. Clinton Avenue (circa 1925)
Angelina and Jennie Lamanna,
Emma Lizzio, Angela Cavallaro,
Jennie Cavallaro,
Mary Lizzio, Angelo Lizzio in front.

Front Steps of House on the Farm
Mary Lizzio, Angela Cavallaro,
Alfred Lizzio & Caterina Lamanna. She
died just 3 months after this was taken.

**The day our Historic Story began
July 1980
(At the home of Mary Lizzio
on Fernwood Pk.)**

Jennie Cavallaro
Lucy Cavallaro
Mary Lizzio
Audrey Lizzio
Theresa Cavallaro

(30 minutes after this
picture was taken,
I began writing down
all the information
my aunts and uncles
remembered of Sicily.)

Three Brothers in 1928
Alfred, Joe, & Roger Cavallaro
Taken at Joe & Jennie Gargana's wedding

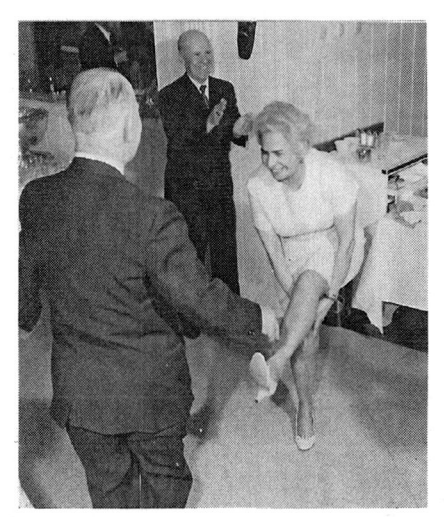

Joe Cavallaro and Lucy Cavallaro
dancing The Tarantella
at Mary & Al Lizzio's
50th Anniversary Party.
(Roger Cavallaro claps
to the beat of the rhythm.)

Three Cousins – 2005
Joe Cavallaro
Roger Cavallaro
Richard Cavallaro

Sons of
Joe Cavallaro
Roger Cavallaro
Alfred Cavallaro

Circa 1916
Mary Lizzio, Jennie Cavallaro,
Joe Cavallaro

Brother & Sister
Joe Cavallaro, Jennie Cavallaro

Back: Jennie Cavallaro, Mary Lizzio,
Theresa Cavallaro
Front: Lucy & Roger Cavallaro

Joe Cavallaro's 1st Birthday Party
August 7, 1938
Around the table: John Samperi, Mary Samperi, Mary Lizzio, Joan Cavallaro, Agatina Samperi, Alfred Lizzio, Frank Samperi with Johnny Samperi, Joe Cavallaro, Angela Cavallaro, Angelina Lamanna, top of head of Frederico Lamanna, Jennie Lamanna, Unknown man, Angelo Cavallaro
Front: Jennie Cavallaro holding Joe, Pat Samperi and unknown female kneeling.

Audrey Lizzio, Theresa Cavallaro, Angelina Lamanna, Mary Lizzio, Joe Cavallaro

My Sicilian Legacy

Jennie & Lucy Cavallaro
Summer 1995

Jennie & Joe Romeo
(Circa summer 1993-95)

Angelo & Joan D'Amanda
San Antonio, TX
(Circa 1943-44 when married)

Roger Cavallaro
Hunting on the farm

Alfred Cavallaro
(Circa 1924)

Sebastiano Cavallaro
(Angelo Cavallaro's brother)

Roger Cavallaro, Mary Lizzio,
Joe Cavallaro
Audrey & Angelo Lizzio

Back: Angelo & Audrey Lizzio,
Joe Cavallaro
Front: Angelina Lamanna, Mary Lizzio,
Joe & Jennie Cavallaro,
Lucy Cavallaro

1939-1940 World's Fair

New York City

September 11-18, 1939

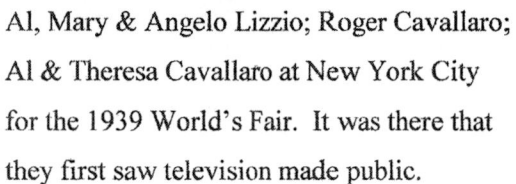

Al, Mary & Angelo Lizzio; Roger Cavallaro; Al & Theresa Cavallaro at New York City for the 1939 World's Fair. It was there that they first saw television made public.

Bond Clothing & Fashion Park Factories

**Shop #1 Bond Clothing
"Finishing sewers"**
Back: Man is unknown, Anna Marzano, Theresa Cavallaro, unknown woman, Anna Weigand,
Front: Anna Fuino, Rose Giordano

Bond Clothing on Martin Street
As it looks currently
(July 1995)

Bond Clothes

In 1933, Barney Ruben moved Bond Clothes from New Brunswick, NJ to Rochester, NY, making it the last firm to enter the men's clothing industry in Rochester. It became the largest retail chain of men's clothing in the United States, best known for selling two-pant suits. In 1936, it had outgrown its factory which prompted a trade with Levy Brothers & Adler-Rochester for their larger, more modern facility. It continued to add annexes to that building and by 1938, it had become the largest employer of textile workers in Rochester, employing over 2,500 people. This included the Cavallaro family. At one time or another, all the brothers and sisters and their families had worked there in different capacities. During WWII, numerous orders for officers' uniforms kept the factories busy, and the early post war years brought increased demands for men's suits; they were at the height of their production by 1947. In 1951, Levy Brothers & Adler-Rochester merged with Michaels-Stern, reducing the number of major companies in the city to five: Bond Clothes, Hickey-Freeman, Fashion Park, Michaels-Stern, and Timely Clothes. As the widespread shift from formal to informal attire slashed the market for men's suits and overcoats, Bond Stores was forced to sell its factory on Goodman Street to General Dynamics, but kept the operation open at the original Martin Street location. In 1977, Michaels-Stern declared bankruptcy, sold their inventory, making Bond Clothing and Hickey-Freeman the only remaining men's clothing manufacturers in Rochester. In 1979, Bond Clothing closed their factory, leaving Hickey-Freeman as the sole manufacturer of men's clothing in the city. By that time, all the Cavallaro family had retired from the clothing industry.*

---

*(no author). ("n.d."), D.222 Bond Clothing Stores, Inc., 1933-1979. University of Rochester, (online), August 14, 2005. http://www.lib.rochester.edu/rbk/Bondclothing.stm

**Fashion Park on Miller Street
Shop #7, Section #2
Canvas Basters Shop**
Alfred Cavallaro can be
seen sitting;
he is in the 4th row
toward the center
of the photo,
with a lamp shade
over his head.
(Circa 1925)

**Fashion Park on Miller Street
Shop #4, Section #2
Lining Makers Shop**
Theresa Cavallaro can be
seen sitting;
she is in the 3rd or 4th row
toward the right side,
the second lady from the post.
It looks like she is
wearing a hat, but she is not.
(Circa 1925)

Cemetery & Grave Information

Unless otherwise noted, all burials listed were at:
Holy Sepulchre Cemetery
2461 Lake Avenue
Rochester, NY 14612

Angelo & Angela Cavallaro
Section: North 24, Lot/Tier 14 - Sites: 32L & 32R
Burial dates: Angelo 4-10-1945 – Age 78
Angela 6-5-1945 – Age 67

Angelina & Frederick Lamanna
Section: South 20, Lot/Tier 38 – Sites 21L & 21R
Burials: Angelina 4-10-1984 – Age 88
Frederick 4-9-1977 – Age 91

Catherine Mary Lamanna
Section: 0, Lot/Tier 20 – Site 102
Burial date: 2-2-1920 – Age 3

Joseph Romeo
Section: South 20, Lot/Tier 43 – Site 11L
Burial Date: 7-9-2003 – Age 86

Alfred F. Romeo
(Infant son of Joe & Jennie Romeo)
Section: North 4, Lot/Tier 5 – Site 143F
Burial Date: 6-9-1943 – Age 7 days
(No Grave Stone at site)

Cemetery & Grave Information

Alfred & Theresa Cavallaro
Section: South 14, Lot/Tier 151 –
Sites 1W-S & 2W-S
Burial Dates: Alfred 9-26-1964 – Age 66
Theresa 1-19-1989 – age 84

Details of Monument and Planters
The Roses and Grape Vines are reminders of
Alfred's two loves:
making his own wine, and
of his prized garden of over 30 rose bushes.

Alfred Angelo Cavallaro Jr.
Section 8, Lot 274
Burial Date: 5-28-1986 – Age 58
Grandview Cemetery
Ft. Collins, Co

Cemetery & Grave Information

White Haven Memorial Park
210 Marsh Road
Pittsford, NY 14534

"Creation Chapel"

Alfred & Mary Lizzio, West Lilac, Tier 2, Row E
Angelo & Audrey Lizzio, East Dogwood, Tier 4, Row F

Burial Dates: Alfred 9-12-1974 – Age 78
  Mary 11-13-2002 – Age 102
Burial Dates: Angelo 10-14-2005 – Age 82
  Audrey 4-6-2004 – Age 80

Joseph & Jennie Cavallaro
Section: South 26, Lot/Tier 529 – Sites 1W & 2W
Burial dates: Joseph 2-9-1983 – Age 80
Jennie 11-20-2001 – Age 94

Cemetery & Grave Information

Roger & Lucy Cavallaro
Queen of Heaven, Lot/Tier 541B – Sites 2W & 3W
Burial Dates: Roger 1-8-2000 – Age 94
Lucy 12-29-2006 – Age 87

Note: At the time of this publishing,
no grave marker was in place for Lucy Cavallaro

Angelo & Joan D'Amanda
Section: South 26, Lot/Tier 530 – Sites 2W & 3W
Burial Dates: Angelo 3-18-1969 – age 66
Joan 6-28-1996 – Age 86

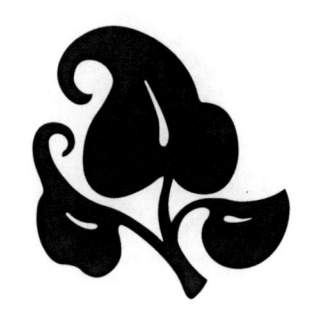

Bibliography

Books

Antinoro-Polizzi, J. (1975). *The Golden Conch.* Rochester, NY: Flower City Printing, Inc.

Brownstone, D.M., Franck, I.M., & Brownstone, D. (2002). *Island of Hope, Island of Tears.* MetroBooks, Friedman/Fairfax Publishers.

Buscaglia, L. (1989). *Papa, My Father: A Celebration of Dads.* Thorofare, NJ: SLACK, Inc.

Ciongioli, A.K., & Parini, J. (2002). *Passage to Liberty: The Story of Italian Immigration and the Rebirth of America.* New York, NY: Harper-Collins Publishers, Inc.

Colletta, J.P. (1996). *Finding Italian Roots: The Complete Guide for Americans.* Baltimore, MD: Genealogical Publishing Co., Inc.

DeBartolo Carmack, S. (1997). *Italian-American Family History.* Baltimore, MD: Genealogical Publishing Co., Inc.

Di Franco, P.J. (1988). *The Italian Americans (The Peoples of North America).* New York, NY: Chelsea House Publishers/Main Line Book Co.

Guzzetta-Jones, A., & Antinoro-Polizzi, J. (1972). *Diceva la Mia Nonna (My Grandmother used to say...).* Rochester, NY: Flower City Printing, Inc.

Italian Americans. (1992). Peterborough, NH: Cobblestone Publishing, Inc.

Mangione, J. (1952). *Mount Allegro.* New York, NY: Alfred A. Knopf, Inc.

Moramarco, F., & Moramarco, S. (2000). *Italian Pride.* New York, NY: MJF Books, Citadel Press – an imprint of Kensington Publishing Corp.

Morreale, B., & Carola, R. (2000). *Italian Americans: The Immigrant Experience.* China: Hugh Lauter Levin Associates, Inc.

Reeves, P. (2002). *Ellis Island.* New York, NY: Barnes & Noble, Inc., and Michael Friedman Publishing Group, Inc.

Sicily, Italy, and Kingdom of the Two Sicilies. World Book Encyclopedia (1994). New York, NY: World Book, Inc.

Sicily Travel Guide. (2000). New York, NY: Dorling Kindersley, Inc.

Spirit Filled Life Bible (New King James Version). (1991) Nashville, TN: Thomas Nelson Publishers.

Viviano, F. (2002). *Blood Washes Blood: A True Story of Love, Murder, and Redemption Under the Sicilian Sun.* New York, NY: Washington Square Press: Simon & Schuster, Inc.

Yans-McLaughlin, V., & Lightman, M. with the Statue of Liberty-Ellis Island Foundation. (1997). *Ellis Island and the Peopling of America (The Official Guide).* New York: The New Press.

Online Sources

1920 United States Federal Census. (Online @ Ancestry Plus), February 26, 2004.
http://www.carlsbadlibrary.org

1930 United States Federal Census. (Online @ Ancestry Plus), March 18, 2005.
http://www.carlsbadlibrary.org

Castiglione di Sicilia. (Online), April 17, 2004.
http://sicilia.indettaglio.it/eng/comuni/ct/castiglionedisicilia/castiflionedisicilia.html

CAVALLARO – L'Italia dei Cognomi. (Online), June 27, 2004.
http://gens.labo.net/en/cognomi/genera.html

Country Life: Travels in the Heart of Sicily. (Online), July 13, 2005.
http://www.bestofsicily.com/country.htm

D.222 Bond Clothing Stores, Inc., 1933-1979, University of Rochester. (Online), August 14, 2005.
http://www.lib.rochester.edu/rbk/Bondclothing.stm

Famous Ellis Island Passenger Arrivals. (Online), May 9, 2005.
http://www.ellisland.org/genealogy/ellisislandfamousarrivals.asp

Modern History: The Modern Era. (Online), May 2, 2005.
http://www.bestofsicily.com/history3.htm

Navy History. (Online), October 5, 2002.
http://www.navyhistory.com/TRANSPORT/CAVALLARO.HTML

O Sole Mio. (Online), April 6, 2007.
http://www.abmusica.com/viaggio.htm

Pandemic Preparedness. (Online), May 21, 2006.
http://www.internationalsos.com/members_home/pandemicpreparedness/index.cfm?content_id=11

Passenger Record. (Online), May 9, 2005.
http://www.ellisisland.org/search/passRecord.asp

Passopisciaro. (Online), May 2, 2005.
http://www.passopisciaro.interfree.it/english/history/htm

Piedimonte Etneo. (Online), April 17, 2004.
http://sicilia.indettaglio.it/eng/comuni/ct/piedimonteetneo/piedimonteetneo.html

Przecha, D. *They Changed Our Name at Ellis Island*. (Online), June 27, 2004.
http://www.genealogy.com/88_donna.html

Ship Image. (Online), October 18, 2002.
http://www.ellisislandrecords.org/search/shipImage.asp

Ship Manifest. (Online), July 23, 2004.
http://www.ellisisland.org/search/viewTextManifest.asp

Sicilian Surnames Search Engine: Cavallaro. (Online), April 17, 2004.
http://sicilia.indettaglio.it/eng/cognomimotore/motore_sql.html

Sicilian Surnames Search Engine: Gravagna. (Online), April 17, 2004.
http://sicilia.indettaglio.it/eng/cognomi/motore/motore_sql.html

Sprangler, G. *Ulithi*. (Online), July 27, 2005.
http://www.laffey.org/Ulithi/Page%201/Ulithi.htm

Taubenberger, J. & Morens, D. *1918 Influenza: the Mother of All Pandemics*. (Online),
   May 21, 2006.
http://www.cdc.gov/ncidod/eid/vol12no01/05-0979.htm

Wikipedia-The Free Encyclopedia. (Online), 2005-2007.
http://www.wikipedia.org/wiki

Printed in the United States
144202LV00002B/2/P